VBA Programming in Business Economics

To my children Louise, Kristoffer, Sebastian, and Mikkel

I hope that you will always
appreciate the joy of learning

Sanne Wøhlk

VBA Programming in Business Economics

DJØF Publishing Copenhagen
2010

Sanne Wøhlk
VBA Programming in Business Economics
First Edition 2010

DJØF Publishing is a company of the
Association of Danish Lawyers and Economists

ISBN 978-87-574-2267-2

Sold and distributed in North America by:
International Specialized Book Services (ISBS)
Portland, OR 97213, USA
www.isbs.com

Sold in all other countries by:
DJØF Publishing Copenhagen
Denmark
www.djoef-forlag.dk

DJØF Publishing
17, Lyngbyvej
P.O.Box 2702
DK-2100 Copenhagen
Denmark

Phone: +45 39 13 55 00
Fax: +45 39 13 55 55
E-mail: forlag@djoef.dk
www.djoef-forlag.dk

Table of Contents

Introduction

This book is about VBA programming and is inspired by the students at the Business School where I work. Motivating business students through the process of learning to program can be a challenging task. With this book I hope to ease the task by presenting a text that is focused precisely on those students.

The structure of this book differs from what you find in most other books on similar topics. After two introductory chapters explaining a.o. the macro recorder, chapter 3 gives the basics on many aspects of VBA programming. Having read that chapter, the readers will be able to create small VBA programs on their own. Chapters 4 through 7 explain the core of VBA programming in detail. After understanding the details of those chapters, the remaining chapters can be read almost independently from each other.

Chapters 8 through 11 are devoted to issues that are closely related to programming: Security and debugging in Chapters 8 and 9, where the latter describes the task of finding bugs. Chapter 10 concentrates on the design of programs - a topic which is often neglected in many introductory books on programming. Chapter 11 focuses on the creation of toolbars, Add-ins, and the like.

Finally, Chapters 12 through 18 are devoted to special topics that deserve special attention: Working with files and strings of text in Chapters 12 and 13, respectively, and the task of creating charts in Chapter 14. Chapter 15 explains the use of built-in dialog boxes and Chapter 16 goes into detail with the creation of custom user forms. Chapter 17 focuses on the Solver Add-in which can be used for optimization, and Chapter 18 focuses on simulation studies, both with and without the Crystal Ball Add-in.

Throughout the book we use numerous examples that are relevant to business and in particular to management science. Some of these examples are based on the assumption that the reader has knowledge of a particular topic. For the reader not familiar with the topic, the book's webpage http://www.djoef-forlag.dk/vare/8757422672 offers a short introduction note. Table 1 provides a list of the background information offered on the book's webpage along with an indication of the sections that are based on the information. Whenever background information is provided on a topic, a *B* is placed in the margin as illustrated here.

TABLE 1 BACKGROUND INFORMATION AVAILABLE ON THE BOOK'S WEBPAGE.

Inventory Control	5.1.2, 6.2.1, 18.2.2, ex17.5, ex18.5-18.7
Sequencing of jobs	6.4.3, ex6.12, ex18.4
Seat Reservation Problem	10.2.2
Branch-and-bound	10.3
Traveling salesman problem	14.3.5, ex7.5, ex18.8
Vehicle routing problem	14.3.6
Linear Programming	Chapter 17
Transportation problem	17.4.2, ex17.8

Since this book is about programming, it contains a lot of code. Most of this code is available on the book's webpage. Whenever the code contained in a figure is available, a *C* is placed in the margin next to that figure. Large examples have their own section and the code is often divided into several figures. In these cases, the *C* is placed next to the header of section, indicating that all code of the section is provided jointly on the book's webpage.

Learning to program requires a lot of practicing. Therefore, each chapter is concluded with a number of exercises. Working through those exercises will help the reader become familiar with the topic of the individual chapter. Many of these exercises are based on a specific data file. These files are also provided on the book's webpage. A *D* in the margin indicates that a data file is necessary to solve the exercise.

In order to master the topic of this book, it is also necessary to practice on problems that are more complex than the exercises of the book. Therefore, the book's webpage offers a number of cases which can be used for practicing.

I hope you find the book useful.

Acknowledgements

I would like to thank my students for their inspiration and Michael Christensen, Head of Department for encouraging me to write this book. I would also like to thank Wilfried Roloff for making the book possible, the department secretaries for their assistance, and my colleagues for their support. The greatest thank goes to my children and my wonderful husband: Thank you for your love and support.

Chapter 1
VBA and Your First Program

In order to get started there are two things you need to become familiar with: The *Developer tab* in Excel, which is explained in Section 1.2 and the *VBA Editor* which is explained in Section 1.3.

The remainder of this chapter is devoted to creating and executing the first macro. In Section 1.4, we explain how to insert a module that can contain your code and in Section 1.5, the macro is created. In Section 1.6, you learn different methods for executing the macro and finally in Section 1.7, we show how to save a workbook that contains code.

1.1 What is VBA

VBA is short for *Visual Basic for Applications* and is a programming language built into the programs in Microsoft Office. In this book, we focus on VBA for the Excel application, but VBA can just as easily be used with Word as the application, for instance.

VBA can be used for manipulating the objects in the application. In the Excel application, the objects are workbooks, worksheets, ranges, charts, etc. The objects of the other applications are different, but the VBA language itself is the same across applications. Like any other programming language, the core of a program created in VBA is variables, loops and decision constructions.

Learning to program is all about learning to write in a language that the computer can understand: If you want to speak Chinese, you must use the Chinese words and phrases, the Chinese grammar, and the Chinese pronunciation. Otherwise, you cannot expect to be understood. Similarly for VBA: In order to create a VBA program that can be executed or to create VBA functions that can be used within the worksheet, it is important to speak VBA to the computer. So far, your computer does not understand plain English. Therefore, you must obey the VBA grammatical rules, which mainly consist of keywords and syntax.

1.2 The Developer Tab

When working with VBA programming, you need the *Developer* tab in Excel, which is shown in Figure 1.1. This is where you find the controls to create and execute macros.

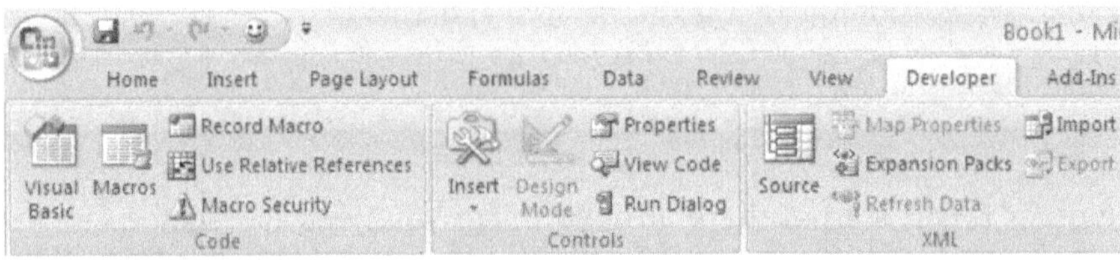

1.1 THE DEVELOPER TAB.

If the Developer tab is not visible in your Excel, locate the *Office* button in the upper left corner of Excel. The Office button is the round one with four colored squares and it is one of the new features in Office 2007. From the Office button, choose *Excel Options* to get the dialog box displayed in Figure 1.2. Select *Popular* in the left-hand side menu and select *Show Developer tab in the Ribbon*. Clicking *Ok* will display the tab as illustrated in Figure 1.1.

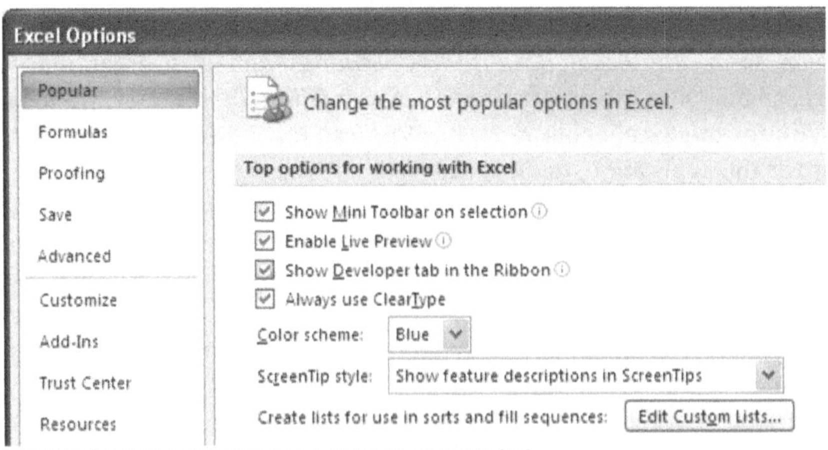

1.2 ACTIVATE THE DEVELOPER TAB FROM THE EXCEL OPTIONS.

The Developer tab consists of three parts. The *Code* part is used to create macros and to execute them. You will learn more about this part below and in Chapter 2. The *Controls* part is used for integrating controls into the worksheets. You will be introduced to this in Section 1.6. In Chapter 16, you will learn a lot about controls on user forms, and you will also learn how they can be integrated into a worksheet. Finally, the *XML* part deals with xml-code and is beyond the scope of this book.

1.3 The VBA Editor

When you develop programs in VBA, you use the *VBA Editor* to do this. There are basically two ways to open the VBA Editor from Excel: Either press the *Visual Basic* control, which is located to the very left on the Developer tab, or press *Alt+F11* from anywhere in Excel. The VBA Editor that appears is shown in Figure 1.3.

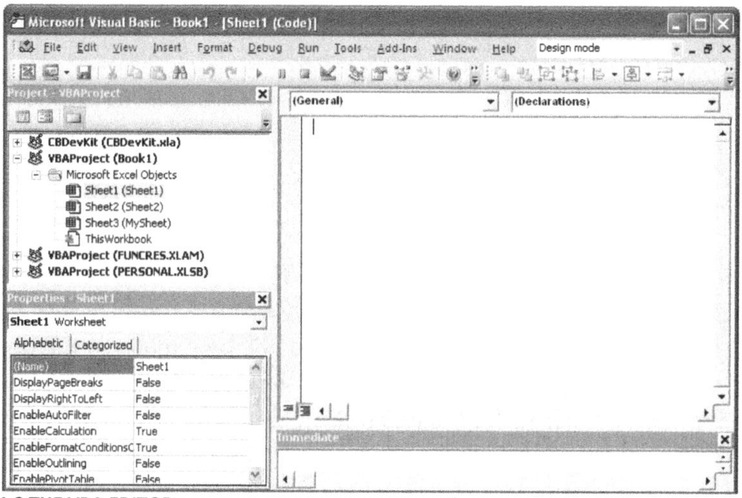

1.3 THE VBA EDITOR.

The VBA Editor has a layout similar to most other Windows programs: At the top you find a *menu bar*, where at least some of the menus are well known: File, Edit, and View, and others that have unfamiliar names such as Debug and Run. After reading through this book, you will be familiar with most of these menus.

Below the menu bar you find a *toolbar*. Figures 1.4 and 1.5 zoom in on the toolbar which we will consider a bit further in the following, so that you know what you are dealing with. From the left-hand side in Figure 1.4, you find the following. The *Excel* control: use this to swap to Excel. *Insert*: use this to insert a module, a user form, or a procedure. *Save*, followed by the traditional *cut*, *copy*, and *paste*. *Find* which is used to search through the code. Finally you have the well-known *undo* and *redo*.

Continuing towards the right, in Figure 1.5 you find the following. Firstly the part that looks like the control panel of a CD player: The triangle, which is used to execute your code, the double vertical bar symbol is used to stop the code from running before it is done, and the square: *reset*, which is mainly used when you try to execute code that contains a bug. In this case, the bug part of your code will be highlighted.

After you have corrected the code by removing the bug, press the square to get out of debugging mode. You will learn a lot more about debugging in Chapter 9. The next control, which looks like tools from a math class, lets you enter and leave design mode. My guess is that you will never want to use this control.

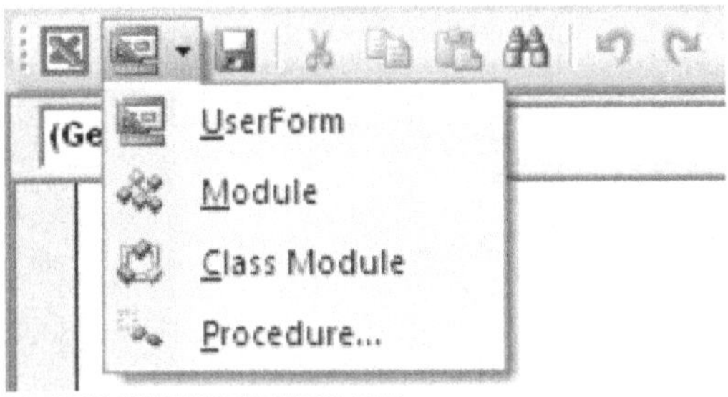

1.4 FIRST HALF OF THE TOOL BAR.

The final five controls are extremely useful. The first two display the *VBA Project Explorer* and the *Properties Window* in case you – more or less by accident – have closed them. These two windows will be explained further below. The control that looks like a yellow box with toys above it opens the *Object Browser*, which will be explained in detail in Chapter 7. The control with the hammer and wrench opens the tool box that is used when designing user forms. You will learn about this tool box in Chapter 16. Finally, the blue question mark control will lead you to the *VBA help system*.

1.5 SECOND HALF OF THE TOOL BAR.

The main part of the VBA Editor consists of three, maybe four, windows. To the right you find a large area that looks much like a note pad. This is the *Code Window*, which is the place where you type in your programming code.

You might, or might not, see an *Immediate Window* below the Code Window. This is used for debugging which is the topic of Chapter 9. We suggest that you close the Immediate Window until you reach that chapter.

At the top to the left, you see the *Project Explorer*, which displays your open Excel files in the same way as the Windows Explorer shows your file system. Let us take a closer look. At this point, if you do not have any Excel file open, please go to Excel and open a new file before returning to the VBA Editor. You now see your Excel file in the Project Explorer.

Now a bit of terminology that will ease your understanding of what you see: When an Excel file is open in Excel, it is referred to as a Workbook. The one you just opened is probably called Book1. Each workbook contains a collection of Worksheets. These are probably called Sheet1, Sheet2, and Sheet3 in your workbook. The Project Explorer lists the sheets of your workbook by stating the sheet number followed by the name of the sheet. In Excel I changed the name of sheet 3 to MySheet. Note how that looks in Figure 1.3.

Below the Project Explorer you find the *Properties Window*. Here you can see and change various properties of your workbooks, worksheets, modules, and user forms. You will not need this window for quite a while, more specifically before Chapter 16, so I suggest that you close it until further notice.

1.4 Insert a Module

You have now become somewhat familiar with the VBA Editor, and you know what the various parts of it can be used for. It is now time to create your very first program.

Code is located in something called a *Module*. You can think of a module as a container that contains one or several programs. A module is contained in a workbook just like worksheets, but they are only used for writing code and you cannot see them in Excel, only in the VBA Editor and the Project Explorer. You can have as much code as you wish in one module, and as many modules in a workbook as you wish.

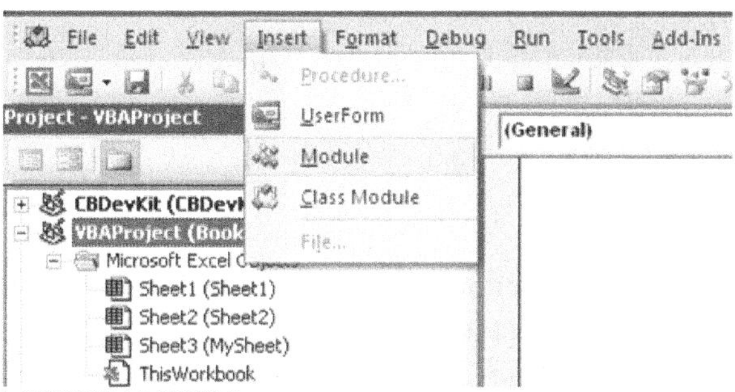

1.6 INSERT A MODULE.

It is possible to have code elsewhere, for example behind a user form as we shall see in Chapter 16. But for now, modules are the only place where you should write code.

Therefore, the first thing you need to do when you want to write a program is to insert the module. Make sure that the workbook where you want to insert your module is highlighted in the Project Explorer. There are several ways to insert a module in your project. The easiest way is to open the VBA Editor, choose the menu *Insert,* and select *Module*, as illustrated in Figure 1.6. Alternatively, select the *insert* control on the tool bar and choose *Module*. Notice that it now appears in the Project Explorer as you can see in Figure 1.7.

1.5 Write Your First Macro

Almost every book about programming starts with a small program that displays the text *Hello World!* on the monitor. This book is no exception.

To open a module for writing, double-click on it in the Project Explorer. Now type in the three lines shown in Figure 1.7 in the Code Window. At this point you are not to worry about understanding what you write. After working your way through Chapter 3 you will have the full understanding about those strange looking lines of text.

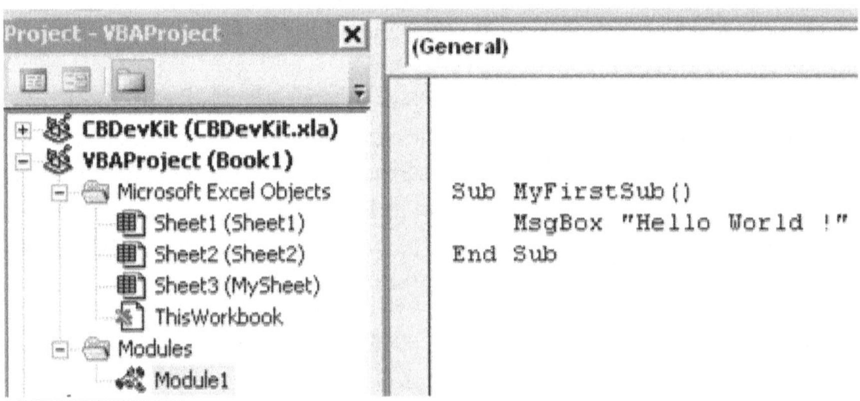

1.7 THE FIRST MACRO.

1.6 Execute your First Macro

In the previous section you wrote a small program. But writing programs is neither fun nor useful if you cannot execute them. There are many ways to execute a macro. Here we explain some of them. Several more advanced ways to execute a macro are explained in Chapter 11.

In the VBA Editor, place the cursor on one of the three lines of code you just wrote. Press the green triangle control on the tool bar. Alternatively, place the cursor on the code and press F5. In both cases the message box shown in Figure 1.8 will be displayed.

1.8 OUTPUT FROM THE FIRST MACRO

While you are programming, the methods above are good ways to execute your code to see that everything is working correctly. But after creating the program it is very inconvenient to have to open the VBA Editor in order to execute a macro. Therefore, macros can also be executed directly from Excel.

Return to Excel by using the Excel control on the toolbar or by using *Alt+Tab* to swap. On the Developer tab, the second control is called *Macros*. Click it to obtain the dialog box displayed in Figure 1.9. Select the macro you want to execute, in this case the one called MyFirstSub, and press *Run*. This will also execute your macro.

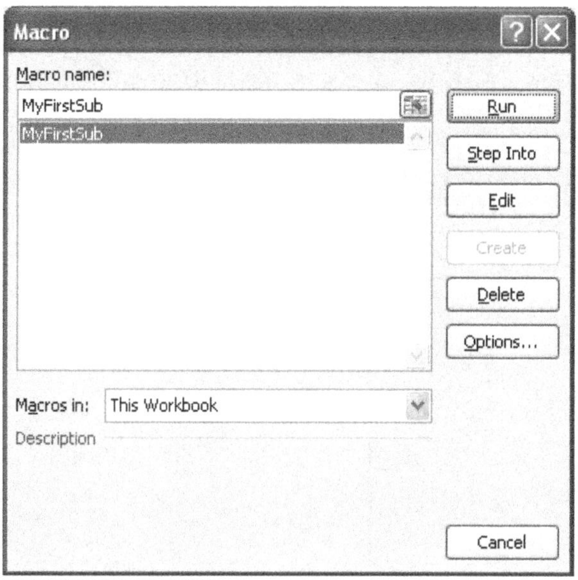

1.9 EXECUTING A MACRO.

The methods above are okay if you only need to execute your macro a couple of times. But if you are going to use it many times, or if someone else is going to use it, you probably would like to be able to execute your macro by pressing a button on the worksheet. Here is how you insert a button: From the Developer tab, select *Insert* to obtain the options displayed in Figure 1.10.

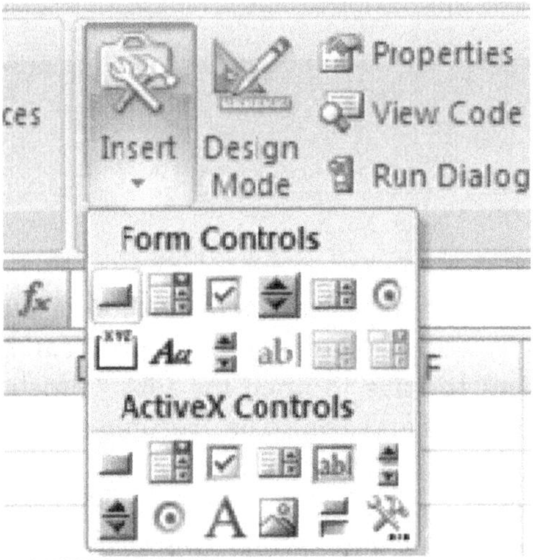

1.10 INSERT A BUTTON.

Choosing the upper left *Form Control*, and clicking somewhere on the worksheet will insert the button. It can be resized and relocated subsequently. The *Assign Macro* dialog box shown in Figure 1.11 is automatically displayed. Select the macro you want to execute when the button is pressed and press *OK*. Now, pressing the button will execute your macro.

1.11 THE ASSIGN MACRO DIALOG BOX.

You are now familiar with the VBA Editor, you have created your first macro and know how to execute it. In the next chapter you will learn how to use the *macro recorder*, and in Chapter 3 we will write more code and you will start to understand the VBA language.

1.7 Save a Workbook that Contains Macros

When a workbook contains VBA code, it cannot be saved in the standard .xlsx or .xls formats. It must be saved as a macro enabled workbook .xlsm (or xlm if you use a pre-2007 version of Excel) as shown in Figure 1.12.

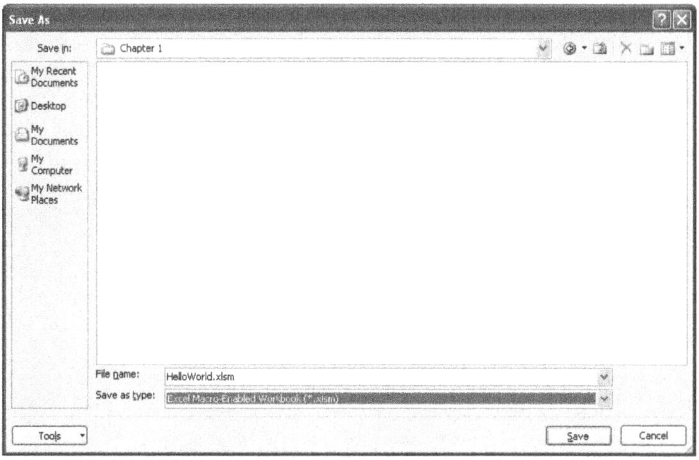

1.12 SAVING A WORKBOOK THAT CONTAINS CODE.

1.8 Exercises

1.1. Follow the steps described in this chapter and end up with the creation of your own *Hello world!* macro.

1.2. Now, let us see what you learned so far.

1. Insert a new procedure – a sub – and call it *HelloX*.
2. Type the body of the procedure to make it look like this:

```
Public Sub HelloX()
    Dim Name As String
    Name = InputBox(“Type your name:”)
    MsgBox "Hello " & Name
End Sub
```

3. Make a button and assign the *HelloX* procedure to it.
4. Run the procedure by pressing the button.

Chapter 2
The Macro Recorder

The easiest way to create a macro is to record it. With the *macro recorder* you can record your actions and execute them at a later point. In that way your routine tasks can be performed by a macro, and you can spend your time on other tasks. In Section 2.1, we explained how to use the macro recorder.

The macro recorder generates VBA code. Often you will need to slightly modify the recorded code. In Section 2.2, we will take a look at the generated code and see how it can be modified.

Just like your worksheet functions can use either absolute or relative references, so can the macro recorder. In Section 2.3, we consider the differences between the two.

Even though the macro recorder is simple to use and can generate VBA code, it has many shortcomings. We consider some of these in Section 2.4.

2.1 How to Record a Macro

In this section you will learn how to use the macro recorder to record a macro. The use of the macro recorder will be illustrated through two examples. For both examples, we use the worksheet illustrated in Figure 2.1. The worksheet states the amount of sales per year for each of four areas of a company over a five year period.

	A	B	C	D	E	F
1				Sales		
2						
3		Year 1	Year 2	Year 3	Year 4	Year 5
4	Area 1	230000	245000	256000	156300	174300
5	Area 2	327500	339000	371000	290000	310500
6	Area 3	432000	447900	468000	350500	367800
7	Area 4	210000	225000	234800	224800	221000
8						

2.1 DATA FOR ILLUSTRATION OF THE MACRO RECORDER.

In the first example we make a macro to format one or several cells. Start by selecting cell B3. Do not change this selection once the recording is started. In order to activate the macro recorder, press *Record Macro* on the Developer tab as illustrated in Figure 2.2.

2.2 PRESS RECORD MACRO TO START RECORDING.

The dialog box shown in Figure 2.3 will be displayed. Here you enter some information about the macro you are about to create: The *name* should be something that relates to the purpose of the macro. We call this macro *FormatCells*. Make sure that the macro is stored in *This Workbook*, which is the default setting. In the *description* field you can write a description of your macro for future use. Click *OK* to start recording.

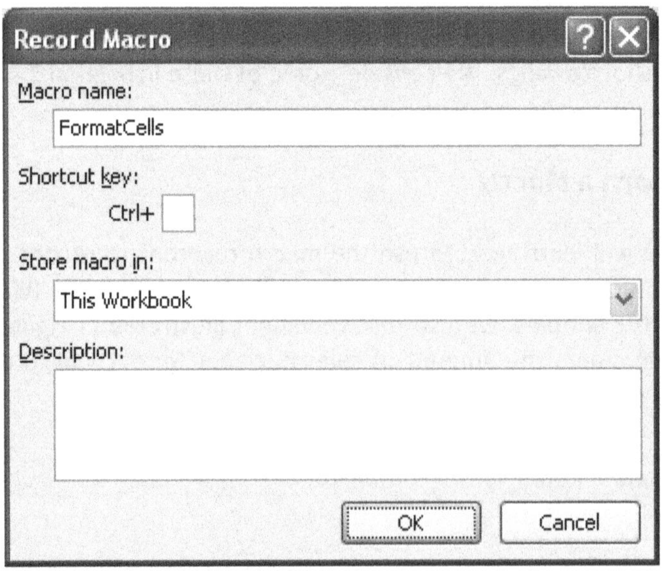

2.3 THE RECORD MACRO DIALOG BOX.

Note how the Developer tab changes by replacing *Record Macro* by *Stop Recording* as shown in Figure 2.4. Everything you do until you press *Stop Recording* will be recorded and turned into a macro.

We change the format of the selected cell by choosing the *Home* tab and selecting *Bold font, font size 16* and change the *font color* to blue. Click *Stop Recording* to stop the recording of your actions.

2.4 PRESS STOP RECORDING TO STOP THE RECORDER.

Now it is time to test that the macro is working correctly. Do this by selecting cell C3 and execute the macro as you learned in Chapter 1: On the *Developer* tab, choose *Macros*, select the macro you just recorded and press *Run*. If the macro has been correctly recorded, the formatting of cells B3 and C3 will now be similar. If this is not the case, do try to follow the steps above once again. Note that if you select several cells, the new formatting will apply to all of them when you execute the macro. Executing the macro for every cell with a heading results in the layout shown in Figure 2.5.

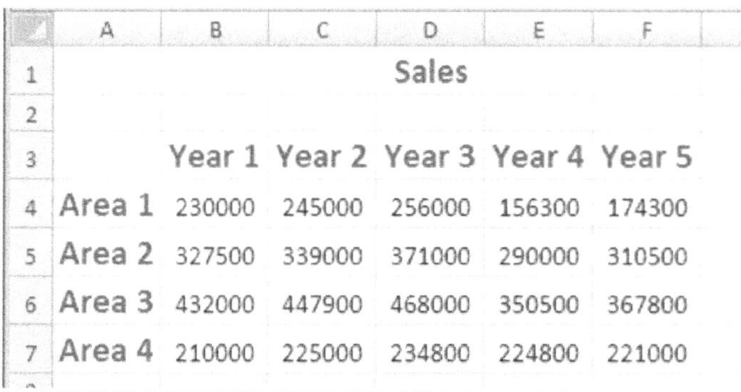

	A	B	C	D	E	F
1				Sales		
2						
3		Year 1	Year 2	Year 3	Year 4	Year 5
4	Area 1	230000	245000	256000	156300	174300
5	Area 2	327500	339000	371000	290000	310500
6	Area 3	432000	447900	468000	350500	367800
7	Area 4	210000	225000	234800	224800	221000

2.5 HEADINGS ARE FORMATTED BY THE RECORDED MACRO.

In the second example, we illustrate how a chart can be created by use of the macro recorder. Creating charts is one of the more tricky tasks in VBA programming, mainly because there are so many possibilities. We go into detail with the creation of charts in Chapter 14. Until you reach that chapter, we recommend that you use the macro recorder to create charts. In the next section, we will shortly point out where you need to change the code in order to make it more flexible.

Start by selecting cell A1 and press the *Record Macro* control on the *Developer* tab. Give your macro a name in the Dialog box that appears, for example ShowChart. Select the area A3:F7, which is the area to be displayed. Select the *Insert* tab and choose the first *2-D Line Chart* as illustrated in Figure 2.6. Then stop the macro recorder.

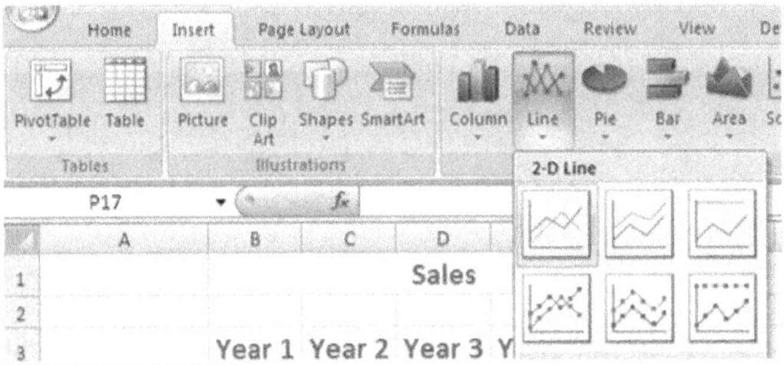

2.6 CREATING A CHART.

When recording this macro, the chart shown in Figure 2.7 will be displayed. Delete the chart and execute the macro to convince yourself that everything is working correctly.

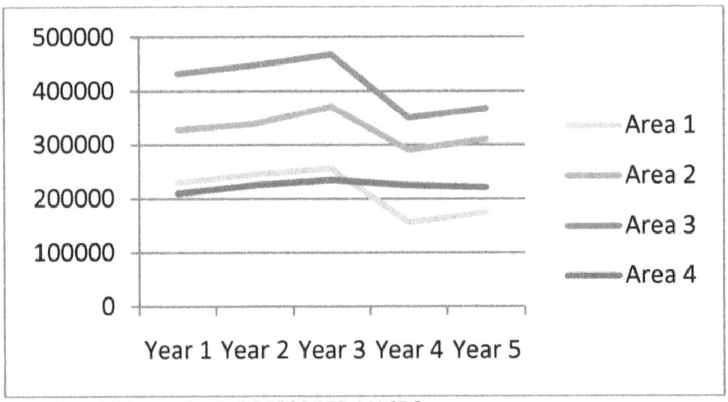

2.7 CHART CREATED BY THE RECORDED MACRO.

2.2 Viewing the Recorded Code

In this section, we will take a look at the code that was recorded in the two examples in the above section. At this point you should not worry about not understanding the details of the code. The purpose is merely to illustrate that even without great programming skills, it is still possible to change the macros slightly.

When you record a macro with the macro recorder, you record your actions, but actually you do a lot more than that: You both record what you do and what you do not do. Here is the explanation. Swap to the *VBA Editor* and take a look at the code you recorded in the first example. It will look like the code in Figure 2.8.

In the code, *Selection* refers to the selected cell or cells. The first real line of code sets Bold to *True*, i.e. states that bold font should be used. The next part of the code changes the Size to 16, but it also states the status of many other font related things which have not been changed, for example that it should not be subscript. This is done even though it is unchanged.

```
Sub FormatCells()
'
' FormatCells Macro
'

'
    Selection.Font.Bold = True
    With Selection.Font
        .Name = "Calibri"
        .Size = 16
        .Strikethrough = False
        .Superscript = False
        .Subscript = False
        .OutlineFont = False
        .Shadow = False
        .Underline = xlUnderlineStyleNone
        .ThemeColor = xlThemeColorLight1
        .TintAndShade = 0
        .ThemeFont = xlThemeFontMinor
    End With
    With Selection.Font
        .Color = -4165632
        .TintAndShade = 0
    End With
End Sub
```

2.8 THE RECORDED CODE.

Every line that states something that is unchanged can be removed without influencing the result. Removing unnecessary lines of code from Figure 2.8 results in the code shown in Figure 2.9.

```
Sub FormatCells()
    Selection.Font.Bold = True
    With Selection.Font
        .Size = 16
    End With
    With Selection.Font
        .Color = -4165632
    End With
End Sub
```

2.9 THE RECORDED CODE AFTER UNNECESSARY CODE HAS BEEN REMOVED.

The code in Figure 2.9 can be cleaned up even further as illustrated in Figure 2.10.

```
Sub FormatCells()
    With Selection.Font
        .Bold = True
        .Size = 16
        .Color = -4165632
    End With
End Sub
```

2.10 FURTHER ADJUSTMENT OF THE CODE IN FIGURE 2.8.

Now consider the *ShowChart* macro, which was recorded in the second example and is shown in Figure 2.11.

```
Sub ShowChart()
'
' ShowChart Macro
'

'
    Range("A3:F7").Select
    ActiveSheet.Shapes.AddChart.Select
    ActiveChart.SetSourceData Source:=Range("'Sheet1'!$A$3:$F$7")
    ActiveChart.ChartType = xlLine
    Range("H3").Select
End Sub
```

2.11 THE RECORDED CODE FOR MAKING CHARTS.

The most interesting line of code for editing purposes is the long one that specifies the *Source*. This line states that the data for the chart should be found on sheet 1 in the range A3:F7. It does not require a lot of imagination to imagine that changing the $F$7 to $F$6 will result in only the first three areas being shown. If you need a chart to display the information that you have stored in the range L9:Q17, enter $L$9:$Q$17 instead.

2.3 Using Relative References

Someone who is used to working with Excel knows the difference between absolute and relative references, but let us shortly refresh this before turning to the use of this in the macro recorder. Consider the small worksheet in Figure 2.12 where the formulas are shown.

	A	B	C
1	1	=A1	=$A$1
2	2		
3			

2.12 ABSOLUTE VERSUS RELATIVE REFERENCES.

Now copying B1:C1 to B2:C2 results in the worksheet shown in Figure 2.13. Why? Well the reference in B1 is relative and points to the cell one step to the left of itself, which when copied to B2 is A2, but the reference in C1 is absolute and points to the specific cell A1, also when copied. The $-sign is the trick.

	A	B	C
1	1	1	1
2	2	2	1

2.13 RESULT OF USING ABSOLUTE VERSUS RELATIVE REFERENCES.

To illustrate the use of *Relative References* which is found right below the *record macro* control on the *Developer* tab, we use the workbook shown in Figure 2.14.

	A	B	C	D	E
1	1			1	
2	2			2	

2.14 DATA FOR USING RELATIVE VERSUS ABSOLUTE REFERENCES.

We record two macros. Firstly select cell A1 and start the macro recorder. Select cell A1 again and press *Ctrl+c* (copy). Then select cell B1 and press *Ctrl+v* (paste). Then stop the recorder. You will see a 1 in cell B1.

Clear cell B1 to be able to test how the macro you just recorded works. Firstly, select cell A1 and execute the macro, then select cell A2 and execute the macro. The result is shown in column B of Figure 2.15.

	A	B	C	D	E
1	1	1		1	1
2	2			2	2

2.15 ILLUSTRATION OF ABSOLUTE AND RELATIVE REFERENCES.

Now activate *Use Relative References* as shown in Figure 2.16. To see the difference we will perform exactly the same steps in columns D and E as follows: Select cell D1 and start the macro recorder. Select cell D1 again and copy. Then select cell E1 and paste. Then stop the recorder. Clear cell

E1 and execute the macro from both cell D1 and D2. The result is shown at the right-hand side of Figure 2.15.

2.16 USE RELATIVE REFERENCES.

Why the difference? Well, in the first macro we used absolute reference and copied cell A1 to cell B1. When executing the macro starting in any other cell, it will still copy A1 to B1. In the second macro we recorded the following: copy the active cell to the cell to the right of it using a relative reference.

2.4 Limitations of the Macro Recorder

At this point a reader or two might believe that there is really no reason to learn VBA programming since the macro recorder can create VBA code for us. Wrong!

There are basically three typical types of tasks that we want to use VBA for. These will be considered in turn below.

Automation of routine tasks: Many people perform the same task over and over again: Create weekly reports on sales, production, etc, perform monthly calculations on employee effectiveness, and so on. These tasks can be done manually in Excel but might take hours. Here, the macro recorder is a great help: Record your actions once, and let the recorded macro perform the tasks in the future.

Functions: We all use worksheet functions such as *=sum*, *=average*, or *=sqrt* in our daily life with Excel. Using VBA code you can create your own functions that can be used from the worksheet just like any built-in function. A sales representative might need a function that can consider the customer's profile, yearly spending etc, to convert a list price to the actual price for the customer to pay. It is not possible to create functions with the macro recorder.

Beyond the recorder: The recorder can only re-play your exact actions, but very often you will need a task to be performed for every customer or product, for every worksheet etc, i.e. we need to iteratively cycle through every item in a set. You cannot record that. Furthermore, you will often need the action to depend on a decision. For example in efficiency analysis, if an employee has been less efficient than some threshold value, the macro should automatically execute another macro that creates a report with an in depth analysis of that employee. This kind of decision making is impossible for the macro recorder to handle.

So what do I think? Well, if you want to go beyond the basics, do read on.

2.5 Exercises

The following exercises will help you get used to the macro recorder.

2.1. The purpose of this exercise is to record a macro to change the font of the text in a cell. Follow the steps described below.

1. Type your first name in cell A1 and your last name in cell A2.
2. Activate cell A1 (click on it).
3. Start the macro recorder.
4. Type a macro name and press *OK*.
5. Change the font size to 16.
6. Stop the macro recorder.
7. Activate cell A2.
8. Run your macro. (the font size of cell A2 should change)

2.2. In this exercise we inspect the code that was recorded in the previous exercise.

1. Open the file from Exercise 2.1.
2. Go to the VBA editor and inspect the macro that you recorded.
3. Clean up the macro to look like:

```
Sub Large()
   With Selection.Font
      .Size = 16
   End With
End Sub
```

4. Type something in cell C1. Activate cell C1 and run the macro. All the stuff you removed was unnecessary.
5. Type numbers in the 4 cells: D1:E2 and activate the 4 cells. Run the macro. Inspect the macro again: The word *Selection* in the second line ensures that the change is performed to all the selected cells. – Try it.

2.3. Record a macro that changes the font color to red. Test that it works.

2.4. Open the data file for this exercise. Record a macro that creates a pie chart displaying the data, create a button in the worksheet and assign your macro to it. Delete the chart you created and test that your macro can make a new one.

2.5. Open the data file for this exercise. Record a macro that creates a pie chart displaying the data and record another macro that creates a column chart displaying the same data. Swap to the VBA editor and compare the code of the two macros.

2.6. Follow the steps of Section 2.3 to become familiar with relative references.

Chapter 3
Try it Out

You are now familiar with the macro recorder. You know how to record a macro and how to execute it. You also know that the recorder cannot always solve the problem. In this chapter you will be introduced to various parts of programming so that you can write programs to do the tasks where the macro recorder cannot help you.

The material in this chapter will enable you to write small VBA programs on your own. In Chapters 4 through 7 we will go further into the material introduced in this chapter. The purpose of this structure is to let you get started with VBA programming without having to worry about a bunch of technicalities and formal definitions.

3.1 Getting Started

In the previous chapter we talked about macros, but when we turn to VBA and the VBA Editor, we refer to code as being clustered in *procedures*, not macros. Actually, the term macro is mainly a leftover from previous versions of Excel. So from now on we will talk about procedures.

There are two kinds of procedures: *Sub* and *Function*. You can use your functions directly from the Worksheet just like any existing Excel function. Functions return a value, but except from that they cannot make changes in the Worksheet. Subs are *executed*, for example by a button. They do not return any value, but can make changes to the Worksheet. When the macro recorder is used, the code is always recorded as a sub and so a sub is what you previously knew as a macro.

To insert a procedure, make sure that you are in the module where you want the procedure to be located. Now choose the menu *Insert* and select *Procedure* as illustrated in Figure 3.1.

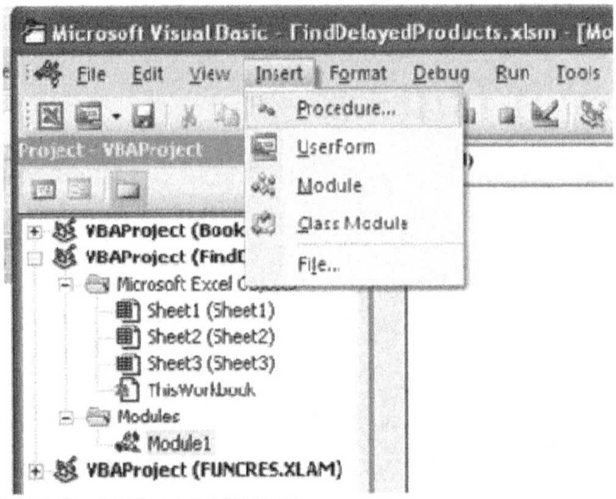

3.1 INSERTING A PROCEDURE.

The *Add Procedure* dialog box will be displayed as shown in Figure 3.2. Here you give your procedure a *name* and choose whether it should be a *sub* or a *function*. You can also choose whether it should be *public* or *private*. So far you should let all your procedures be public. In Chapter 5 you will learn the difference between public and private procedures.

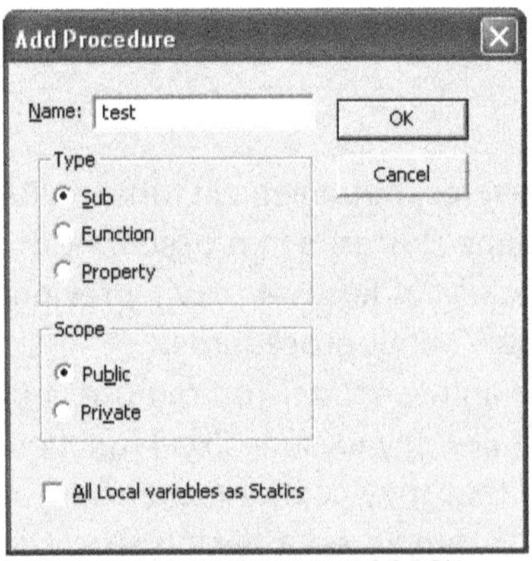

3.2 THE ADD PROCEDURE DIALOG BOX.

When the procedure is correctly inserted, you will see the words as displayed in Figure 3.3 in your module, where *test* is replaced by the name that you gave your procedure. You are now ready to write the content of your procedure.

```
Public Sub test()

End Sub
```

3.3 THE ADD PROCEDURE DIALOG BOX.

Alternatively, you can write the text of Figure 3.3 manually to avoid the *Add Procedure* dialog box.

3.2 Variables

When programming, you can think of variables as being small boxes that can contain a single number or a string of text. Imagine that these boxes are stored in some kind of depot. All you need in order to access the information you put into a box is the name of the variable. If for example you write

x = 7 + 3

the value of the variable *x* will be 10. Writing

ThisVariable = 2 x*

will cause the variable *ThisVariable* to have the value 20.

In Chapter 4 you learn to declare the variables. This basically means specifying that the only thing that may be contained in a certain box, is for example an integer number, a string of text, or a date. The reasons for doing this are many. Most importantly: It saves computer memory and it helps you avoid bugs in your program.

3.3 Accessing the Worksheet

If you know that you are currently in Sheet 1 of a certain file, you can access cell A2 by writing *Range("A2").* But you must be sure that you are in sheet 1 to do this. If you activate your macro from Sheet 2, writing Range("A2") will give you cell A2 of Sheet 2.

Think of it this way: If you know that you are at Park Street, you can say that you live in number 7, and people will know where your house is. If you are at Baker Street and you say that you live in number 7, they will think that you mean Baker Street 7 – and they get the wrong house. You have to specify: Street(Park Street).Number(7). If your house is in London, England, and you are currently in Aarhus, Denmark, you would have to specify this even further: Country(England).City(London). Street(Park Street).Number(7). As you see: the level of specification depends on your location. Writing VBA code is the same: If you know for sure that you are in Sheet 1 you can write *Range("A2"),* but if you could be in another sheet, write *Worksheets("Sheet1").Range("A2").* If you want to refer to A2 in sheet 1 in some other file, you must specify the file name as well. If you are not absolutely sure where you are, please use the long specification to avoid bugs in your program. If you like, you can refer to several cells: *Worksheets("Sheet1").Range("A2:D5").*

If you want to change the value of cell A1 to be 7, you should write *Worksheets("Sheet1").Range("A1").Value = 7,* but because *Value* is the default for *Range*, you may omit this as above and write *Worksheets("Sheet1").Range("A1") = 7.*

Sometimes it is convenient to avoid the letter specification that is needed when using *Range()*. In this case, you can use index. For example, *Cells(2, 1)* refers to cell A2. The syntax is *Cells(row number, column number)*. For example, writing

Cells(27, 3) = "Products"

will cause the word *Products* to be written in cell C27.

3.4 Input and Output

There are several ways to communicate with your user. A very simple way is to use the worksheet for input and output. If for example you want to store the number in cell C2 in a variable called *x*, you write *x = Range("C2").Value*. Note that the program is trying to help you by displaying your options: you can choose *Value* in the drop-down list instead of typing it as illustrated in Figure 3.4. This service comes in handy when you are not quite sure what you are looking for.

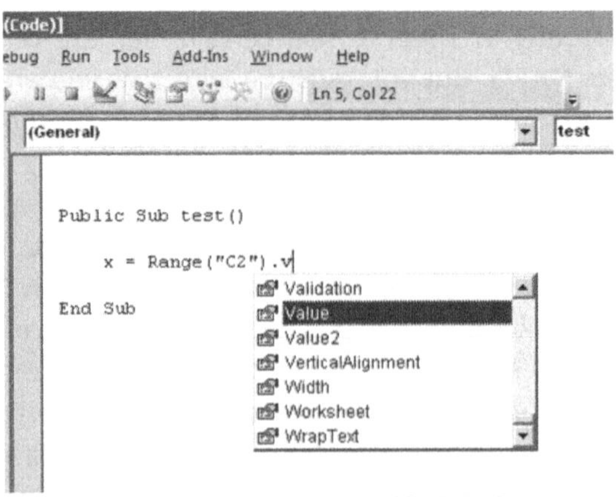

3.4 THE DROP-DOWN LISTS ARE THERE TO HELP YOU.

Similarly, if you want to write the content of the variable *y* to cell B7, you write *Range("B7").Value = y*.

Sometimes you do not want your user to deal with the worksheet or you want the user to pay extra attention to something. Note that even though it seems simple to do so, people seem to have a hard time writing the correct thing, in the correct format, in the correct cell of a worksheet. These are just some of the arguments for learning how to use input boxes and message boxes. Be aware that message boxes can be really annoying (personally I find it quite annoying that my computer asks me if I am sure that I want to delete a file when I just pressed delete.)

3.4.1 Message Box

If you want to display a *message box* with the text *you are done*, you can do it by typing *MsgBox "You are Done !"*. This will display the message box in Figure 3.5.

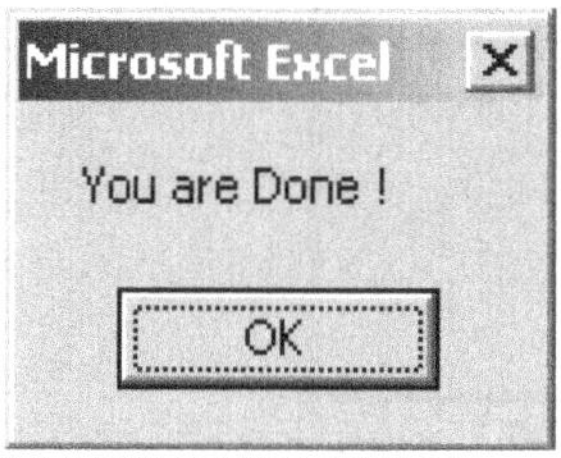

3.5 A SIMPLE MESSAGE BOX.

For this basic box you did not need (), even though *MsgBox* is actually a function. You need them if you want a more advanced message box. For example, if you write *x = MsgBox("Delete Sheet 1 permanently ?", vbOKCancel + vbQuestion)*, you get the message box in Figure 3.6.

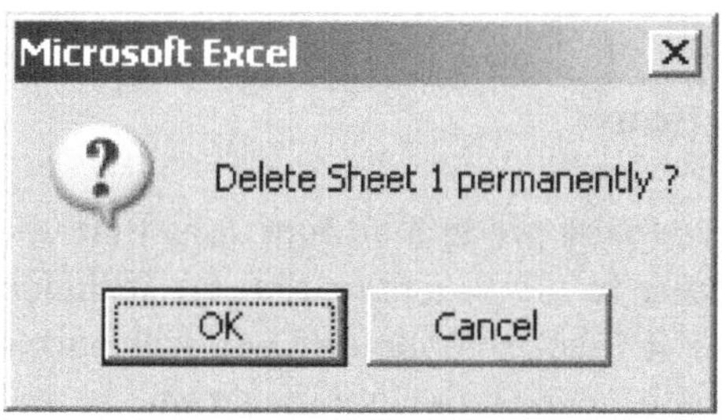

3.6 A MESSAGE BOX THAT GIVES THE USER A CHOICE.

Remember: I just said that *MsgBox* is a function. Hence, it is just like the excel function *=SumProduct*, it returns a value. In the case of our message box example: If the user presses *OK*, the return value is 1 and if the user chooses *Cancel*, the return value is 2. In either case this value will be stored in the variable *x* above. A list of possible return values and a list of options for buttons and icons can be found in Chapter 15, where the message box is explained in detail.

3.4.2 Input Box

Message boxes are good for displaying messages and for getting the yes/no type answers from the user, but often the information you need is not of a yes/no type. You might want to know the name of the product he wants to buy or his personal security number in order to access his employment record. To get this type of information, you can use an *input box*. The standard use of an input box is *s = InputBox("Which product do you want to buy ?")*, which will display:

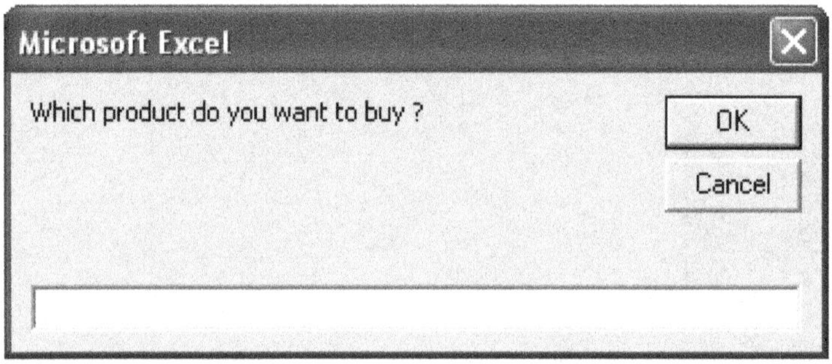

3.7 AN INPUT BOX IS USED TO OBTAIN INFORMATION FROM THE USER.

If the user enters *bananas*, this will now be the value of the variable *s*. Note that your program should also deal with the fact that the user can type nothing or press *Cancel*. If cancel is pressed, the return value is "", i.e. a string of length zero, which is often referred to as an *empty string*. You will learn more about strings in Chapter 13.

3.5 Using Excel and VBA Functions

When you write VBA code, there are many predefined functions that you can use. Furthermore, you have access to the functions that are included in the application which, in this case, is Excel. In Chapter 5 you will learn a lot more about how to use these functions in your program. In the following we shall merely see a few examples. Finally, if you install Add-ins, you have access to the functions of those too. In Chapters 11, 17 and 18 you will learn much more about this.

You have already seen two VBA functions: the *message box* and the *input box*.

```
Sub print_now()
    Range("A1").Value = Now()
End Sub
```

3.8 NOW DISPLAYS THE CURRENT DATE AND TIME.

Some functions deal with date and time: For example you can write the current date and time in cell A1 by using the function *=Now* as shown in Figure 3.8. The result of executing the procedure is shown in Figure 3.9.

	A	B
1	14-08-2009 13:01	
2		
3		
4		

3.9 RESULT OF EXECUTING THE CODE IN FIGURE 3.8.

There are many more functions available. Some deal with numbers, and some deal with strings of text. In Figure 3.10, you see some examples of their use with the result of executing the procedure shown in Figure 3.11.

```
Sub print_vba_functions()
    Range("A2").Value = Abs(15)
    Range("A3").Value = Abs(-12)
    Range("A4").Value = Sqr(16)
    Range("A5").Value = UCase("function")
    Range("A6").Value = Int(13.679)
End Sub
```

3.10 YOU CAN USE BUILT-IN VBA FUNCTIONS IN YOUR CODE.

Above you have seen a few examples of how to use VBA functions. Worksheet functions require more code. For example, to use the *=Sum* function to write the sum of the numbers in cells A2:A4, in cell B2 in the worksheet of Figure 3.11, you write

Range("B2").Value = Application.WorksheetFunction.Sum("A2:A4")

In Chapter 5 you will learn more about this. For now, you just need to know that this is the way to do it.

	A	B
1		
2	15	
3	12	
4	4	
5	FUNCTION	
6	13	
7		

3.11 RESULT OF EXECUTING THE CODE IN FIGURE 3.10.

There are many functions available for your use – both VBA functions and so-called worksheet functions. You can often save time by consulting the *Object Browser*. See Chapter 5 to learn more about the available functions and their use.

3.6 Making Decisions

In order to write programs that actually perform something, you often need the program to make decisions. For example *is this a new customer* (in which case we need to add him to our database), *is the machine ready to perform a new job* (in which case we should select the next job), *or is the order too large or too heavy to be shipped in one box* (in which case we must determine how to split the order). For the purpose of decision making in programming, an *If-Then-Else* construction can be used. Figure 3.12 illustrates the most simple use of this construction. The Else part is illustrated subsequently.

```
Sub SendOrder()
    OrderWeight = Range("B3").Value
    If OrderWeight > 100 Then
        MsgBox "The Shipment must be partitioned into several boxes."
        ' Add code to perform the partitioning here
    End If
    ' Continue here with the rest of the code
End Sub
```

3.12 A SIMPLE IF-THEN-ELSE CONSTRUCTION.

First the weight is read from cell B3 and stored in the variable *OrderWeight*. Then it is checked if it is greater than 100. If that is the case, a message box appears with the information that the shipment must be split. Space is left for adding code to perform the partitioning. Afterwards the program should continue with whatever code is needed. If, on the other hand, the weight is less than or equal to 100, the block with the Message box is ignored and the program jumps to the line where it says *Continue here….*

Now that you have learned how to make simple decisions, let us make it a little more complicated and a lot more useful. Figure 3.12 can be extended to: *If the weight is greater than 100, the shipment should be partition. If the weight is less than or equal to 100, but the length is more than 200 units, the order should be sent by special shipment. Otherwise, if the weight is less than 10, shipment should wait for further orders, and finally, if none of the above is true, the order should be sent by standard shipment.* The code for this is given in Figure 3.13.

```
Sub SendOrderExtendedVersion()
    OrderWeight = Range("B3").Value
    OrderLength = Range("B4").Value
    If OrderWeight > 100 Then
        MsgBox "The shipment must be partitioned into several boxes."
        ' Add code to perform the partitioning here
    ElseIf OrderLength > 200 Then
        MsgBox "Use special shipment."
        ' Add code to send by special shipment
    ElseIf OrderWeight < 10 Then
        MsgBox "Postpone shipment."
        ' Add code to postpone shipment
    Else
        MsgBox "Use standard shipment"
        ' Add code to send by standard shipment
    End If
    ' Continue here with the rest of the code
End Sub
```

3.13 AN IF-THEN-ELSE CONSTRUCTION.

As soon as a condition is true, the code corresponding to that condition will be executed, after which the program jumps to the line where it says *Continue here…*. For example, if the value in B3 is 130, the first condition is true, and the message box shown in Figure 3.14 will be displayed, the program will jump to *Continue here…* and terminate.

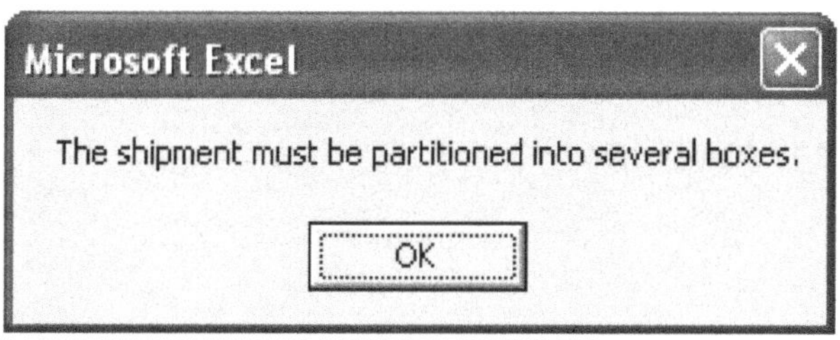

3.14 RESULT OF EXAMPLE 4 IF THE WEIGHT IS 130.

On the other hand, if the value of B3 is 8, the first condition is false. Now the second condition is evaluated. Assuming that the value of B4 is 100, then the second condition is also false, and the program continues by checking the third condition. The third condition is true.

3.15 RESULT OF EXAMPLE 4 IF THE WEIGHT IS 8 AND THE LENGTH IS 100.

Therefore, the code corresponding to this condition is executed, and the message box shown in Figure 3.15 will be displayed. Afterwards, the program will jump to *Continue here...* and terminate.

You must have the *If* and the *End If*, but you can leave out the *ElseIf* and the *Else,* if you do not need them. This is what we did in Figure 3.12. Furthermore, you can include *ElseIf* as many times as you like, though if you need a lot, you might consider using a *Select-Case* construction, which will be explained in detail in Chapter 6. You will also learn more about the *If-Then-Else* construction in Chapter 6.

3.7 Looping

You will often need to search through a list of something. For example, search for a certain product code in a list of products, search for all junior staff members in a list of faculty members, or search for the product with the shortest production time.

There are many different types of looping. For now you will only need to learn one type: the *For-Next* loop. The use of this kind of loop is illustrated in Figure 3.16.

```
Public Sub test()
    For i = 1 To 5
        Sheet3.Cells(i, 1) = i * i
    Next
End Sub
```

3.16 A FOR-NEXT LOOP.

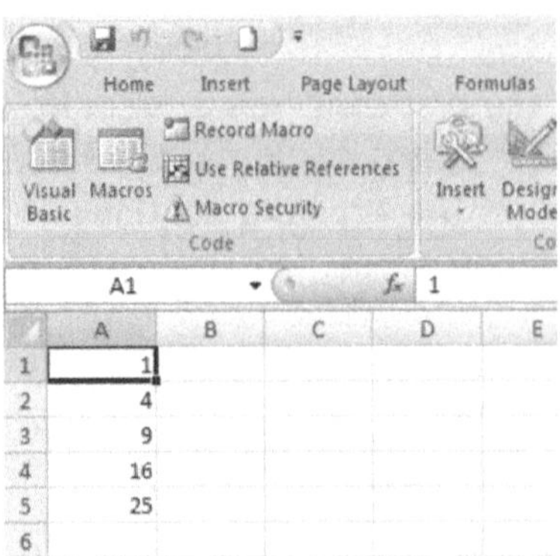

3.17 RESULT OF EXECUTING THE CODE IN FIGURE 3.16.

The lines of code between the *For* and the *Next* are referred to as the *body* of the loop. First, the body of the loop is executed with *i = 1*, in which case, *i * i* is 1, which is written in cell (1,1). Next, *i = 2,* in which case, *i * i* is 4, which is written in cell (2,1). This continues until *i = 5,* which is the value in the final execution of the body. The result of executing the code is shown in Figure 3.17.

3.8 Good Programming Practice

Sometimes you – or somebody else – will probably want to change part of your code. Maybe the code it not quite as perfect for the purpose as you thought it would be, or maybe reality changed and your carefully thought out program needs an update. It can be extremely difficult to return to old code and even more so if you are not the one who wrote the code in the first place. Imagine having to find the right ten lines to change among thousands of lines that are nested in complex ways.

This section will provide you with a few directions for a good programming style. Following these will make it easier to return to existing code. Furthermore, they have the advantage of making the process of finding bugs in your code easier. We will return to the latter issue in Chapter 9.

3.8.1 Structure Your Code

Many programmers have had to re-write part of a program because they had not carefully thought out the structure of their code. We all know the expression *think before you talk*. Translating that into a programming term *think before you code* will spare you many frustrations.

You particularly need to be aware of four things: Firstly: Which input data, or information, is needed in your program, and how can you best obtain it? Can you access the data directly from the worksheet or do you need to import data from an external source such as Access. Maybe you need to obtain some information directly from the user by means of one or several user forms. Secondly: What kind of output should your program provide? You might need a table or a list of information or you might just need a single number. Maybe you need your program to create a report with a bunch of charts.

Thirdly: How should the input be processed in order to provide the output, and in which order should this be done? Maybe you can work with whole tables of information at the same time, and maybe you have to carefully perform calculations with each piece of information separately.

The final matter is more of a technical type. It has to do with breaking your code up into small blocks that are easily maintained and which can be drawn upon several times while executing the code. We will return to the issue of writing well structured code in Chapter 10.

3.8.2 Naming Convention

Sometimes, when programming, people can be misled to think that short variable names result in fast coding. Doing that your program can end up with a bunch of variables called *i, ii, ia, ib, k, kk, x, xx, xa, xb, ni, nj, nn*, etc. Every time a variable is needed, the programmer has to backtrack in order to figure out what that specific variable was called. That is everything but time saving.

Therefore, in order to save yourself a lot of frustrations, give your variables meaningful names such as *NumVehicles*, *number_of_vehicles*, or *vehicle_cnt* for the variable holding the number of vehicles; *CustomerLastName*, *last_name_of_customer*, or *str_cust_l_name* for the variable holding the last name of a customer (here the *str* in the latter suggestion indicates that the variable is of type string).

Only you know which naming convention suits you the best, but a good advice is to use a convention that makes sense to you and to be consistent with that convention – not only in a single program, but across all your programs. That way, naming variables will become a routine to you. The letters *i, j*, and *k* are often used as indices in For-Next loops, unless the loop is going through time, in which case *t* is often used. This book will mainly use the convention illustrated by *NumVehicles* and *CustomerLastName*.

3.8.3 Commenting/Documenting

Computers are very good at reading programming code, but humans are not. Therefore, we should add some information to the code that is quite readable for humans. Such lines of information are called *comments*. You add a comment to your code by starting it with the sign '(apostrophe).

Comments can be short: *'item in inventory*, or long *'we now consider all the customers in order to find the nearest one. The nearest one is added to the route and the current position is updated.* The important thing is that they should help making the flow of the code clear to humans. You can see examples throughout this book on how commenting can be performed in a helpful way.

Note that if you write a rather large program to be used by someone other than yourself, you should make further documentation like a manual and/or a guide of use. We will not consider these issues further in this book.

3.8.4 Indention

Consider the code in Figures 3.18 and 3.19. The code in the two examples is identical. The only difference is that the code in Figure 3.19 is significantly easier to read for humans than the code in Figure 3.18. The longer and more complicated your code gets, the more important it is to use indention properly. After a while, indenting your code becomes just as natural as breaking a long text into paragraphs.

```
Sub without_indention()
For i = 2 To 11
If Cells(i, 2).Value >= 90000 Then
Cells(i, 3).Value = "Major"
ElseIf Cells(i, 2).Value <= 30000 Then
Cells(i, 3).Value = "Minor"
Else
Cells(i, 3).Value = "Medium"
End If
Next
End Sub
```

3.18 CODE WITHOUT INDENTION.

```
Sub with_indention()
    For i = 2 To 11
        If Cells(i, 2).Value >= 90000 Then
            Cells(i, 3).Value = "Major"
        ElseIf Cells(i, 2).Value <= 30000 Then
            Cells(i, 3).Value = "Minor"
        Else
            Cells(i, 3).Value = "Medium"
        End If
    Next
End Sub
```

3.19 CODE WITH INDENTION IS EASIER TO READ.

It is not hard to perform useful indention: Every time a loop or decision structure begins, the indention is increased for the following code, and every time it is ended, the indention is decreased. Indention will be used throughout this book.

3.9 Putting it all Together

In this section we illustrate the use of some of what is presented in this chapter. We do this through an example where we carefully explain the details.

3.9.1 Example: Delayed Products

We consider a list of products to be produced, which is shown in Figure 3.20. For each product we are given the due time and the time at which the production of the product was completed. As can be seen in the figure, planning has not been very good and several products are delayed. At the same time, other products seem to be ready long before their due time.

	A	B	C	D
1	Product	Due Time	Ready Time	
2	3492	25	52	
3	4532	63	36	
4	4267	74	36	
5	7814	93	84	
6	2870	28	62	
7	9387	53	25	
8	8537	83	76	
9	1649	39	47	
10	8242	67	15	
11	7329	84	47	
12				

3.20 DATA FOR THE CODE IN FIGURE 3.21.

In the following we will make a small program that goes through the list of product, and for each product it writes information about the production in column D. If the product is delayed, this is stated. If the product is more than ten time units early, it is stated that the product is very early. Otherwise the product is on time. Furthermore, in the end of the program, a message box should be displayed with information about the number of delayed jobs. A code that solves this problem is shown in Figure 3.21.

The first step is to make a *For-Next* loop that iterates through the products. The following piece of code deals with that part.

```
For i = 2 To 11

Next
```

For each product, the variable *i* will now be the row index when the body of the loop is executed. In the body of the loop we want, for each row, to compare the contents of columns B and C. These can be referred to as *Sheet1.Cells(i, 2)* and *Sheet1.Cells(i, 3)*, respectively. We are going to use an *If-Then-Else* construction to separate the three cases; *delayed*, *very early*, and *on time*. In each case we use *Sheet1.Cells(i, 4)* to write the correct information to column D.

```
Sub FindDelayedProducts()
    NumberDelayed = 0
    For i = 2 To 11
        If Sheet1.Cells(i, 2) < Sheet1.Cells(i, 3) Then
            Sheet1.Cells(i, 4) = "Delayed"
            NumberDelayed = NumberDelayed + 1
        ElseIf Sheet1.Cells(i, 2) > Sheet1.Cells(i, 3) + 10 Then
            Sheet1.Cells(i, 4) = "Very early"
        Else
            Sheet1.Cells(i, 4) = "On time"
        End If
    Next
    MsgBox "There are " & NumberDelayed & " delayed procucts."
End Sub
```

3.21 FIND THE DELAYED PRODUCTS.

Finally, we need to count the number of delayed products. We do this by making a variable, *NumberDelayed*, and setting it equal to zero in the top of the program. Each time we find a delayed product in our *If-Then-Else* construction, we increase the value of the variable by one. After having considered all products we will use a message box to display the value of the variable. The result of executing this code can be seen in Figure 3.22.

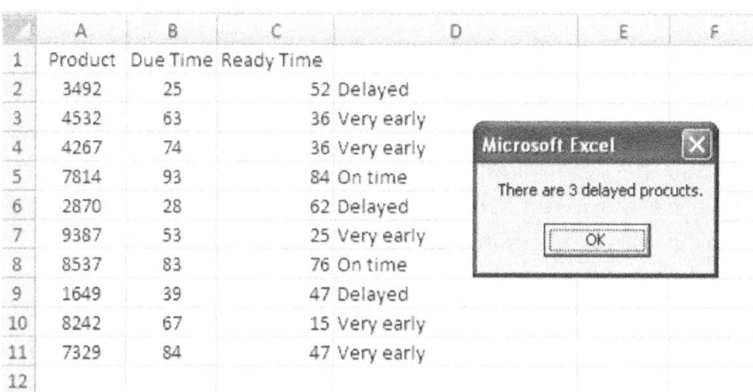

	A	B	C	D	E	F
1	Product	Due Time	Ready Time			
2	3492	25	52	Delayed		
3	4532	63	36	Very early		
4	4267	74	36	Very early		
5	7814	93	84	On time		
6	2870	28	62	Delayed		
7	9387	53	25	Very early		
8	8537	83	76	On time		
9	1649	39	47	Delayed		
10	8242	67	15	Very early		
11	7329	84	47	Very early		
12						

3.22 RESULT OF EXECUTING THE CODE IN FIGURE 2.21.

3.10 Exercises

3.1. Write a Sub that uses an input box to ask for a number. The Sub should determine if the number is positive or negative and make a message box stating: *The number is positive* or *The number is negative*.

3.2. Change the Sub from Exercise 3.1 to read the number from cell E3 of the worksheet and write the information to cell F3.

3.3. Write a Sub that reads two values from the worksheet (e.g. cells D1 and D2) and stores them in two variables. Write the product of the two variables in a cell (e.g. D3) of the worksheet.

3.4. Enter four numbers between -100 and 100 in cells A1, A2, B1, and B2 of the worksheet. Assume that they are coordinates for two points: 1: (A1, B1) and 2: (A2, B2). Write a Sub that reads the four values and uses them to calculate the Euclidean distance between the two points using the formula $\sqrt{(x_1 - x_2)^2 + (y_1 - y_2)^2}$. The Sub should write the distance to the worksheet in cell A3 and display it in a message box.

3.5. Open the file for this exercise. The file already contains a Sub that generates 20 random numbers between -1000 and 1000 and writes them to the range A1:A20 of the worksheet. A button is included to execute the Sub. Write a new Sub that determines the maximum of the generated numbers and writes it to cell D1. The Sub should also write a suitable header, e.g. *Maximum*, in cell C1.

3.6. Open the file with you solution of Exercise 3.5. Expand your Sub to determine the minimum of the numbers and write it to cell D2 along with a suitable header in cell C2.

3.7. Open the file with your solution of the two previous exercises. Expand your Sub to determine the average of the numbers and the number of positive numbers. Write the information to cells D3 and D4, respectively along with headers in cells C3 and C4.

3.8. Open the file for this exercise which is the same as for Exercise 3.5. You can use the file containing your solution of that exercise. It is often not enough to know the value of the maximum number. However, often the index of the row containing the maximum is needed. Write a new Sub that determines the maximum of the 20 values and writes it to cell D1 (just like you did in Exercise 3.5). Furthermore, your Sub should write the index of the row containing the value in cell E1. If the maximum value occurs more than once, the Sub should just write the index of any one of the occurrences.

Chapter 4
Variables

It is now time to go deeper into detail with variables. As mentioned in Chapter 3, variables can be thought of as boxes or envelopes that can store specific information. The label of the box corresponds to the name of the variable, and the content of the box corresponds to the value of the variable.

In Section 4.1, we introduce different types of variables and in Section 4.2, we explain how to declare a variable. In Section 4.3, we give information about the scope of variables and finally, in Section 4.4, we introduce arrays which are used for holding whole lists of information at a time.

4.1 Types of Variables

Depending on the need, different variable types are used. To hold the number of customers or the number of trials in a simulation, variables of *Integer* type are appropriate. To hold the amount of ton to be shipped each day or the expected interest rate, floating point types such as *Single* or *Double* are used. To hold information that can be either true or false, such as whether a product has been ordered or whether a vehicle is in use, a variable of *Boolean* type is suitable.

To hold date and time related information, the *Date* data type is appropriate. To hold information about product name or customer name and address, *Strings* are used. Strings are also used to hold text that should be displayed for the user under certain circumstances.

To hold references to objects such as worksheets, charts, or ranges, special *object* variables are used. These are different from the simple variable types discussed in this chapter and will be considered further in Chapter 7 where we introduce the Excel object model.

If the variable type is not specified, VBA will automatically assume that the variable is of the type *Variant*. The use of this type of variable should be avoided unless strictly necessary because it requires significantly more computer memory than other types.

Details about the information that can be stored in each type of variable can be found in Table 4.1.

4.1 DIFFETENT TYPES OF VARIABLES.

Data type	Bytes used	Range of value
Boolean	2 bytes	True or False
Integer	2 bytes	-32,768 to 32,767
Long	4 bytes	-2,147,483,648 to 2,147,483,647
Single	4 bytes	-3.402823E38 to -1.401298E-45 for negative values and 1.401298E-45 to 3.402823E38 for positive values
Double	8 bytes	-1.79769313486231E308 to -4.94065645841247E-324 for negative values and 4.94065645841247E-324 to 1.79769313486232E308 for positive values
Date	8 bytes	January 1st 100 to December 31th 9999
Object	4 bytes	Any object reference
String	10 bytes + length	1 to about 2 billion characters
Variant (with numbers)	16 bytes	As double
Variant (with characters)	22 bytes + length	As strings

Certain rules have to be respected when using variables. A variable name must begin with a letter and may contain letters, numbers and underscore (_). A variable name may be up to 255 characters long. It is recommended to use variable names that are descriptive with respect to the purpose of the variable.

4.2 Declaring Variables

You declare a variable in your program by stating the name and data type of the variable in the beginning of your procedure. To do this, you use the keyword *Dim* as shown in Figure 4.1. The drop-down list can be useful for selecting the variable type. Variables of numeric types will automatically be assigned the value 0 when they are declared.

By declaring the variables you ensure that the variable can only store the specified type of information. That can help you avoid bugs in your program because VBA will inform you if your program tries to assign information of a different type to a declared variable.

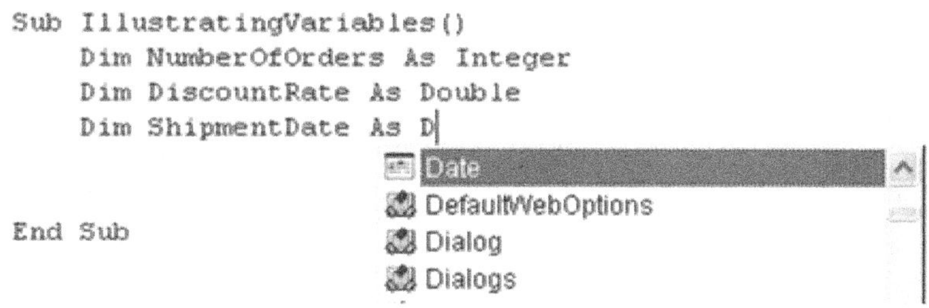

4.1 DECLARE VARIABLES USING DIM.

Furthermore, declaring variables in the top of your procedure can help you by giving you a quick overview of the variables used in the procedure, including their name and their type. If the purpose of the variable is not obvious from its name, it is recommended to include a comment after the declaration to explain the purpose.

Even though the variables in a procedure are declared, it does not prevent you from using a variable that is not declared as well. This also means that if you have a variable called *cost* and somewhere in your procedure make a typo and write *cast*, VBA will automatically assume that this is just a new variable which has nothing to do with the variable called *cost*. This can result in a program that misbehaves, and this type of bug can be really hard to locate.

To prevent you from creating new variables due to typos with the resulting problem of locating bugs, the following strategy can be used. In the top of your module, before any procedure is started, write *Option Explicit* as illustrated in Figure 4.2. That way you are only allowed to use variables that have been declared and you will be prompted if you break that rule. This part of the module is referred to as the declaration part.

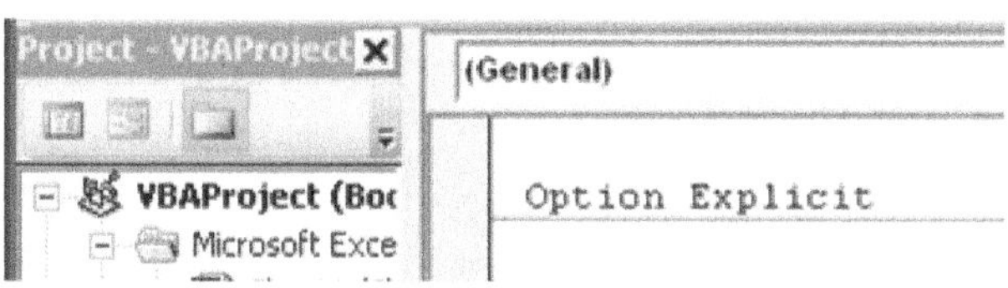

4.2 USE OPTION EXPLICIT TO FORCE VARIABLE DECLARATION.

By selecting *Options* in the *Tools* menu of the VBA Editor and selecting *Require Variable Declaration*, the *Option Explicit* will automatically be entered in any new module that you create. It is highly recommended to do so.

If a variable is not declared before it is used, VBA will assign the data type *variant* to it. That way, it can store any kind of information, and there is nothing to prevent you from using it to hold a string of text for example and later in the procedure use that variable in division as if it was a floating point number. There is no need to explain to you what kind of problems that can course.

A final reason for declaring variables has to do with the use of computer memory. As can be seen from Table 4.1, variables of type variant require significantly more computer memory than other types.

4.3 Scope of Variables

A variable can be either local to a single procedure or it can be at module or global level where the same variable can be used in many procedures. We will discuss this further in the following.

4.3.1 Local Variables

As a general rule a variable is only available within the procedure in which it is declared. Neither the content of the variable nor the variable name is known outside that procedure. Therefore, assuming that *Option Explicit* is used, an error will occur if you try to use the variable outside the procedure. We say that the variable is born with the procedure and dies with the procedure. When leaving the procedure, the computer memory that held the variable information is freed. Next time the procedure is activated, a new variable with the same name and type will be created.

Sometimes it is useful if a variable can remember its value until the procedure is called next time. In Figure 4.3, the variable *Count* is declared by using the keyword *Static* instead of the *Dim* keyword. If *Count* is 5 when *MySub* is called, it will automatically be 6 when the sub is called the next time. Even though this is a smart feature, you should be extremely careful when using it as bugs can easily occur.

```
Sub MySub()
    Dim Amount As Double
    Static Count As Integer

    Count = Count + 1
End Sub
```

4.3 USE THE KEYWORD STATIC TO CREATE A STATIC VARIABLE.

4.3.2 Module and Global Variables

A variable can also be visible for more than one procedure. This can be extremely useful for storing information that is used in many procedures in the program, for example the interest rate, the number of customers, information about available vehicles, or a list of all the employees.

In order to create a variable that can be used from any procedure in a module, the variable should be declared in the *declaration part* of the module, i.e. above any procedure. In Figure 4.4, the variable *cost* is such a variable. The value assigned to *cost* in one procedure can be accessed or changed by any other procedure in the module.

```
Option Explicit

Dim cost As Double

Public InterestRate As Double

Sub MySub()
```

4.4 THE VARIABLE COST IS AVAILABLE IN ALL PROCEDURES OF THE MODULE.

Access to the variable *cost* in Figure 4.4 is limited to the procedures in the current module. By declaring the variable using the keyword *Public* instead of *Dim*, the variable is made available for any procedure in any module in the current workbook. This is illustrated by the variable *InterestRate* in Figure 4.4 which can be accessed and changed by any procedure in any module in the current workbook.

4.3.3 Who is in Charge?

It is not hard to imagine the conflicts and confusions that could arise when several procedures use the same variable name. Fortunately, this issue is automatically dealt with in a rather intuitive manner.

```
Option Explicit

Sub PlanProduction()
    Dim j As Integer
    j = 30
End Sub

Sub NewCustomer()
    Dim j As Integer

End Sub
```

4.5 DIFFERENT PROCEDURES CAN HAVE VARIABLES OF THE SAME NAME.

Consider the code given in Figure 4.5. Here, both the *PlanProduction* procedure and the *NewCustomer* procedure have a variable named *j*. However, since each of these variables are local to each their procedure, they do not conflict. The computer automatically keeps track of which variable belongs to which procedure.

Even if one or both variables are *static*, the computer will still keep them apart, and if one procedure is executing the other, there is still no conflict. This means that you can create and use local variables in your procedures without worrying about which local variables are used in other procedures of your program.

Now, consider the code in Figure 4.6. In this example there is a module level variable called *Cost*. This variable is used in the *TotalCost* procedure and in other procedures which are not shown. In the *CalculateProductCost* procedure a local variable with the same name is defined. When the *CalculateProductCost* procedure is executed the *Cost* variable local to that procedure is created and every reference to the variable *Cost* within that procedure will refer to that local variable. That way, the *CalculateProductCost* procedure does not have access to the module level *Cost* variable.

```
Option Explicit

Dim Cost As Double

Sub TotalCost()
    SimplePrice = 1.3 * Cost
End Sub

Sub CalculateProductCost()
    Dim Cost As Double
    Cost = Range("F7")
End Sub
```

4.6 THE COMPUTER WILL KEEP YOUR VARIABLES APART.

4.4 Arrays

Very often, the information that needs to be stored is not a single value, but a whole list of values. This could be, for example a list of customer locations, a list of possible shipment dates, or a list of available employees to work on new projects.

For the purpose of storing lists of information, arrays are used. An *array* is created by declaring the variable with parenthesis after the name.

In Figure 4.7, two arrays are declared, one to store a list of integer numbers and one to store a list of dates. Numeric arrays are created with the value 0 stored in every location.

```
Dim NumberArray(5) As Integer
Dim DateArray(10) As Date
```

4.7 DECLARATION OF ARRAYS.

When creating an array, the number in the parenthesis defines the last index of the array. By default, arrays are indexed starting with 0. Therefore, the two arrays in Figure 4.7 can store 6 and 11 elements, respectively.

To access the single element of an array, simply write the name of the array followed by parenthesis containing the index of the element you want to access. In Figure 4.8, the values 10, -1, and 100 are inserted in the first, second, and last location of the *NumberArray* from Figure 4.7, respectively. Hereafter the *NumberArray* will have the content as shown in Figure 4.9.

```
NumberArray(0) = 10
NumberArray(1) = -1
NumberArray(5) = 100
```

4.8 STORING DATA IN ARRAYS.

10	-1	0	0	0	100

4.9 THE RESULTING ARRAY.

Sometimes it is convenient to have arrays that are not indexed from 0. For this purpose you can specify the lower and upper index as you declare the array. The array *A* in Figure 4.10 is indexed from 3 through 10 and hence can store 8 integers.

```
Dim A(3 To 10) As Integer
```

4.10 ARRAY INDEXED FROM 3 THROUGH 10.

Another option is to include the statement *Option Base 1* in the declaration part of the module as shown in Figure 4.11. This will cause all arrays to be indexed starting at 1 instead of 0.

```
Option Explicit
Option Base 1
```

4.11 USE OPTION BASE 1.

4.4.1 Dynamic Arrays

When writing a computer program or a small sub or function to make everyday tasks simpler, the number of items to be stored in an array is often not known. The program should be flexible enough to handle this. The length of the array will often be determined while the program is executing. The number of possible shipping dates might be obtained from a user form, a list of customer locations could be read from a worksheet, and so on.

To create a *dynamic array*, you just leave the parenthesis empty. Before storing information in an array, it must be dimensioned by the keyword *ReDim*.

To illustrate, assume that the number of possible shipping dates are given in cell A1 of the current worksheet and that the dates are listed in column B starting from B1. The code in Figure 4.12 reads the number of shipping dates from A1, re-dimensions the array, and stores the list of dates in the array. The code assumes that option base 1 is activated.

```
Sub DynamicArray()
    Dim NumberDates As Integer
    Dim Dates() As Date
    Dim j As Integer

    NumberDates = Range("A1").Value
    ReDim Dates(NumberDates)

    For j = 1 To NumberDates
        Dates(j) = Cells(j, 2)
    Next

    'Here follows the remaining code
End Sub
```

4.12 USE REDIM DO SET THE SIZE OF DYNAMIC ARRAYS.

It is possible to re-dimension a dynamic array as many times as desired. If you want to keep the values you have stored in the array, you must tell the computer to *preserve* them. Otherwise, the values stored in the array may be lost when you re-dimension it.

```
Option Explicit
Option Base 1

Sub IncreasingArraySize()
    Dim n As Integer
    Dim Amount() As Integer

    ReDim Amount(3)
    Amount(1) = 56
    Amount(2) = 71
    Amount(3) = 14
    'Here is some code

    n = 10
    ReDim Preserve Amount(n)
End Sub
```

4.13 USE PRESERVE TO KEEP EXISTING DATA.

This is illustrated in Figure 4.13 where the array *Amount* is first re-dimensioned to length 3 and three values are stored in it. Later in the code the array is re-dimensioned to length 10, while the values are preserved. Figure 4.14 shows the content of the array before and after it is re-dimensioned to length 10.

56	71	14							
56	71	14	0	0	0	0	0	0	0

4.14 THE DYNAMIC ARRAY OF FIGURE 4.13.

4.4.2 Multi Dimensional Arrays

Lists of data are good, but what if you need to store a whole table or matrix of information? It could be a table of distances between pairs of locations, or expected sales numbers for a fruit stand based on number of opening hours, weather, and location. VBA can handle up to 60 dimensions which should be enough for all practical purposes.

Multi dimensional arrays are created exactly the same way as normal arrays which is illustrated by the examples in Figure 4.15.

```
Sub MultiDimensionalArray()

    Dim Dist(10, 10) As Double
    Dim Sales(3 To 14, 3, 5) As Double
```

4.15 CREATING MULTI DIMENSIONAL ARRAYS.

Multi dimensional arrays can be flexible in size just like single dimensional ones. This is illustrated in Figure 4.16 where a matrix of distances is read from the worksheet which is assumed to contain such information. The number of cities to be included is obtained from the user via an input box. This defines the size of the array. The distance information is stored in the array using two *nested For-Next* loops. Again, we assume that *Option Base 1* is activated. Consult Chapter 6 to learn about nested loops.

```
Sub ReadDistances()
    Dim Dist() As Double
    Dim n As Integer
    Dim i As Integer
    Dim j As Integer

    n = InputBox("Please specify the number of cities:")
    ReDim Dist(n, n)

    For i = 1 To n
        For j = 1 To n
            Dist(i, j) = Cells(i, j)
        Next
    Next
End Sub
```

4.16 STORING DISTANCE INFORMATION IN A 2-DIMENSIONAL ARRAY.

4.5 Exercises

4.1. If you have not already done so, turn automatic *Option Explicit* on.

4.2. Open the data file for this exercise. Column A contains a long list of product codes and column B contains the corresponding prices. The number of products is given in cell D1. Write a Sub as follows:

1. Declare two array variables: *price* and *code* and resize them to be able to contain all the products. Declare also any other variable that you may need.
2. Use a For-Next Loop to store all the product codes and prices in the arrays.
3. Use an input box to ask for a product code and store it in a string.
4. Use a For-Next loop to search for the product in the code array.
5. If the product is found, give information about the price in a message box.
6. Test your code by giving different product codes.

4.3. Open the data file for this exercise. The goal of this exercise is to store the numbers of column A in an array in the order given by the numbers in column B. For that purpose, create a sub to do the following:

1. Create an array of length 25 with option Base 1.
2. Use a For-Next loop to iterate through the numbers.
3. For each iteration of the loop, read the index in column B and store it in an integer variable. Use that variable as index of the array and store the corresponding number of column A in that location of the array.
4. To test that you performed step 1 through 3 correctly, create a new For-Next loop and use it to write the numbers from the array to column D of the worksheet.

4.4. Open the data file for this exercise. Column A contains 30 integers. Set Option Base 1. Create an integer array of length 10. Use an integer variable *ArrayLength* to hold the length of the array. Use a For-Next loop to iterate through the numbers in the worksheet. Within the loop, do the following: Check that the array has space for another integer by comparing *ArrayLength* to the index of your loop. If this is not the case, use *ReDim* to increase the size of the array by 3. Remember to *preserve* existing data and update *ArrayLength*. Then read the next number and store it in the array. To check that everything worked correctly, use another For-Next loop to print all values from the array to column B.

Chapter 5
Subs and Functions

You already know that code is contained in procedures and stored in a module. You also know that there are two kinds of procedures: *subs* and *functions*. You know that functions return a value and that subs do not. You also know that subs can be executed by pressing a button and that functions cannot. In this chapter you will learn a lot more about both these types of procedures.

In Section 5.1, you will learn about custom procedures, i.e. procedures that you, the programmer, create. The programming language VBA and Excel also offer a number of pre-defined procedures that you can use when you create your program. You will learn more about these in Sections 5.2 and 5.3. In Chapter 10, you will learn more about partitioning your program into small procedures in a clear and meaningful way.

5.1 Custom Procedures

Any program that you create will be built by a number of subs and functions. You can consider these as being building blocks in your program. In Chapter 10, we consider the more strategic issue of how a program should be partitioned into several subs and functions in a good way. In this section, we will focus on the operational level: How are custom procedures created, what is the difference between subs and functions, how can input information be given to custom procedures, how can one procedure execute another?, and so on. These questions and many more will be answered in the following sections.

5.1.1 Subs

A sub is created by writing the keyword *Sub* followed by the name of the sub at the beginning and the keyword *End Sub* at the end. Everything contained between these two lines will be the content of the sub. This is illustrated in Figure 5.1.

A sub is a collection of code that can be executed to perform some kind of action. When a sub is executed, the lines of code will be executed one at a time, and when the End Sub is encountered, control is given back to the location that called the sub. If the sub was executed by pressing a button in the worksheet, as you learned in Chapter 1, control will return to the worksheet. If, on the other hand, the sub was executed (or called) from within another sub, control is returned to that sub, and execution of that sub will continue at the line of code following the call of the sub.

```
Sub MySub()

    'This is where the code should be.

End Sub
```

5.1 START AND END OF A SUB.

It is important to understand that the system does not worry about a sub until it is called/executed. At that time, memory will be allocated for the variables and execution will start. When the *End Sub* is reached and control leaves the sub, all memory is freed and the system will again not worry about that sub. The only exception to this is the potential use of *static variables*.

A sub cannot return anything. Think about it this way: A sub can be executed by pressing a button in Excel as we did in the *Hello World* example in Chapter 1. If it were to return something when is reached the *End Sub* and control returned to Excel, where would the thing returned end up?

On the other hand, a sub can make all the changes to its surroundings that you can think of. Well, within limitations. Just to mention some of the things that a sub is allowed to do: Delete and insert values in your worksheet, perform formatting, create charts, delete and insert columns and rows and move things around. Subs may also open and close files or even create new files or delete existing ones, turn off screen update or change passwords. And well, when you get to more advanced topics, you can write subs that extract data from an Access database, output your results as a Word report and send it as an attached file by E-mail, or even obtain information from the Internet.

Furthermore, within a sub you can execute as many other subs as you like to execute. You can also call as many functions - both custom, Excel, and VBA – as you want too.

As you see, basically the only limitation of subs is that they cannot return anything.

For an illustration of how one sub can execute another, consider the code in Figure 5.2. The example contains two subs: MainSub which is executed, for example, by a button in Excel and MySub. To keep focus on the execution of the subs, we have left out most other code in both subs.

```
Option Explicit

Sub MySub()
    'This is where the code should be.
    MsgBox "In MySub!"
End Sub

Sub MainSub()
    'This code will be executed before calling MySub
    MsgBox "In MainSub before calling MySub."
    Call MySub
    'This code will be executed after calling MySub
    MsgBox "In MainSub before calling MySub."
End Sub
```

5.2 A SUB CAN EXECUTE ANOTHER SUB.

When *MainSub* is executed, it will start with the code above the *Call MySub* line. When control reaches the *Call MySub* line, control will pass to *MySub* which will be executed. When control reaches the *End Sub* in *MySub*, control will return to *MainSub*, and the execution of that sub will continue from the line following the *Call MySub* statement. When *MainSub* is executed, the three message boxes shown in Figure 5.3 will be displayed in the order from left to right.

5.3 OUTPUT FROM EXECUTION OF THE CODE IN FIGURE 5.2.

5.1.2 Functions

Since subs are so wide in their scope, there is only one reason why we would need anything else: Subs cannot return anything. Functions can *return* something, but besides that, the rights of functions are very limited. Functions cannot make any changes to any worksheet and they may not call any sub that does so.

Because functions can return a value, they can be used within a worksheet just like any Excel function like *=sum* or *=npv*. There is no need to say how useful it can be for a company to have a function

=ShippingCost directly in Excel to calculate the shipping cost or a function *=ExchangeRate* for obtaining the current exchange rate for Yen from the Internet or from a database.

A function is created by writing the keyword *Function* followed by the name of the function at the beginning and the keyword *End Function* at the end. Everything contained between these two lines will be the content of the function. This is illustrated in Figure 5.4.

```
Function MyFunction()

    'This is where the code should be.

End Function
```

5.4 START AND END OF A FUNCTION.

To illustrate the use of functions, consider the information given in Figure 5.5. From the theory on inventory control, it is well known that the optimal order size, Q_0 can be obtained by $Q_0 = \sqrt{\frac{2SD}{c_h}}$.

	A	B	C
1	Order cost per order	S	36000
2	Inventory cost per unit per month	c_h	8
3	Demand per month	D	16000
4			

5.5 DATA FOR THE CODE IN FIGURE 5.6.

Figure 5.6 gives a function that reads the values of *S, D*, and c_h from the worksheet and calculates the optimal order size. Note how the function is created by using the keyword *Function* instead of *Sub*, and ended by the *End Function* keyword.

```
Function OptimalOrderSize_NoInput()
    Dim S As Double
    Dim ch As Double
    Dim D As Double

    S = Range("C1")
    ch = Range("C2")
    D = Range("C3")

    OptimalOrderSize_NoInput = Sqr(2 * S * D / ch)

End Function
```

5.6 FUNCTION TO CALCULATE THE OPTIMAL ORDER SIZE.

In order to return a value from a function, the function creates a variable of the same name as the function itself. In this example, it is called *OptimalOrderSize_NoInput*. The value to be returned by the function must be assigned to the return variable. Note that this return variable is automatically created and should not be declared using the *Dim* keyword.

After the creation of a function, it can be used in the worksheet just like any pre-defined Excel function. This is illustrated in Figure 5.7. After pressing enter, cell C5 will contain the value 12000.

	A	B	C	D	E
1	Order cost per order	S	36000		
2	Inventory cost per unit per month	c_h	8		
3	Demand per month	D	16000		
4					
5	Optimal ordersize		=OptimalOrderSize_NoInput()		

5.7 CUSTOM FUNCTIONS CAN BE USED DIRECTLY IN THE WORKSHEET.

In the example in Figure 5.6, the return value is of type variant because nothing is specified about the type. To specify the type of the return value of a function, the type is stated at the end of the line with the name of the function – using the keyword *As*. This is illustrated in Figure 5.8 where the optimal order size is specified to be of type double.

```
Function OptimalOrderSize_NoInput() As Double
```

5.8 SPECIFYING THE TYPE OF THE RETURN VARIABLE.

5.1.3 Using Arguments in Procedures

Consider again the example in Figure 5.6. The code is suffering from lack of flexibility. In order to work, it must obtain the values of *S*, c_h, and *D* from cells C1, C2, and C3, respectively. What we would really want is to be allowed to give these values to the function as input. That way, we could use our function regardless of where we stored the values of *S*, c_h, and *D*.

Now, consider the code in Figure 5.9. The only difference between this code and the one in Figure 5.6, besides the specification of the type of the return value, is that in Figure 5.9, the values of *S*, c_h, and *D* are given to the function as arguments.

```
Function OptimalOrderSize(S As Double, ch As Double, D As Double) As Double
    OptimalOrderSize = Sqr(2 * S * D / ch)
End Function
```

5.9 USE INPUT ARGUMENTS IN FUNCTIONS.

When considering the code in Figure 5.9, it can be seen that the function takes three arguments and that they are all of type double. When the function is used, the three arguments must be specified in the correct order. Figure 5.10 shows how to use the new function directly from the worksheet.

	A	B	C	D	E
1	Order cost per order	S	36000		
2	Inventory cost per unit per month	C_h	8		
3	Demand per month	D	16000		
4					
5	Optimal ordersize		=OptimalOrderSize(C1;C2;C3)		
6					

5.10 USE FUNCTIONS WITH INPUT ARGUMENTS FROM THE WORKSHEET.

As stated above, besides being used directly from the worksheet, functions can also be used from another procedure. Consider the code in Figure 5.11. The top part is our well-known function for calculating the optimal order size. It is unchanged from Figure 5.9 except the specification of return type. Below, you find a sub containing two variables, *OrderCost* and *Size*. The goal is to use the function to calculate the optimal order size and to store the value in the variable *Size*. As input, the function takes three arguments. For illustration purposes, we use a variable as the first argument. The second argument illustrates that a number can also be stated directly, and the third argument illustrates how a reference to a range containing a value can be used. The return value from the function is stored in the variable *Size* and can be displayed or used subsequently.

```
Function OptimalOrderSize(S As Double, ch As Double, D As Double)
    OptimalOrderSize = Sqr(2 * S * D / ch)
End Function

Sub IllustrateOptimalOrder()
    Dim OrderCost As Double
    Dim Size As Double

    OrderCost = 36000
    Size = OptimalOrderSize(OrderCost, 8, Range("C3"))
    MsgBox Size
End Sub
```

5.11 USE A FUNCTION FROM ANOTHER PROCEDURE.

Both subs and functions can take arguments. In this section, we have illustrated the use of arguments by using functions. Using arguments in subs are equivalent to using them in functions. Note that when a procedure takes arguments, parenthesis must be used when calling them.

It is possible to create procedures with *optional* arguments, but that is beyond the scope of this book. Note that in the help system, optional arguments are marked with [ ].

Note regarding subs that only those subs that do not take any arguments can be executed directly, for example by pressing a button. Subs that take one or more arguments can only be executed from another procedure because they must be given the values of those arguments.

5.1.3.1 ByRef or ByVal

There are two ways that a variable can be passed as argument to a procedure: *by value* or *by reference*.

If the variable is passed *by value*, then only the value of the variable is sent to the procedure. This value is then caught by the appropriate input variable in the procedure. The original variable is not influenced by any change made to this local variable in the procedure.

On the other hand, if a variable is passed *by reference*, then the address of the memory location that stores the variable is sent to the procedure. Even though it is caught by a local variable, any change that is made to this local variable will influence the original variable because the changes will be stored at the address of the original variable.

This calls for an illustration. The code in Figure 5.12 contains two subs: *IllustrateRefVal* and *MySub*. When *IllustrateRefVal* is executed, three variables are created and values are assigned to two of them. Next, *MySub* is called with the three variables as arguments.

```
Sub MySub(ByVal cost As Integer, ByRef R As Double, ByRef SD As Date)
    MsgBox cost & "    " & R & "    " & SD
    cost = 3500
    R = 0.07
    SD = #6/1/2010#
    MsgBox cost & "    " & R & "    " & SD
End Sub

Sub IllustrateRefVal()
    Dim cost As Integer
    Dim Rate As Double
    Dim ShippingDate As Date

    cost = 1000
    Rate = 0.02
    Call MySub(cost, Rate, ShippingDate)
    MsgBox cost & "    " & Rate & "    " & ShippingDate
End Sub
```

5.12 ILLUSTRATION OF BY VALUE AND BY REFERENCE.

In *MySub*, the first variable is accepted by value and the other two are accepted by reference. Before any changes are made, the values of the three variables are displayed in a message box. This is the left message box of Figure 5.13. Next, the values of the first two variables are changed and a value is assigned to the third variable. Again, a message box is displayed to show the current values. This is the middle message box in Figure 5.13. Finally, *MySub* is exited and control returns to *IllustrateRefVal.* Here a final message box displaying the values of the three variables is shown. This is the right message box in Figure 5.13.

First, note that even though no value was assigned to the date variable, there was no problem in sending it to *MySub*. The variable is passed by reference, and hence any value assigned to it will remain after returning to the main sub.

Secondly, note how the double variable is also passed by reference. The value of the variable is changed by *MySub* and the variable retains its value after returning to *IllustrateRefVal*. This is the case even though the name of the variable is different in *MySub*. On the contrary, the integer variable is passed by value. The value of the variable is changed and while we are in *MySub,* this value is in control, but when returning to *IllustrateRefVal*, the new variable disappears and the original variable has exactly the same value as before the execution of *MySub*.

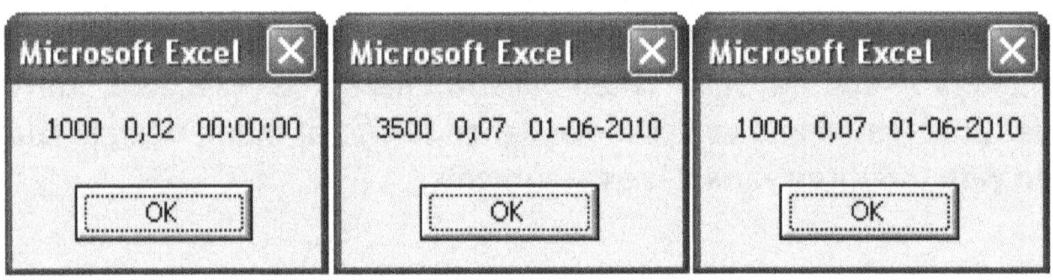

5.13 OUTPUT FROM THE CODE IN FIGURE 5.12.

The default way of passing variables to procedures is by reference. Therefore, you should be careful not to change the value of the input variables by accident.

5.1.4 Public vs Private Procedures

Procedures can be either *public* or *private*. A *private* procedure can only be executed from other procedures that are stored in the same module. Procedures that are supposed only to be used internally by other procedures in larger programs are made private to prevent them from being executed directly by the user. Private functions can be used in the worksheets of the file that contains the private function.

Public procedures can be executed directly from the workbook in which they are contained, but they can also be called from procedures both in the current and other modules of the same workbook.

In order to specify that a procedure is either public or private, write the *Public* or the *Private* keyword before the *Sub* or *Function* keyword. Figure 5.14 illustrates both a public and a private procedure. Procedures are public by default, hence, if nothing else is specified, the procedure will be public.

```
Private Sub MyPrivateSub()
    'This is where the code should be.
End Sub

Public Sub MyPublicSub()
    'This is where the code should be.
End Sub
```

5.14 A PUBLIC AND A PRIVATE SUB.

It is possible to use a procedure that is contained in another file. To do so, a reference to that file must be specified. This is explained in detail in Chapter 17 where a reference to the file containing the *Solver* functions is established.

5.2 VBA Functions

Every programming language contains a number of pre-defined functions that are available to the programmer. VBA is no exception. In this section, we present and illustrate some of the most useful VBA functions. In Section 5.2.1, we consider VBA functions that are related to numbers and mathematics. Section 5.2.2 is concerned with date and time functions. In Section 5.2.3, we consider financial functions and Section 5.2.4 presents some additional functions that are not in any of the above categories. VBA functions that deal with strings are considered in Chapter 13, whereas those related to dealing with files are presented in Chapter 12.

Several other VBA functions can be found by using the *Object Browser* as illustrated in Figure 5.15. In the top left corner of the *Object Browser*, select *VBA*. Selecting *<globals>* in the left-hand side list will display all available functions along with other useful information. Selecting *DateTime* in the left-hand side list will display the functions that deal with date and time, and so on.

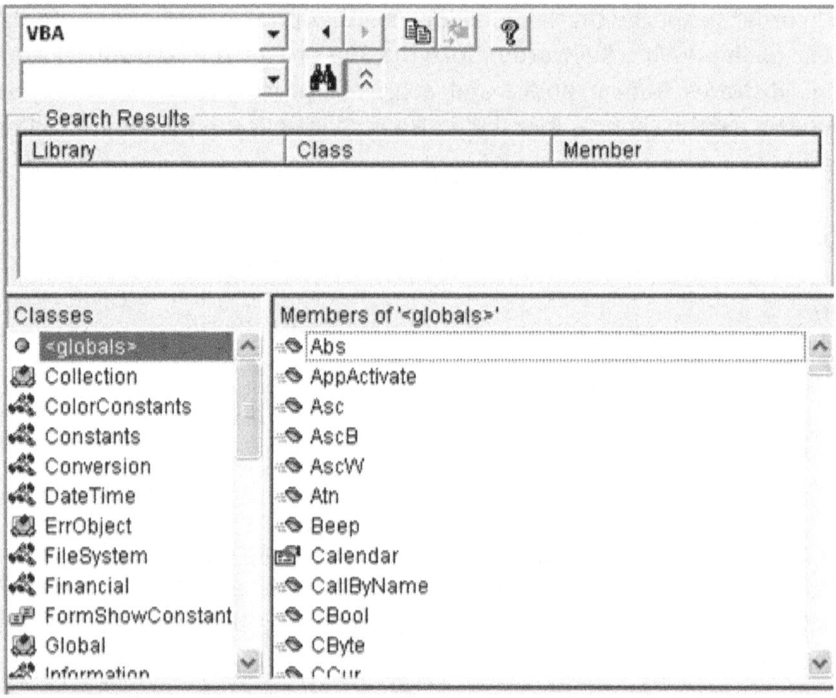

5.15 THE OBJECT BROWSER.

5.2.1 Number and Math Functions

Dealing with numbers is the most obvious things to do in a worksheet application. Table 5.1 gives the most common functions to perform basic operations with numbers.

5.1 MATH AND NUMBER FUNCTIONS.

Abs	Returns the absolute value of the number given as input.
Fix	Returns the integer portion of a number.
Int	Returns the floor af a number. i.e. the largest integer which is <= the number.
Rnd	Returns a random number in the interval [0;1[
Round	Returns a number rounded to the specified number of decimal places. This function is also used to round a number to the nearest integer.
Sgn	Returns an integer representing the sign of a number.
Exp	Returns e (the base of the natural logarithm) raised to a specified power.
Log	Returns the natural logarithm of a number.
Sqr	Returns the square root of a number.

Because it can be hard to tell the difference between some of the functions given in Table 5.1, Figure 5.16 illustrates the use of these functions based on different numbers. Using this figure along with the explanations in Table 5.1, should give the reader a better understanding of the functions.

	3	-3	3,4	-3,4	3,7	-3,7
Abs	3	3	3,4	3,4	3,7	3,7
Fix	3	-3	3	-3	3	-3
Int	3	-3	3	-4	3	-4
Round	3	-3	3	-3	4	-4
Sgn	1	-1	1	-1	1	-1

5.16 ILLUSTRATION OF A NUMBER OF VBA FUNCTIONS.

5.2.2 Date and Time Functions

Working with dates and time is very common in a worksheet. This is used to answer questions such as: How long has the product been in process?, what it the payment deadline?, how old is a member?, and so on. VBA contains many functions to deal with date and time. Some are illustrated below. The most common functions are given in Table 5.2 and a complete list can be found by using the *Object Browser*.

```
Sub IllustrateDateFunctions()
    Dim N As Date
    Dim D As Date

    N = Date
    D = #8/20/2001#

    Range("A1") = N
    Range("A2") = D

    Range("B1") = DateDiff("yyyy", D, N)
    Range("B2") = DateDiff("m", D, N)
    Range("B3") = DateDiff("d", D, N)

    Range("C1") = Now()
    Range("C2") = Time
    Range("C3") = MonthName(Month(N))

    Range("C4") = Year(N)

    MsgBox "Deadline for shipment: " & DateAdd("d", 7, N)

End Sub
```

5.17 ILLUSTRATION OF DATE AND TIME FUNCTIONS.

For an illustration of some useful date and time functions, consider the code in Figure 5.17. The output of the function is shown in Figure 5.18. Two date variables are defined. The function *Date* is used to retrieve the current date and # is used to directly type in a specific date. By using the #, you can type the date in any format which is accepted by Excel. The two dated are written in column A of the worksheet in Figure 5.18.

5.2 DATE AND TIME FUNCTIONS.

Date	Returns the system date in the format dd-mm-yyyy
DateAdd	Returns the date obtained by adding a specified time period to a specified date.
DateDiff	Returns the time between two specified dates. The first argument specifies the unit of measurement (years, months, days etc.).
DatePart	Returns information about a specified date. The type of information requested is specified by the first argument.
DateValue	Converts a string to a Date.
Day	Returns an integer stating the day of the month of a date.
Hour	Returns a number specifying the hour of the day.
Minute	Returns a number specifying the minute of the hour.
Month	Returns a number specifying the month of the year.
MonthName	Returns a string specifying the name of a month.
Now	Returns the current date and time.
Second	Returns a number specifying the second of the minute.
Time	Returns the current system time.
Timer	Returns the number of seconds since midnight.
Weekday	Returns a number specifying the day of the week.
Year	Returns the year of a specified date.

The *DateDiff* function is used to find the time elapsed between two dates. Note that even though the exact time between the two dates is 8 years, 6 months, and 4 days, the *DateDiff* function will state that there are 9 years between the two dates. Hence, when using the *DateDiff* function with respect to years, it will only consider the years. Column B shows the results of using *DateDiff* with respect to years, months, and days, respectively.

In column C, the *Now* and *Time* functions are used to obtain the current time and the date and the current time along with the name of the current month and the current year. Finally, a message box illustrates how to add a specific time, here 7 days, to a date.

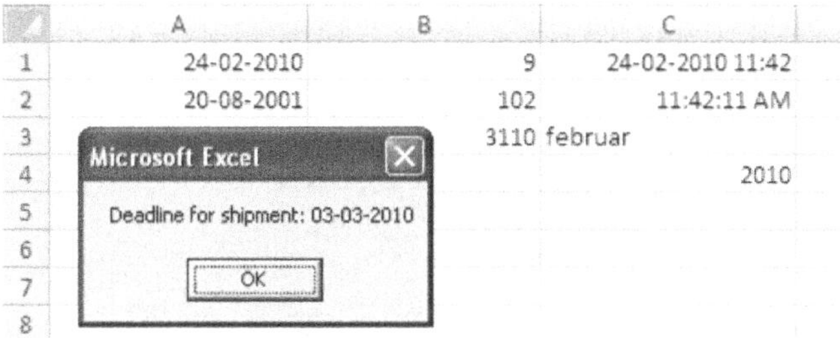

5.18 OUTPUT FROM THE CODE IN FIGURE 5.17.

We saw above that the *DateDiff* function does not return the time between two dates as a combination of years, months, and days. In Figure 5.19, we give the code for a function that can calculate the exact age of a person as such a combination.

```
Function CalculateExactAge(Born As Date)
    Dim N As Date
    Dim Temp As Date
    Dim y As Integer
    Dim m As Integer
    Dim d As Integer

    N = Date

    'Calculate years
    y = DateDiff("yyyy", Born, N)
    Temp = DateAdd("yyyy", y, Born)
    If DateDiff("m", Temp, N) < 0 Or DateDiff("d", Temp, N) < 0 Then
        y = y - 1
        Temp = DateAdd("yyyy", -1, Temp)
    End If

    'Calculate months
    m = DateDiff("m", Temp, N)
    Temp = DateAdd("m", m, Temp)
    If DateDiff("d", Temp, N) < 0 Then
        m = m - 1
        Temp = DateAdd("m", -1, Temp)
    End If

    'Remaining days
    d = DateDiff("d", Temp, N)

    CalculateExactAge = y & " years, " & m & " month, and " & d & " days"

End Function
```

5.19 CALCULATION OF EXACT AGE IN YEARS, MONTHS, AND DAYS.

The function takes the date of birth as argument. It uses *DateDiff* to find the age in years, and then determines whether the person had his birthday the current year. If not, the age in years is adjusted by one. The same procedure is used for number of months, and finally the remaining days are found. In Figure 5.20, the function is illustrated with two random dates of birth.

	A	B	C
1	20-08-2001		8 years, 6 month, and 4 days
2	25-12-1975		34 years, 1 month, and 30 days

5.20 OUTPUT FROM THE CODE IN FIGURE 5.19.

5.2.3 Financial Functions

Various functions are offered for financial use. Some of these are given in Table 5.3. In this section, we will illustrate a few of them.

5.3 FINANCIAL FUNCTIONS.

Function	Description
DDB	Returns the depreciation of an asset.
FV	Returns the future value of an annuity.
IPmt	Returns the interest payment for a period of an annuity.
IRR	Returns the internal rate of return for cash flows.
MIRR	Returns the modified internal rate of return for a series of periodic cash flows.
NPer	Returns the number of periods of an annuity.
NPV	Returns the net present value of a series of periodic cash flows.
Pmt	Returns the payment of an annuity.
PPmt	Returns the principal payment of an annuity.
PV	Returns the present value of an annuity.
Rate	Returns the interest rate for an annuity.
SLN	Returns the straight line depreciation of an asset for a single period.

When determining whether an investment opportunity is advantageous, the net present value can be calculated. This is done by using the *NPV* function. In Figure 5.21, the following investment opportunity is given: At time zero, a down payment of 10000 is made. Each of the following three years, 5000 is received. The discount rate is assumed to be 0.1. In the sub, the cash flows for years 1 through 3 are stored in an array. The net present value is calculated with this array and adjusted for the initial investment. The right-hand side of the figure displays the calculated net present value.

The next example is based on the data in Figure 5.22 where a bank loan of 100000 is obtained. The interest rate is 6% pro anno which corresponds to 1.5% with quarterly payments. We assume that it is an annuity loan and that the horizon is 3 years, corresponding to 12 periods.

```
Option Explicit
Option Base 1

Sub NetPresentValue()
    Dim Payment(3) As Double
    Dim Investment As Integer
    Dim N As Double

    Investment = 10000
    Payment(1) = 5000
    Payment(2) = 5000
    Payment(3) = 5000

    N = NPV(0.1, Payment) - Investment
    MsgBox N
End Sub
```

5.21 CALCULATING THE NET PRESENT VALUE OF AN INVESTMENT.

	A	B
1	Amount	100000
2		
3	Interest rate, % p.a.	6
4	Interest rate, % per period	1,5
5	Number of periods (3 years)	12
6		

5.22 DATA FOR CODE IN FIGURE 5.23.

The code in Figure 5.23 illustrates how the *Pmt* function can be used to determine the quarterly payments. The resulting message box is shown to the right.

```
Sub CalculatePayment()
    Dim rate As Double
    Dim amount As Double
    Dim periods As Integer
    Dim payment As Double

    amount = Range("B1")
    rate = Range("B4") / 100
    periods = Range("B5")

    payment = Pmt(rate, periods, amount)
    MsgBox payment
End Sub
```

5.23 CALCULATE THE PAYMENT OF AN ANNUITY.

For the final example, consider the data in Figure 5.24. A machine is bought for 100000 and is expected to last for 10 years, after which the scrap value is estimated to be 10000.

	A	B
1	Price of machine	100000
2	scrap value	10000
3		
4	Number of years	10

5.24 DATA FOR CODE IN FIGURE 5.25

In the code in Figure 5.25, the *SLN* function is used to determine the yearly depreciation, based on straight line depreciation. The resulting message box is shown to the right.

```
Sub calculateYearlyDepreciation()
    Dim price As Double
    Dim Scrap As Double
    Dim years As Integer
    Dim DEP As Double

    price = Range("B1")
    Scrap = Range("B2")
    years = Range("B4")

    DEP = SLN(price, Scrap, years)
    MsgBox DEP

End Sub
```

5.25 CALCULATE YEARLY DEPRECIATION OF AN ASSET.

5.2.4 Other Functions

VBA also offers a number of functions that cannot be categorized as belonging to any of the previous sections. Some of these functions are considered here. Table 5.4 gives an overview of the most useful of these functions. For example, VBA offers functions that can be helpful in determining the nature of a run-time error, as shown in the top of Table 5.4.

Other functions are useful when working with colors. Two of these are illustrated in Figure 5.26. In the figure, you see three different ways of specifying a color, here used to paint the interior of a cell. *RGB* uses the *red-green-blue* color scheme where the specified amount of each of the three colors is mixed to obtain the color. Using *QBColor*, the basic colors can be obtained by specifying a single number.

5.4 OTHER VBA FUNCTIONS.

Err	Returns information about run-time errors.
Error	Returns the error message corresponding to a specific error number.
EOF	Returns True if the end of a specified file has been reached.
IIf	Returns one of two options based on the evaluation of an expression.
Union	Returns the union of a number of ranges.
Intersect	Returns a range obtained by the intersection of a number of ranges.
QBColor	Returns the RGB color code for specific colors.
RGB	Returns a number representing the RGB color code.

The last line of code illustrates how the return value of the two functions are just integer numbers corresponding to a specific code. For example, *RGB*(0,255,0) is 65280. These numbers can be found by using the macro recorder to change something to the desired color. By inspection of the recorded code the number can be obtained.

```
Sub IllustrationColor()
   Cells(3, 3).Interior.Color = RGB(0, 255, 0)
   Cells(1, 1).Interior.Color = QBColor(9)
   Cells(2, 2).Interior.Color = 192
End Sub
```

5.26 THREE WAYS OF SPECIFYING COLOR.

The *red-green-blue* color scheme is easy to learn, and we recommend using that unless special colors are needed, in which case the recorder process is the way. Table 5.5 gives an overview of the basic *red-green-blue* color codes.

After you have tested all the color functions, it might be useful to know the way to remove the color of a cell in the worksheet. This can be done by the not-so-simple line of code given in Figure 5.27.

```
Cells(1, 1).Interior.Pattern = xlNone
```

5.27 REMOVING COLOR OF A CELL.

5.5 RED-GREEN-BLUE COLOR CODES.

Color	Red value	Green value	Blue value
Black	0	0	0
White	255	255	255
Red	255	0	0
Green	0	255	0
Blue	0	0	255
Cyan	0	255	255
Magenta	255	0	255
Yellow	255	255	0

The *intersection* function calculates the intersection of two or more ranges. Figure 5.28 illustrates the use of this function. The resulting message box will display $D$3:$F$5 which is exactly the range that is contained in both input ranges.

```
Sub IllustrateIntersect()
    Dim R As Range
    Dim S As Range
    Dim T As Range
    Set R = Range(Cells(1, 1), Cells(5, 6))
    Set S = Range(Cells(3, 4), Cells(8, 10))

    Set T = Intersect(R, S)
    MsgBox T.Address
End Sub
```

5.28 THE INTERSECTION FUNCTION RETURNS THE INTERSECTION OF TWO OR MORE RANGES.

5.3 Worksheet Functions

Besides the many functions that are available directly from VBA, the *Excel application* also offers a wide range of functions that you can use in your code. These functions are referred to as *worksheet functions*.

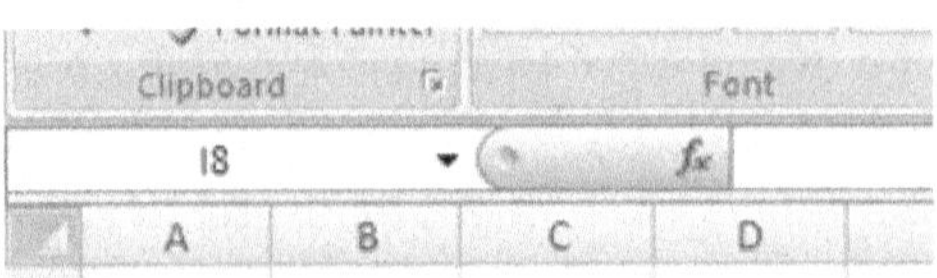

5.29 THE INSERT FUNCTION BUTTON.

Anyone who is used to working with Excel, uses these functions as a routine. Pressing the *Insert function* button, f_x in Excel, as illustrated in

Figure 5.29, displays the dialog box shown in Figure 5.30. Here, the user can choose the function to be inserted into the active cell.

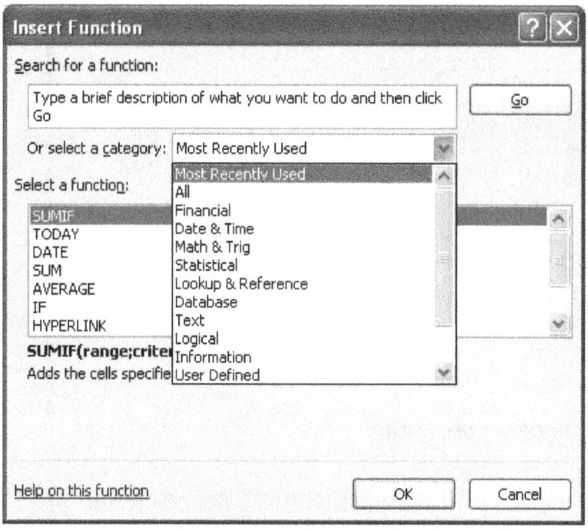

5.30 THE INSERT FUNCTION DIALOG BOX.

As can be seen from the dialog box in Figure 5.30, the functions are categorized much like the VBA functions. Some of these functions have a VBA function counterpart to perform the same task as described in the previous section. Examples of such functions are *ABS, EXP, NPV*, and *NOW*. These functions can only be used in your code as *VBA functions*, not as *worksheet functions*. Many of the Excel functions do not have a VBA function counterpart, and these are available for use in your code as worksheet functions. This will be described below.

5.3.1 Using Worksheet Functions in Your Code

To get an overview of the worksheet functions available for your use, open the *Object Browser* in the *VBA Editor*. In the top left corner of the Object Browser, select *Excel*. Selecting *WorksheetFunction* in the left-hand side list will display all available functions. This is illustrated in Figure 5.31. In order to obtain an explanation of a single function and see examples of its use, mark the function name in the Object Browser and press *F1*.

Note that if you do not know the name of the function you are looking for, it can sometimes be easier to search for the function directly in Excel using the *Insert Function* dialog box as shown in Figure 5.30. The dialog box directly offers a short description of the function.

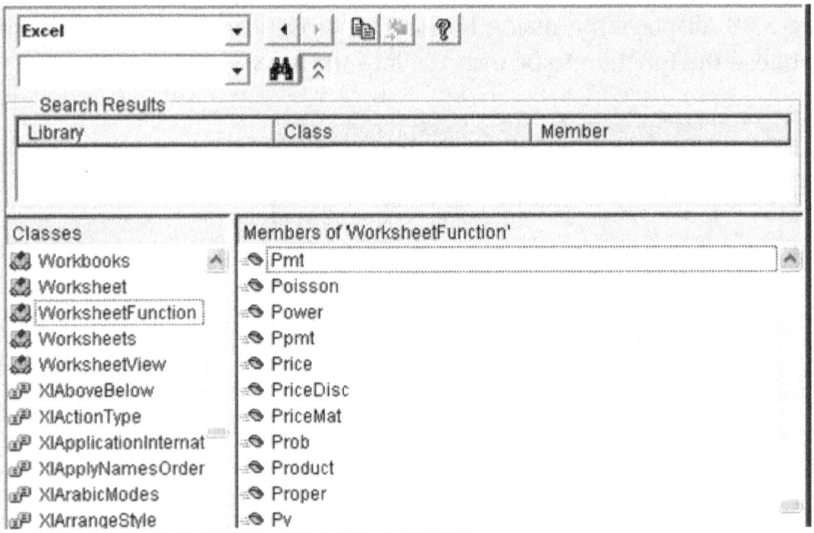

5.31 WORKSHEET FUNCTIONS IN THE OBJECT BROWSER.

Unlike VBA functions, worksheet functions cannot be used by simply typing the function name. Figure 5.32 shows the error message that is displayed if one attempts to do so. As can be seen, the compiler does not recognize the name of the function.

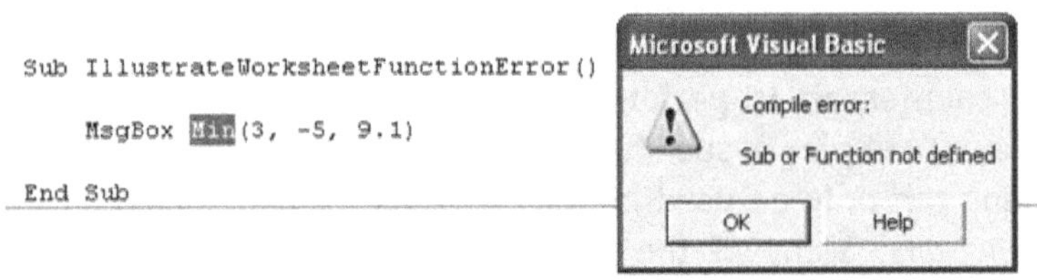

5.32 YOU MUST SPECIFY THAT THE FUNCTION IS A WORKSHEET FUNCTION.

To help the compiler find the function, you must specify that it should search in the *application*, which is *Excel*, and from there, search in *WorksheetFunction*. This is illustrated in the top part of Figure 5.33 where the function *min* is used to display the minimum of three numbers in a message box.

Because the application is assumed by default unless something else is specified this part can be omitted. This is illustrated in Figure 5.33 where the two expressions are equivalent.

```
MsgBox Application.WorksheetFunction.Min(3, -5, 9.1)
```

```
MsgBox WorksheetFunction.Min(3, -5, 9.1)
```

5.33 TWO WAYS TO USE WORKSHEET FUNCTIONS.

5.3.2 Examples of Worksheet Functions

Worksheet functions in Excel are so numerous that only very few people know them all by heart. In this section, we illustrate how a few of them are used from VBA code. Other worksheet functions, which are only defined for ranges, are shown in Chapter 7.

5.3.2.1 Sum

One of the most popular functions in Excel is the *sum* function. It is used to calculate the sum of the content of a range of cells. Clearly, the *sum* function can also be used to calculate the sum of a range from the VBA code as illustrated in the first line of Figure 5.34.

```
Sub IllustrateSum()

    MsgBox WorksheetFunction.Sum(Range("B2:C3"))

    MsgBox WorksheetFunction.Sum(3, 5, 1, 5, 6.3)

    MsgBox WorksheetFunction.Sum(Range("B2:C3"), 2, 5)

End Sub
```

5.34 THE SUM FUNCTION CAN BE USED IN MANY WAYS.

The sum function can take many optional arguments as input, and it need not be ranges, as long as it is of numerical form. In the remainder of Figure 5.34, it is illustrated how the *sum* function can be used to sum a bunch of numbers and a combination of a range and some numbers, respectively.

In Chapter 4, we introduced VBA arrays. In Figure 5.35, we illustrate how the *sum* function can be used to calculate the sum of the values stored in an array. The resulting message box is shown to the right.

```
Sub IllustrateSum2()
    Dim A(3) As Integer

    A(0) = 2
    A(1) = 3
    A(2) = 4
    A(3) = 5

    MsgBox WorksheetFunction.Sum(A)

End Sub
```

5.35 THE SUM FUNCTION CAN BE USED TO SUM THE VALUES IN AN ARRAY.

5.3.2.2 SumProduct

Another very useful function is the *SumProduct* function. Given two vectors, *a* and *b*, it calculates $a_1b_1 + a_2b_2 + a_3b_3 + \ldots + a_nb_n$. For an illustration of how to use this function through VBA code, consider the worksheet shown in Figure 5.36 where an order from a customer is specified with unit price and number of units to buy.

	A	B	C
1	Customer order		
2			
3	Product	Units	Price
4	DH12	23	10,50
5	DF23	35	22,00
6	BS44	3	17,25
7	CN03	20	37,75
8	CN09	12	74,50
9	GF22	7	89,00

5.356 DATA FOR THE CODE IN FIGURE 5.37.

In order to calculate the total order cost, the short code given in Figure 5.37 can be used. The function is simply given two ranges as arguments. The resulting message box is shown in Figure 5.38.

```
Sub IllustrateSumproduct()

MsgBox WorksheetFunction.SumProduct(Range("B4:B9"), Range("C4:C9"))

End Sub
```

5.37 USING THE SUMPRODUCT FUNCTION.

5.38 RESULT OF EXECUTING THE CODE IN FIGURE 5.37.

	A	B	C	D
1	Customer order			
2				
3	Product	Units	Price	Profit Rate
4	DH12	23	10,50	5%
5	DF23	35	22,00	2%
6	BS44	3	17,25	4%
7	CN03	20	37,75	2%
8	CN09	12	74,50	5%
9	GF22	7	89,00	7%

5.39 DATA FOR THE CODE IN FIGURE 5.40.

The *SumProduct* function can easily handle more than two vectors. Given three vectors, it will calculate $a_1b_1c_1 + a_2b_2c_2 + a_3b_3c_3 + \ldots + a_nb_nc_n$. In the worksheet shown in Figure 5.39, an additional column has been added, which states the company's profit rate for each of the ordered products.

In order the calculate the company's profit with respect to the given order, a *SumProduct* of the three columns *Units, Price*, and *Profit Rate* must be calculated. This task can be performed by the code given in Figure 5.40, with the resulting message box shown in Figure 5.41.

```
Sub IllustrateSumproduct2()

MsgBox WorksheetFunction.SumProduct(Range("B4:B9"), _
    Range("C4:C9"), Range("D4:D9"))

End Sub
```

5.40 SUMPRODUCT CAN BE GIVEN MORE THAN TWO ARGUMENTS.

5.41 RESULT OF EXECUTING THE CODE IN FIGURE 5.40.

Finally, we show how the *SumProduct* function can be used with arrays. In Figure 5.42, two arrays are created, and numbers are stored in them. Note how elegant the use of the function looks when internal data structures are used instead of the worksheet. The result of executing the code in Figure 5.42 is shown to the left.

```
Sub IllustrateSumproduct3()
    Dim A(2) As Integer
    Dim B(2) As Integer
    A(0) = 2
    A(1) = 3
    A(2) = 4
    B(0) = 2
    B(1) = 3
    B(2) = 4

    MsgBox WorksheetFunction.SumProduct(A, B)

End Sub
```

5.42 THE SUMPRODUCT FUNCTION CAN BE USED WITH INTERNAL DATA TYPES.

5.3.2.3 Count and CountIf

The final worksheet functions we are considering in this chapter are the *Count* and the *CountIf* functions. *Count* counts how many cells in a range contain a number, and *CountIf* counts the number of cells that respect a specified criterion.

Count and *CountIf* are illustrated in the code in Figure 5.43 which is based on the worksheet in Figure 5.39. The result of executing the code is shown in Figure 5.44.

```
Sub IllustrateCountif()

    MsgBox WorksheetFunction.Count(Range("D4:D9"))

    MsgBox WorksheetFunction.CountIf(Range("D4:D9"), ">4%")

End Sub
```

5.43 THE COUNT AND COUNTIF FUNCTIONS.

5.44 RESULT OF EXECUTING THE CODE IN FIGURE 5.43.

The *Count* function can be used with an array as the first argument, but the *CountIf* function requires the first argument to be a range.

5.4 Exercises

5.1. Create a function called *Shipping* which takes a double as input argument and returns ten percent of the input value. Try to use your function from the worksheet.

5.2. Write a function which takes two integers as arguments. Let the function return 1 if the first is larger than the second and return 0 otherwise. Test your function from the worksheet.

5.3. Write a sub that uses an input box to obtain the total price of an order. The sub should call the function created in Exercise 5.1 to determine the shipping cost based on the total price and display the shipping cost in a message box.

5.4. Open the data file for this exercise. In the file there is a sub, *Main*, whose only job is to call another sub, f. Your job is to write the sub f that takes to arguments: a string and a Boolean. If the value of the Boolean is true, then a message box with the text of the string should appear. If the value of the Boolean is false, then noting should happen. Test your work by executing the main sub.

5.5. Open the data file for this exercise. As you see, there is already a sub that takes as arguments a string and an integer. Write a sub that does the following:

1. Declares two variables: a string and an integer.
2. Uses Input boxes to ask for the users name and age, respectively, and stores these in the variables.
3. Calls the sub *PrintYourNameAge* with these two arguments.

5.6. Open the data file for this exercise. The file contains information about a loan and three subs that are ready to be written by you.

1. Each of the subs *AnnuityLoan* and *NoPayment* should construct a quarterly payment schedule showing quarterly interest, loan repayment and total payment for each quarter until the loan is completely repaid.
   a. *AnnuityLoan*: to total monthly payment is the same each quarter.
   b. *NoPayment:* The first 10 years only interest. After that the loan is repaid using an annuity loan.
2. Please also calculate and display the total amount that is paid in interest for each of the two loans.

5.7. Open the data file for this exercise. The purpose of this exercise is the same as for exercises 3.5 through 3.8 but to use worksheet functions and/or VBA functions to perform the task much simpler. Write a sub that determines the maximum and the minimum of the numbers and writes them to D1 and D2. Determines the average of the numbers and the amount of positive numbers. Writes that to cells D3 and D4. Finally, counts the number of occurrences of the maximum and minimum values. Writes that information to cells D5 and D6. Writes suitable headings in column C.

5.8. Create a sub that displays the current weekday, date, name of the month, and year in four cells of the worksheet.

5.9. Create a function that creates and returns a string with the number of months and days to your next birth day. You can be inspired by the code in Figure 5.19. Test your function from the worksheet.

5.10. Change your solution of exercise 5.9 to take the date of birth as input argument. Test your function by creating a sub form which the function is called and display the string returned in a message box.

5.11. Create a sub and define two ranges which overlap. First color the union of the two by one color, then color the intersection of them by another.

5.12. Open the data file for this exercise. Row 2 gives a number of product profits and row 4 gives the number of units to be produced of each product. First write a sub that uses the *SumProduct* function to determine the total profit based on the ranges and displays the value in a message box. Then write another sub that stores the two lists in arrays and uses the *SumProduct* function based on the arrays to determine and display the total profit in a message box.

Chapter 6
Decisions and Looping

Two of the things that make programming so powerful are the ability to make decisions, and the ability to repeat a task or a process many times: If you want the program to write the first 100 positive integers in a column of your worksheet, you do not want to write 100 lines of code to make it do so. Instead, you want to write just a few lines of code, specifying that, starting from 1, the program should write the next positive integer and repeat it 100 times. Here you use looping.

As another example, you might want to consider each product at a time and based on its category, annual sales, and profit contribution, you might want your program to give an indication as to whether the product should be removed from the product line, be further promoted, or no action should be taken. In this case, a combination of looping and decisions is used.

In Chapter 3, you were introduced to both decisions and looping. In this chapter, we go into more detail. We consider several types of decisions in Section 6.2, and various types of looping in Section 6.3. In Section 6.4, we illustrate how loops can be nested, and in Section 6.5, we show how to jump in the code. When making decisions, it is important to know how the compiler performs comparison. This is, among other things, considered further in Section 6.1.

6.1 Arithmetic and Comparison

In order to write programs, one needs to know how to perform simple arithmetic and how to compare expressions. These are the topics of the next two sections.

6.1.1 Arithmetic

The core of any procedure is arithmetic, i.e. being able to perform simple mathematical calculations such as addition or division. The basic operations are given in Table 6.1.

6.1 BASIC OPERATORS.

+	Addition
-	Subtraction
*	Multiplication
/	Division
\	Integer division
Mod	Modulo gives the remainder when a number is divided by another.
^	Exponential
&	String concatenation

The result of a mathematical expression is assigned to a variable by placing the expression on the right-hand side of an equal sign and the variable on the left-hand side.

Consider the line of code involving *n* in Figure 6.1. At first glance it seems odd that *n* can be equal to itself + one. But remembering that this is an assignment statement, the right-hand side will be evaluated first, and secondly, the value obtained is assigned to the variable on the left-hand side. Therefore, if *n* has the value of 7 at this point, the right-hand side evaluates to 7 + 1, which is 8. This value of 8 will be assigned to the variable *n*. Hence, this line of code increases the value of the variable *n* by one.

```
Sub IllustrateArithmetic()
    Dim price As Double
    Dim n As Integer
    'Other code here

    n = n + 1
    price = 1.2 * price

    'More code here
End Sub
```

6.1 ILLUSTRATION OF ARITHMETICS.

6.1.2 Comparison

Not surprisingly, you will often need to compare one expression with another, or the value of one variable with the value of another. Table 6.2 shows the correct syntax to be used in comparison.

Given two expressions, it is useful to be able to determine if at least one of them is true, or if they are both true, and so on. To help you do that, you can use the logical operators shown in Table 6.3.

6.2 COMPARISON.

=	Equal to
<>	Not equal to
< and >	Strictly less than and strictly greater than
<= and >=	Less than or equal to and greater than or equal to

6.3 LOGIC OPERATORS.

Not	Negation of an expression
And	Logical conjunction on two expressions
Or	Logical disjunction on two expressions
Xor	Logical exclusion on two expressions

To illustrate the use of logical operators, Table 6.4 shows some expressions where the operators are used, along with the value of the expressions. To simplify reading of the table, we have used numbers in the expressions instead of variables.

6.4 ILLUSTRATION OF LOGICAL OPERATORS.

Expression	Value
(-1 < 2) And (2 <=3)	True
(-1 < 2) Or (2 <= 3)	True
(-1 < 2) Xor (2 <= 3)	False
(2 < -1) And (2 <=3)	False
(2 < -1) Or (2 <=3)	True
(2 < -1) Xor (2 <=3)	True
(2 < -1) Or (3 <=2)	False
(2 < -1) Xor (3 <=2)	True

6.2 Decisions

The main purpose of many computer programs is the ability to perform different sets of actions based on the input information given. Within a sub, you might need your program to execute one set of actions if the input format is faulty, another set of actions if some value is too small, yet another if the value is too large, and so on. For this purpose, there are two useful constructions: The *If-Then-Else* construction, which is explained in Section 6.2.1, is used when there are few options. If there are many different options, it might be more convenient to use a *Select-Case* construction, which is explained in Section 6.2.2.

6.2.1 If-Then-Else

The general structure of the *If-Then-Else* construction is shown in Figure 6.2. It consists of a mandatory *If* statement, as many *ElseIf* statements as desired (possibly none) and finally an optional *Else* statement.

First, condition 1 is evaluated. If it is true, then the corresponding code is executed, after which control jumps to the line following the *End If* statement. If condition 1 is false, then condition 2 is evaluated. Again, if it is true, the corresponding code is executed, after which control jumps to the line following the *End If* statement. This continues until all the conditions have been evaluated. If they are all false, control will go to the code corresponding to the *Else* statement.

```
If condition1 Then
   'code
[ ElseIf condition2 Then ]
   'code
[ ElseIf condition3 Then ]
   'code
[ ElseIf condition4 Then ]
   'code
[ Else]
   'code
End If
```

6.2 SYNTAX OF IF-THEN-ELSE.

6.2.1.1 Example: Placing an Order

Firstly, consider the code in Figure 6.3. The function takes three arguments: The current inventory level, the order point, and the order size. The return value of the function is the number of products to order, which is either zero or the given order size. Note in the first line that the space + underscore (_) lets us continue one line of code on the following line. This is useful in order to avoid very long lines.

If the inventory level is below the order point, then an order of the specified size should be placed. Otherwise, no order should be placed. Note that if the condition evaluates to false, then the *Else* part will be executed and the return value is set to zero.

```
Function OrderDecision(ILevel As Double, _
        OPoint As Double, OSize As Double)

    If ILevel < OPoint Then
        OrderDecision = OSize
    Else
        OrderDecision = 0
    End If
End Function
```

6.3 DETERMINE IF AN ORDER SHOULD BE PLACED.

We extend the example to include the possibility of discount. If there is no discount, the decision is as before, but if there is discount, an order should be placed if the inventory level is below twice the order point.

Consider the code in Figure 6.4 where an extra argument is used: a Boolean variable stating whether this is a discount situation. In this example, the condition is more complicated. It evaluates to true if either the inventory level is below the order point, or this is discount and the inventory level is below twice the order point.

```
Function OrderDecisionDiscount(ILevel As Double, _
        OPoint As Double, OSize As Double, _
        Discount As Boolean)

    If ILevel < OPoint Or _
    (Discount = True And ILevel < 2 * OPoint) Then
        OrderDecisionDiscount = OSize
    Else
        OrderDecisionDiscount = 0
    End If
End Function
```

6.4 INCLUSION OF DISCOUNT.

6.2.1.2 Example: Check Data

In the final example, we show how the optional *ElseIf* can be used. Consider the code in Figure 6.5. The goal is to check the correctness of some data. In this case, it is assumed that the date is given in cell A1, but it might as well have been given in an input file, in a user form, or from some other source.

Whenever data is obtained from an external source, it should be checked that it is in the correct format etc. Otherwise, it can cause the program to crash or behave in unintentional ways. In this example, we want to ensure that the data is a positive integer. We use message boxes to display potential problems with the data.

Note that if the type of the input is not known, it is a good idea to start by storing it in a variable of type variant (or to leave it in the worksheet), in order to avoid crashing due to type mismatch.

We first check if there is data at all, then whether it is of numeric type. Knowing that the data is a number of some kind, we can check that it is not negative, and finally, if it is integral.

```
Sub CheckData()
    Dim data
    data = Range("A1")

    If data = "" Then
        MsgBox "There is no input"
    ElseIf IsNumeric(data) = False Then
        MsgBox "The input is not numeric"
    ElseIf data < 0 Then
        MsgBox "Input is negative"
    ElseIf Fix(data) <> data Then
        MsgBox "Input is not an integer"
    Else
        MsgBox "Input ok. Ready to continue"
    End If
End Sub
```

6.5 DATA CHECKING.

6.2.2 Select-Case

When there are many options, the *If-Then-Else* construction is not always the best choice. Sometimes a *Select-Case* is more convenient. The general structure of *Select-Case* is given in Figure 6.6. It is checked which *Case* the test expression falls into, if any. Note that it is only required to have one *Case*, but you can include as many as you want. The *Case Else* is selected if none of the above cases are chosen. The *Case Else* is not required.

```
Select Case TestExpression
   Case Expression1
      'code
   [ Case Expression2 ]
      'code
   [ Case Expression3 ]
      'code
   [ Case Else ]
      'code
End Select
```

6.6 SYNTAX OF SELECT CASE.

In order to understand the *Select-Case* construction, some examples are needed.

6.2.2.1 Example: Determine Discount Rate

In the first example, we consider a company whose customers are partitioned into categories. The discount that the customer can obtain depends on the category. In the function in Figure 6.7, the category is given as input and the discount rate is returned.

The construction should be read as follows: If category is equal to "A", set the rate to 0.2, if category is equal to "B", set the rate to 0.15, etc. Finally, if none of the cases fit, set the rate to zero.

```
Function GetDiscountRate(category As String)
    Select Case category
        Case Is = "A"
            GetDiscountRate = 0.2
        Case Is = "B"
            GetDiscountRate = 0.15
        Case Is = "C"
            GetDiscountRate = 0.05
        Case Else
            GetDiscountRate = 0
    End Select
End Function
```

6.7 SELECT-CASE IS USED TO DETERMINE THE DISCOUNT RATE.

Each *case* can contain as many lines of code as needed. We now illustrate that if there is only one line of code in each *case*, then that line can be placed after the expression, separating them with a colon. Figure 6.8 shows how the function in Figure 6.7 can be changed to follow that strategy.

```
Function GetDiscountRateCompact(category As String)
    Select Case category
        Case Is = "A": GetDiscountRateCompact = 0.2
        Case Is = "B": GetDiscountRateCompact = 0.15
        Case Is = "C": GetDiscountRateCompact = 0.05
        Case Else: GetDiscountRateCompact = 0
    End Select
End Function
```

6.8 A MORE COMPACT FORMULATION.

6.2.2.2 Example: Determine Employee Bonus

The final example illustrates that a *case* can contain a whole interval of values. Consider the function in Figure 6.9. The function calculates the bonus to be given to an employee based on the revenue she has obtained for the company. The sales is given as input to the function and the size of the bonus is returned.

The construction should be read as follows: If sales is <= 400000, set bonus to 0, if sales is between 400000 and 600000, set bonus to 0.5 % of the sales, etc.

```
Function Bonus(sales As Double) As Double
    Bonus = 0
    Select Case sales
        Case Is <= 400000
            Bonus = 0
        Case 400000 To 600000
            Bonus = 0.005 * sales
        Case 600000 To 900000
            Bonus = 6000 + 0.007 * (sales - 600000)
        Case Is > 900000
            Bonus = 9000 + 0.01 * (sales - 900000)
    End Select
End Function
```

6.9 SELECT-CASE IS USED TO CALCULATE EMPLOYEE BONUS.

6.3 Looping

You will often need your program to repeat a specific task over and over again. This section teaches you how to do that. From an intuitive point of view, there are basically two types of repetition. Firstly, you might need to repeat a process a specific number of times. The *For-Next* loop, which is explained in detail in Section 6.3.1, is appropriate for this purpose. Secondly, you might need your program to repeat a task while a condition is true, or until a false condition becomes true. This gives rise for two types of loops: The *While* loop, which is explained in Section 6.3.2, and four types of *Do* loops, all of which are explained in Section 6.3.3. When working with loops, there is a risk of getting trapped in endless looping. Finally, in Section 6.3.4, we explain the concept of endless looping and explain how it can be avoided.

6.3.1 The For-Next Loop

The easiest loop to understand is the *For-Next* loop. In this loop you basically tell the program to count from a start number to an end number, and to execute the content/body of the loop at each count. The basic structure of the *For-Next* loop is given in Figure 6.10. Note that the parts surrounded by [] (square brackets) are optional.

In the following, we will carefully illustrate each part of this structure with small examples. Subsequently, we will give two examples of how the *For-Next* loop works in real action. The statement *Exit For* will be explored in Section 6.5.2.

```
For counter = start To end [step stepsize]
    'code
    [Exit For]
    'code
Next
```

6.10 SYNTAX OF FOR-NEXT LOOP.

6.3.1.1 Illustration of the For-Next Loop

As a first example, consider the code in Figure 6.11. The body of the loop will be repeated three times: First the value of the variable, *i*, is 1, and the content of the loop is executed for that value, displaying the left most message box of Figure 6.12. Next, the variable *i* is automatically increased to 2 and the content of the loop is executed for that value, displaying the middle message box of Figure 6.12. Finally, the value is increased to 3 and the process is repeated, with the right most message box as a result.

```
For i = 1 To 3
    MsgBox i
Next
```

6.11 SIMPLE FOR-NEXT LOOP.

Note that after execution of the loop with the variable *i* equal to 3, the execution will stop, as 3 is the end value of *i*.

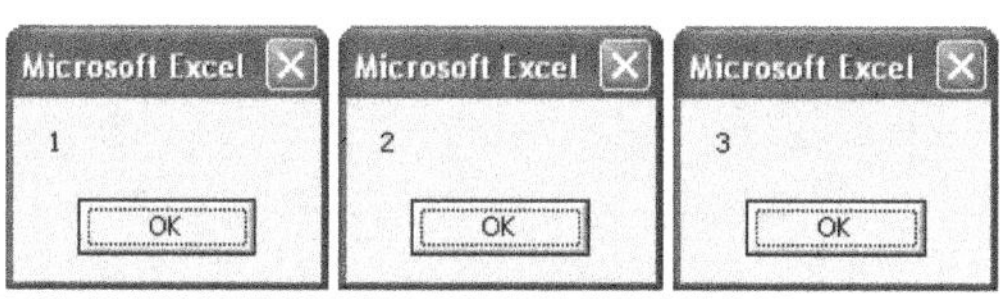

6.12 OUTPUT FROM THE CODE IN FIGURE 6.11.

Consider again the general structure in Figure 6.10. The option *step* at the end of the first line specifies by how much the counter (in our example, *i*) should increase between the repetitions.

In the example of Figure 6.13, the step size is set to 2. Therefore, the value of *i* will increase by 2 at each repetition of the loop. Executing the code in Figure 6.13 will result in four message boxes, displaying the values 2, 4, 6, and 8, respectively.

The default value of the step size is 1. Hence, if no step size is specified, the value of the counter will be increased by 1 for each repetition.

```
For i = 2 To 8 Step 2
     MsgBox i
Next
```

6.13 ILLUSTRATION OF STEP.

Sometimes – but not very often – it is advantageous to have the value of the counter variable decrease instead of increase. This is illustrated in Figure 6.14 where the *step* size is set to -0.5. This will cause the variable *i* to take on the values 1, 0.5, 0, -0.5, -1, -1.5, and -2, respectively, for the execution of the content of the loop.

```
For i = 1 To -2 Step -0.5
     MsgBox i
Next
```

6.14 NEGATIVE STEP SIZE.

Note that you must ensure that the stop value of the counter can be reached with the specified step size.

Now, the structure of *For-Next* loops is clear, and we turn our attention to a couple of examples where we can see the loop in action.

6.3.1.2 Example: Find Product

For the first example, assume that a list of product codes are given in the first column of a worksheet, as illustrated in Figure 6.15. Clearly, for practical applications there would be further information in the worksheet, but this has been omitted here in order to keep focus on the parts that are used in the code.

	A	B	C
1	Product		
2	DJ4761		
3	KG3734		
4	GY3456		
5	EN3463		
6	YM3854		
7	WH5715		
8	WE5143		
9	QG5247		
10	WC5465		
11	IM5458		

6.15 DATA FOR THE CODE IN FIGURE 6.16.

It if not hard to imagine the need for being able to search for a specific product in such a list in order to obtain further information on the product. In this example, we focus on finding the product in the list. Consider the code in Figure 6.16. In Section 6.5.2, we will further develop code.

```
Sub FindProduct()
    Dim Product As String
    Dim Found As Boolean
    Dim i As Integer

    Product = InputBox("Please enter a product code:")
    Found = False

    For i = 2 To 11
        If (Product = Cells(i, 1).Value) Then
            Found = True
        End If
    Next

    If Found = True Then
        MsgBox "Product found"
    Else
        MsgBox "Product not found"
    End If
End Sub
```

6.16 FIND A SPECIFIC PRODUCT IN A LIST.

Firstly, a string, containing the product code to search for, is obtained by an input box. Next, the Boolean variable *Found* is set to False, indicating that the product has not been found so far.

Using a *For-Next* loop, we iteratively consider product from 2 to 11 (corresponding to the rows containing the information). We use the variable *i* to do so. Hence, *i* corresponds to the row number. For each value of *i*, we check whether the content of the first column of that row equals our product code. If this is the case, we set the Boolean variable *Found* equal to true, indicating that the product has been found.

After executing the *For-Next* loop, we know that if the product is found, then the value of *Found* has been set to true. Therefore, if the value is still false, it means that the product has not been found in the list. We use an If-Then-Else construction, based on this knowledge, to display the appropriate message box at the end of the sub.

6.3.1.3 *Example: Members*

In the second example, we consider the members of an organization. Available information is the name of the member, along with the gender and date of birth. Information about the members is given in a worksheet, as illustrated in Figure 6.17. Note that cell C3 gives the number of members.

The task to be performed in this example is to create a table showing the age distribution of each gender separately and of the members as a whole. Swap to Figure 6.20 to get a preview of the table to be constructed. This table is used in Chapter 14, as a base for constructing charts showing the age distribution. Even though this example is about age distribution, it is not hard to see that the same structure can be used for other objects that need to be categorized.

	A	B	C
1	Number of member:		151
2	Name	Gender	Birth
3	Mikkel	Male	15-03-2002
4	Louise	Female	04-04-2001
5	Kristoffer	Male	20-08-2001
6	Sebastian	Male	14-07-1995
7	Lars	Male	03-12-1993

6.17 DATA FOR THE CODE IN FIGURE 6.19.

Firstly, consider the code in Figure 6.18. The function *CalculateExactAgeYears* takes the date of birth as input and returns the current age in years. The function is similar to the function in Figure 5.19, except that here we only calculate the age in years.

```
Function CalculateExactAgeYears(Born As Date)
    Dim N As Date
    Dim Temp As Date
    Dim y As Integer

    N = Date
    'Calculate years
    y = DateDiff("yyyy", Born, N)
    Temp = DateAdd("yyyy", y, Born)
    If DateDiff("m", Temp, N) < 0 Or DateDiff("d", Temp, N) < 0 Then
        y = y - 1
    End If
    CalculateExactAgeYears = y
End Function
```

6.18 FUNCTION TO DETERMINE AGE IN YEARS.

Now, consider the code in Figure 6.19, which is the main sub. Firstly, the headings of the table are create, and a *For-Next* loop is used to write the list of ages in column F. Secondly, the number of members are stored in the variable *children*.

```
Public Sub PrepareDataFromDates()
    Dim i As Integer
    Dim children As Integer
    Dim d As Integer

    ' Prepare data area:
    Range("F1:I20").Clear
    Range("F5").Value = "Age"
    Range("G5").Value = "Male"
    Range("H5").Value = "Female"
    Range("I5").Value = "Total"
    For i = 6 To 19
        Cells(i, 6) = i
    Next

    children = Range("C1").Value

    For i = 3 To children + 2
        d = CalculateExactAgeYears(Cells(i, 3).Value)
        If Cells(i, 2) = "Male" Then
            Cells(d, 7) = Cells(d, 7) + 1
        ElseIf Cells(i, 2) = "Female" Then
            Cells(d, 8) = Cells(d, 8) + 1
        End If
            Cells(d, 9) = Cells(d, 9) + 1
    Next
End Sub
```

6.19 STRUCTURING DATA IN A TABLE.

The main part of the sub consists of a *For-Next* loop that iterates through the list of members. Note that the first member is stored in row 3, and the last row is found by the value of the *children* variable + 2 where the 2 is for the two top rows that do not contain a member.

For each member, the age is calculated using the above function and is stored in the variable *d*. This value also immediately gives us the row index, of that age, in column F, due to the location of this table. Now, using an If-Then-Else construction, the correct column – either 7 or 8 - is found based on the gender. The value, in the row determined by *d*, of that column, is increased by one. Finally, the value in column 9, which is the total, is also increased. The resulting table, showing the age distributions, can be seen in Figure 6.20.

	A	B	C	D	E	F	G	H	I	J
1	Number of member:		151							
2	Name	Gender	Birth							
3	Mikkel	Male	15-03-2002							
4	Louise	Female	04-04-2001							
5	Kristoffer	Male	20-08-2001			Age	Male	Female	Total	
6	Sebastian	Male	14-07-1995			6	3	1	4	
7	Lars	Male	03-12-1993			7	4	3	7	
8	Lasse	Male	28-03-2002			8	11	3	14	
9	Anders	Male	30-12-1999			9	7	1	8	
10	Lone	Female	20-09-2002			10	8	5	13	
11	Mia	Female	08-01-1996			11	8	1	9	
12	Maria	Female	08-01-1996			12	24	6	30	
13	Bob	Male	19-06-1999			13	7	9	16	
14	Erik	Male	27-10-2002			14	9	7	16	
15	Tenna	Female	05-11-1999			15	5	8	13	
16	Bodil	Female	24-05-1996			16	8	3	11	
17	Jens	Male	05-05-1996			17	2	1	3	
18	Peter	Male	04-09-1997			18	4		4	
19	Hans	Male	19-03-1999			19	2	1	3	
20	Gert	Male	13-09-1999							
21	Søren	Male	16-04-1998							

6.20 TABLE CONSTRUCTED BY THE CODE IN FIGURE 6.19.

6.3.2 The While Loop

The *While* Loop is significantly different from the For-Next loop: Regarding the for loop, we know exactly how many times the loop will be repeated. This is not the case for the *While* loop, which will be repeated as long as a certain condition is true.

The basic structure of the *While* loop is given in Figure 6.21. Note that *While* loops are often referred to as *While-Wend* loops. The *While* loop works as follows: First, the condition is checked. If the condition is true, then the body of the loop if executed. Then, the condition is checked, and if it is true, then the body is executed, and so on. The body is executed as long as the condition is true. When the condition evaluates to false, then the program skips the body and jumps directly to the *Wend* statement in order to leave the loop.

```
While condition
   'code
Wend
```

6.21 SYNTAX OF WHILE LOOP.

Note, that the condition is not checked during the execution of the code in the body of the loop. Therefore, if the condition were to become false in the middle of the body, but true when it reaches the end of the body and the condition checking, then the looping would continue. Hence, the only thing that matters is the value of the condition at the points where it is checked.

6.3.2.1 Illustration of the While Loop

As a first example, consider the code in Figure 6.22. In the body of the loop, the variable *i* is first displayed in a message box. Then, the value is increased by one. Execution of the loop is repeated as long as the value of *i* is less than or equal to 3. When *i* becomes strictly greater than 3, the body will not be executed. Instead the program jumps to the *Wend* statement, and leaves the loop.

```
Public Sub IllustrateWhile()
    Dim i As Integer

    i = 1
    While i <= 3
        MsgBox i
        i = i + 1
    Wend

End Sub
```

6.22 SIMPLE WHILE LOOP.

Execution of the code in Figure 6.22 results in the three message boxes shown in Figure 6.23.

6.23 OUTPUT FROM THE CODE IN FIGURE 6.22.

The next example is given in Figure 6.24. In the body of the loop, the value of *i* is first increased by two, then *i* is displayed, and finally, the value is decreased by one. When the sub is executed, three message boxes are shown, displaying the values 3, 4, and 5, respectively. If it is not completely clear to you why this is the case, it is recommended that you read this section again.

```
Public Sub IllustrateWhile2()
    Dim i As Integer

    i = 1
    While i < 4
        i = i + 2
        MsgBox i
        i = i - 1
    Wend
End Sub
```

6.24 THE COUNTER CAN HAVE ANY VALUE WITHIN THE BODY OF THE LOOP.

As a final example, we show how a while loop can be used to force the user of the program to enter something in an input box. Consider the code in Figure 6.25. First the string variable, *Product*, is initialized to be an empty string. In the body of the while loop, the variable *Product* is set equal to the return of an input box, i.e. the variable now contains the input that the user has typed.

The loop is repeated as long as the string is empty. Note that an input box returns an empty string if *Enter* has been pressed without anything being typed. Therefore, the only way that the program will stop repeating the loop is by the user typing something in the input box.

```
Public Sub IllustrateWhileInput()
    Dim Product As String

    Product = "" 'Empty string
    While Product = ""
        Product = InputBox("Please enter product id:")
    Wend

End Sub
```

6.25 FORCE THE USER TO WRITE SOMETHING.

Clearly, a similar method can be used to force the user to enter numerical input, or only letters, etc.

6.3.2.2 Example: Find Product - Revisited

In Section 6.3.1.2, we illustrated how a *For-Next* loop can be used to find a specific product in a list of products. Here, we will show how the same can be done by using a *While* loop. Assume that the first column in a worksheet contains a list of products, and consider the code in Figure 6.26.

```
Sub FindProduct()
    Dim Product As String
    Dim i As Integer
    Product = InputBox("Please enter a product code:")

    i = 2
    While Cells(i, 1) <> Product And i < 100
        i = i + 1
    Wend

    If (Cells(i, 1) = Product) Then
        MsgBox "Product found"
    Else
        MsgBox "Product not found"
    End If
End Sub
```

6.26 USING A WHILE LOOP TO FIND A PRODUCT IN A LIST.

The string variable is used to store the product id to search for, which is obtained through an input box. The variable *i* is used to iterate through the rows of the worksheet. In the body of the *while* loop, the value of *i* is increased such that the next product will be considered.

The loop is repeated as long as the content of the cell does not equal the string we are looking for, i.e as long as we do not have a match, and as long as *i* is less than 100. The last part is only there to ensure that even if there is no match, the looping will eventually stop. The value 100 should be high enough to ensure that all products are considered.

The looping can stop for two reasons. Firstly, if a match is found, the first part of the condition becomes false. In this case, the condition of the if statement is true, and the appropriate message box is displayed. Note that in this example, we know the index of the row that contains the product. Secondly, the looping can stop because *i* grows to 100 without finding a match. In this case, the condition in the if statement evaluates to false, and a message box states that the product was not found.

6.3.2.3 Example: Investment

The final example is based on the worksheet shown in Figure 6.27. Assume that we have an amount of 200 to buy shares in a range of products. For each product, the price and the expected profit is given in columns C and B, respectively. Column D gives the ratio between the two. The products are sorted in decreasing order by expected profit. There is a limit on the number of shares that may be bought of each product. This limit is given in column E. Note that only whole numbers may be bought. The goal of the problem is to determine the number of shares to buy of each product in order to maximize expected profit.

In this example, we will use the following investment strategy: Consider each product at a time, in the order in which they appear in the worksheet, and buy as much as possible of that product.

Note that the goal of this example is not to determine an optimal investment strategy, but rather to implement the above strategy.

	A	B	C	D	E	F
1	Product	Profit	Price	Profit/Price	Max	Buy
2	DJ4761	31	23	1,35	2	
3	KG3734	28	17	1,65	3	
4	GY3456	23	13	1,77	1	
5	EN3463	18	11	1,64	3	
6	YM3854	14	10	1,40	4	
7	WH5715	13	6	2,17	6	
8	WE5143	9	5	1,80	6	
9	QG5247	5	3	1,67	10	
10	WC5465	3	2	1,50	20	
11	IM5458	1	1	1,00	20	
12						

6.27 DATA FOR THE CODE IN FIGURE 6.28.

Consider the code in Figure 6.28. We first explain the function *Buy*. The function takes as argument two integers: *Money* is the amount of money left for further investment, and *product* is the row index of the current product to be considered for investment. The return value of the function is the number of shares of the current product to buy.

In the first line of code, we calculate the number of shares that we can afford to buy, by taking the integer portion of the ratio of the available amount of money, to the price of a share.

In the second line of code, we determine the minimum of the number of shares that we want to buy, and the number of shares that we are allowed to buy. This value is the number of shares that we will buy and is the value returned by the function.

We now turn our attention to the main sub in Figure 6.28. The variable *money* holds, at any time, the amount of money left for further investment, and is initialized to 200. *Product* is the row index of the product currently considered for investment, and *Amount* is used to hold the number of shares of the product to buy.

In the body of the loop, the *Buy* function is first used to determine the number of shares of the current product to buy. This is entered in column F in the worksheet, as can be seen in Figure 6.29. Next, the amount of money left for further investment is adjusted by the amount just spent. Finally, the row index is increased by one to consider the next product.

```
Sub Invest()
    Dim product As Integer
    Dim Amount As Integer
    Dim money As Integer

    money = 200
    product = 2
    While money > 0 And product <= 11
        Amount = Buy(money, product)
        Cells(product, 6) = Amount
        money = money - Amount * Cells(product, 3)
        product = product + 1
    Wend

    Range("C13") = money
    Range("C14") = Application.WorksheetFunction.SumProduct _
            (Range("B2:B11"), Range("F2:F11"))
End Sub
```

```
Function Buy(money As Integer, product As Integer)
    Buy = Fix(money / Cells(product, 3))
    Buy = Application.WorksheetFunction.Min(Buy, Cells(product,
End Function
```

6.28 USING A WHILE LOOP TO DETERMINE AN INVESTMENT STRATEGY.

The loop is repeated as long as there are still both money left and further products to consider. When all money is spent, and the value reduces to 0, the first condition evaluates to false and execution will jump to the line following the *Wend* statement. Furthermore, when the *product* index increases above 11, the second condition evaluates to false, and again execution jumps to the line following the *Wend* statement.

Finally, the amount of money left is written in cell C13, and the expected return is calculated by *SumProduct* and written in cell C14. The resulting worksheet is shown in Figure 6.29.

	A	B	C	D	E	F	G
1	Product	Profit	Price	Profit/Price	Max	Buy	
2	DJ4761	31	23	1,35	2	2	
3	KG3734	28	17	1,65	3	3	
4	GY3456	23	13	1,77	1	1	
5	EN3463	18	11	1,64	3	3	
6	YM3854	14	10	1,40	4	4	
7	WH5715	13	6	2,17	6	2	
8	WE5143	9	5	1,80	6	1	
9	QG5247	5	3	1,67	10		
10	WC5465	3	2	1,50	20		
11	IM5458	1	1	1,00	20		
12							
13	Money invested		0				
14	Profit		314				
15							

6.29 OUTPUT OF THE CODE IN FIGURE 6.28.

6.3.3 The Do Loops

If you fully understand the *While* loop, you will have no problems understanding the *Do* loops as well. The basic idea of the *While* loop and the *Do* loops is the same.

There are four types of *Do* loops which we will briefly discuss in the following two sections.

6.3.3.1 The Do-While Loop and the Do-Until Loop

The *Do-While* loop works as the *While-Wend* loop, considered in the previous section. The syntax is a little different, though: *While* is replaced by *Do-While*, and *Wend* is replaced by *Loop*. Figure 6.30 shows the syntax of the *Do While* loop along with a flowchart that illustrates the loop. Note that just like the while loop, here the condition is evaluated before entering the body of the loop. The body of the *Do-While* loop is executed as long as the condition is true.

```
Do While condition
    'code
    [Exit Do]
    'code
Loop
```

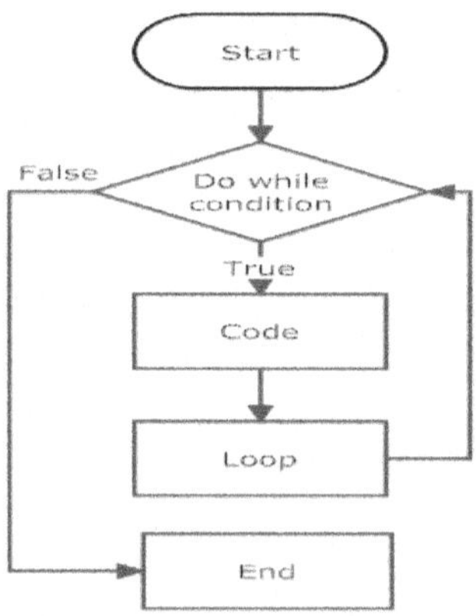

6.30 SYNTAX AND FLOWCHART OF THE DO-WHILE LOOP.

The *Do-Until* loop is similar, except that here, the body is executed until the condition becomes true. That is, the condition starts out false, and the body is repeated until it becomes true, at which point the looping stops. This kind of looping is intuitive in situations where some tasks should be repeated until all products are scheduled, or until a vehicle is found, and so forth. Figure 6.31 shows the syntax of the *Do-Until* loop along with a flowchart that illustrates the loop.

You have probably already noted that these to loops can replace each other by using the negation of the condition. This means that everything that can be coded, using one of the two loops, can just as easily be coded using the other. The only reason for making both types available is that depending on the programmer and the task, one often seems more intuitive than the other.

```
Do Until condition
   'code
   [Exit Do]
   'code
Loop
```

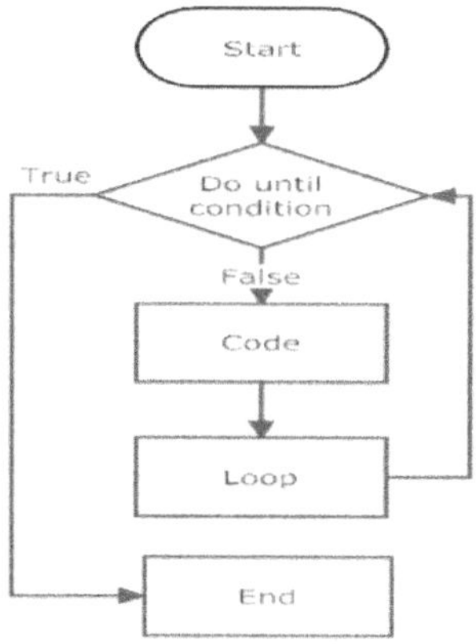

6.31 SYNTAX AND FLOWCHART OF THE DO-UNTIL LOOP.

For an illustration, consider the code in Figure 6.32. The two pieces of code are identical, except that they use each their type of loop. Both codes display three message boxes, showing the numbers 1, 2, and 3, respectively.

```
Sub ShowDoWhileLoop()
    Dim j As Integer
    j = 1
    Do While j <= 3
        MsgBox j
        j = j + 1
    Loop
End Sub
```

```
Sub ShowDoUntilLoop()
    Dim j As Integer
    j = 1
    Do Until j > 3
        MsgBox j
        j = j + 1
    Loop
End Sub
```

6.32 COMPARISON OF A DO-WHILE LOOP AND A DO-UNTIL LOOP.

6.3.3.2 The Do-Loop-While and the Do-Loop-Until

The *Do-Loop-While* and the *Do-Loop-Until* loops are significantly different from the two loops introduced in the previous section. We start with the loop that repeats while a condition is true. The syntax of the *Do-Loop-While* is shown in Figure 6.33 along with a flowchart of the loop. Try to compare the flowchart to the one given for the *Do-While* Loop in Figure 6.30. Note how the code in the body is executed the first time before the condition is evaluated. Hence, independently of the condition being true or false, the body will be executed at least once.

This calls for an example. In the left-hand side of Figure 6.34, we show an example of a *Do-While* Loop which is described in the previous section. The condition of this loop will clearly evaluate to false, and the body of the loop will not be entered. Hence no message box is displayed when the left-hand side code is executed.

```
Do
   'code
   [Exit Do]
   'code
Loop While condition
```

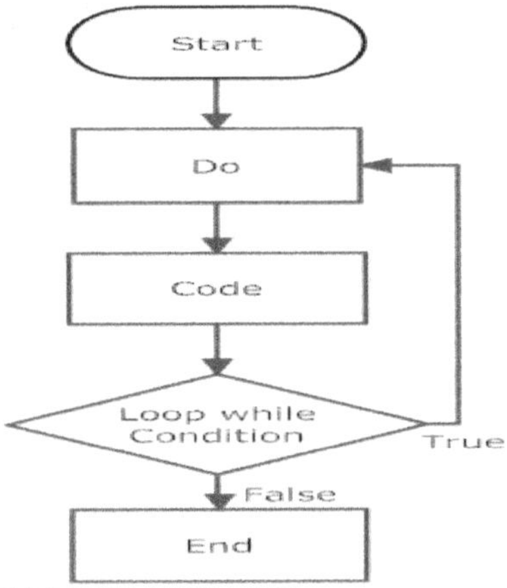

6.33 SYNTAX AND FLOWCHART OF THE DO-LOOP-WHILE LOOP.

To the right we give a code that looks very similar, except that a Do-*Loop-While* loop is used. However, note that the initialization of the variable *j*, and the condition used in the two pieces of code, is exactly the same. When executing the right-hand side code, a message box showing the value 1 will be displayed.

If it is not clear to you why this is the case, then take a second loop at the two flowcharts in Figures 6.30 and 6.33. For the *Do-While* Loop, the procedure is: First check the condition to determine if you want to execute the body, next execute it if this is what you wanted. Repeat that. For the *Do-Loop-While* loop, the procedure is: First execute the body, next check the condition to determine if you want to execute the body again. Repeat that. See the difference?

This kind of looping is useful when you want to ensure that the body is executed at least once.

```
Sub NotOnce()
    Dim j As Integer
    j = 1
    Do While j < 0
        MsgBox j
        j = j + 1
    Loop
End Sub
```

```
Sub AtLeastOnce()
    Dim j As Integer
    j = 1
    Do
        MsgBox j
        j = j + 1
    Loop While j < 0
End Sub
```

6.34 COMPARISON OF A DO-WHILE LOOP AND A DO-LOOP-WHILE LOOP.

We now turn our attention to the last of the four loops, the *Do-Loop-Until* loop. As you might have guessed, this loop is structured like the *Do-Loop-While* loop, but executes until the condition becomes true. The syntax of the *Do-Loop-Until* is shown in Figure 6.35 along with flowchart of the loop.

```
Do
   'code
   [Exit Do]
   'code
Loop Until condition
```

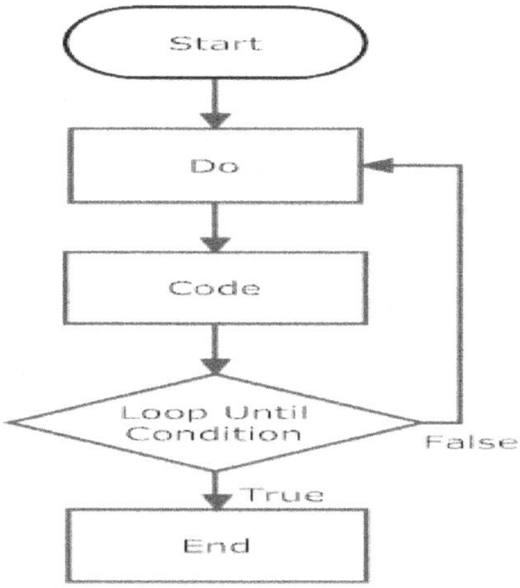

6.35 SYNTAX AND FLOWCHART OF THE DO-LOOP-UNTIL LOOP.

To see how this loop is different from the *Do-Until* Loop, consider the code in Figure 6.36. The loop in the right-hand side is repeated until *j* becomes positive, but since *j* is already positive, the body of the code is never executed and no message box is displayed when executing the code.

```
Sub UntilNotOnce()
    Dim j As Integer
    j = 1
    Do Until j > 0
        MsgBox j
        j = j + 1
    Loop
End Sub
```

```
Sub UntilAtLeastOnce()
    Dim j As Integer
    j = 1
    Do
        MsgBox j
        j = j + 1
    Loop Until j > 0
End Sub
```

6.36 COMPARISON OF THE DO-UNTIL LOOP AND THE DO-LOOP-UNTIL LOOP.

The left-hand side code is similar, except that here we use a *Do-Loop-Until* loop instead. Note that the condition in the two pieces of code is the same. When executing this code, the body of the loop is executed once before the condition is evaluated. The condition is evaluated to be true which forces the looping to stop. Hence, one message box, showing the value 1, is displayed.

Again, a comparison of the flowcharts of Figures 6.31 and 6.35 gives us the explanation: Regarding the *Do-Until* Loop, first the condition is checked to see is we want to execute the body. Next, the body is executed if this is what we wanted. With the *Do-Loop-Until*, first the body of the loop is executed. Next, the condition is checked to determine if we want to execute the body again. This is repeated.

Just like the two loops in the previous section could replace each other by a simple negation of the condition, so can the two loops described in this section. From the above explanation, is should be clear why execution of any of the two subs in Figure 6.37 results in three message boxes, with the values 1, 2, and 3, respectively, being displayed.

```
Sub ShowDoLoopWhile()
    Dim j As Integer
    j = 1
    Do
        MsgBox j
        j = j + 1
    Loop While j <= 3
End Sub
```

```
Sub ShowDoLoopUntil()
    Dim j As Integer
    j = 1
    Do
        MsgBox j
        j = j + 1
    Loop Until j > 3
End Sub
```

6.37 COMPARISON OF A DO-LOOP-WHILE LOOP AND A DO-LOOP-UNTIL LOOP.

6.3.4 Be Aware of Endless Looping

Making your computer break down is not a difficult task, and using *While* or *Do* loops make it even easier.

Consider the small code in Figure 6.38. How many times will the body of the loop be executed? 1?, 5? 100? 1 million? The truth is, execution will continue until you force it to break because the stopping criterion is never met: *i* will not stop being greater than zero. This situation is referred to as *endless looping*.

```
Sub Endless_loop2()
    Dim i As Integer
    i = 1
    While i > 0
        MsgBox Cells(1, 1)
        i = i + 1
    Wend
End Sub
```

6.38 EXAMPLE OF AN ENDLESS LOOP.

Sometimes you need to search through a list of something to find a specific element. Consider for example the *Find Product* example that we have used several times before in this chapter. Figure 6.39 gives a code for finding the product and displaying the row index of it. The *While* loop is executed as long as the entered product code is different from the content of the current cell. When a match is found, the looping is stopped. But what if a faulty product code is entered – one that is not in the list. In that case, the loop is endless. To avoid this problem, a safety condition can be inserted, just as we did in Figure 6.26.

```
Sub FindProduct_Endless()
    Dim Product As String
    Dim i As Integer

    Product = InputBox("Please enter a product code:")
    i = 2
    While Product <> Cells(i, 1)
        i = i + 1
    Wend

    MsgBox "Product found at row " & i
End Sub
```

6.39 FIND PRODUCT EXAMPLE WITH RISK OF ENDLESS LOOPING.

You have now seen a couple of examples of endless loops. We have used *While* loops for illustration purposes, but *Do* loops can be just as endless. There is no need to point out that you should avoid endless loops at all times.

If you accidently make an endless loop anyway, you should learn how to stop your computer from total meltdown: *Fn + Break* does the trick. Note that this might depend on your computer. Well, so does *Ctrl + Alt+ Delete*, but if you use that, you could lose your unsaved work.

Endless looping mainly occur for two reasons: The first one is that you want to iterate through a list of items, but forget to include the line to increase the value of the variable that helps you iterate. The second reason is that your code assumes that you find what you are looking for, and you forget to take into account that you might not find it.

6.4 Nested Loops

Loops and decision constructions can be nested. This means that within the body of one loop, you can place another loop, or a number of decision structures. Within one decision structure you can place another, or a bunch of loops, and so forth.

In the following, let structure refer to any kind of loop or decision construction. Common to all of them is that they have a specific start line and a specific end line: *For* has *Next*, *If* has *End If*, *While* has *Wend*, and so on. With this in mind, Figure 6.40 shows two ways of nesting loops – you can create any combination that you can come up with.

There is only one rule that must be respected: For any two structures, A and B: if the start line of B is after the start line of A in the code, then the end line of B must be before the end line of A, i.e. the whole B structure must be within the body of A. As long as this rule is respected, the only limit is the imagination of the programmer.

```
Start structure A
   Start structure B
      Start structure C
         Start structure D
            Start structure E

            End structure E
         End structure D
      End structure C
   End structure B
End structure A
```

```
Start structure A
   Start structure B
   End structure B

   Start structure C
   End structure C
End structure A
```

6.40 NESTED LOOPS.

To see what this can look like in VBA code, consider Figure 6.41. Here you see how two *For-Next* loops, a *While* loop, and a *If* construction can be nested. Note that there can be further code in between the nested loops.

```
Sub IllustrateNesting()
    Dim i As Integer
    Dim k As Integer
    Dim t As Double

    'code
    For i = 1 To Range("A1")
        'code
        While t > 0
            'code
            If cell(i, 3) > Range("A2") Then
                'code
                For k = 100 To Range("A3") Step -2
                    'code
                Next
                'code
            Else
                'code
            End If
            'code
            t = t - 0.05
        Wend
        'code
    Next
End Sub
```

6.41 EXAMPLE OF NESTED LOOPS.

6.4.1 Example: Calculate Distances

This example is based on the worksheet shown in Figure 6.42. A number of cities are located in a coordinate system where x- and y-coordinates for each city are given in columns B and C. Cell E1 states the number of cities. The goal is to make a distance table, using the Euclidian distance, based on the given information.

	A	B	C	D	E
1	Number	X	Y	Number of cities	10
2	1	6	1		
3	2	1	5		
4	3	6	3		
5	4	7	4		
6	5	4	6		
7	6	4	7		
8	7	5	2		
9	8	1	4		
10	9	4	2		
11	10	6	5		
12					

6.42 DATA FOR THE CODE IN FIGURE 6.43.

Consider the code in Figure 6.43. Given two city indexes, the function *Distance* calculates and returns the Euclidian distance between the cities.

```
Public Sub MakeDistanceMatrix()
    Dim n As Integer
    Dim i As Integer
    Dim j As Integer

    n = Range("E1")
    For i = 1 To n
        Cells(i + 1, 6) = Cells(1 + i, 1)
        Cells(1, 6 + i) = Cells(1 + i, 1)
    Next

    For i = 1 To n
        For j = 1 To n
            Cells(i + 1, j + 6) = Distance(i, j)
        Next
    Next
End Sub
```

```
Public Function Distance(i, j)
    Dim x As Single
    Dim y As Single

    x = Cells(i + 1, 2) - Cells(j + 1, 2)
    y = Cells(i + 1, 3) - Cells(j + 1, 3)
    Distance = Sqr((x * x) + (y * y))
End Function
```

6.43 CREATION AF A DISTANCE TABLE IN A WORKSHEET.

Before reading on, it might be useful to take a look at Figure 6.44 which shows the resulting distance table. The variable *n* is used to store the number of cities.

The first *For-Next* loop writes the horizontal and the vertical city numbering of Figure 6.44. Note that the list with information is shifted one row down compared to the row index. That explains the +1 on the right-hand side of the equal sign. The vertical city numbering of the distance table is located in column 6 which explains the 6 in the first line of the body. The vertical city indexing starts in column 7, which corresponds to 6 + *i*, when *i* is 1. That explains the second line of the body.

The second part consists of two nested *For-Next* loops which iterates through each origin city and each destination city. For each pair, the distance is determined by the *Destination* function and written in the distance table. Note how the 1 and the 6 on the left-hand side take us to the cell above and to the left of the table. Figure 6.44 gives the final table.

F	G	H	I	J	K	L	M	N	O	P
	1	2	3	4	5	6	7	8	9	10
1	0,00	6,40	2,00	3,16	5,39	6,32	1,41	5,83	2,24	4,00
2	6,40	0,00	5,39	6,08	3,16	3,61	5,00	1,00	4,24	5,00
3	2,00	5,39	0,00	1,41	3,61	4,47	1,41	5,10	2,24	2,00
4	3,16	6,08	1,41	0,00	3,61	4,24	2,83	6,00	3,61	1,41
5	5,39	3,16	3,61	3,61	0,00	1,00	4,12	3,61	4,00	2,24
6	6,32	3,61	4,47	4,24	1,00	0,00	5,10	4,24	5,00	2,83
7	1,41	5,00	1,41	2,83	4,12	5,10	0,00	4,47	1,00	3,16
8	5,83	1,00	5,10	6,00	3,61	4,24	4,47	0,00	3,61	5,10
9	2,24	4,24	2,24	3,61	4,00	5,00	1,00	3,61	0,00	3,61
10	4,00	5,00	2,00	1,41	2,24	2,83	3,16	5,10	3,61	0,00

6.44 OUTPUT OF THE CODE IN FIGURE 6.43.

Often distance tables for symmetric distances only display the upper right half of the distanced, as shown in Figure 6.45.

F	G	H	I	J	K	L	M	N	O	P	Q
	1	2	3	4	5	6	7	8	9	10	
1		6,40	2,00	3,16	5,39	6,32	1,41	5,83	2,24	4,00	
2			5,39	6,08	3,16	3,61	5,00	1,00	4,24	5,00	
3				1,41	3,61	4,47	1,41	5,10	2,24	2,00	
4					3,61	4,24	2,83	6,00	3,61	1,41	
5						1,00	4,12	3,61	4,00	2,24	
6							5,10	4,24	5,00	2,83	
7								4,47	1,00	3,16	
8									3,61	5,10	
9										3,61	
10											

6.45 OUTPUT OF THE CODE IN FIGURE 6.46.

In Figure 6.46, we have changed the code so that it produces the table of Figure 6.45. Note that the only difference in the code is in the inner of the two nested loops. The outer loop indexes the origin cities, while the inner loop indexes the destination cities. Here, we only consider destination indexes that are larger than the origin cities, resulting in the triangular structure.

```
Public Sub MakeDistanceMatrix()
    Dim n As Integer
    Dim i As Integer
    Dim j As Integer

    n = Range("E1")
    For i = 1 To n
        Cells(i + 1, 6) = Cells(1 + i, 1)
        Cells(1, 6 + i) = Cells(1 + i, 1)
    Next

    For i = 1 To n
        For j = i + 1 To n
            Cells(i + 1, j + 6) = Distance(i, j)
        Next
    Next
End Sub
```

6.46 CREATING A SYMMETRIC DISTANCE TABLE.

Finally, we show how simple the creation of a distance table is, if it is stored in an internal array instead of being written to the worksheet. Consider the code in Figure 6.47. In the main sub, an array is dimensioned and given to the *MakeDistArray* along with an integer stating the number of cities.

The *MakeDistArray* mimics the *MakeDistanceMatrix* from above. The first loop is removed, because the city indexing of the table is not used when the table is stored in an array. Note also how simple the indexing in the nested loops is, compared to the code above.

```
Sub main()
    Dim n As Integer
    Dim A() As Double

    n = Range("E1")
    ReDim A(n, n)
    Call MakeDistArray(A, n)
End Sub
```

```
Sub MakeDistArray(ByRef D() As Double, ByVal n As Integer)
    Dim i As Integer
    Dim j As Integer

    For i = 1 To n
        For j = 1 To n
            D(i, j) = Distance(i, j)
        Next
    Next
End Sub
```

6.47 CREATING A DISTANCE TABLE IN AN ARRAY.

6.4.2 Example: Gantt Chart

In this example we create a program to produce a *Gantt Chart*. Given the worksheet presented in Figure 6.48, the code should produce the Gantt Chart shown in Figure 4.49. The numbers shown for each period for each activity in the Gantt Chart are the use of resources given in column D. Below the Gantt Chart, the program is supposed to sum up the resources used in each period. The code should be flexible in the sense that it works with any given number of activities.

	A	B	C	D
1	Number of Activities		9	
2				
3	Activity	Duration	Start	Resources
4	1	3	1	6
5	2	2	1	3
6	3	1	3	3
7	4	1	7	3
8	5	2	4	6
9	6	4	6	5
10	7	1	4	3
11	8	2	5	4
12	9	2	7	3

6.48 DATA FOR CREATING A GANTT CHART.

The first task to perform is to determine the last period for each activity. For example, the fifth activity starts in period 4 and lasts for two periods. Hence, the activity is ended in period 5 (4+2-1). This is obtained by the following piece of code where the variable *i* iterates through the activities.

```
Range("E3") = "End"
For i = 4 To 3 + NumActivities
   Cells(i, 5) = Cells(i, 3) + Cells(i, 2) - 1
Next
```

In order to set up the Gantt Chart, we need to know the finishing time for the activity that finishes last. For this purpose we will use the worksheet function *Max* which can take a range as an argument, as follows.

```
FinishTime = Application.WorksheetFunction.Max( Range(Cells(5, 4),
                         Cells(NumActivities + 3, 5)))
```

H	I	J	K	L	M	N	O	P
1	2	3	4	5	6	7	8	9
6	6	6						
3	3							
		3						
						3		
			6	6				
					5	5	5	5
			3					
				4	4			
						3	3	
Total use of resources								
9	9	9	9	10	9	11	8	5

6.49 RESULT OF EXECUTING THE CODE IN FIGURE 6.50.

The next piece of code writes the period numbers above the Gantt Chart. The variable *j* iterates through the periods until the finishing time. The period index is written to column 7+*j*. For example, in the first period, *j =1*. Hence we write to column 8 (7+1).

```
For j = 1 To FinishTime
   Cells(2, 7 + j) = j
Next
```

After setting up the Gantt Chart, it is now the time for filling in the activities. This is done by using two *For-Next* loops. The first loop uses *i* to iterate through all rows, containing activities. For each activity, *i*, the body of the outer loop is executed. The body of the outer loop contains another *For-Next* loop where *j* is used to iterate through the periods where the activity is active. For example for *i = 9*, we have *j = Cells(9,3)*, which is 6, To Cells(9,5) which has previously been determined to be 9. Hence, *j* will iterate from 6 through 9 and execute the body of the inner loop, still with *i = 9*. In the body of the inner loop, we write to row *i*, column *7+j* which in our example are columns 13 (7+6) through 16 (7+9). In each of these cells, the value of column 4 is written which is the Resources. This will be repeated for every *i*.

```
For i = 4 To 3 + NumActivities
   For j = Cells(i, 3) To Cells(i, 5)
      Cells(i, 7 + j) = Cells(i, 4)
   Next
Next
```

Finally, using a *For-Next* loop to let *j* iterate through the periods, we use the worksheet function *Sum* to calculate the total resources for each period.

```
Cells(4 + NumActivities, 8) = "Total use of resources"
For j = 1 To FinishTime
   Cells(5 + NumActivities, 7 + j) = _
      Application.WorksheetFunction.Sum( Range(Cells(4, 7 + j),
                  Cells(3 + NumActivities, 7 + j)))
Next
```

The complete code can be found in Figure 6.50.

```
Sub MakeGanttChart()
    NumActivities = Range("C1")

    'Find end time for each activity:
    Range("E3") = "End"
    For i = 4 To 3 + NumActivities
        Cells(i, 5) = Cells(i, 3) + Cells(i, 2) - 1
    Next

    'Find end time for total project:
    FinishTime = Application.WorksheetFunction.Max( _
            Range(Cells(5, 4), Cells(NumActivities + 3, 5)))

    'Prepare Gantt Chart:
    For j = 1 To FinishTime
        Cells(2, 7 + j) = j
    Next

    'Place each activity in Gantt Chart:
    For i = 4 To 3 + NumActivities
        For j = Cells(i, 3) To Cells(i, 5)
            'Each period where the activity is active
            Cells(i, 7 + j) = Cells(i, 4)
        Next
    Next

    'Determine use of resources:
    Cells(4 + NumActivities, 8) = "Total use of resources"
    For j = 1 To FinishTime
        Cells(5 + NumActivities, 7 + j) = _
            Application.WorksheetFunction.Sum( _
            Range(Cells(4, 7 + j), _
            Cells(3 + NumActivities, 7 + j)))
    Next
End Sub
```

6.50 CODE FOR CREATING A GANTT CHART.

6.4.3 Example: Sequencing of Jobs

This example is about sequencing of jobs and is based on the worksheet shown in Figure 6.51. The number of jobs is given in cell C3, and the jobs are indexed starting from 1. Figure 6.51 gives the setup cost for each ordered pair of jobs. Index 0 indicates the initial setup. The goal of the problem is to determine the processing order of the jobs which minimizes the total setup cost.

	A	B	C	D	E	F	G
1	Number of jobs		5				
2							
3	From \ To	1	2	3	4	5	
4	0	27	28	32	35	26	
5	1		35	22	44	12	
6	2	49		46	38	17	
7	3	46	12		29	41	
8	4	23	37	31		26	
9	5	17	23	28	34		
10							

6.51 DATA FOR THE CODE IN FIGURE 6.52.

We consider the following greedy strategy: Start by selecting the job with smallest initial setup cost. Then, as long as there are unscheduled jobs, select the job with the smallest setup cost based on the current setup. Note that the goal of this example is not to determine an optimal sequence of the jobs, but rather to implement the strategy described.

For this purpose, consider the code in Figure 6.52 which is one of the most difficult so far in this book. The variable *n* holds the number of jobs, and the array *used*, with the length of *n*, contains for each job a 1 if the job has been scheduled and zero otherwise. Note that *used* is initialized with zero at each location.

M is an arbitrary number, larger than the number of jobs. At this point you might want to swap forward to Figure 6.53 to take a look at the format of the output: Every setup cost that is selected is indicated by green (gray in this printed version). This gives the ordering of the jobs. In this example, the order is 0 – 5 – 1 – 3 – 2 – 4. Note that after the last job, which is job 4, no setup is required. The total setup cost is given in cell F1. In the code, the sub *CleanUp* clears this output information, and is not shown here.

The variable *i* is used to index the current job. Note that the initial situation is indexed as zero. The outer loop is repeated *n* times. The variable *k*, which indexes the loop is not used in the code, and is only there to ensure that the process is repeated *n* times.

```
Sub SequencingJobs()
    Dim n As Integer ' number of jobs
    Dim used() As Integer
    Dim i As Integer, j As Integer
    Dim t As Integer, k As Integer
    Dim M As Integer
    Dim cost As Integer

    n = Range("C1").Value
    ReDim used(n)
    M = 1000

    i = 0
    Call CleanUp
    For k = 1 To n
        t = M
        For j = 1 To n
            If used(j) <> 1 And (t = M Or _
            Cells(i + 4, j + 1) < Cells(i + 4, t + 1)) Then
                t = j
            End If
        Next
        Cells(i + 4, t + 1).Interior.Color = RGB(0, 200, 0)
        cost = cost + Cells(i + 4, t + 1).Value
        used(t) = 1
        i = t
    Next

    Cells(1, 5) = "cost"
    Cells(1, 6) = cost
End Sub
```

6.52 GREEDY STRATEGY FOR SEQUENCING JOBS.

The inner loop ensures that we consider each job as a candidate to follow the current one. Hence, the inner loop iterates through the columns of the table, using the index *j*. Therefore, within the body of the inner loop, *i* is the index of the current job, and *j* is the index of the job being considered to follow *i*.

	A	B	C	D	E	F
1	Number of jobs		5		cost	115
2						
3	From \ To	1	2	3	4	5
4	0	27	28	32	35	26
5	1		35	22	44	12
6	2	49		46	38	17
7	3	46	12		29	41
8	4	23	37	31		26
9	5	17	23	28	34	
10						

6.53 OUTPUT OF THE CODE IN FIGURE 6.52.

We use the variable *t* to hold the best candidate among the columns considered so far. Note that before iterating through the columns, we set *t* = *M* which is used as a sign that no candidate has been found so far.

Consider the inner loop. Here, we check that job *j* is unscheduled, and that it is either the first unscheduled job considered in this loop (in which case *t* = *M*), or is a better candidate than the current best (smaller setup cost). If that holds true, *j* is now the best candidate so far, and we set *t* = *j* (remember that *t* should hold the best candidate).

After executing the inner loop, the job to be scheduled after job *i* is therefore found and stored in the variable *t*. We paint the cell corresponding to the decision, update the total setup cost, and state that job *t* is now scheduled. Finally, we set *i* = *t* to indicate that this is now the current job. With this, the process can be repeated.

6.5 Jumping

So far in this chapter, you have learned a lot about controlling the flow of your program. The only thing left is to learn how to jump in your program. There are basically two types of jumping: The *GoTo* statement which is considered in Section 6.5.1, and the *Exit* statement which is considered in section 6.5.2.

6.5.1 GoTo

The core idea behind the *GoTo* statement is to allow you to jump within a procedure. The *GoTo* statement consists of a *label* followed by a colon which is placed at the destination of the jump. At the origin of the jump, the keyword *GoTo* is followed by the name of the *label*.

```
Sub IllustrateGoTo()
   'code
   If (a problem occurs) Then
      'code
      GoTo Terminate
   End If

Terminate:
   'code
End Sub
```

6.54 ILLUSTRATION OF THE GOTO STATEMENT.

To illustrate the use of the *GoTo* statement, consider the code in Figure 6.54. Within an if statement, it is realized that a problem occurs. Possibly, the correct information is not available, the input file does not exist, or there are not enough employees to handle all the tasks. In this case, you do not want to program to execute the next part of the code. Instead, you want to program to jump to the label *Terminate.* Here a piece of code closes the open files and resets what needs resetting, before the sub ends. This is a very common use of the *GoTo* statement.

```
Sub Without_GoTo_Confusion()
    Dim FromCity As Integer
    Dim ToCity As Integer
    Dim Distance As Double

    FromCity = InputBox("Travel from city number:")
    ToCity = InputBox("Travel to city number:")
    Distance = Cells(FromCity, ToCity)
    MsgBox "The distance is " & Distance

End Sub
```

6.55 SIMPLE CODE WITHOUT GOTO STATEMENT.

You can place as many *labels* and *GoTo* statements in your code as you want to. It should be noted, however, that even though your program do not care, excessive use of *GoTo* statements will make it hard for humans to read your code. To get a feeling of this, consider first the simple code in Figure 6.55 which assumes to have a distance table available in the worksheet. Input boxes are used to obtain two city indexes, and the distance is calculated and displayed.

```
Sub With_GoTo_Confusion()
    Dim FromCity As Integer
    Dim ToCity As Integer
    Dim Distance As Double

    GoTo First
Fourth:
    MsgBox "The distance is " & Distance
    Exit Sub
Second:
    ToCity = InputBox("Travel to city number:")
    GoTo Third
First:
    FromCity = InputBox("Travel from city number:")
    GoTo Second
Third:
    Distance = Cells(FromCity, ToCity)
    GoTo Fourth
End Sub
```

6.56 HARD TO READ CODE WITH SEVERAL GOTO STATEMENTS.

Now, consider the code in Figure 6.56. The only difference between the two pieces of code is that now the lines of code have been shuffled, and *GoTo* statements are inserted to ensure that the lines are executed in the correct order. To help you read the code, the names of the labels give you information about the order.

With the above, it should be clear that *GoTo* statements can be useful, but that they should be used carefully.

6.5.2 Exit

It can be useful to break out of a sub before the end of it is reached, for example, if an error occurs, or if no further processing of the data is necessary. The illustration in Figure 6.57 shows how to use the keyword *Exit Sub* to break out of a sub. When the statement is reached, control will return to the unit that called the sub, whether it being another sub or a control in the workbook.

```
Sub IllustrateExit()
   'code
   If (a problem occurs) then
      'code
      Exit Sub
   End If
End sub
```

6.57 ILLUSTRATION OF THE EXIT STATEMENT.

You can break out of loops in a similar way by using the keywords *Exit For* or *Exit Do*. We use the *Find Product* example from Section 6.3.1.2 to illustrate the *Exit For* statement. The others are used similarly. Consider the code in Figure 6.58 which should look almost familiar by now. The new in this code is that when the product is identified, *Exit For* is used to escape from the loop.

Just as it was the case in the example where we used the *While* loop in this example, using the *Exit For* statement ensures that the index of the product is known after the looping.

Note that if you use the *Exit* statement with nested loops, it will help you escape from the inner most loop only. If you need to break out of several loops simultaneously, you can use a *GoTo* statement to do so.

```
Sub FindProductwithExit()
    Dim Product As String
    Dim i As Integer

    Product = InputBox("Please enter a product code:")

    For i = 2 To 11
        If (Product = Cells(i, 1).Value) Then
            Exit For
        End If
    Next

    If (Cells(i, 1) = Product) Then
        MsgBox "Product found - row " & i
    Else
        MsgBox "Product not found"
    End If
End Sub
```

6.58 USING AN EXIT FOR STATEMENT TO ESCAPE FROM A LOOP.

6.6 Exercises

The purpose of the first couple of exercises is to give you total control of the different types of loops and of the indexing of loops. In each of these exercises, you are asked to write 6 small subs: One for each of the looping types introduced in this chapter: The For-Next loop, the While loop, and the 4 Do loops. The subs should write information to a worksheet. Use a separate column for each of the six subs.

6.1. Using the different types of loops, each sub should write the numbers 1,2,3, and 4 in rows 1 through 4 of the worksheet.

6.2. Using the different types of loops, each sub should write the numbers 1,2,3, and 4 in rows 7 through 10 of the worksheet.

6.3. Using the different types of loops, each sub should write the numbers -1,-2,-3, and -4 in rows 1 through 4 of the worksheet.

6.4. Using the different types of loops, each sub should write the numbers 3,4,5, and 6 in rows 1 through 4 of the worksheet.

6.5. Using the different types of loops, each sub should write the numbers 1,3,5, and 7 in rows 1, 3, 5, and 7 of the worksheet.

6.6. Using the different types of loops, each sub should write the numbers 1,3,5, and 7 in rows 1 through 4 of the worksheet.

6.7. Using the different types of loops, each sub should write the numbers -4,-1,2, and 5 in rows 2 through 5 of the worksheet.

At this point you should be familiar with all types of loops, but the chances are that you already found your favorite type.

6.8. Write a sub that uses an input box to ask for an integer. The sub should determine if the number is even or odd and display a message box stating: *The number is even* or *The number is odd*.

6.9. Write a function that takes an integer as input and uses Select-Case to return 1 (negative), 2 (zero), or 3 (positive). Test the function from the worksheet.

6.10. Open the data file for this exercise. The file contains – in columns A-C a list of flights with flight number, origin, and destination city. Columns E and F contain a small list of desired origin and destination cities. Cells E2 and F2 give the number of different origin and destination cities, respectively. Your job is to write a procedure to list the possible flights from each of these origins to each of the destinations and write the result in columns H-J.

1. Take a look at the format of the solution in columns H-J before you erase it by pressing the upper button (the code for erasing it is already there).
2. Write the code of *FindFlights* to solve the problem described above. You should use arrays to store the flight information. Doing that you search through arrays and not columns which is faster for large amounts of data.

6.11. Open the file for this exercise. The problem is to convert a starting amount of 1000 Euros into Mars-dollars in order to maximize the amount of Mars-dollars obtained. New exchange rates (given as Mars-dollars per Euro) arrive in real time every hour and any fraction can be exchanged at a time. Future exchange rates are unknown but can be assumed to be within a minimum value of V and a maximum value of M. The file contains a function, Rate, which takes two doubles representing V and M as input and returns a randomly generated exchange rate within that interval – also a double. We consider the following trading strategy: Only exchange when the rate is above $\sqrt{VM}$. When exchanging, exchange everything if less than 10 Euros are left. Otherwise exchange half of the remaining amount of Euros. Use a loop to repeatedly obtain a new exchange rate and make a decision based on the above rule. Stop when no more Euros are left. Use arrays or the worksheet to keep track of the exchanged amounts and the amount of Mars-dollars obtained and present the result. After obtaining a maximum of 500 exchange rates, the remaining amount of Euros should be exchanged at that rate.

6.12. Consider the Sequencing of jobs as in Section 6.4.3 and the file of that example. If you have implemented the greedy strategy yourself, you can use that file. The goal of this exercise is to implement another well-known strategy for solving the problem: For each column, subtract the smallest setup time from the other setup times of that column. Then apply the greedy strategy to that table to obtain the scheduling order. Note that the total setup time should be based on the original data. Create a sub that uses this strategy for solving the problem.

Chapter 7
Workbooks, Worksheets, and Ranges

In this chapter, we consider the *Object Model* of Excel. The Object Model is the core of the *Excel Application*, and also of your VBA program. Even though you might not be fully aware of it at this time, much of what you do in your VBA programs is a matter of manipulating various *objects*.

In Section 7.1, we introduce the concept of the Object Model and discuss various details, such as an objects *properties* and *methods* and *collections* of objects.

In section 7.2 through 7.5, we discuss the four main types of objects: *Ranges, Worksheets, Workbooks,* and the *Application.*

In Section 7.6, we introduce yet another type of loop called the *For-Each* loop, which is special to objects, and in Section 7.7, we introduce the *With-End-With* statement, which can ease your life if you need to perform many operations with the same object.

7.1 The Object Model

Worksheets, ranges, charts, windows, comments, etc.: they are all objects and are nicely ordered in a hierarchical model called the Excel Object Model. This is illustrated in Figure 7.1 for the main types of objects.

For explanation purposes, we start with a workbook, which is a *Workbook object*. A workbook can contain a number of *Worksheet objects* – these are the worksheets that you usually see in Excel plus the ones that might be invisible. Your workbook object also contains a large number of other objects, for example charts, names, windows, and sheets. The latter of which contains both worksheets and chart sheets. Each worksheet in the collection of worksheets in your workbook object will again contain a number of objects: ranges and pivot tables, for example. Now, just to make the confusion complete: your workbook object is itself contained in another object: the *Application Object* (Excel) along with the other open workbooks, and along with other objects such as Add-Ins and Dialogs.

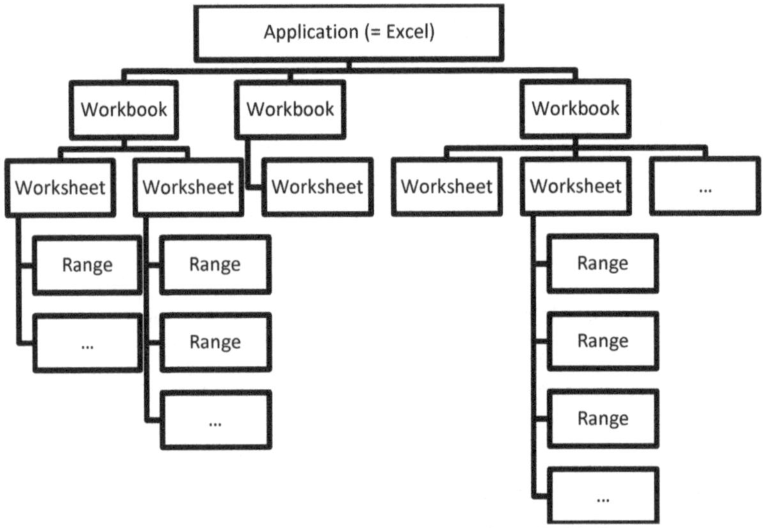

7.1 WORKBOOKS, WORKSHEETS, AND RANGES IN THE OBJECT HIERARCHY.

7.1.1 Referring to an Object

When referring to an object, you must follow the path through the hierarchy. If you need to access cell *D3* in *Sheet2* of *Book3*, you write *Workbooks("Book3.xlsx").Worksheets("Sheet2").Range("D3").*

Giving the complete path of every object can be quite a job, so tools are provided for simplifying your work. First of all, if an incomplete path is given, the computer will start from the *active object*. Hence, writing *Range("D2")* will give you cell *D2* in whatever sheet is currently the active one. If, for example, the active object is a chart instead, you get an error.

If you are absolutely sure that you are currently in the right workbook, it is enough to write *Worksheets("Sheet2").Range("D3")*. If you are sure to be in the right worksheet, writing *Range("D3")* is enough, and so on. But you have to be certain about the active object.

You can make a specific object the active one by using the *Activate* method as in Figure 7.2, where it is shown how to make a workbook and a worksheet, respectively, the active object. It is advisable to use the activate method in your programs, to ensure that the correct object is active.

```
Workbooks("Book3.xlsx").Activate

Workbooks("Book3.xlsx").Worksheets("Sheet4").Activate
```

7.2 USE THE ACTIVATE METHOD TO MAKE AN OBJECT THE ACTIVE ONE.

Another tool to help you refer to the correct object is the special term *ThisWorkbook*, which you have probably seen in the *Project Explorer* in the

VBA editor already. ThisWorkbook will always be the workbook containing the code which is currently being executed, i.e. the workbook of the code. That way, you can use *ThisWorkbook.Worksheets("Sheet2").Range("D3")* to refer to cell *D3* of *Sheet2* in the workbook containing the code.

7.1.2 Properties and Methods

Properties can be thought of as attributes that an object can have. A worksheet can be visible or invisible, it has a name, and it can be either allowed or not allowed to contain pivot tables. A range can have a value, an address, a formula, a name, etc. It also has a width and a height. These are some of the properties of the worksheet object and the range object, respectively. You can change the value of some properties, whereas others are read-only.

Objects also have *methods*. Methods are like procedures; some of them return a value and some do not. For ranges, there are methods to clear the content and methods for sorting. For worksheets, there are, for example, methods to delete or move a sheet, to print or to protect a worksheet. For workbooks there are methods to save, close, or send as E-mail, among others.

Both properties and methods of an object are accessed by specifying the object and the name of the property or method, separated by a dot as illustrated in Figure 7.3, where *w* is an object variable holding a worksheet.

```
Range("A3").Value = 23

w.Visible = xlSheetVisible
```

7.3 USE A DOT TO SEPARATE THE OBJECT FROM THE PROPERTY OR METHOD.

By displaying the *Properties Window* in the VBA editor, you can see and change properties of the open workbooks and the worksheets of these.

7.1.3 Collections

Some objects are organized in collections as well, and to make the confusion complete, these collections are objects themselves. Consider for example the worksheets of a workbook. They are all members of the *Worksheets Collection* of that workbook. All open workbooks are members of the *Workbooks Collection*, and so on. Note the plural terms when dealing with collections.

Collections help us find the object we are looking for. Assume that you need to access cell *D3* of a sheet in the currently active workbook. Consider the code in Figure 7.4. If you know the name of the sheet, you can specify that this is the sheet in the worksheets collection that you want. If you know that the sheet is the second one in the workbook, use the latter method.

```
Worksheets("Products").Range ("D2")

Worksheets(2).Range ("D2")
```

7.4 USE THE COLLECTIONS TO FIND THE OBJECT YOU NEED.

Because collections are objects themselves, they also have both properties and methods.

7.1.4 Object Variables

Special object variables are used to hold objects. Object variables are declared using the keyword *Dim* just like the variables considered in Chapter 4. This is shown for three illustrative objects in the top of Figure 7.5. When assigning an object to an object variable, the keyword *Set* is used. This is illustrated in the same figure. After the assignment, the objects are ready to use the properties and methods belonging to it and can be used for other purposes.

```
Dim W As Workbook
Dim my As Worksheet
Dim R As Range

Set W = Workbook("Book3.xlsx")
Set my = ThisWorkbook.Worksheets("Sheet1")
Set R = W.Worksheets("Products").Range("G24")

R.Value = "New Products"
my.Visible = xlSheetHidden
W.Close
```

7.5 USE THE KEYWORDS DIM AND SET WHEN WORKING WITH OBJECTS.

7.1.5 The Object Browser

There are many different types of objects, and every object has many properties and methods. Probably you are never going to use most of them, but they are there if you need them. To help you find an object, a property, or a method that are useful for the task you want your program to perform, you can use the *Object Browser*.

The control to open the Object Browser from the VBA editor looks like a yellow box with toys above it. You can also open the Object Browser by pressing *F2*. The Object Browser is shown in Figure 7.6.

In the upper left corner of the Object Browser you choose the library that you want to search in. Choose *VBA* if you are looking for a built-in

VBA function, choose *VBAProject* to search among your custom procedures, and choose *MSForms* if you are looking for user form related issues. For most other matters you can choose *Excel* or you can leave it at *<All Libraries>* if you like.

In the left-hand side menu, you choose the class you are considering. Choose *WorksheetFunction* to obtain a list of all worksheet functions in the right-hand side window. Choose *Range* to see the range properties and methods in the right-hand side window. Select *Workbook* to see the workbook properties and methods, but choose *Workbooks* (plural) to see those of the workbooks collection. Note that the small icons can help you tell properties from methods, etc

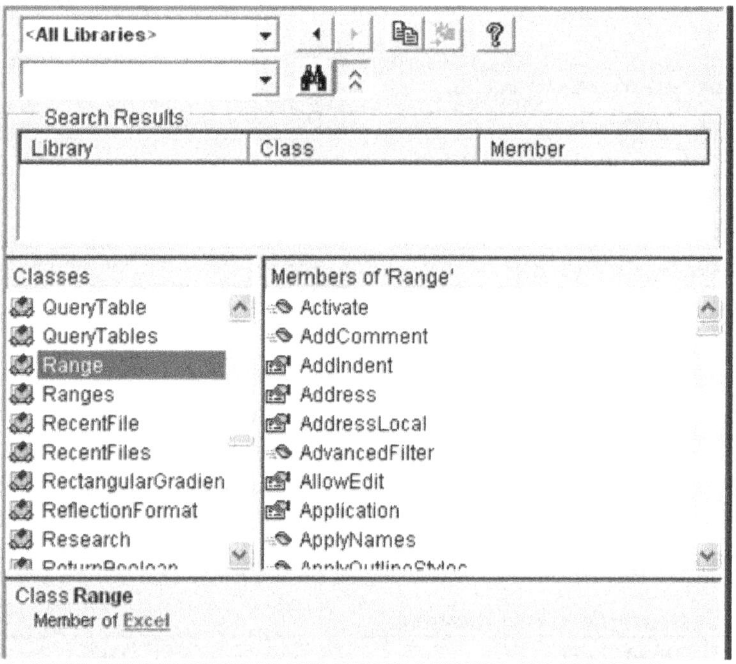

7.6 USE THE OBJECT BROWSER TO FIND OBJECTS, METHODS, AND PROPERTIES.

Basically the only information you get is the name and the membership relation, but highlighting the element that might be of interest to you in the right-hand side window and pressing *F1* will provide you with the Excel help on the topic, which is usually quite descriptive.

7.2 Ranges

A range object consists of a number of cells – possibly one. Such a thing as a cell object does not exist, and hence, even a single cell is a range object.

Let *R* be a range object variable. There are basically two ways to specify a range: Firstly, you can use the column letter and row index as in *Set R = Range("A1")*. This is sometimes referred to as A1-style and is very convenient when you know exactly which cell to use. Secondly, you can use the cells property and specify row index and column index. For example, *Set R = Cells(2,4)* will give you the cell *D2*. The syntax of this property is *Cells(row index, column index)*. This is sometimes referred to as R1C1-style. The cells property is convenient when dealing with ranges of flexible size and when using the index of a loop to specify the cell.

Table 7.1 shows how the range and the cells property can be used to specify both single and multiple cells ranges in various ways. The left-hand side states the VBA code and the right-hand side shows the corresponding cells.

7.1 USE RANGE OR CELLS TO REFER TO RANGES.

Range("D3")	D3
Cells(5, 1)	A5
Range("A1:C5")	A1:C5
Range("J7:G5")	G5:J7
Range(Cells(3, 5), Cells(5, 8))	E3:H5
Range(Range("D15"), Range("H17"))	D15:H17

The *Offset* property can be used to move a specified number of cells down to the right from a starting point. For illustration purposes, let *n* and *k* be integers and let *R* be a range. The expression *R.Offset(n,k)* will return the range obtained by sliding *R n* cells down and *k* cells to the right. If *n* is negative, *R* is slid upwards, if *k* is negative, *R* is slid to the left. Table 7.2 provides examples of the use of the *Offset* property.

7.2 USE OFFSET TO SPECITY THE RELATIVE LOCATION.

Range("B3").Offset(7, 2)	D10
Range("B3:C4").Offset(7, 2)	D10:E11
Range(Range("B3"), Range("B3").Offset(7, 2))	B3:D10
Range(Range("D2"), Range("F4").Offset(0, 5))	D2:K4
Range(Range("A1").Offset(5, 7), Range("A1").Offset(8, 9))	H6:J9

Very often, the size of a range is not known in advance, but rather obtained based on one or two integer variables. Let *n* and *k* be two integer variables with positive values. Table 7.3 illustrates different ways of specifying ranges of flexible size.

7.3 SPECIFYING RANGES OF FLEXIBLE SIZE.

Code	Range
n = 13 Range("A7:D" & n)	A7:D13
n = 2, k = 6 Cells(3 + n, 2 + k)	H5
n = 2, k = 6 Range("B3").Offset(n, k)	H5
n = 2, k = 6 Range("B3").Offset(10 + n, 2 + k)	J15
n = 10, k = 6 Range(Range("D2"), Range("D2").Offset(n, k))	D2:J12
n = 10, k = 6 Range(Cells(2, 4), Cells(2 + n, 4 + k))	D2:J12

Ranges have many useful properties and methods. We illustrate some of these in the following. Consult the Object Browser and the remaining help system for many more.

7.2.1 Size of the Region

The *CurrentRegion* property is extremely useful when the size of a table is not known. Given a range *R*, *CurrentRegion* returns the smallest range containing *R*, which is surrounded by a whole box of empty cells.

Transportation costs

	Destination									
Origin	W1	W2	W3	H2	H27	H28	Y35	Y45	Y66	Y69
F1	3	9	37	18	2	24	32	5	46	46
F2	27	4	31	8	23	8	12	28	23	14
F3	3	42	21	15	5	27	3	2	25	7
D42	67	6	2	32	9	7	16	35	5	17
D26	10	26	9	3	54	2	6	16	73	36
G5	35	6	51	11	7	25	16	6	8	2
G6	28	38	33	7	43	16	31	32	54	27
V1	8	68	38	16	67	12	7	25	7	9

7.7 DATA FOR THE CODE IN FIGURE 7.8

Consider the sheet of data shown in Figure 7.7 and the code in Figure 7.8. First the *CurrentRegion* property is used to obtain the current region and the *address* property is used to display the address of the range. Note in the resulting message box shown in Figure 7.9 that the region is expanded in all directions. Next, we use the *rows* and *columns* property, respectively and the *count* property to determine the number of origins and destinations, respectively. The 2 and 1 that are subtracted is due to the rows and columns containing headings. The result is shown in Figure 7.9.

```
Sub IllustrateCurrentRegion()
    Dim R As Range
    Dim NumOrigins As Integer
    Dim NumDest As Integer
    Set R = Range("C5")

    MsgBox R.CurrentRegion.Address

    NumOrigins = R.CurrentRegion.Rows.Count - 2
    NumDest = R.CurrentRegion.Columns.Count - 1

    MsgBox NumOrigins & " origins and " & _
           NumDest & " destinations"
End Sub
```

7.8 USE CURRENTREGION TO DETERMINE THE SIZE OF A DATA AREA.

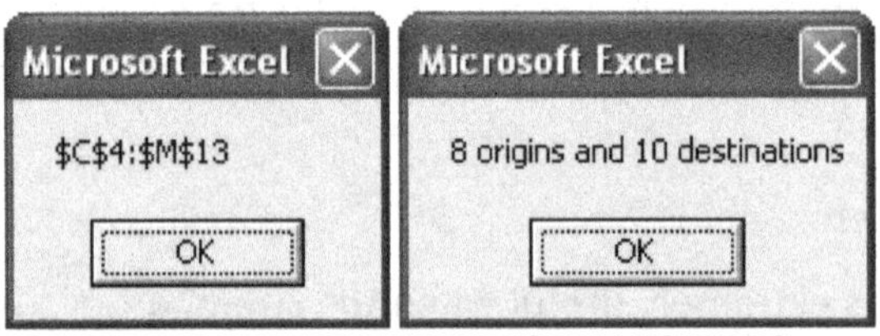

7.9 OUTPUT FROM EXECUTING THE CODE IN FIGURE 7.8.

7.2.2 Sorting

Most Excel users have tried to sort a range of data by the Excel sorting method found in the *Home* menu. This is done by specifying the column that should primarily determine the sorting, and specifying whether to sort the elements in increasing or decreasing order. Next a secondary column can be specified, etc. We use the worksheet in Figure 7.10 to illustrate how the range method *sort* can be used for the same purpose.

	A	B	C	D
1	Number of products		10	
2				
3		Processing time		
4	Product	Machine 1	Machine 2	
5	1	2	8	
6	2	4	7	
7	3	7	5	
8	4	4	4	
9	5	10	3	
10	6	2	9	
11	7	4	5	
12	8	8	3	
13	9	4	6	
14	10	9	1	
15				

7.10 DATA FOR THE CODE IN FIGURE 7.11

Consider the code in Figure 7.11, which illustrates the *sort* method through three examples. First, *R* is defined to be the data range excluding headings. Assuming that the products are shuffled, the first example shows how to sort the products in increasing order by product number, as shown in Figure 7.10. *Key1* is set to be a cell in the primary sorting column, and *Order1* specifies that the data should be sorted in increasing (*Ascending*, when speaking VBA) order with respect to *Key1*.

```
Dim n As Integer
Dim R As Range
n = Range("C1").Value
Set R = Range(Cells(5, 1), Cells(4 + n, 3))

'Example 1:
R.Sort Key1:=Range("A4"), Order1:=xlAscending, Header:=xlNo

'Example 2:
R.Sort Key1:=Range("B4"), Order1:=xlAscending, Header:=xlNo

'Example 3:
R.Sort Key1:=Range("B4"), Order1:=xlAscending, _
        Key2:=Range("C4"), Order2:=xlDescending, Header:=xlNo
```

7.11 DIFFERENT WAYS OF SORTING A RANGE OF DATA.

The final argument specifies that the first row is not a header row. Now, consider example 4 in Figure 7.4. Here the range is extended to include the header row and the *Header* argument reflects this.

```
'Example 4:
Set R = Range(Cells(4, 1), Cells(4 + n, 3))
R.Sort Key1:=Range("A4"), Order1:=xlAscending, Header:=xlYes
```

7.12 INCLUDING HEADERS IN THE RANGE.

4	Product	Machine 1	Machine 2	4	Product	Machine 1	Machine 2
5	1	2	8	5	6	2	9
6	6	2	9	6	1	2	8
7	2	4	7	7	2	4	7
8	4	4	4	8	9	4	6
9	7	4	5	9	7	4	5
10	9	4	6	10	4	4	4
11	3	7	5	11	3	7	5
12	8	8	3	12	8	8	3
13	10	9	1	13	10	9	1
14	5	10	3	14	5	10	3

7.13 RESULT OF SORTING USING THE CODE IN FIGURE 7.11.

Output from examples 2 and 3 is shown in the left and right-hand side of Figure 7.13, respectively. In example 2, the products are sorted in increasing order with respect to processing time at machine 1, whereas in example 3, they are primarily sorted in increasing order with respect to processing time at machine 1 and secondarily in decreasing order with respect to processing time at machine 2.

7.2.3 Other Range Properties and Methods

The code in Figure 7.14 illustrates how to copy and paste a range. The specified destination cell is the upper left cell of the destination range.

```
Dim R As Range
Set R = Range("D6:E8")
R.Copy Destination:=Range("D20")
```

7.14 COPY AND PASTE.

The code in Figure 7.15 illustrates how to remove the content of a range. The *Clear* method removes both content and formatting whereas *ClearContents* only removed the content of the range. The *Delete* method deletes the range by shifting the cells below it upwards.

```
Range("F8:G9").Clear
Range("F8:G9").ClearContents
Range("F8:G9").Delete
```

7.15 DIFFERENT METHODS FOR REMOVING DATA.

7.3 Worksheets

The tasks that you are most likely to perform with worksheets are adding a new one, deleting, and changing the name.

```
Sub CreateNewWorksheet(id As String)

    Dim W As Worksheet

    Set W = ThisWorkbook.Worksheets.Add

    W.Name = id
    W.SetBackgroundPicture (ThisWorkbook.Path & "/Logo.jpg")

    ActiveWindow.DisplayGridlines = False
End Sub
```

7.16 CREATE WORKSHEET AND SET BACKGROUND PICTURE.

Consider the code in Figure 7.16. Given a *customer id*, the goal is to create a new worksheet with the customer id as the name, and to set it up with a background picture. We use the *Worksheets collection* to *add* a new worksheet to the workbook that contains the code. The variable *W* will hold the new sheet. Next, the *Name* property of the worksheet object is used to assign the customer id as the name of the sheet we just created. Note that specifying a name that already exists in the collection will result in an error message. We use the *SetBackgroundPicture* method to add a background picture to the sheet. Note that to do this, we use the *Path* property of the *Workbook* object and assume that the image file is located in the same folder as the workbook of the code. Finally, we use the *DisplayGridlines* property of the *ActiveWindow* object to hide the gridlines.

Another useful task related to worksheets is accessing the number of worksheets in a workbook. The code in Figure 7.17 shows how the *Count* property of the worksheets collection can be used for this purpose. The code also shows how to *delete* a worksheet. Note about the latter that if a sheet does not exist with the specified name, an error message will occur. Before the actual deletion, you will be asked if you are sure. In Section 7.5, we show how to avoid this.

```
Sub DeleteAndDisplayNumber()
    Dim W As Worksheet

    MsgBox Worksheets.Count

    Worksheets("Sheet1").Delete
End Sub
```

7.17 COUNTING AND DELETING WORKSHEETS.

7.4 Workbooks

In this section we consider some of the basic tasks that you might want to perform in relation to workbooks. Because handling workbooks is closely related to handling files, you can find much more workbook related information in Chapter 12.

For illustration purposes, consider the following situation. A small company keeps a workbook for each customer. In this workbook, the first sheet provides information about the customer. Each remaining sheet corresponds to a separate order from the customer. Consider the code in Figure 7.18, which creates and prepares the file for new customers.

```
Sub CreateCustomerFile(id As String)
    Dim W As Workbook
    Dim k As Integer

    Set W = Workbooks.Add

    'Turn prompting off
    For k = 2 To W.Worksheets.Count
        W.Worksheets(2).Delete
    Next

    W.Worksheets(1).Name = "Info"
    'Turn prompting back on

    W.SaveAs (id)
    W.Close
End Sub
```

7.18 CREATE A CUSTOMER FILE.

A new workbook is created using the *Add* method for the *Workbooks* collection. As a default, new workbooks contain three worksheets. All but one is deleted and the remaining sheet is renamed. The workbook is saved using the customer id as the name. The *xlsx* extension is automatically added unless otherwise specified, and the file is, by default, stored in the same folder as the workbook containing the code, unless otherwise specified. Finally, the workbook is saved. As before, prompts will occur when deleting worksheets. Note that if a file with the given name already exists, a prompt will appear before you overwrite. You might want to keep that prompt in the code in order to avoid overwriting files - unless you check for file existence first (in which case the prompt should not appear anyway).

7.5 The Application Object

Let us start with a warning: Messing around with the application object can be a dangerous game. This section is where you learn the task of deleting files without being warned - for example. So be careful.

Be aware that when you change application settings, they will stay changed – until you change them back. Turn automatic recalculation off and your Excel program will not recalculate your formulas anymore. Not even when you are just doing worksheet stuff. So remember to turn it back on.

At this point, the *GoTo Terminate* that was introduced in Section 6.5, comes in handy. You simply ensure that all application settings are restored in the terminate part of your code and that the structure ensures that the terminate part is always executed.

But: If your program stops with an error, for example while developing, you do not reach the terminate part. So for safety, you might want to write a small sub with the purpose of resetting the mess you made. Just for safety.

Now, after all these warnings, why would you ever want to mess with the applications settings? There are three reasons – possibly more: 1) To speed up your program: If you work with large files it takes time to automatically recalculate everything. 2) To stop the monitor flickering that occurs when the worksheet is updated repeatedly. 3) To create programs that are not annoying due to numerous alerts being displayed.

Figure 7.19 illustrates how to turn off the *automatic screen updating* – and how to turn it back on. Try to write large amounts of data to the worksheet with and without screen updating, respectively to see the speed difference.

```
'S automatic screen updating
Application.ScreenUpdating = False

'code

'Turn screen updating back on:
Application.ScreenUpdating = True
```

7.19 TURN AUTOMATIC SCREEN UPDATING ON AND OFF.

Figure 7.20 shows how to turn off *automatic recalculation*. If you need something to be calculated while the automatic calculation is turned off, use the method *calculate*, which works on a workbook, a range or all open workbooks, depending on the object using it. Do remember to turn automatic recalculation back on.

```
'Turn automatic recalculation off
Application.Calculation = xlCalculationManual

'Code

'Turn it back on:
Application.Calculation = xlCalculationAutomatic
```

7.20 TURN AUTOMATIC RECALCULATION ON AND OFF.

Computer programs have an annoying tendency of asking if you are sure you want it to perform the task you asked it to perform – delete is a good example of this. In the previous sections we deleted sheets and mentioned that the alert can be avoided by messing with the application object. Figure 7.21 illustrates how to turn the alerts off – and back on again. But make sure that your program cannot accidently delete or overwrite wrong files if executed from the wrong location.

```
'Do not display alerts:
Application.DisplayAlerts = False

'code

'Start displaying them again:
Application.DisplayAlerts = True
```

7.21 TURN ALERTS ON AND OFF.

The application object is also useful for less harmful issues. Consider for example the code in Figure 7.22, where ten numbers are written to a worksheet. The interesting part of the code is the use of the method *Wait* of the application object. It makes the computer wait with the execution of the next line of code until a certain time. In the example it will wait until the current time plus a second, i.e. it will pause for one second. This method is useful when making animations, but do only use it when needed as it clearly slows your program.

```
Sub animation()
   For i = 1 To 10
    Cells(i, 1) = i
    Application.Wait (Now() + TimeValue("0:00:01"))
   Next
End Sub
```

7.22 USE THE WAIT METHOD TO PERFORM ANIMATION.

7.6 For-Each Loops

In Chapter 6 you were introduced to several different types of loops, but the *For-Each* loop was postponed to the current chapter. The *For-Each* loop iterates through each object in a collection of objects, for example each worksheet in the worksheets collection of a workbook. The syntax of the *For-Each* loop is shown in Figure 7.23.

```
For Each element In Group
    'Code
Next
```

7.23 SYNTAX OF THE FOR-EACH LOOP.

When working with Excel, one can often end up having quite a few files open. The code in Figure 7.24 saves and closes all open workbooks except from those whose name is *Book*-something, which can be closed manually afterwards. Code could have been included to open the windows *SaveAs* dialog box for these. In Chapter 11 you will see how to place this code in a location where it will always be accessible.

```
Sub SaveCloseAllOther()
    Dim w As Workbook
    For Each w In Workbooks
        If w.Name <> ThisWorkbook.Name Then
            If Left(w.Name, 4) Like "Book" Then
                MsgBox (w.Name & " must be closed manually")
            Else
                w.Save
                w.Close
            End If
        End If
    Next
End Sub
```

7.24 SAVE AND CLOSE ALL OPEN WORKBOOKS.

For-Each loops can be used to search for a specific element in a collection. In Figure 7.25 such a loop is used to search through all worksheets in the worksheets collection. Whenever a hidden sheet is found, the name is displayed and the worksheet is made visible.

```
Sub MakeVisibleAndShowName()
    Dim w As Worksheet

    For Each w In Worksheets
        If w.Visible = xlSheetHidden Then
            MsgBox w.Name
            w.Visible = xlSheetVisible
        End If
    Next
End Sub
```

7.25 USE A FOR-EACH LOOP TO FIND HIDDEN WORKSHEETS.

It might be a little hard to get used to the idea, but the *For-Each* loop can also be used to search through every element of a range. The elements of a range are (single cell) ranges, hence the loop will iterate through every range in a range. We illustrate this with the code in Figure 7.26. *L* and *R* are both range variables, where the former will be used to hold the range we want to iterate through and the latter is used to iterate. We let *m* be the largest value found in *L* – a range containing only integer numbers.

Now, a *For-Each* loop is used to consider every element that is: every (single cell) range, *R* in *L*. If the value of *R* equals *m*, a message box stating the row and column index of that range (single cell) is displayed.

```
Sub FindMax()
    Dim L As Range
    Dim R As Range
    Dim m As Integer

    Set L = Range("A2:D4")
    m = WorksheetFunction.Max(L)

    For Each R In L
       If R.Value = m Then
          MsgBox "Row " & R.Row & ", column " & R.Column
       End If
    Next
End Sub
```

7.26 FOR-EACH LOOPS CAN BE USED TO ITERATE THROUGH ALL RANGES IN A RANGE.

It should be mentioned that the *For-Each* loop can also be used to iterate through each element of an array.

7.7 With Statements

Sometimes; in particular when performing formatting of worksheets, several properties are set simultaneously. When this is the case, you can save a bit of typing by using the *With-End-With* structure.

The use of this kind of structure is shown in Figure 7.27, where we first perform a number of actions based on the worksheet *W*, and secondly perform actions based on the *application* with another *With-End-With* structure.

Note in the first structure, how the object *W* is indirectly assumed at the beginning of every line. That is exactly what the *With-End-With* is doing. In the second part, the *Application* is the assumed object at every line of code.

```
Sub IllustrateWith()
    Dim W As Worksheet

    Set W = ThisWorkbook.Worksheets(1)
    With W
        .Name = MonthName(Month(Now()))
        .Columns.ColumnWidth = 5
        .ScrollArea = "A1:K15"
        .Columns.Interior.Color = 1234
    End With

    With Application
        .Width = 365
        .Height = 400
    End With
End Sub
```

7.27 THE WITH STRUCTURE.

7.8 Exercises

7.1. Write a sub called *declaring that* declares a range variable *r* and sets it to A1:G5. Write a function called *MakeBlue* that takes a range as argument. Write a code in the function that changes the color of the cells in the range to blue. Add a line to call *MakeBlue* from *declaring* using the range *r* as parameter. Execute *declaring*.

7.2. Open the data file for this exercise. Give the 10X10 area with numbers a range name *MyRange*. Use a For Each-Loop to go through every cell in *MyRange.* Within the For Each-loop: Use your favorite type of loop to determine if the number is prime and change the color to red and the font to bold if this is the case.

7.3. Open the file for this exercise. Pressing the existing button will result in the generation of numbers in a range of uncertain size. Though cell C6 will always be contained in the range. Write a sub that determines the number of rows and columns in the range and the index of the last row and last column in the range and writes the information in the top of the worksheet.

7.4. Consider the investment example of Section 6.3.2.3 and open the file with the code of that example. Implement a similar strategy where the products are considered in decreasing order with respect to profit/price.

7.5. This exercise considers the Traveling Salesman problem. Open the data file for this exercise. The file contains a procedure for generating data for the problem. You can use the procedure in Figure 6.47 to create a distance matrix. Write a procedure that solves the problem by visiting the cities in increasing order by x-coordinate, calculates the cost and writes the solution to the worksheet.

7.6. Create two nested For-Next loops to iterate from fx 1 to 100 each (possibly more). In each cell determined by those loops, write the product of the index of the loops. Use the *timer* function to determine how long time it takes. Now turn off *automatic screen update* and try again (remember to turn it back on). If you do not see a large difference in the time it takes, increase the values and try again.

7.7. Open the data file for this exercise. The file only has one worksheet which contains a list of employee names in column A. Write a sub that loops through the list of employees, creates a new worksheet for each and renames the sheet using the name of the employee. Create another sub which deletes all employee worksheets but not the main sheet without displaying alerts. Before a sheet is deleted, the name of the sheet should be written to column B. Test that you get the same names as in column A. Remember of turn alerts back on.

7.8. Open the data file of this exercise. The file contains a procedure that generates products to be produced on two machines. All products must be processed first on machine 1 then on machine 2 and only one product can be processed at a time. Headers for a production plan are also given in the file. Create a production plan where the products are processed in the following order: Primarily in decreasing order with respect to machine 2, secondarily in increasing order with respect to the processing time on machine 1. Display the make-span, i.e. the finishing time of the product that finishes last. Note that your procedure should be flexible enough to determine the number of products based on the given data.

Chapter 8
Security

Security is of upmost importance when dealing with macros. It is not hard to create a damaging macro that executes automatically when a file is opened. Therefore, it is important to set a rather high macro security level on your computer. We show how to set the macro security level in Section 8.1.

You probably consider some files as being safe. That could, for instance, be the files that you created yourself, or the files created by your trusted colleague, or the files belonging to this book. In Section 8.2, we discuss how to specify trusted sources.

When you create programs yourself, you can sign them with a digital certificate. That way, others can see that you created the program, and decide whether you are a trusted source to them. You will learn how to create a digital certificate in Section 8.3.

From another perspective, security is also about keeping your code safe, such that others cannot copy it. Maybe you even want to prevent others from executing your macros. In Section 8.4, we discuss issues of protecting your own code.

8.1 Set Macro Security

If you open external files on your computer, you should be concerned with macro security. You know by now that you need to save your files with code as macro enabled files. If you save them in the standard Excel format, your code does not work. Similar pairs of file extensions exist for the other Office programs. Therefore, you only need to be concerned with macro security when you open the macro enabled versions. But since this is a book about VBA programming, it is reason enough to, at least, consider macro security.

To set the macro security level, you need to locate the Office *Trust Center*: In Excel, click the Office button in the upper left corner and select *Excel Options*. Select *Trust Center* in the left-hand side menu and click the *Trust Center Settings* button to open the *Trust Center*. In the Trust Center, select *Macro Settings* as illustrated in Figure 8.1. You can skip the first two steps by pressing *ALT + F, i* in Excel.

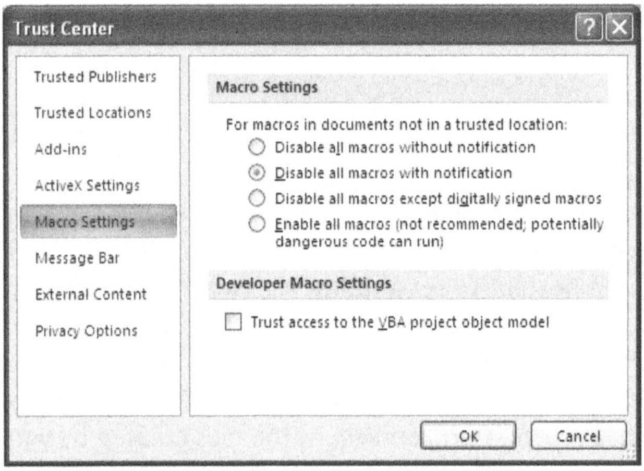

8.1 SET THE MACRO SECURITY LEVEL IN THE TRUST CENTER.

Microsoft offers four levels of macro security, which will be explained in the following.

The highest security is obtained by selecting *Disable all macros without notification*. With this setting you will be able to view and edit code, but you will not be allowed to execute it. Exceptions are files that are stored in a *Trusted location*, as explained in Section 8.2.

The *Disable all macros with notification* is the default setting. With this setting macros do not execute unless you specifically allow them to. Instead, you will be confronted with a dialog box as in Figure 8.2 or a message bar as in Figure 8.3 where you can choose either to temporarily allow the macros of the file or to forbid them.

8.2 SECURITY WARNING DIALOG BOX.

An exception is files that are stored in a trusted location, as explained in Section 8.2. They will open without further warning.

8.3 SECURITY WARNING MESSAGE BAR.

The *Disable all macros except digitally signed macros* is slightly more convenient than the previous ones. Here, both macros in trusted locations and macros that are digitally signed by a publisher that you trust will be executed without further notice. Other macros will give you a security warning where you can choose to execute or forbid the macro, but you can also choose to trust the publisher in the future. With this setting, you can, for example, choose to trust the macros that are digitally signed to belong to this textbook. Learn more about trusted publishers in Section 8.2.

The *Enable all macros* setting is not recommended as it allows any macro – also the ones that erase your hard disk – to execute without further notice.

8.2 Trusted Sources

When the macro security is set relatively high, you have to give special permission to enable macros. Or even worse, you might not be able to get permission to enable macros - even your own macros. After a while you might be so annoyed that you want to lower the security. Do not do that.

In Section 8.2.1, you learn to specify trusted locations. Macros in files stored in a trusted location will be executed without security warning. In Section 8.2.2, you learn to specify trusted publishers.

8.2.1 Trusted Locations

You can point out special *trusted locations* such that macros from these locations can be executed without security warning. For example, on my laptop, the folder that contains all the excel files for this book is specified as a trusted location. The only catch is that it is your own responsibility not to store potentially harmful files in your trusted locations. You should only store files that you really trust to be safe in your trusted locations.

To specify a trusted location, open the *Trust Center* as described in the previous section (From Excel, click *ALT +F,I,* select *Trust Center* in the menu and press the *Trust Center Settings* button) and select *Trusted*

Locations in the left-hand side menu. As you can see in Figure 8.4, there are already a number of trusted locations – specified by Office.

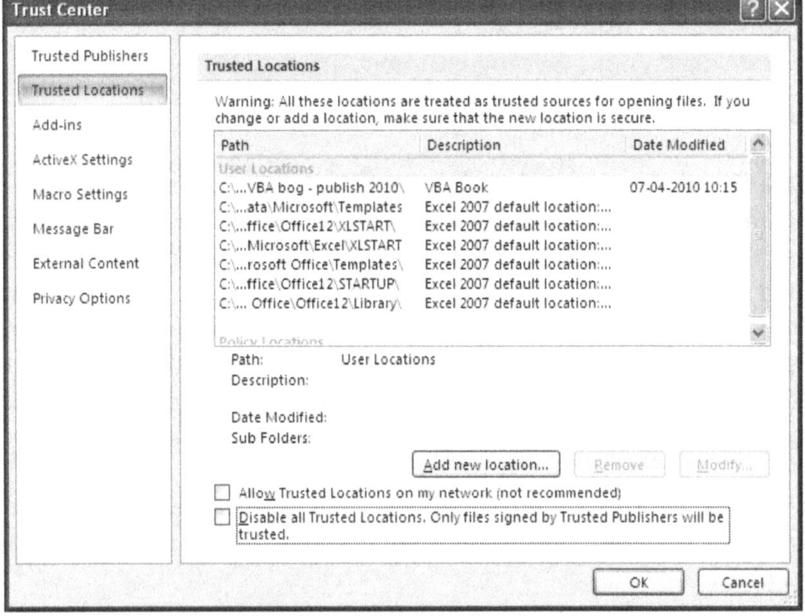

8.4 SPECIFY YOUR TRUSTED LOCATIONS IN THE TRUST CENTER.

To add a trusted location to the list, press the *Add new location* button to get the dialog box shown in Figure 8.5. Here you specify the location of the folder to add and indicate whether to include subfolders in the trust. It is a good idea to write a description, as it will be shown in the overview in Figure 8.4. Click *OK* a couple of times, and you are done.

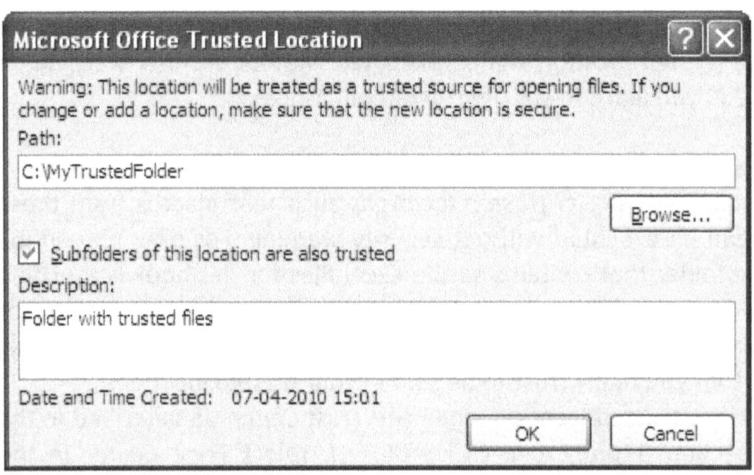

8.5 ADD A NEW TRUSTED LOCATION.

8.2.2 Trusted Digital Certificates

You can choose to trust files that are created by a specific publisher. That way, you can get rid of those, at times annoying, security warnings, discussed in Section 8.1. You might, for example, choose to trust the files created by a close colleague, a friend, or those belonging to this book. Files in the latter category are all digitally signed.

But be aware: Do not trust a file just because it is digitally signed. It is not the signature itself you can trust, it is a matter of trusting the people behind the signature.

To see which digital certificates you trust already, search for the file called *Certmgr.msc*. When you open that file, you see your *Certificate Center*, as shown in Figure 8.6.

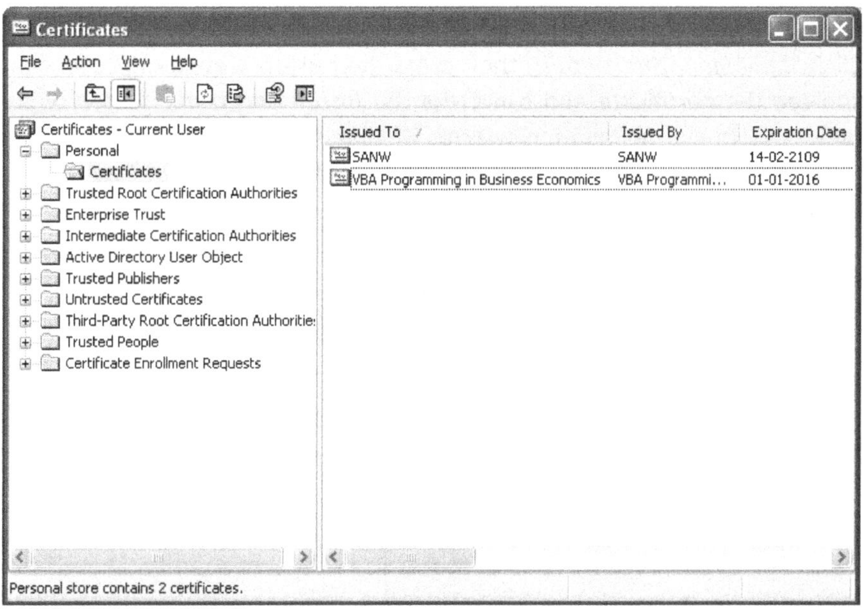

8.6 THE CERTIFICATE CENTER.

As you see, on my laptop, the certificate of this book is located in the *personal certificates* category. The simplest way to specify that you want to trust a new publisher is the following which requires that you are in one of the medium security settings.

If the warning comes in the form of a bar as in Figure 8.3, click the *options* button to get the dialog box of Figure 8.7.

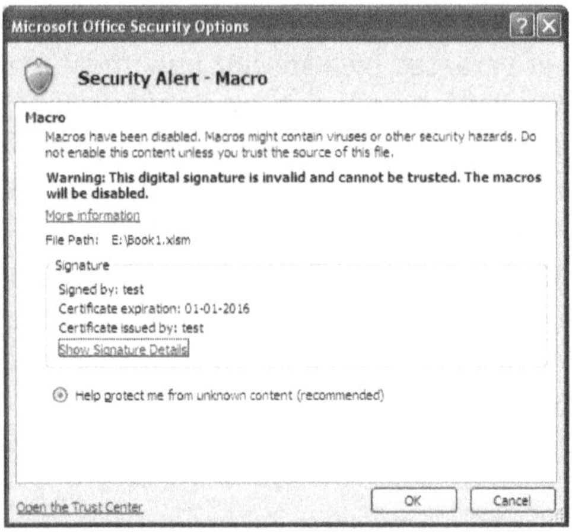

8.7 ON YOU WAY TO VIEW THE CERTIFICATE OF A FILE.

Click *Show Signature Details*, then press the button *View Certificate*. Now you see the certificate and can press the *Install Certificate button* which takes you to the installation wizard. (If that does not work, then follow these steps again, but now force the store to be *Trusted Root Certification Authorities* – But only do that if you have to.)

If, on the other hand, the warning comes in the form of a dialog box like the one shown in Figure 8.8, simply press the *Trust all from publisher* button and feel free to be gently guided through the process.

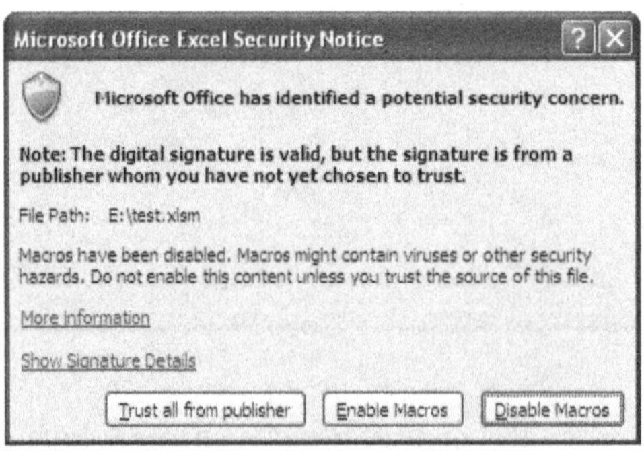

8.8 SPECIFY THAT YOU TRUST THE PUBLISHER.

8.3 Create a Digital Certificate

You can create your own digital certificate. That way, others can specify that they trust the files you have created. Clearly, you can also specify that you trust files signed with your own certificate and thereby be allowed to execute your own code without security warning, independently of the location of the code. Note that only people who really trust you will accept a certificate that you created by the following method. If you create code of more public nature, you should obtain a certificate from a more official source.

To create a digital certificate, press the *Windows start* button, choose *Programs*, then *Microsoft Office*. Here you choose *Microsoft Office Tools* and select *Digital Certificate for VBA Projects* to obtain the dialog box shown in Figure 8.9. Specify the name you want to give your certificate and click *OK*.

8.9 CREATE A DIGITAL CERTIFICATE.

You might want to export your digital certificate to install it on another computer or just for backup purposes. Do not save the backup on your hard disk, due to the security risk. To export your certificate, search for the file called *Certmgr.msc* to open your *Certificate Center*. Locate your certificate in the *Personal* store. The right click menu gives you an export option.

8.3.1 Sign Your Code with Your Digital Certificate

When you create a project containing VBA code, you can sign it with your digital signature. To do this, select *Digital Signature* from the *Tools* menu in the VBA editor. You obtain the dialog box shown in Figure 8.10.

8.10 SIGN YOUR CODE WITH YOUR DIGITAL CERTIFICATE.

Press the *Choose* button to get the *Select Certificate* dialog box shown in Figure 8.11. Select the certificate you want to use to sign your project and press *Ok* a couple of times. Finally, save your project again to apply the change.

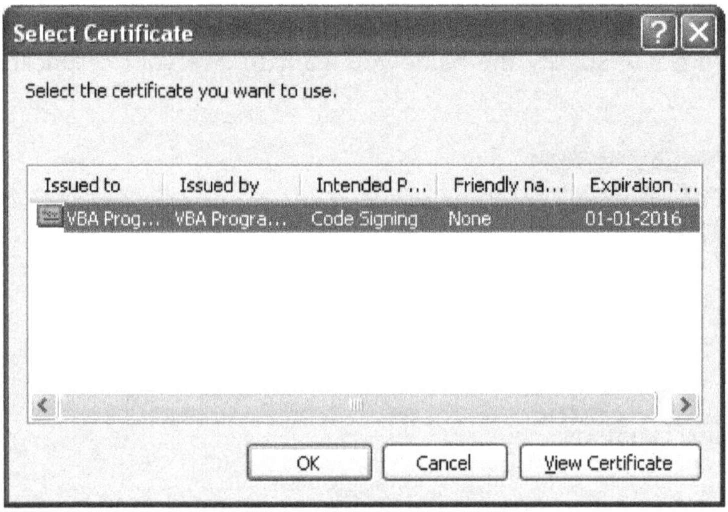

8.11 CHOOSE THE CERTIFICATE YOU WANT TO USE TO SIGN.

8.4 Protecting Your Work

One thing is to protect yourself and your computer from evil macros. Another is to protect the work that you have done from being copied or used by others.

Note that code crackers do exist and that the methods explained here do not set a high security level, but they do work for many purposes.

In Section 8.4.1, we explain how you can password protect your code such that it cannot be changed or viewed by others. Others can still use your program, but they cannot mess up your work. This is useful if you let others use your program, but do not want others to take credit for your work, or if you want to prevent others from destroying the program that you have carefully created.

In Section 8.4.2, we show how you can write a program that requires a password to execute. That way you can ensure that only the people who know the password can use the program – or part of the program. This is useful if only few of several users are allowed to change the customer status or overload a machine. Note again that the security level of the explained method is not high, but it is good enough for many purposes.

8.4.1 Prevent Others from View or Changing Your Code

There can be numerous reasons for wanting to protect your code from being edited or seen by others. In the following, we explain how you can password protect your code.

If your code is password protected, others can view the code and execute it, but they cannot change the code. To activate password protection, select *VBA Project Properties* from the *Tools* menu in the *VBA editor* to obtain the dialog box shown in Figure 8.12. In the *Protection* tab, enter your favorite password twice to protect your code. This protects your code from being edited without the password being entered first.

If you want to prevent others from seeing your code, you should both enter a password and tick the *Lock project for viewing* option.

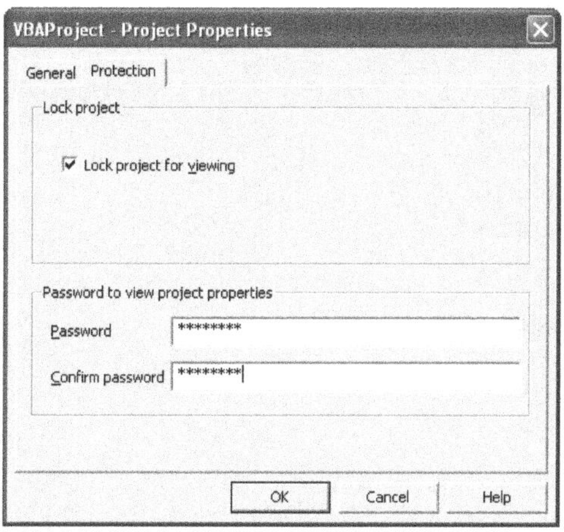

8.12 LOCK AND PASSWORD PROTECT YOUR CODE

8.4.2 Prevent Others from Executing Your Program

There can be situations where it is not enough for you that no one can edit or see your code, but you do not even want to let others execute your code. In the following, you find three ways of forcing the user to enter a password in order to be allowed to execute a program – a sub.

The main idea in all three examples is to use an *input box* to let the user enter the password which is stored in the variable *user*. The true password is predefined and stored in the variable *pw*. Now, the value of *user* is compared to the value of *pw*. If there is a mismatch, the program is terminated by an *Exit Sub* statement. If the two values match, the program can start executing.

Clearly, the code should still be password protected and locked for viewing as explained in the previous section. Otherwise a potential harmful user can obtain the predefined value of *pw* by inspection of the code.

An obvious drawback of this method is that the text is visible when entering it in an input box. Another drawback is that this kind of protection is not encrypted in any way – except from the encryption that prevents the user from viewing the code in the first place.

Firstly, consider the code in Figure 8.13. In this example, the user gets a single attempt to get the password right. If it is not correct, the user is prompted and the program is exited. Otherwise the execution continues.

```
Sub PasswordOneTry()
    Dim pw As String
    Dim user As Variant

    pw = "wk4F9Gaz7"

    user = InputBox("Please enter the password:")
    If user <> pw Then
        MsgBox "You are not allowed to execute this program."
        Exit Sub
    End If
    'Correct password was entered:
    MsgBox "Ok to execute program"
    'code
End Sub
```

8.13 ONE ATTEMPT TO GET THE PASSWORD RIGHT.

```
Sub ForcePassword()
    Dim pw As String
    Dim user As Variant

    pw = "wk4F9Gaz7"
    Do
        user = Application.InputBox("Please enter the password:")
        If user = False Then
            'cancel was pressed
            Exit Sub
        End If
    Loop Until user = pw

    'Correct password was entered:
    MsgBox "Ok to execute program"
    'code
End Sub
```

8.14 INFINITE NUMBER OF ATTEMPTS TO GET THE PASSWORD RIGHT.

Knowing that we all make typos, only providing the user with one attempt to get the password right might be a little too cruel. At the other extreme, the code in Figure 8.14 allows the user to try as many times as desired. Here, a *Do-Loop-Until* loop is used to repeatedly display the input box. In the body of the loop it is checked if the cancel button was pressed, in which case the program is terminates. Note that in this example, another version of the *input box* is used. Please consult Chapter 15 to learn more about the different types of input boxes. The loop is repeated until the value of the variable *user* equals the value of *pw*, at which point the execution of the program continues.

Usually, the user is given three attempts to get a password right. The code in Figure 8.15 follows this practice. The variable *TryMax* specifies the number of attempts the user is allowed. Here the value is set to 3. The variable *try* counts the attempts. As in the previous example, we use a Do-Loop-Until loop to repeatedly display the input box. In the body of the loop, the program is terminated if the *cancel* button was pressed. Furthermore, the value of *try* is increased. The loop is repeated until the password is correct or *TryMax* attempts have been used. After the looping, it is checked if the password is still not correct, in which case the program is terminated. Otherwise execution of the program continues.

```
Sub ForcePassword3Times()
    Dim try As Integer
    Dim TryMax As Integer
    Dim pw As String
    Dim user As Variant

    TryMax = 3
    pw = "wk4F9Gaz7"
    try = 0

    Do
        user = Application.InputBox("Please enter the password:")
        If user = False Then
            'cancel was pressed
            Exit Sub
        End If
        try = try + 1
    Loop Until try >= TryMax Or user = pw

    'false password (or nothing) was entered TryMax times:
    If (user <> pw) Then
        MsgBox "You are not allowed to execute this program."
        Exit Sub
    End If

    'Correct password was entered:
    MsgBox "Ok to execute program"
    'code
End Sub
```

8.15 THE USER IS GIVEN THREE ATTEMPTS TO GET THE PASSWORD RIGHT.

Chapter 9
Debugging

Debugging is the art of finding and correcting bugs in a program. In Section 9.2, we introduce the reader to the debugging tools of the VBA editor and in Section 9.3, we consider Run-Time Errors. In Section 9.1, we give some advice on how to avoid the creation of bugs in the first place.

9.1 Avoid the Need for Debugging

Having to debug is never desirable and hence our best advice is to avoid the need for debugging in the first place. Unfortunately, that is easier said than done, but in this section we give some advices that can help you reduce the need for debugging.

Variations of *index out of range* constitute one of the most common sources of error - either when indexing arrays or when referring to cells in a worksheet. This type of error occurs when you refer to an index that does not exist – for example row zero, or *A(6)* when the array *A* is only defined up to index 5. This type of bug will be detected by the computer and you will be met with an *index out of range* error message.

Another source of errors deals with the variables. When variables are sent to a procedure using the *ByRef* statement there is a risk of changing the value of the variable even though it is not intended. You can avoid this by only sending variables *ByRef* if the procedure is allowed to change the value. Otherwise the *ByVal* statement should be used.

When using Module or Global variables there is always a risk of creating a local variable with the same name, which would then be the one responding when referring to a variable of that name, so be extra careful regarding names of variables when you have Module or Global variables in your code. Furthermore, Option Explicit should be used to prevent errors due to typos.

The next source of errors might be considered more a matter of frustration than a source of errors. When working with nested loops and/or decision constructions it can be extremely difficult to place the statements that end the loops and constructions correctly. The best advice here is to always write the *Next* right after the *For*, then add empty lines between the two statements, and finally place code between them. Another piece of advice is to place a comment by the *Next* statement stating which *For* loop ends. Similarly for the other kinds of loops.

The final and maybe most important advice of this section is to never write five lines of code without testing them before continuing. Add some lines of code to print to the worksheet, use a bunch of message boxes, or use the Immediate Window, which is introduced in Section 9.2.8, to ensure that the code does exactly what you would expect. Then delete those print statements and move on to coding the next five lines. It might seem tedious, but it is clearly more fun than debugging. Similarly, after finishing one procedure, test it thoroughly before moving on to the next one to ensure that potential errors are caused by the new, not the old, code.

Following the above advices along with those in Section 3.8 will probably reduce the need for debugging when you code, but at the end of the day, having to debug is just something that every programmer has to do once in a while. In the next sections we introduce some debugging tools that can help you in the process.

9.2 VBA Debugging Tools

9.1 DEBUGGING TOOLS.

Control	Short cut	Method
	F8	Step Into
	Shift + F8	Step Over
	Ctrl + Shift + F8	Step Out
	F9	Break Point
	Ctrl + Shift + F9	Clear All Break Points
		View Locals Window
	Ctrl + G	View Immediate Window
		View Watch Window

The VBA editor offers a number of debugging tools. The main tools are explained in this section, where we also go into detail with the so-called Break Mode. Table 9.1 gives a quick overview of the various tools along with the control and the short cut key to activate the tool.

9.2.1 Step Into or Single Stepping

The first tool to be considered is the *Step Into* method – also called *Single stepping*. Using this tool, you can execute your code one line at a time. Pressing *F8* will execute the first line of code, pressing *F8* again will execute the next, and so forth. At any time, the next line of code to be executed will be highlighted. When single stepping is used, the code is in *Break Mode*.

By single stepping through your code in this way, you can follow the changes made to the worksheet and observe how execution moves through your nested loops, decision constructions, and procedure calls.

Furthermore, because the code is in Break Mode, you can use the tools described in the following sections to observe the values of your variables.

F5 can be pressed at any point during the single stepping process. This will cause the remainder of the program to be executed without single stepping.

9.2.2 Step Over

Many of your procedures contain calls to other procedures. Often – at least if you followed the advice of the previous section – you will have already tested those procedures and trust that they work correctly.

When single stepping through your code, the single stepping will proceed line by line through the procedures called by your code. If you already know that the procedure works correctly, you might want to execute the whole procedure by a single key stroke and continue single stepping after the procedure call. This is called to *Step Over* the procedure and is done by pressing *Shift + F8*.

9.2.3 Step Out

Sometimes you may want to Step Into a procedure called by your code and single step through the first part of it. After ensuring that everything works correctly, you may want to execute the remainder of that procedure in one key stroke to return to the main code and continue single stepping after the procedure call. This is called to *Step Out* of a procedure and is done by pressing *Ctrl+Shift+F8*.

9.2.4 Break Point

No matter how useful Single Stepping through your code can be, if you know that the bug occurs in the last part of your code, you might not want to single step through the first couple of hundred lines of code to reach the bug.

Instead you want the code to execute normally, as if you had pressed F5, until it reaches a specific line of code, at which point you want to start single stepping. You can do that by placing the cursor on the line where the execution should stop and press *F9* to set a *Break Point* at that line. Pressing *F5* will then execute your code until the *Break Point* and wait there in break mode.

When setting a *Break Point* at a line of code, the line will be marked in brown and a brown dot will occur in the margin of the code. You can also set and remove *Break Points* by clicking in the margin of the code.

Note that you can place as many *Break Points* in your code as you want to. Pressing *F5* will cause your code to be executed until the next *Break Point* or until the end of the code if there are no more *Break Points*. *Break Points* are removed automatically when the file is closed.

As an alternative to setting a *Break Point*, a *Stop* statement can be used within the code. The effect is the same: Execution will stop and the VBA editor enters *Break Mode*. Note that unlike *Break Points*, Stop statements are not removed automatically when the file is closed and hence they must be removed manually after the debugging process.

9.2.5 Break Mode

When you single step through your code and when stopping at a Break Point, the VBA Editor will enters *Break Mode*. *Break Mode* is also entered when a bug is reached and causes execution of the code to stop. *Break Mode* is automatically left when the code is executed through to the end and you can leave *Break Mode* by pressing the *Stop* control.

When the VBA Editor is in *Break Mode*, the line of code to be executed next is highlighted and a yellow arrow is placed in the margin of the code.

When the code is in *Break Mode*, you can move the yellow arrow to another line of code. This will cause that line to be executed next. That way you can repeat lines of code or skip lines of code. Note that if you repeat lines of code, the values of your variables are not reset to the value they had when the code was originally executed.

If you hold the pointer over a variable during *Break Mode*, you will see the value of that variable. This tool is very useful if you want to examine a portion of your code in order to determine the cause of the bug. In the next three sections we introduce other tools for viewing the values of variables during *Break Mode*.

9.2.6 Locals

The *Locals* window makes it a lot easier to inspect the value of the variables in Break Mode than holding the pointer over the variable. When the *Locals* window is open it automatically displays the value of all variables local to the current procedure when in Break Mode.

9.2.7 Watch

If you know or suspect that the error in your code occurs when a certain expression is True, the *Watch* window is useful. Examples could be when *j > 10*, when *Inventory < OrderPoint*, or when *j=3 and Route>17*.

You add a *Watch* by selecting *Add Watch* from the *Debug* menu to obtain the dialog box shown in Figure 9.1. Here the expression to watch is entered and the action to be taken is specified.

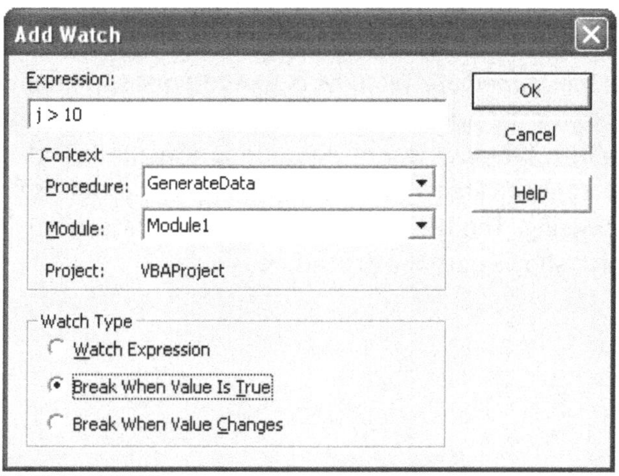

9.1 ADD A WATCH.

Executing the code with the setting shown in the figure will cause the execution to break and the editor to enter Break Mode whenever the value of the expression becomes true.

9.2.8 The Immediate Window

The *Immediate Window* can be thought of as a combination of a calculator, scratch paper, an output window, and an oracle. If it is not already open, use *Ctrl+G* to open the *Immediate Window*.

You can enter code directly in the *Immediate Window* as shown in Figure 9.2. The question mark is used to get an answer, for example, when entering the line *?n*, the answer 7 automatically occurs. VBA code can be used in the *Immediate Window*, but must be placed on a single line and separated by colon.

```
Immediate
a = 3
b = 4
n = a+b
?a
 3
?n
 7
?5+5
 10
```

9.2 USE THE IMMEDIATE WINDOW.

During Break Mode, the *Immediate Window* can be used in the same way to obtain the current value of variables by using the question mark followed by the variable name.

Another way to use the *Immediate Window* is to add *print* statements to the code which automatically print the current value of one of several variables to the *Immediate Window* when the code is executed. This is considered to be more sophisticated than the common method of using message boxes for debugging. The use of this type of print statements is shown in Figure 9.3 which shows part of a procedure.

```
Order = GetOrder()
Inv = Inv + Order

Debug.Print Inv
```

9.3 PRINT TO THE IMMEDIATE WINDOW FROM THE CODE.

9.3 Run-Time Errors

Run-Time Errors sometimes seem to occur out of the blue. Maybe your program executed without problems many times and then suddenly an error occurs during the next execution. Typical examples of Run-Time Errors are trying to divide by zero, trying to open a file that is already open, trying to access cells of the active workbook when a chart is selected, trying to take action based on the selected range when no range is selected, etc.

As can be seen from the above list, it is extremely hard to imagine all the potential errors that could occur and hence it is hard to take them all into account.

In the following, we show two ways to handle Run-Time Errors, which will at least prevent the program from crashing. Please note that these methods should not replace efforts to make the program stable, but they can supplement that.

The first method is illustrated by the code in Figure 9.4. If an error occurs in the code, here illustrated by the zero division, the *GoTo* statement will take effect and control jumps to the *HandleError* label where proper action should be taken. If no error occurs, the sub is exited right before the error handling.

In the error handling part of the code, the *Error* object can be used to obtain further information on the error.

```
Sub IllustrateError()
    On Error GoTo HandleError

    MsgBox 7 / 0
    Exit Sub
HandleError:
    MsgBox ("An error occurred")
End Sub
```

9.4 USING THE ON ERROR GOTO STATEMENT.

The second method is illustrated by the code in Figure 9.5. The *On Error* statement in this code ensures that if an error is encountered in a line of code, that line should be ignored and execution of the code should continue at the next line. Note that sometimes this is a smart way of handling errors, whereas in other cases it is critical if a line of code is not executed.

```
Sub IllustrateResumeNext()
    Dim k As Integer
    Dim Amount As Double
    Dim Shipment As Double

    On Error Resume Next

    For k = 1 To 20
        Amount = GetAmount()
        Shipment = GetShipment
        Cells(k, 3) = Amount / Shipment
    Next
End Sub
```

9.5 USING THE ON ERROR RESUME NEXT STATEMENT.

9.4 Exercises

9.1. Write a sub that uses a For-Next Loop to iterate from 0 to 40 with step size 1. Use the *Immediate Window* and the statement *Debug.Print* to print every fourth value (i.e. 0, 4, 8, 12, etc).

9.2. Write a procedure that uses a Do-Until Loop to iterate through the numbers from 1 to 11 with a step size of 2 and prints the numbers to the *Immediate Window*.

9.3. Open the file of this exercise. The file contains the following small sub: First execute the code.

```
Public Sub f()
  i = 32
  i = "text"
  j = i + 3
  MsgBox i
End Sub
```

Then, single step through the code and inspect the values of all variables to figure out what went wrong.

9.4. Open the file with your solution of Exercise 7.5. Include statements in the code to print the cities to the Immediate Window when they are selected.

9.5. Open the file with your solution of Exercise 6.11. Include statements that print to the *Immediate Window* enough information in each iteration to check that the strategy is correctly implemented. It is up to you to determine which information is necessary.

Chapter 10
Design of programs

When you set out to create a program, digging right into coding the first procedure might not be the smartest decision. If you do, chances are that you will have to re-write part of your code due to some issues that you did not think of when you first started.

Instead, the program should be thought out in detail before even opening the VBA editor. This process is called the design phase and is the focus of this chapter. Roughly speaking, if enough effort is put into the design phase, the coding task becomes relatively simple and the risk of having to delete code is minimized.

It should be pointed out that the material in this chapter has focus on relatively small programs that can be created by a single person within a couple of weeks.

In Section 10.1, we go into more detail with the different phases of creating a program. In Section 10.2 we consider the issue of designing a program and finally in Section 10.3, we shortly consider the use of flow charts in the design phase.

10.1 The Process of Creating a Program

The process of creating a program is illustrated in Figure 10.1. We emphasize that the process described here is in relation to relatively small programs. For larger programs, the connection between designing and coding/testing must be much more flexible as the needs in large programs will often change before the developing time is over.

The first phase is an analysis of the problem at hand. If the problem is given to you from an external source, for example a colleague or a company, this is the part where you are to obtain a full understanding of the goal of the problem.

It should be ensured that both parties agree what the exact output of the program should be. If a report is to be created, exactly what should it contain, what should possible charts show and how, etc.

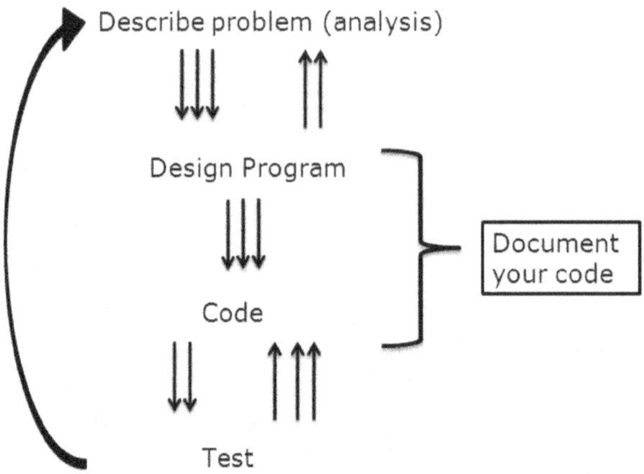

10.1 THE PROCESS OF DEVELOPING A PROGRAM.

It should be analyzed what kind of input is available and whether this is sufficient for obtaining the desired output. It should also be agreed how the input can be obtained and in which format. If the program is to have some degree of user interaction, the person you are creating the program for might have an opinion regarding the design of the interface, which may also influence your program.

Finally, if you are creating the program on your own behalf, or even for yourself to use, you will still have to clarify the above matters before the program can be created. But clearly, in this case you have a higher degree of flexibility.

After performing an in-depth analysis of the problem to be solved, the program can be designed. During the design phase, the layout of the program is determined.

In the rough design, the flow of the program is determined. It is determined how the program should be broken into smaller procedures. The purpose of each procedure should be described, including the input and output variables and the order and type of these. The use of global variables should also be determined at this level.

In a detailed design, the structure of each procedure is described in more detail with data structures, loops, decision making etc.

The design should in all cases be detailed enough that the code phase is just a matter of coding what has been described in the design. When the code phase is reached there should preferably not be any changes in the design of the program and hence all potential problems of the program should be dealt with in the design phase.

For complex problems, it is often necessary to swap back to the problem description several times during the design phase with the purpose of clarification of various issues.

During the design phase and the code phase, the documentation of the program should be created.

After the code phase follows the test phase. This is where it is ensured that the program works correctly. Clearly, there is a great deal of interaction between the code phase and the test phase, as the easiest way to create a bug free program is to test every single piece of code while creating it. But regardless of that, there will be a significant test phase at the end of the process.

It should be pointed out that even though the code phase and the test phase are clearly partitioned in Figure 10.1, in reality they are much more integrated. It should also be pointed out that test of the output should take place during the analysis phase to ensure that the type and format of the output is accepted by the user of the program.

It is now in its place to answer the questions: Why is the design phase so important? Why is there no arrow going backwards from the code phase to the design phase? And why are the two phases so separated from each other?

When proper attention is not paid to the design phase, there is an increased risk of having to delete large amounts of code or create clumsy quick fix solutions. The problem can be anything from the proper data not being available in the single procedure where needed, double storage of data, or the need of changing the format of data forth and back several times, to coding of similar tasks several times instead of reusing code. It could also be even more serious, as the smart solution in the head of the programmer simply not leading to the goal of the problem. If the program is carefully designed, these issues, and many more, can be discovered and handled during the design phase instead of say half way through the code phase.

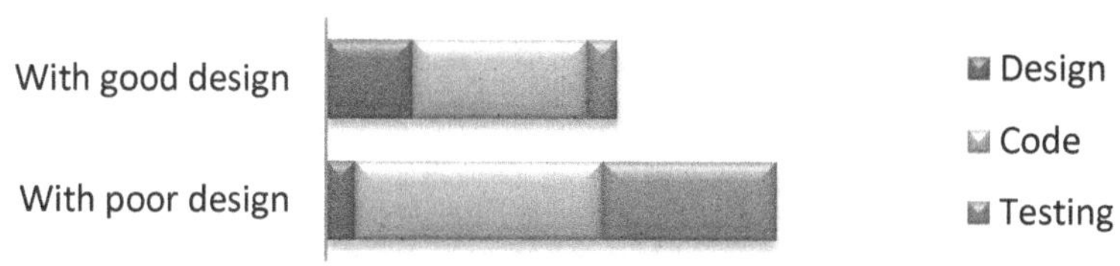

10.2 TIME CAN BE SAVED BY HAVING FOCUS ON THE CREATION OF A GOOD DESIGN.

Creating a design of a program takes time. Creating a good detailed design takes even more time. But the time spent during the design phase comes back as time saved during the code phase and in particular during the test (and correct) phase. This is illustrated in Figure 10.2, where the time usage during the design, code, and test phases when effort is put into creation of a good design is compared to the time usage in the three phases when the design phase is neglected.

In Figure 10.1, there is an arrow going backwards from the test phase to the analysis phase. It should be clear from the above that following this arrow should be avoided through careful design and even more careful analysis. Nevertheless, if the task of developing the program is given to you from someone else, there will always be a risk that someone will not be satisfied with the result. In this case there is only one way: back – and through the phases again and pray that most of your work can be used after all. The best advice for avoiding this is to devote sufficient time to the analysis and design phases.

10.2 Designing a Program

There are almost as many ways to design programs as there are programmers. When several programmers work jointly on a program, professional design tools are needed.

When working on smaller projects, the easiest way to create a design for a program is to use pen and paper, which is the method considered in this section. An advantage of this method is that it is relatively fast compared to other methods. A great disadvantage is that it is not very presentable to others and it can end up rather messy if several corrections are made. We suggest using the suggested method or something similar first and possibly supplementing with a nicer looking computer created design.

In this section we focus on the overall design of how the program as a whole is partitioned into several procedures. The design of the single procedure is done using pseudo code and is easier.

10.2.1 Example: Simple Production Planning

The first example to be considered is partly based on Case 3, which is to be found on the book's webpage. Here we consider a simplified version of the case. A number of products are to be processed first on either machine 1 or 2 and then on machine 3 as illustrated in Figure 10.3.

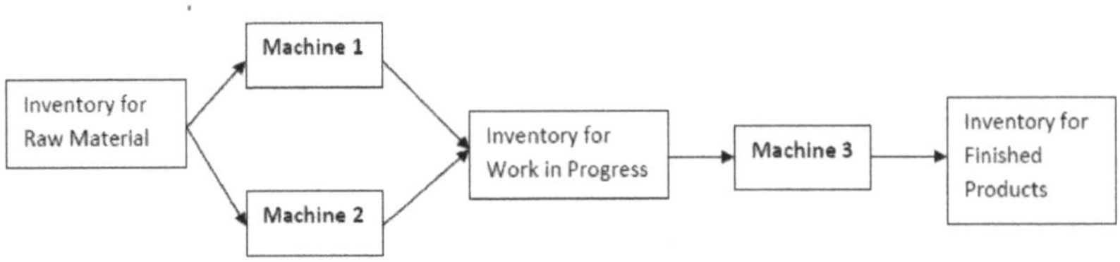

10.3 PRODUCTION LINE.

For each product, information regarding processing times and due time for each product is given in a worksheet as shown in Figure 10.4.

5		Due time		Processing Time	
6		D_j	M_j^1	M_j^2	M_j^3
7	11	58	22	13	5
8	19	77	22	11	9
9	4	20	21	14	4

10.4 AVAILABLE DATA.

The goal is to produce a production plan like the one indicated in Figure 10.5, where the figure spans columns *H* through *U*. Furthermore, a message box should be displayed stating a number of key quality measures based on the generated production plan.

In Figure 10.5, the first two columns are the product index and an indication of the choice between M1 and M2. The next four columns should contain the start and finish time on machine M1 and M2 for each product. Next is the time each product enters the inventory for work in progress and the time the product leaves that inventory, followed by the start and finish time on machine M3. The final four columns should give information regarding time in inventory for work in progress, time elapsed from the product started its processing, an indication of whether the product is delayed, and the delay time of the product.

						Inventory for WIP				Time		Job	Size
Job index	Machine	Start M1	End M1	Start M2	End M2	Enter	Leave	start M3	End M3	Inv. WIP	Elapse Time	Delayed	Delay

10.5 HEADINGS OF THE PRODUCTION PLAN.

The rules to determine the processing order of the products and the choice between M1 and M2 are described in the case text. They will not be repeated here and are not important for this example.

In Figure 10.6, we show a possible design for the program. The program has been partitioned into six procedures, each indicated by a box. In the lower left corner, information regarding location of global information is given. In this example, all global information is to be found in the worksheet.

The only task of the main procedure, *MakeProdPlan*, is to control the flow of the program and call the remaining procedures in the correct order. The asterisk next to the main procedure indicates that a button should be included in the worksheet to execute the procedure. This is important in the design because procedures to be executable by a button may not return a value, nor may they take any input arguments.

The *Setup* procedure should clear the production plan area of the worksheet and create new headings. The actual clearing is taken care of by another procedure called *Clear*. That way the actual clearing can also be done directly by pressing a button in the worksheet as indicated by the asterisk next to the *Clear* procedure.

Creation of the new production plan is partitioned into two procedures: Machines 1 and 2 in *PlanM1M2* and machine 3 in *PlanM3*. The main reason for this choice is to ensure that each procedure is kept relatively short and that they can easily be tested for correctness separately.

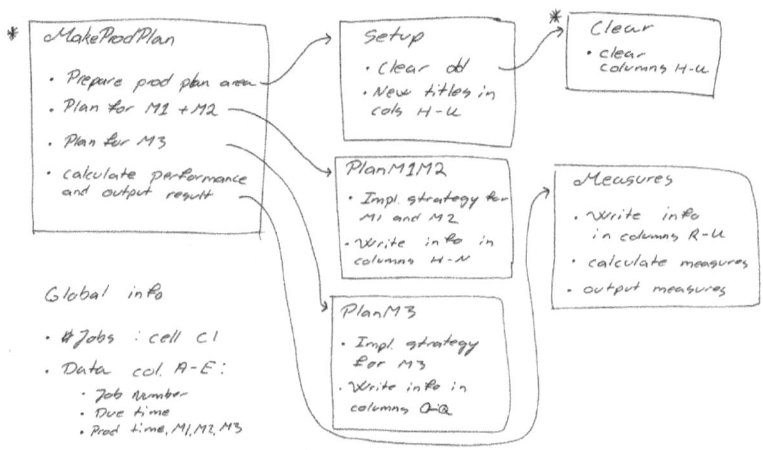

10.6 DESIGN OF THE SIMPLE PRODUCTION PLANNING PROGRAM.

The calculation and presentation of the quality measures of the production plan is kept in a separate procedure. That way, if a second method for planning the production is developed, this procedure can be reused.

10.2.2 Example: Reservation Problem

The second example is concerned with a seat reservation problem and is based on Case 4 on the book's webpage. In the following, enough information will be provided to understand the design phase. Detailed understanding of the assignment methods and the quality measures are not necessary in the following.

Even though the example is based on reservation of train seats, similar methods can be used for handling reservations of hotel rooms, rental of summer cabins or booking of meeting facilities. For that purpose, stations in the following should be replaced by appropriate timeslots.

The setup is as follows. A train with a fixed number of seats is traveling from a start station to an end station with a number of stops in between. A number of reservation requests arrive online and a decision must be made to either assign the passenger to a specific seat or reject the passenger. We use two strategies for this decision: *First interval* and *Best interval.* Start and destination station for each request is given in columns *B* and *C* in Figure 10.7.

The resulting assignment, using the two strategies, is shown in graphical manner starting in column *G*. Furthermore, the assignment and the rejected requests are given in columns *D* and *E*.

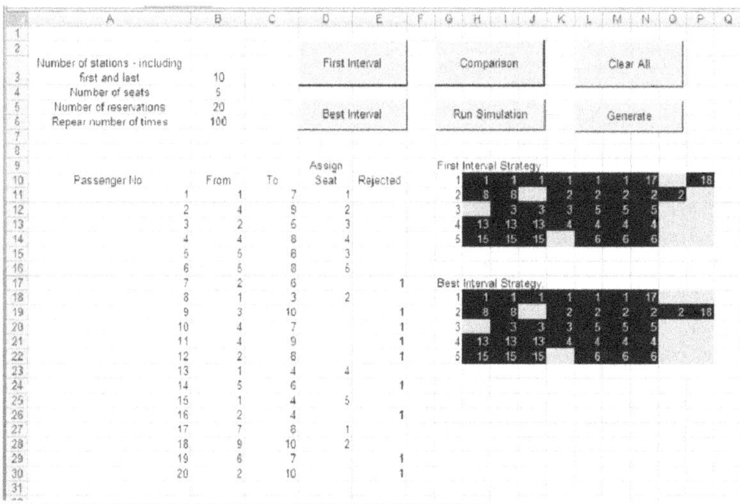

10.7 WORKSHEET FOR THE SEAT RESERVATION PROBLEM.

Pressing the *Generate* button should generate a new list of requests based on the information in the top left corner of the worksheet. Pressing either of the two leftmost buttons should assign passengers based on the corresponding method, display the graphical layout, and display a message box stating the quality measures for the assignment. Pressing the *Compare* button should assign and create graphical layout for both methods and display a joined message box comparing the quality of the two solutions. Pressing the *Run Simulation* button should repeatedly generate new data and assign with each of the two strategies without displaying graphics and finally display a message box concluding which of the two strategies is best based on the experiment. Finally, pressing the *Clear All* button should clear the graphics and the assignments in columns *D* and *E*.

The design for this example, which is shown in Figure 10.8, is far more complex due to the wish for integration of comparison. Clearly the procedures to be created for the two strategies should be used both when these are executed separately and when used within one of the two comparison methods. In the following, we focus on the explanation of the *First interval* strategy. The procedures for the *Best interval* strategy are designed similarly.

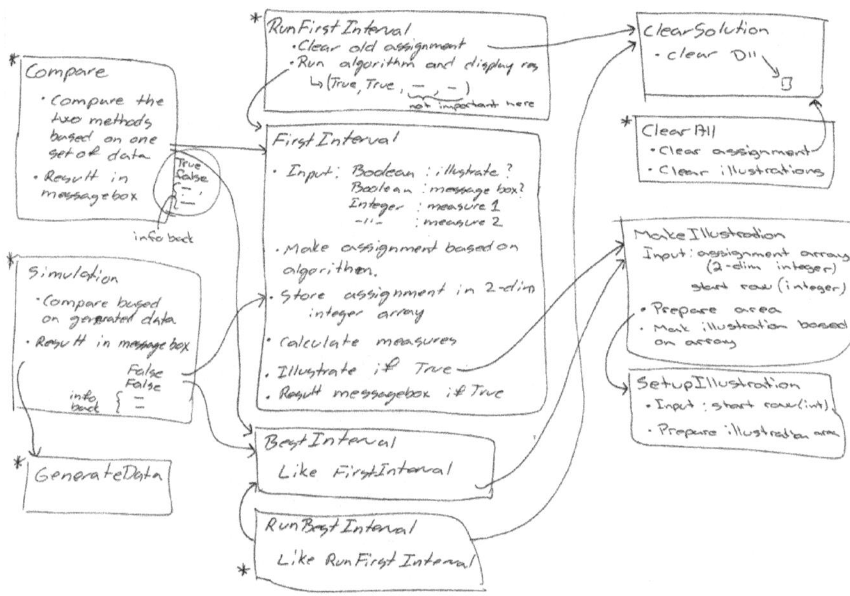

10.8 DESIGN OF THE SEAT RESERVATION PROGRAM.

Because of the simulation we want to create the assignment in an array, which can be used for quality measuring. When graphical display is wanted we can call a separate procedure to create this based on the array. This procedure is called *MakeIllustration* and takes our array as input. We can use the same illustration procedure for the two strategies by using an index stating the row where the graphics should start. Hence *MakeIllustration* needs both the array with the assignment and a row index as input. We have decided to use a separate procedure, called *SetupIllustration*, to prepare the area for showing the assignment. The only input needed for this procedure is the index of the start row.

The procedure that should actually create the assignment is *FirstInterval*. The procedure takes as input four variables. A Boolean indicating if graphics should be displayed. If this variable is true, the *MakeIllustration* procedure is called. A Boolean indicating if a message box should be displayed with the result. The final arguments are two integers which are used for returning the two quality measures. The procedure should make the assignment based on the given strategy, store the assignment in an array and calculate the two quality measures.

In order to be able to execute the first interval strategy by pressing a button, a small procedure, called *RunFirstInterval* is created. The only purpose of this procedure is to call *FirstInterval* with the correct input arguments: True for graphics, True for message box, and two integer variables that are not used for anything here as the two final arguments. Furthermore, this procedure should call the *ClearSolution* which clears the assignment in columns *D* and *E*.

The same is done for the best interval procedures. Note that it is really not necessary to duplicate the details for this strategy in the design when it is just the same. The *ClearAll* procedure calls *ClearSolution* to clear columns *D* and *E*, and clears all graphical illustration.

The *Compare* procedure should first call *FirstInterval*, then *BestInterval*, both with input parameters True for graphics, False for separate message boxes, and two integers to catch the quality measures. Next the total of four integers are used in a joined message box displaying a comparison.

Finally, the *Simulation* procedure should repeatedly call *GenerateData*, which generates new requests, and the two strategies *FirstInterval* and *BestInterval*. These should be called with input arguments False for graphics, False for separate message boxes, and two integers to return the quality measures. The latter are used in summing up the quality comparison, which is finally displayed. Note that the number of repetitions can be directly obtained from the worksheet.

10.3 Use of Flow Charts in Designs

The reader may have a feeling that *Flow Charts*, also called activity diagrams, could supplement the design of a program. Flow charts are good tools for clarifying the problem and could be used with advantage in the process of analyzing the problem. An example of this is in Section 10.2.1, where we used a small flow chart to clarify the production line.

Flow charts can also be used to make a more detailed design of the single procedure. But note that flow chart should supplement, not replace, a design that considers input and output of the separate procedure.

A detailed introduction to flow charts is beyond the scope of this book. In order to illustrate the use of flow charts, Figure 10.9 shows a Pseudo code of a standard branch-and-bound algorithm. Figure 10.10 shows a corresponding flow chart. We leave it to the reader to compare the two.

As long as there are still active nodes, repeat:

- Select an active node A
- Solve LP-relaxation of A
- If LP-relax is infeasible -> close A
- If the solution in A is integral, then
    - Close node
    - Update best feasible solution if this solution is better
- Else (the solution is fractional)
    - If LP-relax value ≤ best value, then
        - Bound node
    - Else Branch, i.e. partition A into sub nodes and make them active

10.9 PSEUDO CODE OF A BRANCH-AND-BOUND ALGORITHM.

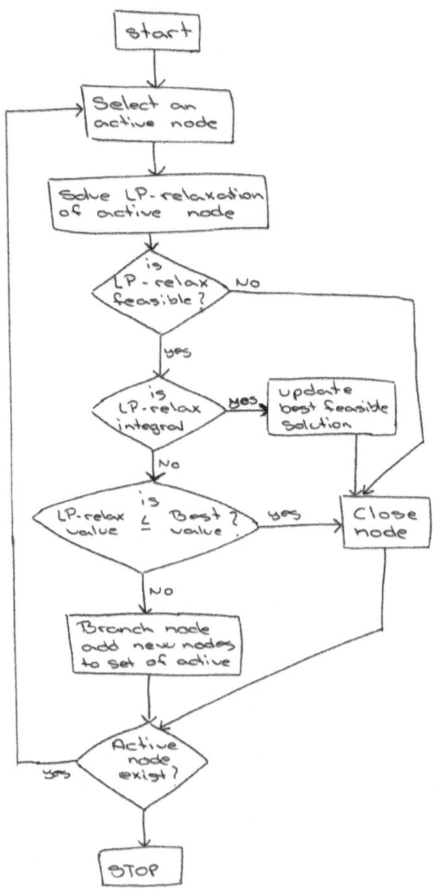

10.10 FLOW CHART OF A BRANCH-AND-BOUND ALGORITHM.

Chapter 11
Making it Easier to Use Your Code

Up to this point, all code has been located in a module of the workbook in which it was to be used. That is, in the specific Excel file. In this chapter we will make exceptions from this rule. We start by introducing a special workbook called *Personal.xlsb*, which will make it significantly more convenient to use your code in practice. We continue in Section 11.2, by discussing several ways to execute your code. Section 11.3 illustrates how to use the *Quick Access Toolbar* to execute your own macros, and Section 11.4 demonstrates how to construct and maintain a *customized toolbar*. Finally, Section 11.5 deals with the construction and installation of *Add-Ins*.

11.1 The Personal Workbook

In order to execute a macro, the workbook which contains the code, must be open. Once the workbook is open, the macro can be executed directly or indirectly from that workbook or from any other open workbook. This is not a problem for code which is designed for a specific workbook, but consider again the macro *SaveCloseAllOther* from Chapter 7. This small sub is very useful when working with many files as it saves and closes all currently open workbooks except the one containing the code. But in order to use your macro you must first open the workbook which contains the code, which limits the usefulness significantly.

Now imagine having that sub located in a workbook that automatically opens and closes with Excel so that your code would always be available for you. That would significantly increase the usefulness of your code. *Personal.xlsb* is exactly such a workbook. Once it contains code, it will automatically be loaded when Excel is opened. The *Personal.xlsb* can be used for storing both subs and functions. Under normal conditions, you will not see the workbook in Excel, but it will be available for you in the *Project Explorer* in the *VBA editor* as illustrated in Figure 11.1.

Personal.xlsb will not be shown in the *Project Explorer* until it contains code. In order to activate it, you start by recording a dummy macro and choose to store it in *Personal Macro Workbook* as shown in Figure 11.2.

The content of the macro is unimportant as the macro will be deleted subsequently. Now the *Personal.xlsb* will be available in the *VBA editor* and you can insert modules and store subs and functions in it. After having written some code in the *Personal.xlsb*, you can delete the dummy macro.

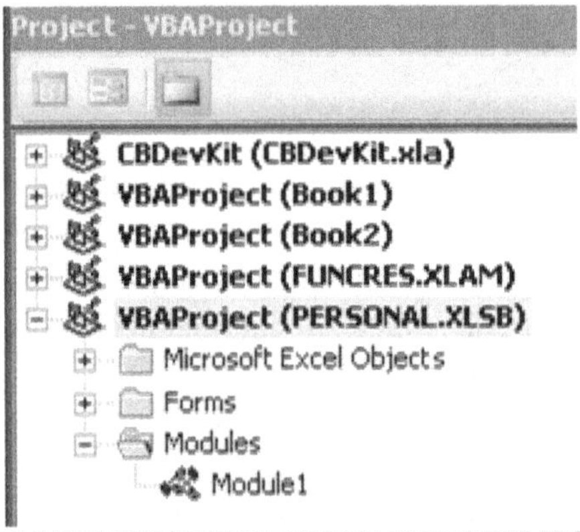

11.1 YOU CAN SEE THE PERSONAL.XLSB IN THE PROJECT EXPLORER.

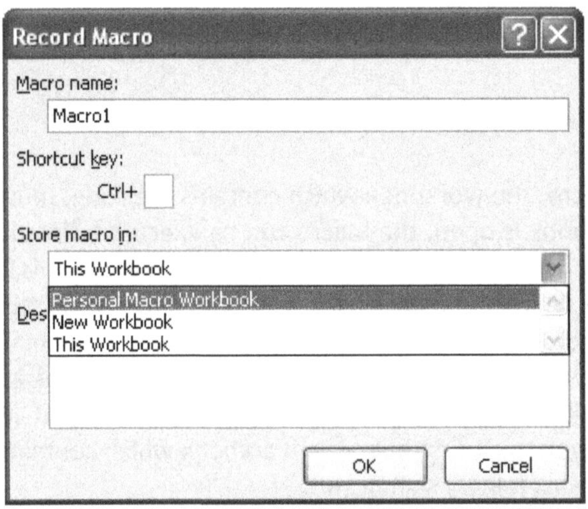

11.2 RECORD A DUMMY MACRO AND STORE IT IN THE PERSONAL MACRO WORKBOOK.

11.2 Executing a Macro

There are several ways to execute a macro. You are already familiar with some of them: In Chapter 1 you learned how to use the button *Macros* in the Excel *Developer* tab to select a macro to be executed and you learned how to create a button and assign a macro to it. In Chapter 1 you also learned that you can use *F5* to execute a macro directly from the VBA editor, and in Chapter 5 you learned how to execute one macro from another. In Chapter 16, you will learn how to execute your macros from a user form. In the following, we will show you two alternative ways to execute your macro.

11.2.1 Use Alternative Buttons to Execute a Macro

Not only standard buttons can be used to execute a macro. Nearly anything you can imagine inserting into your worksheet can function as a button to execute a macro: Pictures, Clip Art, Shapes, and SmartArt. Even Charts and WordArt can be used.

All you need to do is the following: Choose your favorite object from the *Insert* menu in Excel to insert the object in your workbook and adjust it to fit your needs. Right-click the object and choose *Assign Macro* from the menu to obtain the *Assign Macro dialog box*. Select the macro you want to assign to your object and press *OK*.

11.2.2 Use a Shortcut Key to Execute a Macro

If you press *ctrl+s* in Excel, the active workbook is saved. If you press *ctrl+f*, the find and replace procedure is started. These are called *shortcut keys*. It is easy to create a shortcut key for your macro so that it will be executed when you press for example *ctrl+a*. This is how it is done: Choose *Macros* on the *Developer* tab in Excel. Select the macro for which you want to set up a *shortcut key* and press the *Options* button. The *macro options dialog box*, shown in Figure 11.3, is displayed. Select the *shortcut key* that you prefer and press *OK*.

Note that when you assign a macro to a shortcut key, you automatically overwrite any previous assignment for that shortcut key. Hence, if you choose *ctrl+s*, this key combination will no longer save the active workbook, but will execute your macro instead. Therefore it is recommended that you only assign shortcut keys that you do not use in your daily work.

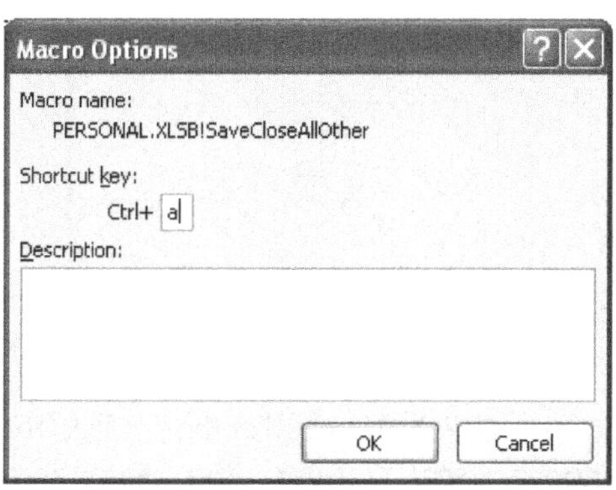

11.3 OPEN THE MACRO OPTIONS DIALOG BOX TO ASSIGN A SHORTCUT KEY.

11.3 Quick Access Toolbar

In the upper left corner of Excel you find the *Quick Access Toolbar* as shown in Figure 11.4. You can add controls to the *Quick Access Toolbar* to execute either standard Excel Macros or your own macros. For example, clicking the *smiley face* in Figure 11.4 will execute the *SaveCloseAllOther* macro from Chapter 7.

11.4 THE QUICK ACCESS TOOLBAR.

You can add controls to execute macros from both the *Personal.xlsb* and normal workbooks. If the workbook containing the code is not open, it will automatically be opened when the control is chosen. As a general rule, it is recommended only to add controls to execute macros from the *Personal.xlsb*, unless there are specific reasons for doing differently.

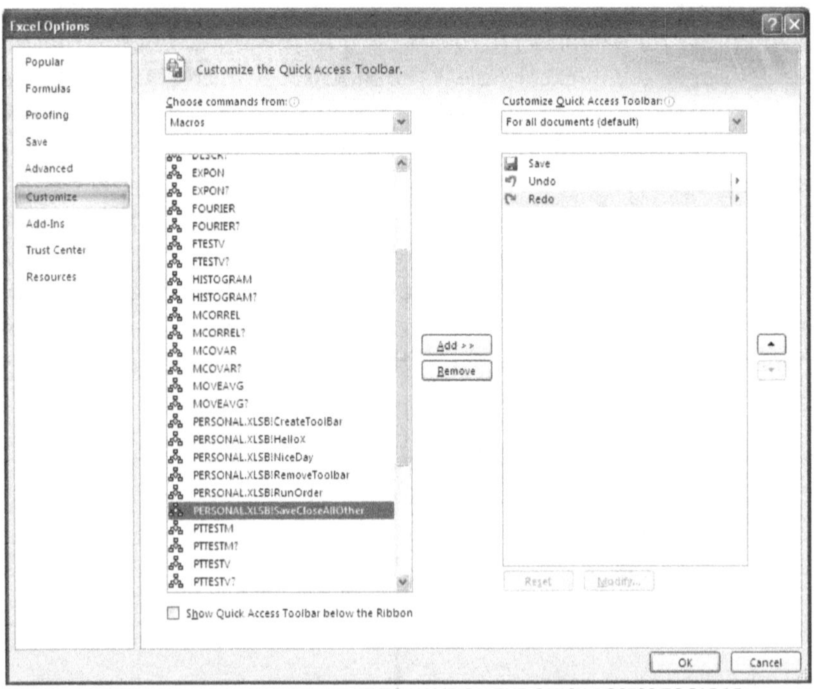

11.5 SELECT THE MACROS THAT YOU WANT TO HAVE ON THE QUICK ACCESS TOOLBAR.

This is how you add a control to the *Quick Access Toolbar*: Click the *Windows Button* in Excel and choose *Excel Options*. The dialog box displayed in Figure 11.5 appears. Select *Customize*. Alternatively, right click on the *Quick Access Toolbar* and select *Customize Quick Access Toolbar*. Here you can choose a macro to add. This is also the place to go if you want to remove controls from the Quick Access Toolbar. In order to add a control for a custom macro, select Macros in the top of the left-hand side window to get a list of available macros. Locate the desired macro and press the *Add* button. In order to change the face of the control, select your macro in the right-hand side window and press the *Modify* button. Press *OK* a couple of times and you are done.

11.4 Toolbar in the Ribbon

There is a simple and a more advanced way to make a *custom toolbar* in the *Ribbon* of Excel. In this book we will only deal with the simple method. In order to create good looking toolbars which are nicely divided into groups, it is necessary to use *XML* code, which is beyond the scope of this book. By using a relatively simple VBA code, it is, however, possible to make a toolbar which will be located in the *Add-Ins* menu as *Custom Toolbars* as illustrated in Figure 11.6.

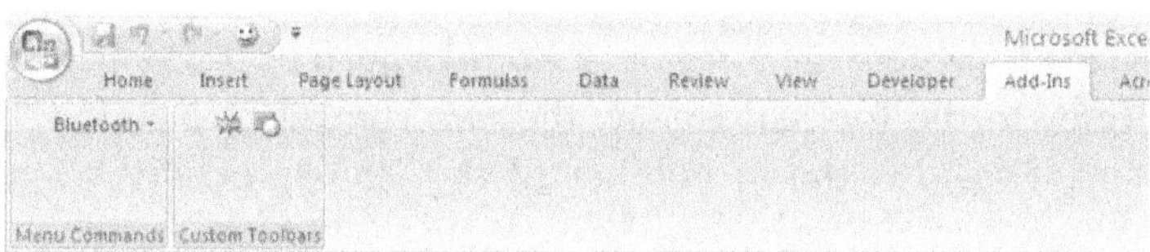

11.6 CUSTOM TOOLBARS ARE FOUND IN THE ADD-INS MENU OF THE RIBBON.

Before creating a toolbar, it is advisable to test the macros thoroughly and store them in the *Personal.xlsb*. Remember that the personal workbook is never the active workbook in Excel, so it is important to test the macros from another workbook.

In order to create the toolbar and be able to remove it again, two special subs are needed. These are stored in the *Personal.xlsb* as well. Consider the code in Figure 11.7, which creates the toolbar illustrated in Figure 11.6. The toolbar has two controls which execute the *SaveCloseAllOther* and the *MakeVisibleAndShowName*, respectively. Both are described in Chapter 7.

Two special types of variables are needed: *bar*, which refers to the *toolbar* itself, and *c*, which is used to refer to the single *control* on the toolbar. Do not get confused about the fact that VBA uses the term *Commandbar* instead of *toolbar*. Firstly, a sub for removing the toolbar, in case it is already there, is called. By doing this, our sub can also be used to update the toolbar. Next, a new toolbar is added to the Excel application.

```
Sub CreateToolBar()
    Dim bar As CommandBar
    Dim c As CommandBarControl

    Call RemoveToolbar
    Set bar = Application.CommandBars.Add
    bar.Name = "My Toolbar"
    bar.Visible = True

    Set c = bar.Controls.Add
    c.FaceId = 643
    c.OnAction = "SaveCloseAllOther"
    c.TooltipText = "Save and close all Workbooks"


    Set c = bar.Controls.Add
    c.FaceId = 168
    c.OnAction = "MakeVisibleAndShowName"
    c.TooltipText = "Make sheets visible"

End Sub
```

11.7 SUB TO CREATE A TOOLBAR WITH TWO CONTROLS.

The toolbar is made visible and given a *name* which is used in the application to refer to the toolbar. Finally, the two controls are added to the toolbar. Here, *FaceId* is the id number of the icon to be displayed, *OnAction* is the name of the macro to be executed when the control is pressed, and *TooltipText* is the text to be displayed when the mouse is held over the control. These are the basic properties. Please refer to the *Object Browser* for more. The code in Figure 11.8 removes the toolbar.

```
Sub RemoveToolbar()
    On Error Resume Next
    Application.CommandBars("My Toolbar").Delete
End Sub
```

11.8 SUB TO REMOVE A TOOLBAR.

11.5 Create and Use Your Own Add-In

There are two main reasons for wanting to make a custom *Add-In*: First of all, if you want to share your subs and functions with colleagues or others, you probably do not want them to change your code or even see it. Second, it is simpler to use a function from an Add-in than to use a function of one workbook in another.

11.5.1 Preparing the Workbook

In order to create an *Add-In*, you first create a normal macro-enabled workbook with the subs and functions you want to have included in your Add-In. For Add-Ins, the worksheets cannot be made visible, but you may still use them in your code to store and obtain information and to perform calculations, as long as you remember that it will not be possible for the user of your Add-In to view this information after you have converted the file into an Add-In.

Just as the *Personal.xlsb*, an Add-In is never the active workbook. Therefore it is important that you test the subs and functions thoroughly while another workbook is active.

After transforming the workbook to an Add-In, any function in the Add-In can be used from any active workbook simply by using the function name.

If your Add-In will contain any subs, you should make sure to create a way to execute the subs. Subs that are contained in an Add-In will not be available in the *Macro dialog box* activated by choosing *Macros* on the *Developer* tab in Excel.

Add-Ins often contain a toolbar with controls for executing the subs contained in it. To make this work, include two subs similar to the ones shown in Figures 11.7 and 11.8. In order for the toolbar to appear automatically when the Add-In is installed and be removed automatically, two extra subs are needed. These subs are so called *Event Programming*, i.e. they will be executed when a certain event occurs. In this case right before the workbook with the code is closed, in which case the sub to remove the toolbar is called, and when the workbook is opened, in which case the sub to create the toolbar is called. The name of the two subs must be as in Figure 11.9, and they must be placed directly under *ThisWorkbook*, not in a module. Refer to Chapter 16 for further information on *Event Programming*.

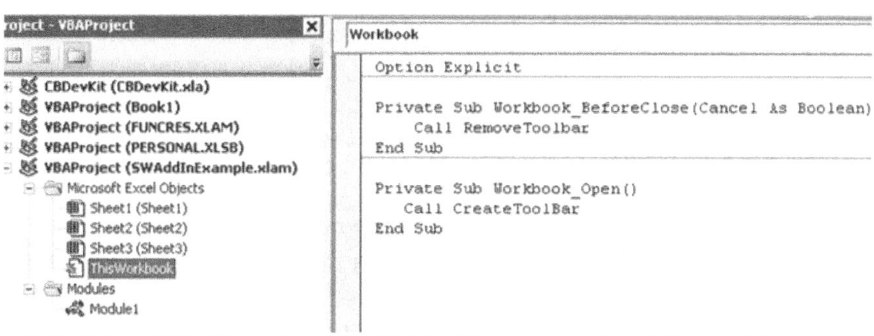

11.9 THE SUB TO REMOVE THE TOOLBAR MUST BE CALLED RIGHT BEFORE THE WORKBOOK CLOSES. THE SUB TO CREATE THE TOOLBAR MUST BE CALLED WHEN THE WORKBOOK IS OPENED. BOTH THESE SUBS MUST BE PLACED DIRECTLY UNDER THISWORKBOOK – NOT IN A MODULE.

Note that subs and functions that should only be used internally in the Add-In can be protected by the keyword *Private* as illustrated in Figure 11.10.

```
Private Function MyInternalFunction(i As Integer)

End Function
```

11.10 PROCEDURES TO BE USED INTERNALLY IN THE ADD-IN CAN BE MADE PRIVATE.

11.5.2 Creating the Add-In

After creating and testing the code to be contained in your *Add-In*, only three things are left: The *properties* should be set, the code should be *password protected*, and the file should be stored as an Add-In in the correct location. Before following the steps below, we recommended that you save the file as a normal macro enabled excel file. In that way you can always access your code, even if you forget the password.

In order to set the *properties* of the Add-In, select *VBAProject Properties* from the *Tools* menu in the *VBA Editor* in order to obtain the dialog box shown in Figures 11.11 and 11.12.

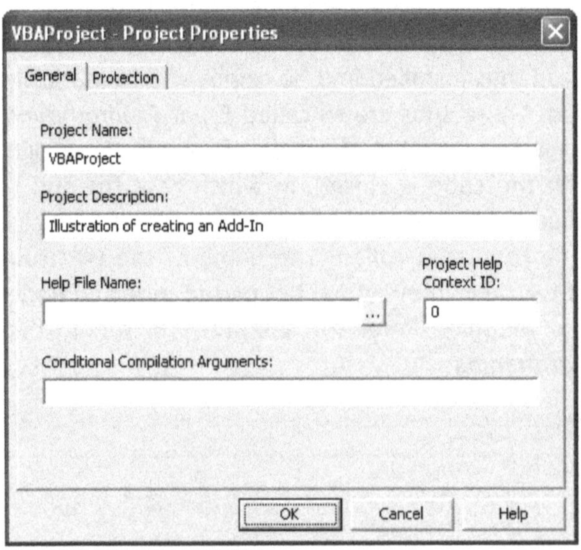

11.11 THE ADD-IN PROPERTIES.

On the *General* tab, the Add-In is given a *name* and a *descriprion* is added as shown in Figure 11.11. On the *Protection* tab, a *password* in entered in order to protect the code from being edited. If you do not want other people to view the code, you should tick the *Lock project for viewing* box.

It should be mentioned that products exist that can recover the password.

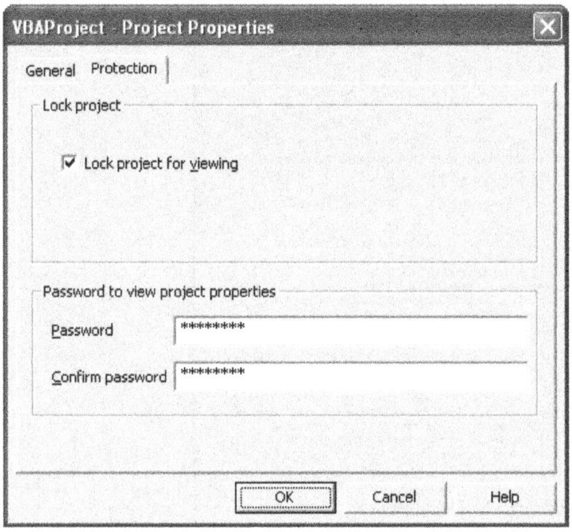

11.12 PASSWORD PROTECT YOUR FILE AND LOCK IT FOR VIEWING.

In order to save the project as an Add-In, choose *Save As* from the *Office Button* to obtain the dialog box displayed in Figure 11.13. Select the file type to be *Excel Add-In (*.xlam)* and give the file a name. Do save the file in the suggested location.

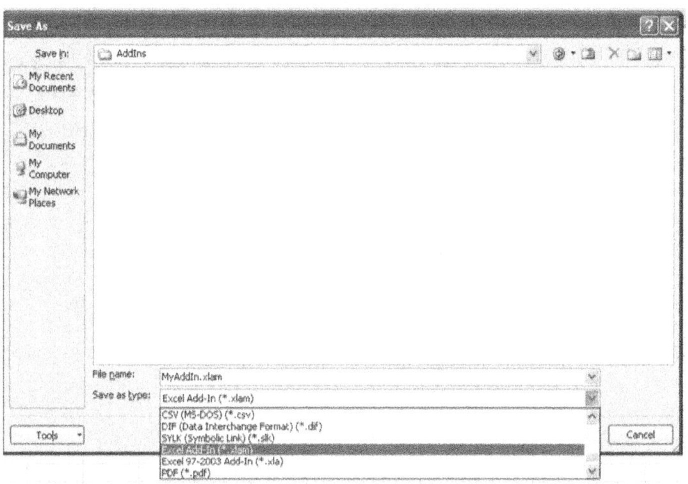

11.13 SAVE YOUR FILA AS AN EXCEL ADD-IN IN THE SUGGESTED LOCATION.

11.5.3 Installing an Add-In

The following procedure for installing an *Add-In* can be followed no matter if the Add-In has been obtained with Excel as for example the *Analytical ToolPak* or *Solver*, or has been created by the above method.

In order to install the Add-In, choose *Excel Options* from the *Office Button* in Excel. Select *Add-Ins* in the left-hand side menu of the dialog box that appears to obtain the view displayed in Figure 11.14.

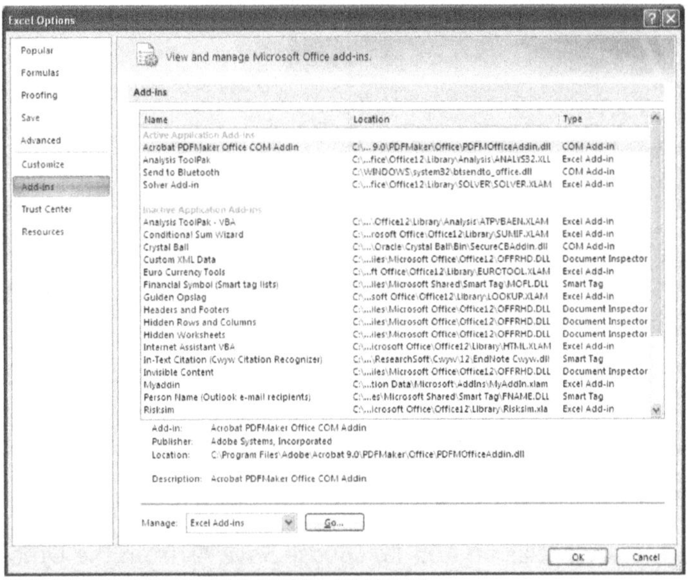

11.14 USE EXCEL OPTIONS TO INSTALL AN ADD-IN.

In the bottom, select *Excel Add-ins* and click the *Go* button. This will give you a list of the available Excel Add-Ins, both preinstalled and custom, as illustrated in Figure 11.15. Select the Add-In you want to install. If, for some reason, you did not save your Add-In in the standard location, you can find it by using the *Browse* button. Pressing *OK* will install the Add-In, and you can start using the subs and functions contained in it. If the Add-In contains a toolbar, it will be available.

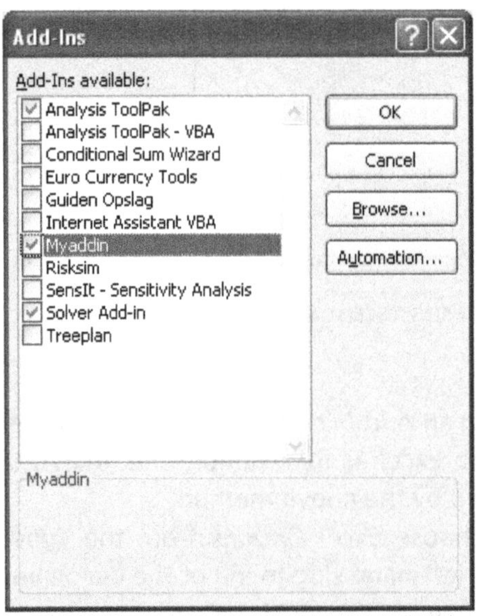

11.15 SELECT THE ADD-IN YOU WANT TO INSTALL.

11.6 Exercises

11.1. Locate your *Personal.xlsb* by recording a dummy macro. Copy a sub or two into the *Personal.xlsb* and remove the dummy macro. Restart Excel and check that the *Personal.xlsb* is still available.

11.2. Create a Shortcut Key for one of your subs in the *Personal.xlsb* and try to execute the sub from another file.

11.3. Make an alternative button, a picture for example, to execute one of the subs in your *Personal.xlsb*.

11.4. Add a control that executes one of the subs in your *Personal.xlsb* to the Quick Access Toolbar.

11.5. Create a sub in your *Personal.xlsb* that removed all but one sheet in the active workbook. Add a control for executing the sub to the Quick Access Toolbar. Open a new file in Excel and test your sub.

11.6. Create a toolbar in the Ribbon with two or more controls that execute subs from your *Personal.xlsb*. Remember to write a sub that can remove the toolbar again. Test that it works.

11.7. Open a new workbook and copy a couple of your favorite subs and functions into it. Test that they work properly when another workbook is active. Write code that creates a toolbar for the subs when the workbook is loaded and a sub that removes the toolbar when the workbook is closed. Test that it works. Turn the workbook into an Add-In and install it. Check that it works.

Chapter 12
Files

The ability to deal with files is important when creating computer programs. It makes you able to open and read from external data files and to save output in other files. This is particularly important when creating code that is generic enough to work on several data sets.

In Section 12.1, we give a short introduction to the file system. In Section 12.2, we offer material that makes you able to work with folders, and in Section 12.3, we consider the issue of working with files. Finally in Section 12.4, we show how to work with text files.

12.1 The File System

Many of the procedures presented below require that you work directly with the *file system object*. These are the ones with a variable of type *FileSystemObject* which we often call *sys*.

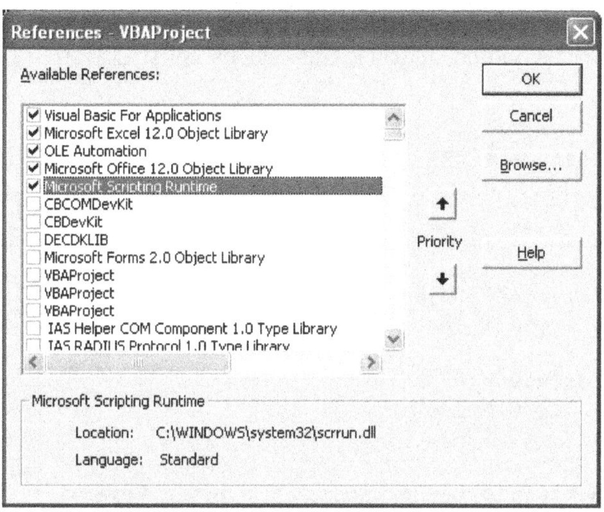

12.1 SET A REFERENCE TO MICROSOFT SCRIPTING RUNTIME TO WORK WITH FILES.

To be allowed to work with the file system object, you must first establish a connection. To do this, choose *References* from the *Tools* menu in the

VBA editor to obtain the dialog box shown in Figure 12.1. Select *Microsoft Scripting Runtime* and press *OK.*

12.2 Working with Folders

It can be very convenient to be able to create and delete folders from within your program, or even to be able to check whether a specific folder exists. In this section, we consider one way of doing that.

In all examples in this section, *sys* is an object variable for the *file system* and *F* is a *Folder* object variable. All examples start by setting a reference to the file system object and setting *F* to be the folder containing the file of the code.

12.2.1 Create a New Folder

In the example in Figure 12.2, we check if there is a sub folder called *First* in the folder *F*. We do that with the *FolderExists* method of the *Folder* object. If there is no such folder, we want to create it. This can be done with the *CreateFolder* method of the *Folder* object. Note that attempting to create a folder with a name that already exists will cause an error.

Next, we create a folder whose name is to be the concatenation of the string *Orders* and the current date. The latter is merely to illustrate how values of variables can be used as part of the folder name. In the last part, to illustrate the *GetParentFolderName* method of the *Folder* object, we check whether the name of the parent folder of the folder we just created is the same as the name of *F*, which clearly is the case by construction.

```
Sub CreateFolders()
    Dim sys As FileSystemObject
    Dim F As Folder
    Dim A As Folder
    Dim D As Folder

    Set sys = New FileSystemObject
    Set F = sys.GetFolder(ThisWorkbook.Path)

    If Not sys.FolderExists(F & "\First") Then
        Set A = sys.CreateFolder(F & "\First")
    End If

    If Not sys.FolderExists(F & "\Orders " & Date) Then
        Set D = sys.CreateFolder(F & "\Orders " & Date)
        MsgBox (sys.GetParentFolderName(D) = F.Path)
    End If
End Sub
```

12.2 CREATE A FOLDER.

12.2.2 Delete a Folder

Sometimes you might also want to delete an existing folder. The code in Figure 12.3 illustrates how to do that using the *DeleteFolder* method of the *Folder* object. Note that to avoid errors, it is important to check that the folder exists before trying to delete it.

```
Sub DeleteFolder()
    Dim sys As FileSystemObject
    Dim F As Folder

    Set sys = New FileSystemObject
    Set F = sys.GetFolder(ThisWorkbook.Path)
    If sys.FolderExists(F & "\Orders " & Date) Then
        sys.DeleteFolder (F & "\Orders " & Date)
    End If
End Sub
```

12.3 DELETE A FOLDER.

12.2.3 Display Sub Folders

In the final example, we show how a For-Each construction can be used to iterate through every sub folder of a folder. Consider the code in Figure 12.4 where we use a *Folder* object variable *A* to do this. For each sub folder we display the name of the folder along with the date of creation in the worksheet.

```
Sub DisplayFolders()
    Dim sys As FileSystemObject
    Dim F As Folder
    Dim A As Folder
    Dim i As Integer

    i = 1
    Set sys = New FileSystemObject
    Set F = sys.GetFolder(ThisWorkbook.Path)

    For Each A In F.SubFolders
        Cells(i, 1) = A.Name
        Cells(i, 2) = F.DateCreated
        i = i + 1
    Next
End Sub
```

12.4 DISPLAY SUB FOLDERS.

12.3 Working with Files

In Chapter 7 you learned how to create new workbooks and how to save and close a workbook. In that chapter we also presented a procedure to save and close all open workbooks. In this section, we teach you further tasks that you will need to be able to deal with files from your VBA code.

12.3.1 Get Information about Files

The first thing you might need is the ability to obtain information about your files. We show two different ways of doing this.

Consider first the code in Figure 12.5. We start by opening a workbook by the *Open* method of the *workbooks* collection. Note that we give the *full path* to the file as input to this method. If only the name of the file is given, the computer will search in the standard file location which is *MyDocuments* on most computers. In this code, we assume that the workbook is located in the same folder as the file of the code.

```
Sub OpenInfoSaveAsClose()
    Dim W As Workbook
    Dim WBName As String

    WBName = ThisWorkbook.Path & "\wb2.xlsx"
    Set W = Workbooks.Open(WBName)

    ThisWorkbook.Activate
    Range("A1") = W.Name
    Range("A2") = W.Path
    Range("A3") = W.FullName
    Range("A4") = W.HasPassword
    Range("A5") = W.FileFormat

    W.SaveAs FileName:="newfile", FileFormat:=51
    W.Close
End Sub
```

12.5 BASIC FILE OPERATIONS.

Next, we write a list of information about the workbook: The *name* of the file, the *path*, and the *FullName*. The latter contains both the name and the path. *HasPassword* returns either *True* or *False,* and *FileFormat* is an integer number specifying the type of the file. See Table 12.1 for a list of the main file formats that you are likely to use in your program. Other formats can be found in the help system.

Next in Figure 12.5, we use the *SaveAs* method to save the workbook. Here, we specify the name and the file format. You can give the full name, including the path to ensure that the file is stored in the right location. If the file is only modified and not new, the *Save* method can be used instead. Finally, the workbook is closed using the *Close* method of the *workbook* object.

12.1 THE BASIC FILE FORMATS.

51	Standard Workbook format
52	Macro Enabled Workbook
35	Text Format
44	HTML format

Using the above method you can only obtain information for open workbooks, but you can obtain information about other files by accessing the file system as we do in Figure 12.6. We let *sys* be a *FileSystemObject* variable, let *F* hold a folder, and let *MyFile* hold a file.

First, we make sure to get in touch with the file system and we use that to reach the folder we are interested in. Next, we use a For-Each loop to consider each file in the folder, and write information about the file to the active workbook.

```
Sub GetFileInformation()
    Dim sys As FileSystemObject
    Dim F As Folder
    Dim MyFile As File
    Dim count As Integer

    count = 1
    Set sys = New FileSystemObject
    Set F = sys.GetFolder(ThisWorkbook.Path)

    For Each MyFile In F.files
        Cells(count + 1, 1) = MyFile.Name
        Cells(count + 1, 2) = MyFile.DateCreated
        Cells(count + 1, 3) = MyFile.DateLastAccessed
        Cells(count + 1, 4) = MyFile.ShortName
        Cells(count + 1, 5) = MyFile.Size
        Cells(count + 1, 6) = MyFile.Type
        Cells(count + 1, 7) = MyFile.ParentFolder
        count = count + 1
    Next
End Sub
```

12.6 OBTAIN FILE INFORMATION.

12.3.2 Check if a File Exists

Trying to open a file that does not exist causes and error. Therefore, before opening a specific file it is always a good idea to check if the file exists. Consider the code in Figure 12.7 where *FileName* is the name of the file we are looking for, and *Pa* is the path to the folder we want to search in. In the last part of the procedure we show two ways of using the *FileExists* method for checking if a file exists. First, we only specify the name of the file. By default the search will take place in the folder of the file containing the code. Next, we specify the whole path of the file to search for. The method returns *True* if the file exists and *False* otherwise.

```
Sub CheckFileExists()
    Dim sys As FileSystemObject
    Dim FileName As String
    Dim Pa As String

    Set sys = New FileSystemObject
    Pa = ThisWorkbook.Path
    FileName = "test.xlsx"

    'check in this folder:
    MsgBox sys.FileExists(FileName)
    'check in specific folder:
    MsgBox sys.FileExists(Pa & "\First\" & FileName)
End Sub
```

12.7 CHECK IF A GIVEN FILE EXISTS.

12.3.3 Check if a Workbook is Open

It is not enough to know that a file exists. We must also ensure that it is not already open before we try to open it. Trying to open a file that is already open will cause an error. In Figure 12.8, there are two procedures. The function *CheckWorkBookOpen* returns *True* if the file is open, and *False* otherwise.

```
Function CheckWorkBookOpen(WBName As String) As Boolean
    'Input is full path of workbook
    Dim W As Workbook

    CheckWorkBookOpen = False
    For Each W In Workbooks
        If W.FullName = WBName Then
            CheckWorkBookOpen = True
        End If
    Next

End Function

Sub UseCheckWorkBookOpen()
    Dim WBName As String
    Dim answer As Boolean

    WBName = ThisWorkbook.Path & "\First\test3.xlsx"

    answer = CheckWorkBookOpen(WBName)
    MsgBox answer
End Sub
```

12.8 CHECK IF A GIVEN WORKBOOK IS OPEN.

We are given a string which contains the full name of the file we are looking for, including the path. Using a For-Next loop, we search through every open workbook to check if their *FullPath* matches the string we are looking for, in which case we conclude that the file is open. The sub illustrates how to use the function.

12.3.4 Count Workbooks in Folder

The final procedure in this section is shown in Figure 12.9. It looks for specific file names in a folder. In this case we look for files that are called *WB*.xlsx*. The code can be modified to look for all excel files or all customer files etc.

We do this by iterating through the files of a folder using a For-Each loop. In the body of the loop, we check if the name matches the name we are looking for. If so, we write the name in the active worksheet and open the file. Besides opening the files, they are counted and at the end of the code the number is displayed.

```
Sub CountAndOpenAllWorkbooks()
    Dim sys As FileSystemObject
    Dim F As Folder
    Dim MyFile As File
    Dim W As Workbook
    Dim fileext As String
    Dim count As Integer

    fileext = "xlsx"
    count = 0
    Set sys = New FileSystemObject
    Set F = sys.GetFolder(ThisWorkbook.Path)

    For Each MyFile In F.files
        If UCase(MyFile.Name) Like "WB*." & UCase(fileext) Then
            Cells(count + 1, 1) = MyFile.Name
            Set W = Workbooks.Open(ThisWorkbook.Path & "\" & MyFile.Name)
            count = count + 1
        End If
    Next

    MsgBox "There are " & count & " files of type ." & fileext
End Sub
```

12.9 FIND WORKBOOKS IN A FOLDER.

12.4 Working with Text Files

In this section, we show how to read from and write to text files. In the examples we use a *TextStream* object variable which we call *textfile* and we let *sys* be a *FileSystemObject* variable. We use *P* to hold the path to the files we are working with and let *N* hold the name of the text file. That way it should be easy to keep focus on the new material in this section. In the examples we assume that the files are located in the same folder as the file containing the code.

In the code in Figure 12.10, we first create a new text file. The second argument indicates that if a file of the specified name already exists, it may be overwritten. After the creation, a single line of text is written to the file which is then closed.

```
Sub CreateTextFile()
    Dim sys As FileSystemObject
    Dim textfile As TextStream
    Dim P As String
    Dim N As String

    P = ThisWorkbook.Path
    N = "datafile.txt"

    Set sys = New FileSystemObject
    Set textfile = sys.CreateTextFile(P & "\" & N, True)

    textfile.WriteLine ("First line in text file.")
    textfile.Close
End Sub
```

12.10 CREATE A TEXT FILE.

The code in Figure 12.11 illustrates different ways of writing to a file. First, the text file is opened using the *OpenTextFile* method of the *TextStream* objects. Text files are opened either for reading or writing. The second argument in this example indicates that the file should be opened for appending text, i.e. for writing.

```
Sub WriteToTextFile()
    Dim sys As FileSystemObject
    Dim textfile As TextStream
    Dim P As String
    Dim N As String

    P = ThisWorkbook.Path
    N = "datafile.txt"

    Set sys = New FileSystemObject
    Set textfile = sys.OpenTextFile(P & "\" & N, ForAppending)

    textfile.Write ("This is a line without break.")
    textfile.WriteLine ("This is a line with break.")
    textfile.WriteLine ("Name of the file is " & N)
    textfile.WriteBlankLines (2)
    textfile.WriteLine ("This is the final line.")

    textfile.Close
End Sub
```

12.11 WRITING TO A TEXT FILE.

The *TextStream* object supports three write methods which are all used in this example: *Write, WriteLine*, and *WriteBlankLines*. The *WriteLine* method writes a string and adds a newline character at the end. The *Write* method writes the string without adding a newline character, and finally, the *WriteBlankLines* merely writes the specified number of newline characters. Figure 12.12 shows the file resulting from executing the code in Figure 12.10 followed by the one in Figure 12.11.

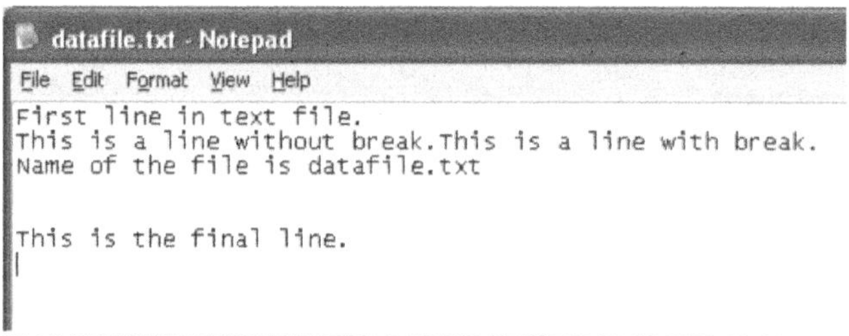

12.12 RESULT OF EXECUTING THE CODE IN FIGURES 12.10 AND 12.11.

Figure 12.13 illustrates how to open a text file for reading. Note how the second argument of the *OpenTextFile* method now specifies that the file should be opened for reading. In the example we read a whole line at a time – including the newline character – using the *ReadLine* method. We continue until the *AtEndOfStream* property is True, indicating that we reached the end. Note that empty lines, i.e. lines only containing the newline character, are also lines. Alternatively, the *Read* method can be used to read a specified number of characters.

```
Sub ReadFromTextFile()
    Dim sys As FileSystemObject
    Dim textfile As TextStream
    Dim P As String
    Dim N As String
    Dim i As Integer

    P = ThisWorkbook.Path
    N = "datafile.txt"

    Set sys = New FileSystemObject
    Set textfile = sys.OpenTextFile(P & "\" & N, ForReading)

    i = 1
    While Not textfile.AtEndOfStream
        Cells(i, 1) = textfile.ReadLine()
        i = i + 1
    Wend
    textfile.Close
End Sub
```

12.13 READING FROM A TEXT FILE.

Data is sometimes stored in space-separated text files. Such files can be opened in excel, writing each line in a new row and shifting one cell to the right when a space character is met. The code in Figure 12.14 illustrates how to do this. The second argument specifies that the space character should determine the shifting to the right, and the third argument states that consecutive spaces should be read as one.

```
Sub ReadSpaceSeparatedFile()
    Dim P As String
    Dim N As String
    Dim W As Workbook

    P = ThisWorkbook.Path
    N = "A10A.dat"

    Workbooks.OpenText Filename:=P & "\" & N, _
            Space:=True, _
            ConsecutiveDelimiter:=True

    Set W = Workbooks(N)
    W.Worksheets(1).Name = "Data"
End Sub
```

12.14 OPEN A TEXT FILE IN A WORKBOOK.

Sometimes you might also need to create your output as a space separated text file. The code in Figure 12.15 gives an example of doing this.

```
Sub SaveAsSpaceSeparatedFile()
    Dim W As Workbook
    Dim P As String
    Dim N As String

    P = ThisWorkbook.Path
    N = "datafile.txt"

    Set W = Workbooks.Add
    'Code to add data

    W.SaveAs Filename:=P & "\" & N, FileFormat:=xlTextPrinter
    W.Close (False)
End Sub
```

12.15 SAVE A WORKBOOK AS A TEXT FILE.

12.5 Exercises

12.1. Save the file. Create a sub that writes the *name*, the *path,* and the *full path* of this file to sheet1.

12.2. Make a sub that does the following:
1. Makes a new file.
2. Writes something in sheet1 of the new file.
3. Writes something else in Sheet1 of this file (the file of the code).
4. Uses *SaveAs* to save the new file.
5. Closes the new file.

12.3. Write a sub that
1. Opens the file you made in Exercise 12.2.
2. Writes something to the file.
3. Uses *Save* to save the changes.
4. Closes the file.

12.4. Open a few Excel files. Write a sub that uses the *Count* method to count and display the number of open files.

12.5. Include a reference to the FileSystemObject. Write a sub that counts and displays the number of files in the current folder.

12.6. Open the data file for this exercise. Create a text file. Create a sub that writes the information of sheet 1 of the data file to the text file and closes is.

12.7. Write a sub that opens the text file you created in Exercise 12.6 and reads the information from the text file to the worksheet.

The following exercises create a file system to keep track of the employees of a company.

12.8. Write a sub that creates two folders called *FormerEmployees* and *Employees*. You will need to know the exact or the relative path to these folders in the following exercises.

12.9. Write a sub that can be used when a new employee is hired. The sub should locate the *Employees* folder and create a subfolder of it. This folder should be named using the name of the Employee: Peter Hansen,

Jannie Skov, or Claus Madsen, for example. Use an input box to obtain the name of the employee. Furthermore, the sub should create three Excel files in the folder. These should be called *PersonalData*, *Training*, and *Salary*. In each of these files should cell A1 contain the name and cell A2 the date of employment start. The latter can also be obtained through an input box. All the files should be closed by the end of the sub.

12.10. Write a sub that can be used when the employment of a person stops. The sub should move the person's folder – including the files in it – to the *FormerEmployees* folder.

12.11. White a sub that iterates through all current employees and writes the name and date of employment start in the workbook of the code.

Chapter 13
Strings

A *string* is a piece of text. It can be as short as one or even zero characters and as long as about 2 billion characters. Strings are not numbers, so you cannot perform arithmetic operations on strings. Instead you can concatenate strings and perform a number of other operations.

In Section 13.1, we introduce the string variable and the basic string operations and in Section 13.2, we discuss some of the built-in functions that work on strings.

13.1 Working with Strings

Just like any other variable, String variables are declared using the *Dim* keyword. There are two types of strings: *fixed length* strings and *variable length* strings. Declaration of the two types is illustrated in Figure 13.1.

```
Dim VS As String

Dim FS As String * 25
```

13.1 DECLARATION OF STRING VARIABLES

A *variable length* string can hold as many as approximately 2 billion characters, but the memory usage is 10 bytes + the number of characters used. The variable VS in Figure 13.1 is a variable length string.

For *fixed length* strings, the programmer must specify in the declaration how many characters the string should hold. This is illustrated with FS in Figure 13.1. If the string exceed this limit, it will automatically be truncated. The maximum length of a fixed length string is approximately 64000 characters, and the memory usage for fixed length strings corresponds to the maximum number of characters given in the declaration.

Even though using fixed length strings can potentially save memory, it is recommended to use variable length strings due to the risk of unintentional truncation.

To assign text to a string variable, the text should be surrounded by quotation signs as shown for the variable *s* in Figure 13.2. Here, it is also shown how the value of a string variable can be used in a range or displayed in a message box. The variable *t* is used to show how an *empty string* can be assigned to a variable.

```
Dim s As String
Dim t As String

s = "Customer information"
t = ""

Range("A4") = s
MsgBox s
```

13.2 ASSIGNING A STRING TO A STRING VARIABLE.

Strings can be concatenated, i.e. glued together, using the & character. This is illustrated in Figure 13.3 where *s* is the concatenation of a string containing the word *Vehicle* and a space, the value of the variable *k* which is 4, and a string containing first a space, then the phase *of 10.* The message box on the left-hand side of Figure 13.4 displays the value of *s*. The value of the string *t* is the concatenation of a string consisting of the word *Secondary* followed by a space and the string *s*. The right-hand side message box of Figure 13.4 displays the value of *t*.

```
Dim s As String
Dim t As String
Dim k As Integer
k = 4

s = "Vehicle " & k & " of 10."
t = "Secondary " & s

MsgBox s
MsgBox t
```

13.3 CONCATENATION OF STRINGS.

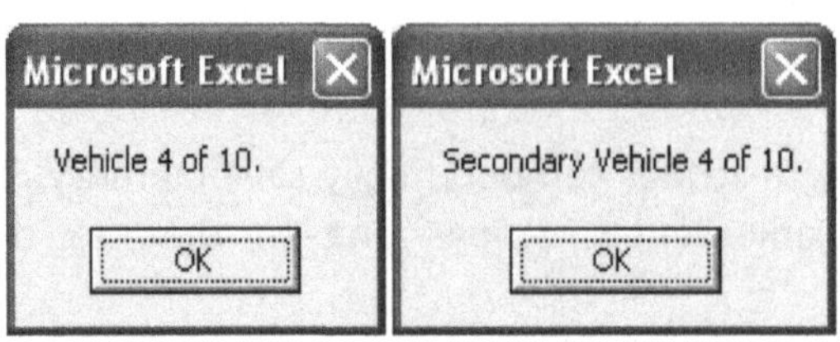

13.4 MESSAGE BOXES CREATED BY THE CODE IN FIGURE 13.3

Special constants are provided for the purpose of breaking the text into a new line and for tabbing. The most important ones are shown in Table 13.1.

13.1 SPECIAL STRING VALUES.

vbTab	Tab character
vbCr	Carriage return character
vbNewLine	Platform-specific new line character; whichever is appropriate for current platform

The code in Figure 13.5 illustrates how *vbTab* and *vbCr* can be used for displaying a table. It is assumed in the code that *text* is a string variable and that *Load* is an array containing five integer values. The resulting message box is shown in Figure 13.6.

```
text = "Vehicle " & vbTab & "Load" & vbCr
For j = 1 To 5
   text = text & j & vbTab & Load(j) & vbCr
Next

MsgBox text
```

13.5 USING THE SPECIAL STRING VALUES OF TABLE 13.1.

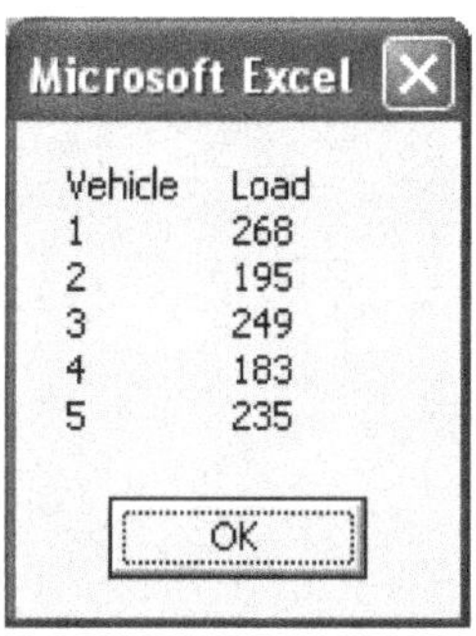

13.6 MESSAGE BOX CREATED BY THE CODE IN FIGURE 13.5.

13.2 String Functions

VBA offers many functions for manipulating strings. Some of these are shown in Table 13.2.

The code in Figure 13.7 illustrates the use of many of these functions. The result of executing the code is given in Figure 13.8. The example uses the string variable *text* which contains a name. The functions *LCase* and

UCase convert text to lowercase and uppercase letters, respectively, whereas *StrReverse* reverses the string.

13.2 STRING FUNCTIONS.

Join	Returns a string obtained by concatenating a number of strings.
LCase	Returns a string that has been converted to lowercase.
Left	Returns the specified number of characters from the left side of a string.
Len	Returns the number of characters in a string.
Mid	Returns a string with the specified number of characters starting at a specific location of a string.
Right	Returns the specified number of characters from the right side of a string.
Space	Returns a string consisting of a specified number of spaces.
Split	Splits a string into an array.
Trim	Returns a copy of a string without leading and trailing spaces. See also LTrim and RTrim.
UCase	Returns a string that has been converted to uppercase.

```
text = "Hans Peter Jensen"

Range("A1") = text
Range("A2") = LCase(text)
Range("A3") = UCase(text)
Range("A4") = StrReverse(text)

Range("C1") = Left(text, 7)
Range("C2") = Right(text, 7)
Range("C3") = Mid(text, 3, 4)
Range("C4") = Left(text, 4) & _
              Space(7) & Right(text, 6)
```

13.7 ILLUSTRATION OF STRING FUNCTIONS.

Left, *Right*, and *Mid* return a partial string as follows. *Left* returns as many characters as stated by the second argument – starting from the left. *Right* does the same, but from the end of the string, and *Mid* starts at the location specified by the second argument and returns as many characters as given by the third argument. Note that spaces are also characters, which explains why the content of cell C2 starts with a space.

Finally, the *Space* function returns a string containing as many spaces as specified, which can be seen in cell C4 where 7 spaces are placed between first name and last name.

	A	B	C
1	Hans Peter Jensen		Hans Pe
2	hans peter jensen		Jensen
3	HANS PETER JENSEN		ns P
4	nesneJ reteP snaH		Hans Jensen

13.8 RESULT OF EXECUTING THE CODE IN FIGURE 13.6.

The Trim function returns a string with leading and trailing spaces removed. This is illustrated in Figure 13.9 where the content of cell C5 is shown below the code. Note how the spaces surrounding *Y* are removed before the three strings are concatenated.

```
Range("C5") = "X" & Trim("  Y     ") & "Z"
```

XYZ

13.9 ILLUSTRATION OF THE TRIM FUNCTION.

The final example illustrates how the *Split* function can be used to partition a string and store the parts in an array. By default, the delimiter is *spaces*, but others can be used. The function places one word in each location of the array. Consider the code in Figure 13.10 where the corresponding worksheet is shown to the right. The function *UBound* gives the highest index of an array.

```
Sub IllustrateSplitArray()
    Dim A() As String
    Dim s As String
    Dim j As Integer

    s = "VBA Programming in Business Economics "

    A = Split(s)

    For j = 0 To UBound(A)
        Cells(j + 1, 1) = A(j)
    Next
End Sub
```

	A
1	VBA
2	Programming
3	in
4	Business
5	Economics
6	

13.10 SPLITTING A STRING INTO AN ARRAY OF SMALLER STRINGS.

13.3 Exercises

13.1. Open the file for this exercise. Write a sub iterates through the names and writes the first name in column B, the family name in column D, and any middle names in column C.

13.2. Open the file with your solution of Exercise 13.1. Write a sub that iterates through the names and writes a short version of the names, for instance S. Wøhlk or P. Madsen, in column E.

13.3. Open the file with your solution of Exercise 13.2. Write a sub that displays a message box showing a table with the information of the worksheet.

13.4. Write a sub that renames sheet 1 of the active workbook to be the current date.

13.5. Write a sub that obtains a string through an input box and checks if the string is a palindrome, i.e. a word that is spelled equivalently forwards and backwards (for example radar, Hannah, or 2002). If this is the case a confirmation message box should be displayed.

Chapter 14
Charts

Charts are extremely useful because many people absorb information much better when it is visualized in a chart rather than a table. In this chapter we show how to create charts through the VBA code.

The chart object of Excel is very comprehensive and we will not be able to cover all of it in this book. Instead we show examples of how to create and modify charts. To perform tasks that are not explained here, the reader can use the help system and the Internet for inspiration. Furthermore, the macro recorder is useful for obtaining the name of specific settings etc.

In Section 14.1, we introduce the two different types of objects for charts and show how to create and access charts. In Section 14.2, we present some basic chart operations such as deleting charts and determining if a given chart exists. Finally in Section 14.3, we consider a number of chart cases and through these we show how to create charts and how to modify them.

14.1 Chart Sheets and Embedded Charts

Charts can be created in two ways: As a *Chart Sheet* or as an *Embedded Chart*. A *chart sheet* is a sheet in the workbook just like the worksheets, except that the only purpose of chart sheets is to hold a chart. No data or other information can be stored in a chart sheet. Each chart sheet is included in the *Charts* collection object which is member of the *WorkBook* object. Chart sheets are also included in the *Sheets* collection which is a collection of all sheets in a workbook – including both worksheets and chart sheets. An *embedded chart* is a chart that is places in a worksheet along with data and other information. Such a chart object is located in a special container called a *ChartObject* object which is a member of the *ChartObjects* collection of a worksheet.

The difference between the two ways of creating charts is illustrated in Figure 14.1 where we first show how to create an embedded chart and then how to create a chart sheet.

Note that to create a chart sheet, we create a variable of type *Chart*, whereas to create an embedded chart, a variable of type *ChartObject* is needed. Note also how the embedded chart is under a worksheet in the object hierarchy, whereas the chart sheet is right below the workbook.

```
'Create an embedded chart:
Dim MyChart As ChartObject
Set MyChart = ThisWorkbook.Worksheets(1).ChartObjects.Add

'Create a chart sheet:
Dim YourChart As Chart
Set YourChart = ThisWorkbook.Charts.Add
```

14.1 CREATION OF EMBEDDED CHART AND CHART SHEET, RESPECTIVELY.

After creating a chart, it is recommended that the chart is given a name using the *name* property of the *ChartObject* object and the *Chart* object, respectively. This is illustrated in Figure 14.2. Note that these are different objects and hence the names do not conflict.

```
MyChart.name = "Sales"

YourChart.name = "Sales"
```

14.2 GIVE YOUR CHART A NAME.

To access an existing chart, the same strategy is used. This is illustrated in Figure 14.3 where we show two ways of accessing each of the two kinds of charts. Accessing a chart by specifying the name is preferable, but it is possible to use and index instead. In the figure, it is assumed that the file contains a chart sheet called *Sales* and that the first worksheet contains a chart called *Sales* as well.

```
'Access an embedded chart:
Dim MyChart As ChartObject
Set MyChart = ThisWorkbook.Worksheets(1).ChartObjects("Sales")
Set MyChart = ThisWorkbook.Worksheets(1).ChartObjects(2)

'Access a chart sheet:
Dim YourChart As Chart
Set YourChart = ThisWorkbook.Charts("Sales")
Set YourChart = ThisWorkbook.Charts(2)
```

14.3 ACCESS EXISTING CHARTS.

An obvious way to proceed is to specify the type of the chart (bar chart, column chart, doughnut chart, etc) followed by specifying the data to be used, and concluding with a bunch of formatting.

Figure 14.4 shows how the type is specified for each of the two charts. For *YourChart*, which refers to a chart sheet, this is done by specifying the value of the *ChartType* property of the *Chart* object. For *MyChart*, which is an embedded chart, the process is a little different. Remember from above that *MyChart* is a *ChartObject* object which is a container for the Chart. Hence, to specify the type, we use the *ChartType* property of *Chart* of the *ChartObject* object. You will find the same difference between charts in chart sheets and embedded charts for most of the tasks you want to perform – for embedded charts there is an extra level in the object hierarchy.

```
MyChart.Chart.ChartType = xlLine

YourChart.ChartType = xlLine
```

14.4 SPECIFY THE TYPE OF YOUR CHART.

If you are used to working in Excel, you know that there are many types of charts. From the *Insert* menu in Excel you can open the *Insert Chart* dialog box shown in Figure 14.5. The name of the type is displayed if the pointer is held over the illustration.

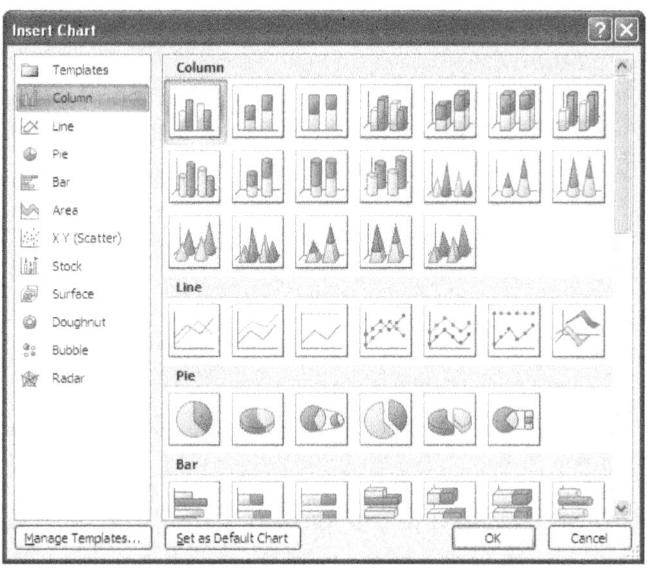

14.5 THE INSERT CHART DIALOG BOX.

Each type has its own value in VBA. By selecting *XlChartType* in the Object Browser, a list of chart type values is displayed as shown in Figure 14.6. The names are rather descriptive, so it should not be hard to match them with the chart illustrations in Figure 14.5.

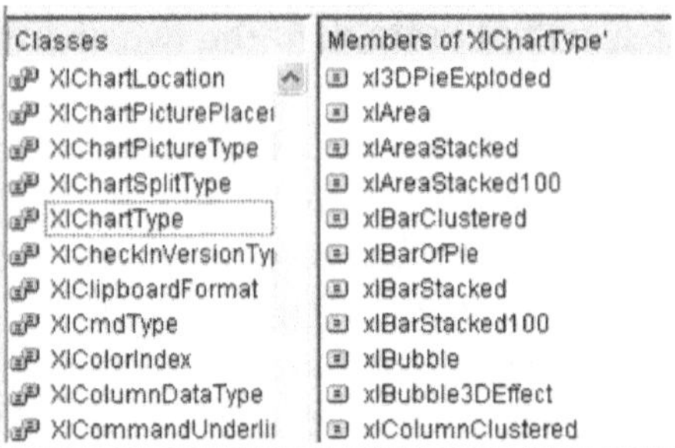

14.6 THE CHART TYPES TO USE IN YOUR CODE ARE FOUND IN THE OBJECT BROWSER.

14.2 Basic Chart Operations

Most of this chapter is about creating and modifying charts but there are several other small tasks that are useful when working with charts. Some of these will be considered in this section.

14.2.1 Check if a Chart Exists

Trying to create a chart sheet with the same name as an existing chart sheet will cause an error. It is therefore useful to be able to check whether a given chart sheet name is already being used. The *SheetExists* function in Figure 14.7 returns *True* if a chart sheet exists with the name given as input, and returns *False* otherwise.

We let *S* be a *Chart* object variable and use a For-Each loop to let *S* iterate through all *Chart* objects in the *Charts* collection of the workbook. In the body of the loop we check the *name* of the current sheet.

```
Function SheetExists(name As String) As Boolean
    Dim S As Chart
    SheetExists = False
    For Each S In ThisWorkbook.Charts
        If S.name = name Then
          SheetExists = True
        End If
    Next
End Function
```
14.7 CHECK IF CHART SHEET EXISTS.

Trying to create a *ChartObject* object in a worksheet with the same name as another *ChartObject* object in the same worksheet will not cause an error. It is, however, highly recommended not to allow the use of the same name twice as it will be uncertain which object is returned when the name is subsequently used to obtain the object.

The *ChartExists* function in Figure 14.8 returns *True* if a *ChartObject* with the input name exists in the worksheet and returns *False* otherwise.

The structure of the function is the same as for the one above, except that we are now working with embedded charts instead of chart sheets.

```
Function ChartExists(name As String) As Boolean
    Dim s As ChartObject
    ChartExists = False
    For Each s In ThisWorkbook.ActiveSheet.ChartObjects
        If s.name = name Then
          ChartExists = True
        End If
    Next
End Function
```

14.8 CHECK IF AN EMBEDDED CHART EXISTS.

14.2.2 Delete Charts

The procedure in Figure 14.9 deletes all embedded charts in a worksheet. This can easily be done by iterating through the members of the *ChartObjects* collection and using the *Delete* method on each *ChartObject* object.

```
Sub DeleteAllEmbeddedCharts()
    Dim MyChart As ChartObject
    For Each MyChart In ActiveSheet.ChartObjects
        MyChart.Delete
    Next
End Sub
```

14.9 DELETE ALL EMBEDDED CHARTS IN A WORKSHEET.

The procedure in Figure 14.10 deletes all chart sheets in a workbook. When deleting a worksheet, an alert will appear asking if you are sure you want to delete the sheet. The same is true when you try to delete a chart sheet. Therefore, before we start deleting chart sheets, we turn off the alerts. We do, of course, remember to turn the alerts back on at the end of the code.

```
Sub DeleteAllChartSheets()
    Dim C As Chart

    Application.DisplayAlerts = False
    For Each C In ThisWorkbook.Charts
        C.Delete
    Next
    Application.DisplayAlerts = True
End Sub
```

14.10 DELETE ALL CHART SHEETS IN A WORKBOOK.

14.2.3 Display Names of Charts

The procedure in Figure 14.11 displays a series of message boxes with the names of the embedded charts in the active worksheet. Names of chart sheets can be displayed in a similar way.

```
Sub DisplayNamedEmbeddedCharts()
    Dim W As Worksheet
    Dim MyChart As ChartObject

    Set W = ThisWorkbook.ActiveSheet
    For Each MyChart In W.ChartObjects
        MsgBox MyChart.name
    Next
End Sub
```

14.11 DISPLAY THE NAMES OF ALL EMBEDDED CHARTS IN A WORKBOOK.

14.3 Charts in Action

In this section, we illustrate the creation and modification of charts through a number of examples. This should give the reader a base for working with charts.

14.3.1 Example: Sales

In the first example, which was also used in Chapter 2, we consider the sales information given in Figure 14.12 for each of four areas over a five year period. The goal is to create a line chart where each of the four areas represents a data series. Skip forward to Figure 14.14 to get a preview of the chart we want to create.

We use this example to show two different ways of creating an embedded chart, and finally we show how the same chart can be created as a chart sheet.

	A	B	C	D	E	F
1				Sales		
2						
3		Year 1	Year 2	Year 3	Year 4	Year 5
4	Area 1	230000	245000	256000	156300	174300
5	Area 2	327500	339000	371000	290000	310500
6	Area 3	432000	447900	468000	350500	367800
7	Area 4	210000	225000	234800	224800	221000
8						

14.12 SALES DATA.

14.3.1.1 Basic Creation of Charts

In the first method, we leave as much as possible to Excel. Consider the code in Figure 14.13. As explained in Section 14.1, we first declare a *ChartObject* object variable. We call it *MyChart*. Remember, this is an embedded chart, so *MyChart* is the container of the chart – not the chart itself.

Next, we want to use the *Add* method of the *ChartsObjects* collection to add a new chart to the collection. Because we are dealing with objects, we use the *Set* keyword to let *MyChart* hold the newly created object. The *Add* method takes four arguments to specify the location of the chart on the worksheet and to size of the chart: The distance from the *left* side and the *top* of cell A1 to the upper left corner of the chart, respectively, followed by the *width* and the *height* of the chart. All values are given here in absolute terms. Subsequent examples show other ways of specifying the location and size of a chart.

After creating the chart container, we use the *name* property to specify a name. That way we can always find the chart again. Note that the name is not displayed anywhere on the chart, but is only used to identify them. Think about is this way: What is displayed is the chart, but the name belongs to the container – not the chart. For *Chart Sheets* the name is displayed just like the names of worksheets are displayed.

Everything else that we need to do in this example deals with the chart itself, so we use a With-End-With construction to take us to *MyChart.Chart*, i.e. to the chart contained in the *ChartObject* object.

```
Sub Simple()
    Dim MyChart As ChartObject

    Set MyChart = _
        ThisWorkbook.ActiveSheet.ChartObjects.Add _
        (300, 300, 300, 200)

    MyChart.name = "Sales Chart"
    With MyChart.Chart

        .ChartType = xlLine
        .SetSourceData Source:=Range("A3:F7")
        .HasTitle = True
        .ChartTitle.Text = Range("B1")

        .HasLegend = True 'default

        .Axes(xlCategory).HasTitle = True
        .Axes(xlCategory).AxisTitle.Caption = "Year"
        .Axes(xlValue).HasTitle = True
        .Axes(xlValue).AxisTitle.Caption = "Area"
    End With
End Sub
```

14.13 CREATE A SIMPLE LINE CHART.

We use *ChartType* to specify that the chart should be of type *xlLine* which is a standard line chart. Next, we use *SetSourceData* to give the range containing the data. By letting the range contain the top and left headings, Excel automatically assumes that the left-hand side headings specify the names of the series and the top headings give the categories.

Executing the code that we have so far would give us the chart of Figure 2.7 in Chapter 2. The remaining part of the code is formatting. We use *HasTitle* to state that the chart has a title and use *ChartTitle.Text* to specify the text to be displayed. For this you can use a reference to a cell, the content of a variable, or specify a string of text. If you want to change the formatting of the title text, you can do that using *ChartTitle.Font* followed by *.Size*, *.Bold*, or *.Name*, etc.

We use *HasLegend* to ensure that the legend is displayed. The legend is the little box that is usually displayed on the right-hand side of the chart giving information about the color coding and names of the different series. The legend is displayed by default, and you can leave that line of code out if you prefer.

The final four lines of code ensure that the two axis titles are displayed. We use the *Axes* collection to take us to the specific axis: *xlCategory* is the x-axis and *xlValue* is the y-axis. Here we use *HasTitle* to state that a title should be displayed and *AxisTitle.Caption* to specify the text to be displayed. It should come as no surprise by now that you can use *AxisTitle.Font.Size* and *AxisTitle.Font.Color*, etc. to change the formatting of the text being displayed on the axes. Furthermore, you can use *AxisTitle.Orientation*, etc to further specify how the axis text should be displayed. The object browser is extremely helpful in figuring out the correct keyword to use to perform the formatting you want. The chart created by the code in Figure 14.13 is displayed in Figure 14.14.

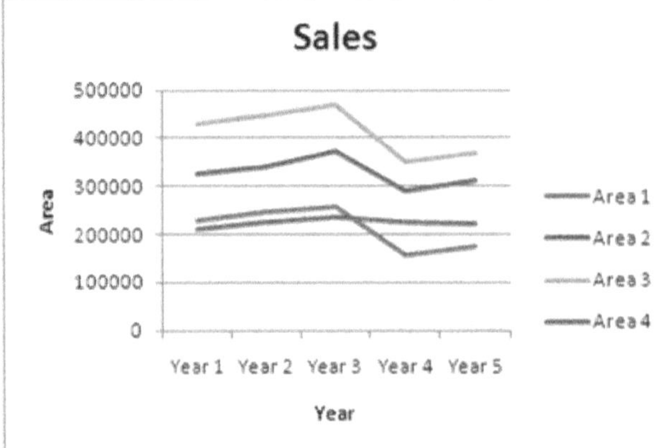

14.14 LINE CHART CREATED BY THE CODE IN FIGURE 14.13.

14.3.1.2 Another Way of Creating the Sales Chart

Even though in this example we can find the headings right to the left and above the data area, respectively, this is not always the case. Sometimes there is a huge amount of data which we only want to display a small fraction of. In that case, the cells with headings are not adjacent to the data area. The code in Figure 14.15 is a modified version of the code just described. In the new code we manually specify the location of the headings.

```
Sub MakeSales()
    Dim MyChart As ChartObject
    Dim S As Integer

    Set MyChart = _
        ThisWorkbook.ActiveSheet.ChartObjects.Add _
        (300, 300, 300, 200)

    MyChart.name = "Second Sales Chart"
    With MyChart.Chart

        .ChartType = xlLine
        .SetSourceData Source:=Range("B4:F7")
        .HasTitle = True
        .ChartTitle.Text = Range("B1")
        .HasLegend = True 'Default

        For S = 1 To 4
            .SeriesCollection(S).name = Cells(3 + S, 1)
        Next

        .SeriesCollection(1).XValues = Range("B3:F3")

        .Axes(xlCategory).HasTitle = True
        .Axes(xlCategory).AxisTitle.Caption = "Year"
        .Axes(xlValue).HasTitle = True
        .Axes(xlValue).AxisTitle.Caption = "Area"
    End With
End Sub
```

14.15 CREATES THE SAME LINE CHART AS THE CODE IN FIGURE 14.13, BUT NOW WE SPECIFY THE HEADINGS MANUALLY.

The first difference to the code in Figure 14.13 is the specification of the source data where we now give the range including the data only.

The next difference is to be found about halfway through the code. Note in Figure 14.12 that the left-hand side headings, i.e. the series, are to be found in cells A4 through A7. In the code in Figure 14.15 we use a For-Next loop to iterate through the four series in order to specify the name of each of them – which corresponds to the content of those cells. Notice that we are within a With-End-With construction, so the statement actually reads *MyChart.Chart.SeriesCollection(s).name* where *s* is the index of the series. Hence, we consider each of the series in the *SeriesCollection* of our chart and set the name.

Setting the categories is a lot simpler. Here, we just consider one of the series – the first one, for instance – and state that the *XValues* are to be found in a given range. Here, cells B3 through F3. The remaining code in figure 14.15 is similar to the code in Figure 14.13.

14.3.1.3 Creating a Chart Sheet

In this section, we show how to modify the code of Figure 14.13 to create the chart as a *Chart Sheet* instead of an embedded chart. The resulting chart sheet is shown in Figure 14.16.

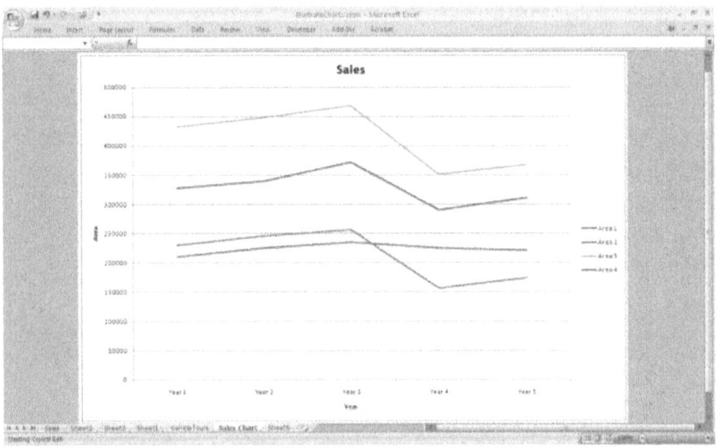

14.16 A LINE CHART IN A CHART SHEET.

Consider the code in Figure 14.17. The first thing to notice is that now *MyChart* is created to be a *Chart* object. Because an error message will appear if we try to create a chart sheet with the same name as an existing chart sheet, we start by obtaining a unique name. The *SheetExists* function is explained in section 14.2.

Next, the chart sheet is added and placed after the existing sheets. Since it is a chart sheet, we need not worry about the size and the location of the chart. Finally, the With-End-With construction works directly on *MyChart* because, unlike embedded charts, for chart sheets this is the chart itself.

Try to compare the code in Figure 14.17 to the code in Figure 14.13 to see how few changes it takes to create a chart sheet instead of an embedded chart.

```
Sub SalesChartSheet()
    Dim W As Worksheet
    Dim MyChart As Chart
    Dim name As String

    name = "Sales Chart"
    While SheetExists(name)
        name = InputBox("Sheet exists. Please specify another name:")
    Wend

    Set W = ThisWorkbook.Worksheets("Sales")
    Set MyChart = ThisWorkbook.Charts.Add(After:=Sheets(Sheets.Count))

    With MyChart
        .name = name
        .ChartType = xlLine
        .SetSourceData Source:=W.Range("A3:F7")
        .HasTitle = True
        .ChartTitle.Text = W.Range("B1")
        .HasLegend = True 'default

        .Axes(xlCategory).HasTitle = True
        .Axes(xlCategory).AxisTitle.Caption = "Year"
        .Axes(xlValue).HasTitle = True
        .Axes(xlValue).AxisTitle.Caption = "Area"
    End With
End Sub
```

14.17 CREATING A CHART SHEET.

14.3.2 Example: Advertisement

In this section, we consider the data in Figure 14.18 which shows the percentage of the advertisement budget spent in each of eight national regions. We use this example to illustrate some formatting issues.

	A	B
1	North	20%
2	South	55%
3	West	10%
4	S. East	1%
5	Central	4%
6	City A	3%
7	N. East	2%
8	Rest	5%
9		

14.18 ADVERTISEMENT DATA.

14.3.2.1 Basic Pie Chart

The code in Figure 14.19 creates a simple pie chart which is shown in Figure 14.20. This is an embedded chart so we let *MyChart* be a *ChartObject* object variable and add a new chart to the *ChartObjects* collection of the worksheet.

```
Sub MakePie()
    Dim W As Worksheet
    Dim MyChart As ChartObject

    Set W = ThisWorkbook.ActiveSheet
    Set MyChart = W.ChartObjects.Add(100, 100, 300, 200)

    MyChart.name = "Pie Chart"
    With MyChart.Chart
        .ChartType = xlPie
        .SetSourceData Source:=Range("B1:B8")

        .HasTitle = True
        .ChartTitle.Text = "Advertisement"

        .HasLegend = True
        .SeriesCollection(1).XValues = Range("A1:A8")
        .SetElement (msoElementDataLabelInsideEnd)
    End With
End Sub
```

14.19 CREATION OF A SIMPLE PIE CHART BASED ON THE DATA IN FIGURE 14.18

The *ChartType* is set to *xlPie* which is a standard pie chart and the source is given as cells B1 through B8, only - i.e. no headings. We let the headings be the categories in the chart by setting the *XValues* of *SeriesCollection(1)*. Notice that for pie charts, only one series can be used.

Finally, we want the data values to be displayed in the chart itself. This can be done with the *SetElement* method. Notice that a list of the allowed values for the argument of this method can be found by choosing *MsoChartElementType* in the left-hand side of the object browser. In this example we choose to place the data labels inside the colored area, but at the end of it.

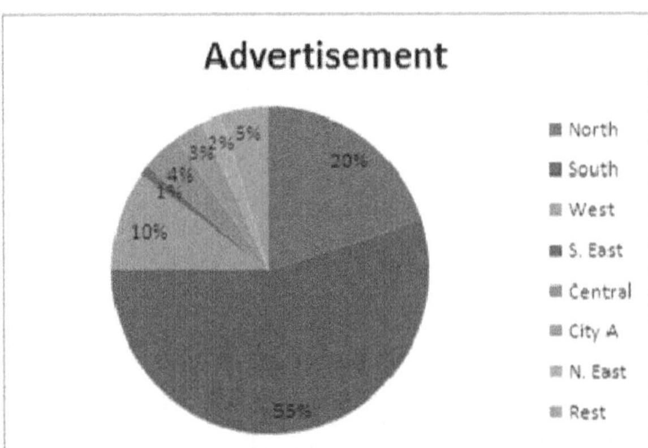

14.20 PIE CHART CREATED BY THE CODE IN FIGURE 14.19.

14.3.2.2 Formatting the Pie Chart

In this section, we show how the pie chart of the previous section can be modified with a nice modern styling. We do this by using the built-in styling system. The resulting chart is shown in Figure 14.21.

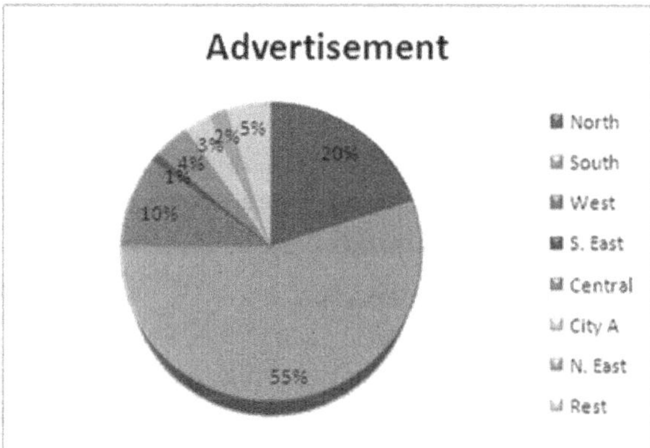

14.21 PIE CHART FORMATTED BY THE CODE IN FIGURE 14.22.

In the code in Figure 14.22 we let the object variable *MyChart* hold the existing chart created in the previous section. Note that if the chart does not exist, an error will occur at this point, so some code should be included to check for existence.

```
Sub FormatPie()
    Dim MyChart As ChartObject
    Set MyChart = Worksheets(1).ChartObjects("Pie Chart")

    With MyChart.Chart
        .ChartType = xl3DPie
        .ChartStyle = 25
        .ClearToMatchStyle
        .HeightPercent = 250
    End With
End Sub
```

14.22 CODE TO PERFORM FORMATTING OF THE PIE CHART.

Within the With-End-With construction, where we consider the chart, we start by changing the *ChartType* to be a nice 3D version of the pie chart. From your work in Excel, you know that if you activate a chart and select the *Design* menu in the Ribbon, you can choose between a wide range of predefined styles for your chart as illustrated in Figure 14.23 for the 3D pie chart. These are numbered, e.g. the left choice in row four is style number 25.

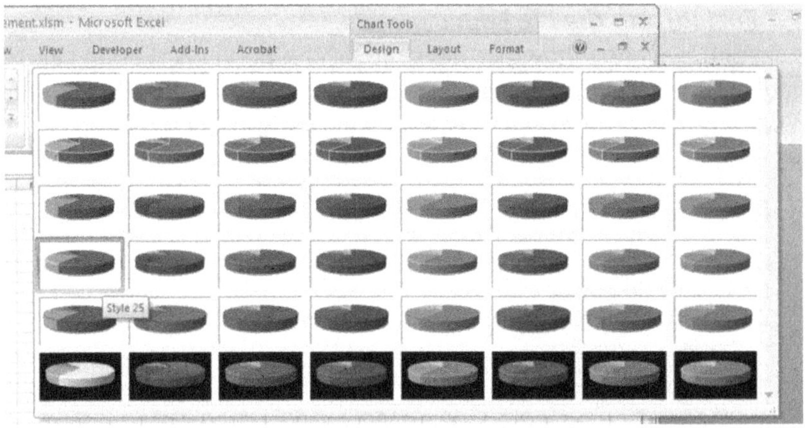

14.23 CHOOSE YOUR FAVORITE STYLE AND USE IT IN YOUR VBA CODE.

We access the predefined styles by using the *ChartStyle* property of the chart. After choosing a style, the *ClearToMatchStyle* method removes odd styling that may remain from any previous code. Note that the labels in the colored area remain because they are not part of the styling. Finally, we change the height of the pie to emphasize the 3D effect.

14.3.2.3 Create Bar of Pie Chart

As can be seen from the pie charts of Figures 14.20 and 14.21, some of the slices are really small. Therefore it might be desirable to use a so-called *Bar of Pie* chart instead. The code in Figure 14.24 creates such a chart. As you can see, the code is very similar to the one constructed in the previous sections.

```
Sub MakeBarOfPie()
    Dim W As Worksheet
    Dim MyChart As ChartObject

    Set W = ThisWorkbook.ActiveSheet
    Set MyChart = W.ChartObjects.Add(100, 100, 300, 200)

    MyChart.Name = "Bar of Pie Chart"
    With MyChart.Chart
        .ChartType = xlBarOfPie
        .SetSourceData Source:=Range("A1:B8")
        .ChartGroups(1).SplitValue = 5
        .HasTitle = True
        .ChartTitle.Text = "Global Sales Distribution"
        .ChartStyle = 9
        .SetElement (msoElementDataLabelCenter)
    End With
End Sub
```

14.24 CREATE A BAR OF PIE CHART.

The *ChartType* property is set to *xlBarOfPie*. Note that if you know what the chart is called, it is not hard to find the correct value for this property. To ease the coding, we give both the data and the labels as source and let the program figure out that column A contains the categories.

To specify that the last five categories are the ones to be included in the *bar* part of the chart, we set the *SplitValue* to 5. Note that the bar part is always the last part of the data.

Finally, we select the *ChartStyle* to be the fifth of the available styles for this type of chart and we set the labels to be shown in the center of the colored areas. The resulting chart is shown in Figure 14.25.

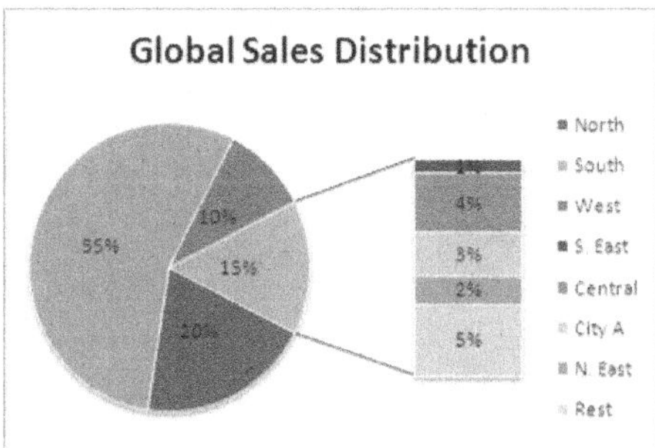

14.25 BAR OF PIE CHART CREATED BY THE CODE IN FIGURE 14.24.

14.3.3 Example: Members

In Chapter 6, we considered the problem of categorizing the members of an organization. The result of the work we did in that chapter was a table like the one shown in Figure 14.26 where the upper left corner is located in cell F5.

Age	Male	Female	Total
6	3	1	4
7	4	3	7
8	11	3	14
9	7	1	8
10	8	5	13
11	8	1	9
12	24	6	30
13	7	9	16
14	9	7	16
15	5	8	13
16	8	3	11
17	2	1	3
18	4		4
19	2	1	3

14.26 DATA ABOUT MEMBERS.

In this section, we consider the last part of the Membership problem, namely the creation of a chart that shows the age and gender distribution. This is also the section where we show how to copy charts.

14.3.3.1 Create Clustered Column Chart

Consider the code in Figure 14.27 where we first create a very basic embedded chart. Note that when we add the new *ChartObject* to the *ChartObjects* collection, we do not specify the arguments as fixed numbers. Instead, we state the location and size relative to the worksheet as follows. Let the left-hand side of the object be aligned with the left-hand side of cell K2 and let the top be aligned with the top of cell K2. Let the object be as wide as the range K2:P2 and as high as the range K2:K12, however wide and high these ranges are. Using this method you can ensure that your chart does not overlap with existing data, but you lose control of the actual size of your chart because the size of the cells might have been changed since you created the code.

```
Sub MakeMemberChart()
    Dim W As Worksheet
    Dim C As ChartObject

    Set W = ThisWorkbook.ActiveSheet
    Set C = W.ChartObjects.Add( _
        Left:=Range("K2").Left, _
        Top:=Range("K2").Top, _
        Width:=Range("K2:P2").Width, _
        Height:=Range("K2:K12").Height)

    C.name = "Clustered Column Chart"
    With C.Chart
        .ChartType = xlColumnClustered
        .SetSourceData Source:=Range("G5:I19")
        .HasTitle = True
        .ChartTitle.Text = "Age distribution of members"

        .HasLegend = True
        .SeriesCollection(1).XValues = Range("F6:F19")
        .Axes(xlCategory).HasTitle = True
        .Axes(xlCategory).AxisTitle.Caption = "Age"
        .Axes(xlValue).HasTitle = True
        .Axes(xlValue).AxisTitle.Caption = "Members"
    End With
End Sub
```

14.27 CODE TO CREATE THE CHART IN FIGURE 14.28 BASED ON THE DATA IN FIGURE 14.26

In this example we only specify the data area as source and hence, we have to specify the categories subsequently using the *XValues* property. The resulting chart is shown in Figure 14.28.

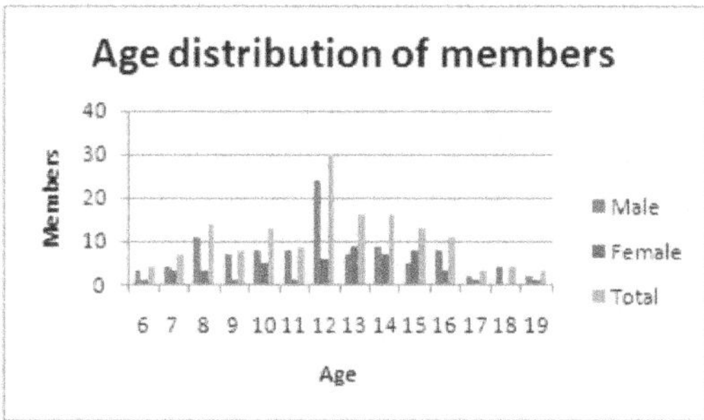

14.28 COLUMN CHART CREATED BY THE CODE IN FIGURE 14.27.

14.3.3.2 Copy Chart and Change Type

We now show how to copy one chart to another. Consider the code in Figure 14.29. We create two *ChartObject* object variables – one to hold the chart we want to copy and one to hold the destination. We start by letting the former hold the chart created in the previous section and use the *copy* method. Next, we create a new chart, or rather a new container for a chart and *paste* the copied chart into this container.

```
Sub CopyMembers()
    Dim W As Worksheet
    Dim C As ChartObject
    Dim n As ChartObject

    Set W = ThisWorkbook.ActiveSheet
    Set C = W.ChartObjects("Clustered Column Chart")
    C.Copy

    Set n = W.ChartObjects.Add( _
        Left:=Range("K25").Left, _
        Top:=Range("K25").Top, _
        Width:=Range("K25:S25").Width, _
        Height:=Range("K25:K40").Height)

    n.Chart.Paste
    n.Chart.SeriesCollection(3).Delete

    n.Chart.ChartType = xlCylinderCol
    n.Chart.ChartStyle = 33
    n.Chart.ClearToMatchStyle

End Sub
```

14.29 COPY A CHART.

Finally, we are ready to do some formatting. We start by removing the third series which is the *total*. Then we set the *ChartType* and the *ChartStyle*. The resulting chart is shown in Figure 14.30.

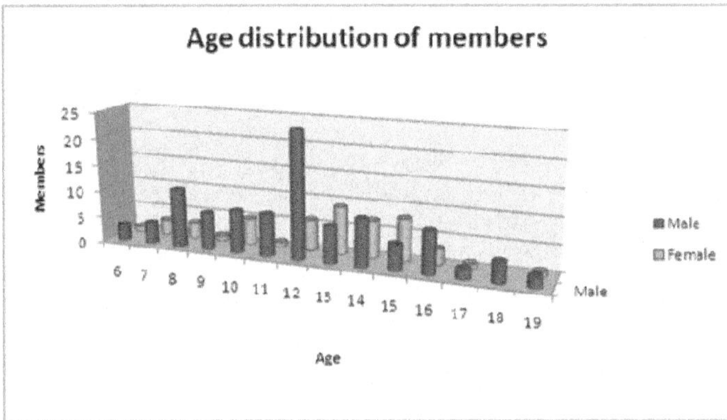

14.30 CHART CREATED BY THE CODE IN FIGURE 14.29.

14.3.4 Example: Sales – Revisited

In this section, we revisit the Sales example from Section 14.3.1. In this section, the goal is to add a *data table* to the chart. Consider the code in Figure 14.31 where we assume that the *Simple* procedure from Figure 14.13 has been executed to create a line chart based on the *Sales* data.

```
Sub MakeChartWithDataTable()
    Dim W As Worksheet
    Dim MyChart As ChartObject
    Set W = ThisWorkbook.ActiveSheet
    Set MyChart = W.ChartObjects("Sales Chart")

    MyChart.Width = 400
    MyChart.Height = 300

    With MyChart.Chart
        .HasLegend = False
        .HasDataTable = True
        .DataTable.ShowLegendKey = True
        .ChartArea.Format.Line.Visible = False
    End With
    ActiveWindow.DisplayGridlines = False
End Sub
```

14.31 INCLUDE A DATA TABLE IN A CHART.

We start by letting the variable *MyChart* hold the existing chart. Next, the size of the chart is changed using the *Width* and the *Height* properties. The *HasDataTable* property is set to *True* in order to show the data table. The *HasLegend* property is set to *False* in order to hide the legend because the legend will be shown as part of the data table by setting *DataTable.ShowLegendKey* to *True*.

Finally, to let the chart blend in with its surroundings, we remove the border by setting *ChartArea.Format.Line.Visible* to *False* and remove the gridlines from the worksheet itself using the active window. The resulting chart is shown in Figure 14.32.

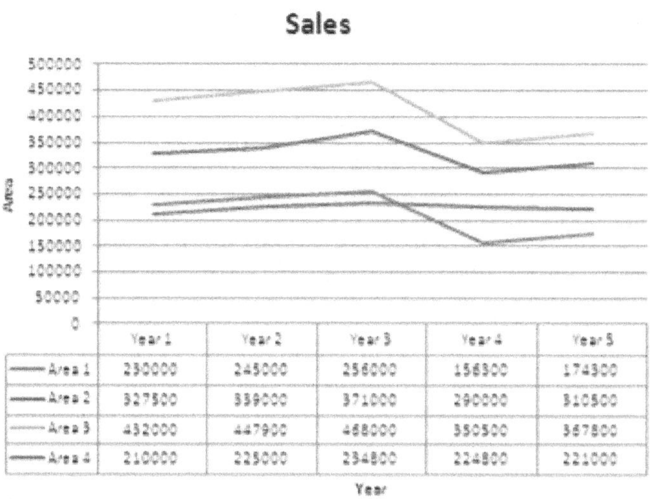

14.32 CHART WITH DATA TABLE CREATED BY THE CODE IN FIGURE 14.13 AND MODIFYED BY THE CODE IN FIGURE 14.31.

14.3.5 Example: The Traveling Salesman Problem

In this section, we show how charts can be used to show solutions of the Traveling Salesman Problem (TSP). The data is, as shown in Figure 14.33, a list of cities where the location of each city is specified by x and y coordinates.

	A	B	C	D
1	Number	X	Y	
2	1	4,118718	4,145115	
3	2	7,084759	3,296821	
4	3	6,305153	2,134099	
5	4	1,922932	5,816918	
6	5	0,891004	4,58812	
7	6	8,976152	2,661409	
8	7	7,79508	3,813245	
9	8	2,938717	9,109895	

14.33 DATA FOR THE TRAVELING SALESMAN PROBLEM.

The goal of this section is to show how charts can be used for illustration, not to solve the problem itself. The code, which is shown in Figure 14.35, uses three procedures which are not shown here: First, *MakeNewData* which creates the data as shown in Figure 14.33, and next *MakeDistanceMatrix* calculates the distance between each pair of cities.

Finally, *NearestNeighbor* constructs a solution to the problem using the Nearest Neighbor heuristics. Output from this procedure is an index for each city stating the order of the cities in the solution. These are placed in column D in Figure 14.33. Furthermore, this procedure also dublicates the first city such that this city appears in the list twice – with the smallest and with the highest index. That way, the tour returns to the start city.

Consider the code in figure 14.35. After the creation of data, the chart is constructed and the type is set to be a XY Scatter chart. First, we want to display the location of the cities. We set the range with the coordinates as the source. Note that *n* is the number of cities. We set a title but remove the legend. Next, we scale the axis to be bounded by 10 which is the highest value of any of the coordinated in the data creation and finally, we remove the grid lines within the chart. The chart constructed so far is shown in Figure 14.34.

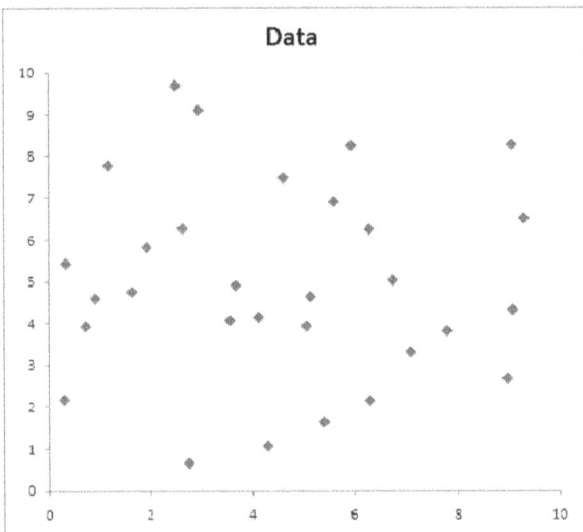

14.34 EXECUTE THE FIRST HALF OF THE CODE IN FIGURE 14.35 TO SEE THE CITY LOCATIONS.

At this point, we are ready to construct the solution and sort the data to list the cities in the order in which they appear in the solution. Then a small message box is displayed. The only practical purpose of the box is to let the user see the chart with the city distribution.

In the second part of the code we change the chart type to be a scatter chart with lines. Since the cities are listed in the order by visit, these lines will show the traveled route.

The purpose of the remainder of the code is to display the city name as labels next to the points in the chart area. We do that by specifying the label of each point to be the corresponding value found in column A. The resulting chart, which shows the Nearest Neighbor solution to the problem, is shown in Figure 14.36.

```
Sub CreateTSPTour()
    Dim n As Integer
    Dim W As Worksheet
    Dim MyChart As ChartObject
    Dim k As Integer

    Call MakeNewData
    Call MakeDistanceMatrix

    Set W = ThisWorkbook.Worksheets(4)
    n = W.Range("A2").CurrentRegion.Rows.Count - 1

    Set MyChart = W.ChartObjects.Add(300, 50, 500, 500)

    MyChart.name = "TSP Chart"
    With MyChart.Chart
        .ChartType = xlXYScatter
        .SetSourceData Source:=Range(Cells(2, 2), Cells(n + 2, 3))
        .HasTitle = True
        .ChartTitle.Text = "Data"
        .HasLegend = False
        .Axes(xlValue).MaximumScale = 10
        .Axes(xlCategory).MaximumScale = 10
        .Axes(xlValue).HasMajorGridlines = False
    End With

    Call NearestNeighbor
    Range(Cells(2, 1), Cells(n + 1, 4)).Sort _
            key1:=Range("D1"), order1:=xlAscending
    MsgBox ("GO!")

    With MyChart.Chart
        .ChartType = xlXYScatterLines
        .ChartTitle.Text = "Nearest Neighbor Solution"
        .SeriesCollection(1).ApplyDataLabels _
            (Type:=xlDataLabelsShowValue, _
            AutoText:=True, _
            LegendKey:=False) = True
    End With

    For k = 1 To n + 1
        MyChart.Chart. _
        SeriesCollection(1). _
        Points(k). _
        DataLabel.Text = Cells(k + 1, 1)
    Next
End Sub
```

14.35 CODE TO DISPLAY A TRAVELING SALESMAN TOUR AS SHOWN IN FIGURE 14.36.

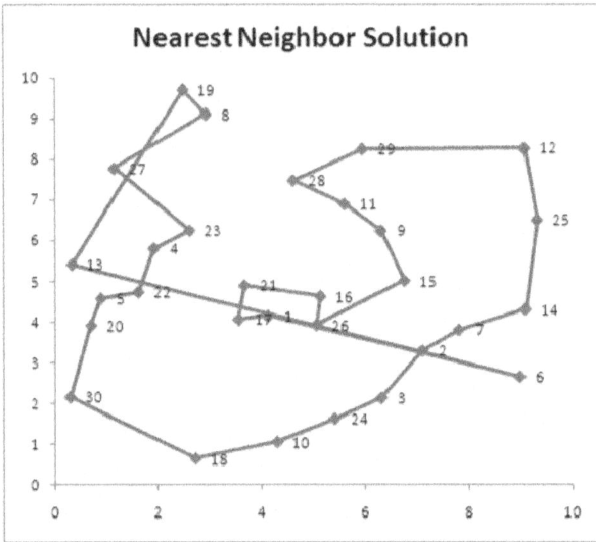

14.36 THE TOUR CONSTRUCTED BY THE CODE IN FIGURE 14.35.

14.3.6 Example: The Vehicle Routing Problem

In this section, we show how charts can be used to show solutions of the Vehicle Routing Problem (VRP). The data is, as shown in Figure 14.37, a list of cities where the location of each city is specified by x and y coordinate. For each city a demand is also given. The data is assumed to be available before execution of the code begins. Routes are constructed for several vehicles such that no vehicle services more demand than some pre-specified capacity.

	A	B	C	D
1	Number	X	Y	Demand
2	15	0,891004	4,58812	8
3	30	0,696979	3,924856	5
4	6	2,998574	3,843705	5
5	27	3,564032	4,067375	7
6	11	4,118718	4,145115	4
7	9	2,827144	1,672327	4

14.37 DATA FOR THE VEHICLE ROUTING PROBLEM.

We point out that the purpose of this section is to show the illustration rather than creating the solution. We use a procedure called *CreateTours* to create tours for the vehicles using the *Sweep* method. Output from this procedure is a list of vehicle tours as the one shown in Figure 14.38 along with the number of tours created, which is written to cell F1.

	A	B	C	D
34	Vehicle 1		load	46
35	0	5	5	
36	15	0,891004	4,58812	
37	30	0,696979	3,924856	
38	6	2,998574	3,843705	
39	27	3,564032	4,067375	
40	11	4,118718	4,145115	
41	9	2,827144	1,672327	
42	28	2,743369	0,644816	
43	5	2,887907	0,547362	
44	0	5	5	
45				
46	Vehicle 2		load	50
47	0	5	5	
48	20	4,298872	1,060143	
49	3	5,736801	1,080512	
50	2	6,726524	0,253898	
51	26	5,134627	4,637204	

14.38 THE VEHICLE TOURS CONSTRUCTED BY CREATETOURS.

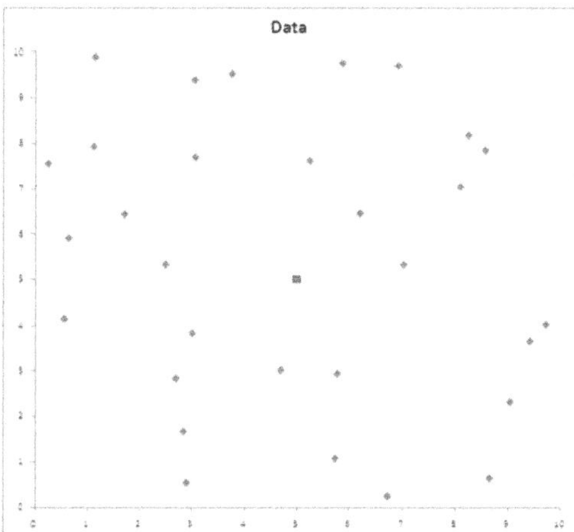

14.39 CHART CREATED BY THE FIRST HALF OF THE CODE IN FIGURE 14.40.

For the creation of charts, consider the code in Figure 14.40. The first half of the code creates the chart shown in Figure 14.39 where all the city locations are shown. This part of the code mimics the similar code from the previous section, except from the last four lines in the first With-End-With construction. These lines add a new series of data to the chart. This series contains only one point: The depot with coordinates (5,5). It is clear in Figure 14.39 that this point is of a different series than the others.

After creation of the chart, the tours are created using the CreateTours procedure and the message box is displayed in order to pause the program and allow the user to see the chart that was created.

```
Sub MakeVehicleTours()
    Dim n As Integer
    Dim k As Integer
    Dim S As Integer
    Dim R As Range
    Dim T As Range
    Dim W As Worksheet
    Dim MyChart As ChartObject

    'Make Data Chart:
    n = Range("A2").CurrentRegion.Rows.Count - 2
    Set W = ThisWorkbook.Worksheets("VehicleTours")
    Set MyChart = W.ChartObjects.Add(300, 50, 550, 500)

    MyChart.name = "Vehicle Chart"
    With MyChart.Chart
        .ChartType = xlXYScatter
        .SetSourceData Source:=Range(Cells(2, 2), Cells(n + 2, 3))
        .HasTitle = True
        .ChartTitle.Text = "Data"
        .HasLegend = False
        .Axes(xlValue).MaximumScale = 10
        .Axes(xlCategory).MaximumScale = 10
        .Axes(xlValue).HasMajorGridlines = False

        .SeriesCollection.Add _
            Source:=Range(Cells(n + 2, 3), Cells(n + 2, 3))
        .SeriesCollection(2).XValues = _
            Range(Cells(n + 2, 2), Cells(n + 2, 2))
    End With

    Call CreateTours
    MsgBox ("GO!")

    S = n + 5
    For n = 1 To Range("F1")
        If n = 1 Then
            k = S + Cells(S, 1).CurrentRegion.Rows.Count - 2
            Set R = Range(Cells(S, 2), Cells(k, 3))
            With MyChart.Chart
                .ChartType = xlXYScatterLines
                .HasLegend = True
                .SetSourceData Source:=R
                .ChartTitle.Text = "Tours"
                .SeriesCollection(n).name = "Vehicle " & n
            End With
        Else
            S = k + 3
            k = S + Cells(S, 1).CurrentRegion.Rows.Count - 2
            Set R = Range(Cells(S, 2), Cells(k, 2))
            Set T = Range(Cells(S, 3), Cells(k, 3))
            With MyChart.Chart
                .SeriesCollection.Add Source:=T
                .SeriesCollection(n).XValues = R
                .SeriesCollection(n).name = "Vehicle " & n
            End With
        End If
    Next
End Sub
```

14.40 CODE FOR DISPLAYING THE VEHICLE TOURS AS SHOWN IN FIGURE 14.41.

In the second half of the code, we use a For-Next loop to consider each of the constructed vehicle tours as displayed in the list in Figure 14.38. For the first vehicle tour, the *if* part of the If-Then-Else construction is entered. The remaining tours enter the *else* part.

For the first vehicle, we change the chart to be a Scatter chart with lines. We force the legend to be displayed and change the title. Then we set the source data to be the cities visited by the first vehicle. The *SetSourceData* overwrites any existing source data and sets the new. At this point, the chart contains one series of data displaying the first vehicle tour. We set the name of the series, which will be displayed in the legend, to be *Vehicle 1*.

For the remaining vehicles, the ranges *R* and *T* are set to contain the data and we use these to add a new series of data to the *SeriesCollection*. Finally, the name of the added series is also set. The resulting chart, which displays all the vehicle tours, is shown in Figure 14.41.

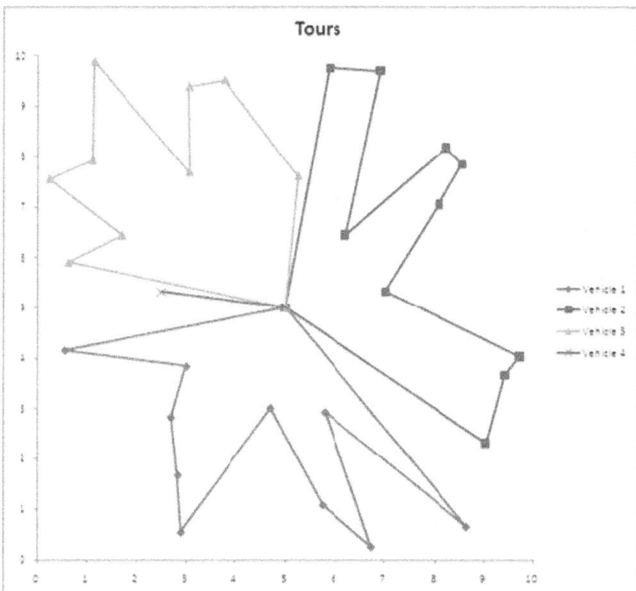

14.41 THE VEHICLE TOURS DISPLAYED BY THE CODE IN FIGURE 14.40.

14.4 Exercises

14.1. Open the data file of this exercise. Write a sub that creates a pie chart illustrating the data.

14.2. Open the data file of this exercise. Write a sub that creates a column chart with the given data.

14.3. Open the file with your solution of Exercise 5.6. Write a sub that creates a chart sheet with a stacked cylinder chart showing the payments (interest, repayment, and total payment) of the annuity loan.

14.4. Open the data file for this exercise. In the file you see a number of tasks to be performed. The execution of each task is partitioned into five phases. The file gives the start time for the first phase and the duration of each phase. There should be no slack time between the phases. The time horizon is partitioned into 74 time slots – corresponding to the next two years. Write a sub that creates a stacked bar chart to illustrate the planning of the tacks. Hint: It is possible to remove the fill of one or several series.

14.5. Open the file with your solution of Exercise 14.4. Add a couple of new tasks to the table. Write a sub that can modify the chart you created to include new tasks. The sub should automatically obtain the total number of tasks.

14.6. Open the data file for this exercise. In the file, sales data are given for 10 teams over a period of a year. Write a sub that creates a chart displaying the sales of June, July, and August for 4 selected teams. The four teams can be obtained from sheet 2. The chart should include a data table.

14.7. Open the file with your solution of Exercise 6.11. Modify the code to have a maximum of 100 periods. Extend the code to create a chart sheet that shows the variations of the exchange rate as a line chart and the amount of exchanged Euros in each period as a column chart.

Chapter 15
Built-in Dialog Boxes

Throughout this book we have used message boxes to display information to the user. In Section 15.1, we illustrate how the appearance of the basic message box can be modified and how the message box can be used for obtaining simple information from the user. Previously we have also used input boxes for obtaining input from the user. In Section 15.2, we show how the appearance of the input box can be modified and in Section 15.3, we present the application input box. Finally in Section 15.4, we consider the use of other built-in dialog boxes.

15.1 Message Boxes

So far we have only used *message boxes* with one argument: The text to be displayed and with one button: An OK button. In the following we show how the text box function can be used in more useful ways. The syntax of the message box is shown in Figure 15.1.

Function **MsgBox**(*Prompt*, [*Buttons* As VbMsgBoxStyle = vbOKOnly], [*Title*], [*HelpFile*], [*Context*]) As VbMsgBoxResult
Member of VBA.Interaction

15.1 SYNTAX OF THE MESSAGE BOX.

As can be seen in Figure 15.1, the message box can take several optional arguments. The first argument is, however, not optional. This is the *prompt*, i.e. a string specifying the text to be displayed in the message box and is the only argument we have used so far.

If only the first argument is used, the message box will be displayed with a single *OK* button. Such a message box is shown in Figure 15.2, where the left-hand side shows the code that generated the message box.

The second argument is used to change the appearance of the message box and should be one of several pre-defined values. The purpose of this argument is threefold: Changing the *buttons* to be shown, including an *icon* to be displayed in the message box, and selecting which should be the *default* button.

```
MsgBox "Continue."
```

15.2 A SIMPLE MESSAGE BOX.

```
MsgBox "Generate Report?", vbYesNo
```

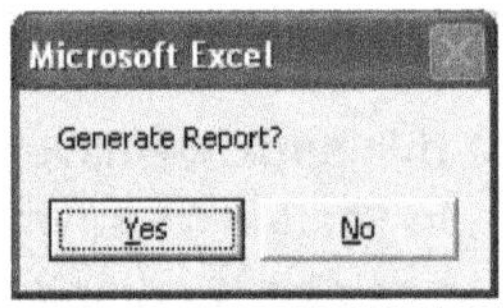

15.3 CHANGE THE BUTTONS BY USING THE SECOND ARGUMENT OF THE MESSAGE BOX.

In Table 15.1, we show the possible button combination along with the value of the second argument to generate them. In Figure 15.3, we show how to use the second argument to obtain Yes and No buttons.

15.1 POSSIBLE BUTTON COMBINATIONS

Value	Displays
VbOKOnly	OK
VbOKCancel	OK Cancel
VbMsgBoxHelpButton	OK Help
VbYesNo	Yes No
VbYesNoCancel	OK
VbRetryCancel	Retry Cancel
VbAbortRetryIgnore	Abort Retry Ignore

15.2 POSSIBLE ICONS TO BE DISPLAYED ON THE MESSAGE BOX.

Value	Displays	Explanation
vbCritical		Displays Critical message icon
vbExclamation		Displays Warning message icon
vbInformation		Displays Information message icon
vbGuestion		Displays Question mark icon

You can include one of four standard icons in your message box. The four options are shown in Table 15.2.

In order to include both an icon and specify the buttons, the two values are simply included with a plus sign separating them. This is illustrated in Figure 15.4 where the code to display the message box is shown to the left.

```
MsgBox _
    "Execution may take a few minutes.", _
    vbOKCancel + vbInformation
```

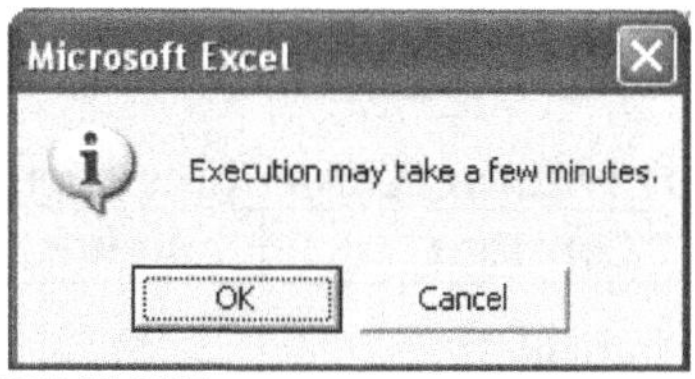

15.4 USE THE SECOND ARGUMENT TO ADD AN ICON TO A MESSAGE BOX.

The first button is always the default button. Hence, if *Enter* is pressed, the program executes as if the first button was pressed. In order to force another button to act as default button, a third value must be added to the second argument. For example, changing the second argument in the code in Figure 15.4 to be *vbOKCancel + vbInformation + vbDefaultButton2* will result in the *Cancel* button being the default.

```
MsgBox "Go.", vbExclamation, "Processing"
```

15.5 USE THE THIRD ARGUMENT TO ADD A TITLE.

The third argument is a string containing the *Title* of the message box, i.e. the text being displayed in the top blue area. Figure 15.5 shows how to include a title argument. The final two arguments are used to include a user defined help file for the message box, and this is beyond the scope of this book.

```
Dim answer As Integer

answer = MsgBox("Generate Report?", vbYesNo)

If answer = 6 Then
    'Code to generate report
Else
    'Code if no report is generated
End If
```

15.6 USE THE RETURN VALUE OF A MESSAGE BOX.

As can be seen from the syntax of the message box in Figure 15.1, a message box is a function and can return a value. The possible return values are shown in Table 15.3 along with a specification of the button to be pressed in order for the value to be returned.

Figure 15.6 illustrates how the return value of a message box can be used in a program. Notice that when the message box is used as a function, i.e. when returning a value, the arguments should be surrounded by parenthesis as in Figure 15.6.

15.3 POSSIBLE RETURN VALUES OF MESSAGE BOXES.

Constant	Value	User clickes
vbOK	1	OK
vbCancel	2	Cancel
vbAbort	3	Abort
vbRetry	4	Retry
vbIgnore	5	Ignore
vbYes	6	Yes
vbNo	7	No

15.2 Input Boxes

Input boxes are used for obtaining information from the user in text format. Throughout this book, we have used input boxes with one argument. In this section, we show how the input box can be adjusted by using one or more of the optional arguments as well. The syntax of the input box is shown in Figure 15.7.

```
Function InputBox(Prompt, [Title], [Default], [XPos], [YPos], [HelpFile], [Context]) As String
    Member of VBA.Interaction
```

15.7 SYNTAX OF THE INPUT BOX.

Note that the input box is a function and that the return value is a string. If the user presses the *OK* button, the value of the string is the text typed by the user. If the user presses the *Cancel* button, an empty string is returned. It should be pointed out that if the user presses the *OK* button without typing anything, an empty string is also returned.

The first argument of an input box is the only one that is required. This is the *Prompt*, i.e. the text to be displayed in the gray area of the input box. Figure 15.8 shows a simple input box where only the first argument is used, along with the code generating it.

```
Dim ID As String

ID = InputBox("Enter customer Id:")
```

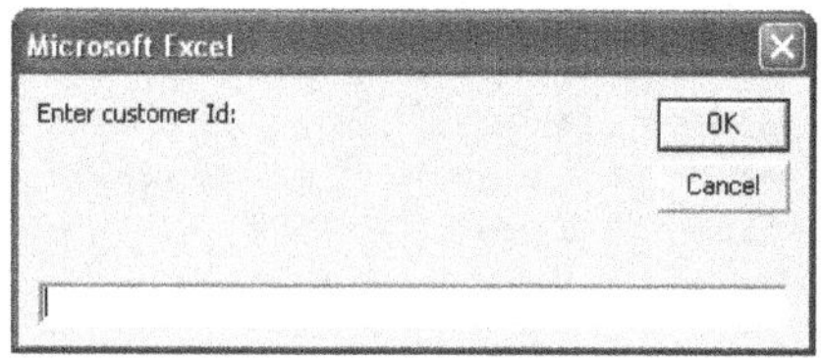

15.8 A SIMPLE INPUT BOX.

The second argument is the *Title*, i.e. the text to be displayed in the blue top bar of the input box. The third argument is the default string to be returned by the input box if nothing is entered by the user. This text will be pre-displayed in the text area of the input box. Figure 15.9, with the result shown in Figure 15.10, illustrates how to use these two arguments.

```
r = InputBox("How is responsible for the project?", _
        "New Project", "Professor Peter Hansen")
```

15.9 USING OPTIONAL ARGUMENTS OF AN INPUT BOX.

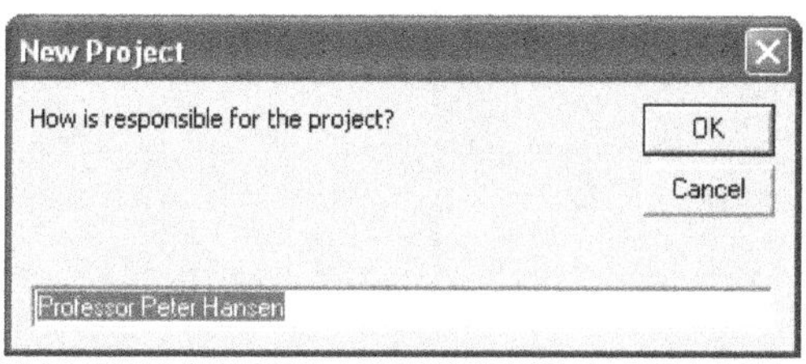

15.10 USING OPTIONAL ARGUMENTS OF AN INPUT BOX.

The next two arguments, called *xpos* and *ypos*, respectively, specify where on the monitor the input box will be displayed. *Xpos* defines the horizontal distance to the left edge of column A and *ypos* defines the vertical distance to the top of row one. If these two arguments are omitted, the input box is displayed centred.

Finally, the last two arguments are used to include a user-defined help file to supplements the input box.

There is nothing to prevent the prompt of an input box from being very long. This is illustrated by the code in Figure 15.11. Note in the final part of the text that the line is automatically broken when the column width is met. The resulting input box is shown in Figure 15.12.

```
Dim Acronym As String
Dim pr As String

pr = "Please provide an Acronym for the project."
pr = pr & vbCr & vbCr
pr = pr & "Remember that an appropriate Acronym should be"
pr = pr & vbCr
pr = pr & vbTab & "- Easy to remember." & vbCr
pr = pr & vbTab & "- Relatively short." & vbCr
pr = pr & vbTab & "- Easy to procance" & vbCr
pr = pr & vbCr & vbCr
pr = pr & "Note that before you assign an acronym " & _
    "to your project you must check the company " & _
    "database to ensure that the acronym is not " & _
    "used for any other project which have been " & _
    "in process for the past four years."

Acronym = InputBox(pr, "New Project")
```

15.11 CONSTRUCTION OF INPUT BOX WITH LONG PROMPT.

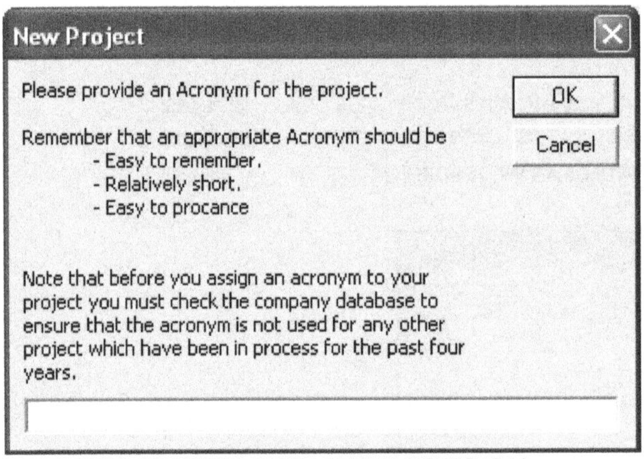

15.12 INPUT BOX CREATED BY THE CODE IN FIGURE 15.11.

15.3 The Application Input Box

The Excel application also offers an input box, but it is different from the VBA input box in several ways. Most importantly, you can specify the type of return values to be accepted. If the input entered by the user is of another type, an alert will automatically be displayed and the user gets a chance to correct the input.

Function **InputBox(***Prompt As String*, [*Title*], [*Default*], [*Left*], [*Top*], [*HelpFile*], [*HelpContextID*], [*Type*]**)**
Member of Excel.Application

15.13 SYNTAX OF THE APPLICATION INPUT BOX.

The syntax of the *Application input box*, which is shown in Figure 15.13, is similar to that of the VBA input box except from the last argument which specifies the type of the accepted input. Table 15.4 shows the possible types along with the corresponding value of the *Type* argument.

15.4 TYPES ACCEPTED BY THE APPLICATION INPUT BOX.

Value	Accepted input
0	Formula
1	Number
2	String of text
4	Logical value (True or False)
8	Range reference
16	Error value
64	Array of values

Figure 15.14 illustrates the use of the application input box with the result displayed in Figure 15.15. Note that if the Type value 8, i.e. a Range, is accepted, then the user can mark a range directly in the worksheet.

```
Dim K As Range

Set K = Application.InputBox( _
        Prompt:="Please enter the range to adjust:", _
        Type:=8)
```

15.14 USE THE APPLICATION INPUT BOX TO SPECIFY THE TYPE OF USER INPUT TO BE ALLOWED.

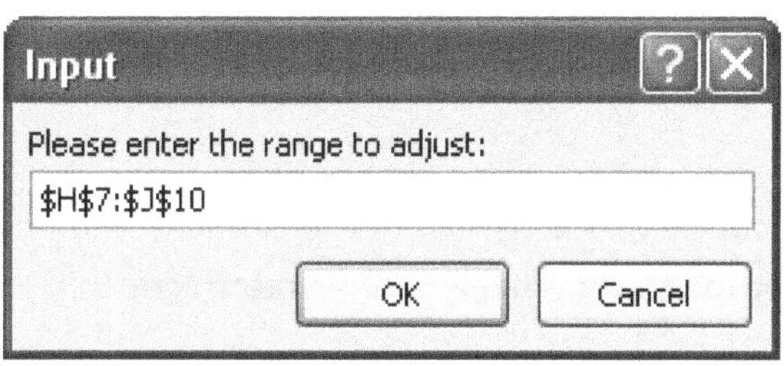

15.15 ILLUSTRATION OF THE APPLICATION INPUT BOX.

In case several types of input are accepted, the values corresponding to those types can be added. This is illustrated in Figure 15.16 where both numbers and logical values are accepted.

```
Dim r As Variant

r = Application.InputBox( _
        Prompt:="Please enter the range to adjust:", _
        Type:=1 + 4)
```

15.16 APPLICATION INPUT BOX WITH TWO TYPES ALLOWED.

15.4 Other Built-in Dialog Boxes

When writing a program, the dialog boxes that you usually meet when working with Excel are available for you to use.

For example, to let the user select a file to open via the well-known *Open File* dialog box, the *GetOpenFilename* method can be used. As illustrated in the code in Figure 15.17, this method returns a string specifying the full path of the selected file. This string can subsequently be used in the *Open* method of the *Workbooks* collection.

Similarly, the *GetSaveAsFilename* displays the well-known *Save File As* dialog box. Again, the method returns a string representing the full path of the file to save, which can subsequently be used as input for the *SaveAs* method which does the actual saving.

```
Dim s As String
Dim W As Workbook

s = Application.GetOpenFilename()
Set W = Workbooks.Open(s)

'Code

s = Application.GetSaveAsFilename()
W.SaveAs (s)
```

15.17 USING THE APPLICATION METHOD TO OBTAIN THE FULL PATH OF THE FILE TO OPEN.

Many dialog boxes can be integrated in the code by using the *Dialogs* property of the application. Here, a constant representing the dialog box to display is used as argument. Figure 15.18 illustrates how this is done by displaying the format font and the zoom dialog boxes.

```
Application.Dialogs(xlDialogFormatFont).Show

Application.Dialogs(xlDialogZoom).Show
```

15.18 USING THE DIALOGS METHOD.

Chapter 16
User Forms

User forms are powerful tools for obtaining information from the user of a program, while minimizing the risk of the user messing up the worksheets. They are also far more user-friendly than a workbook, and done correctly they can handle all the interaction the user will need to have with the program.

In Section 16.1, we introduce the various *form controls* that are available to be used in user forms. Working with user forms requires an understanding of *Event Programming*, so we provide the basics on that topic in Section 16.2

In Section 16.3, we show step by step how to create a user form and make it work, and in Section 16.4, we present a number of examples to show how more advanced user forms can be created.

16.1 Controls

In this section, we present the various controls that can be used on user forms. In the following sections, we give examples of how to use many of the controls.

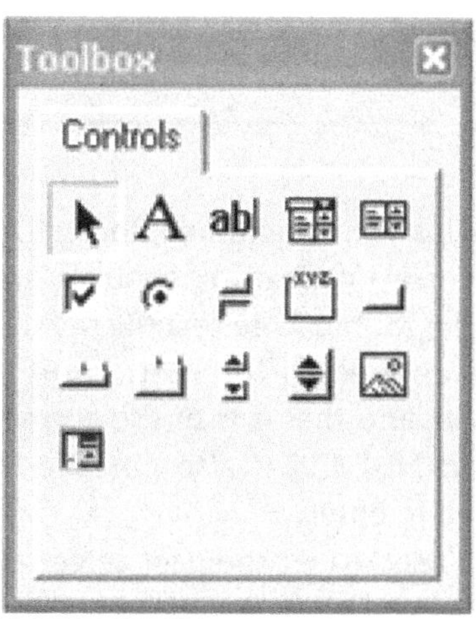

16.1 THE USER FORM TOOLBOX.

When working with user forms a *Toolbox* containing the controls is available as shown in Figure 16.1. The controls are simply added to the user form by dragging them from the Toolbox. Table 16.1 gives an overview of the types of the controls, and Figure 16.2 illustrates the appearance of the controls on a user form. Here, the controls are in the same order as in the Toolbox.

16.1 THE AVAILABLE USER FORM CONTROLS.

	Label	TextBox	ComboBox	ListBox
CheckBox	OptionButton	ToggleButton	Frame	CommandButton
TabStrip	MultiPage	ScrollBar	SpinButton	Image
RefEdit				

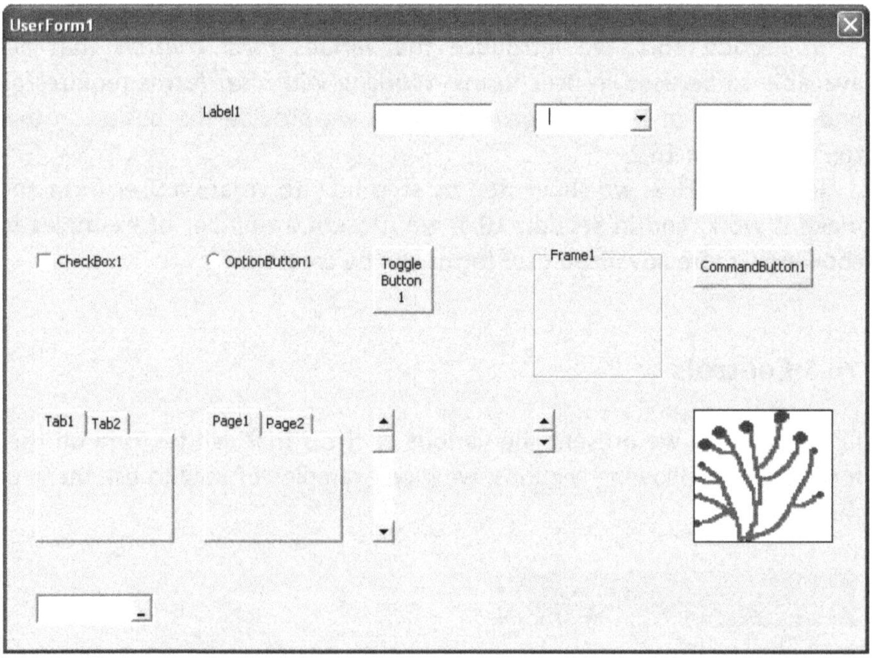

16.2 THE AVAILABLE USER FORM CONTROLS

The *Label* is used to add text to the form. This text should be informative and help the user fill out the user form correctly. *TextBox* controls are used to let the user provide information in the form of free text. By default there are no limits to the type of the text entered by the user, but it is possible to check the text subsequently to ensure that it is of the correct type. We investigate that further in Section 16.4.3. It is also possible to limit the length of the text the user is allowed to enter.

The *ComboBox* and the *ListBox* are both used to let the user select an item from a list. The main difference is that in a *ComboBox,* the user also has the option of entering text freely. When using a *ListBox* in a user form, it should be determined if the user can select one item only or several items simultaneously. This is done by specifying the value of the *MultiSelect* property.

Both the *CheckBox* and the *ToggleButton* is used for matters that can either be on or off, or *True* or *False*. You know the *CheckBox* from for example the *Font* dialog box in Word where the user can check *Subscript, Shadow*, etc. The *ToggleButton* looks differently, but works the same way.

The *OptionButton* and the *Frame* is almost always used together to let the user choose exactly one of several options. You know the *OptionButton* from the *Print* dialog box in Word where the user can choose to print *All, Current page,* or *Pages*. The *Frame* is used to cluster the *OptionButtons* in Groups.

The *CommandButton* works exactly like the button to execute a sub which you have enclosed in your worksheet many times by now. Typical *CommandButtons* on user forms are *OK, GO, Cancel*, etc.

Both the *TabStrip* and the *Multipage* is used to break a large user form into smaller pieces. You know them from many built-in dialog boxes, for example the *Page Setup* dialog box in Word which has three pages: *Margins, Paper*, and *Layout*. In this book we focus on the *MultiPage* control.

It is probably safe to assume that everybody is familiar with *ScrollBars* from working with Word, Excel, or Internet. The *ScrollBar* control can be used on user forms to let the user slide towards the desired value between a minimum and a maximum value determined by the creator of the form. A *Label* control would usually be used to display the value of the *ScrollBar*.

The *SpinButton* control works much like the *ScrollBar* control but is much more commonly used on forms. For example, the *Paragraph* dialog box in Word uses *SpinButtons* to let the user increase or decrease several values by clicking a small arrow. *SpinButtons* are often used jointly with a *TextBox*, displaying the value and also offering the user the option of typing the desired value directly.

The *Image* control is used for displaying – well, images. A common use is to display some kind of a logo, but it might as well be used as a decision support tool displaying an image corresponding to the selection made in a *ListBox*, which, used correctly, could help the user make the right selection.

The final control, called *RefEdit*, is used to let the user enter a range by selecting it directly on the worksheet. This is similar to the control that lets the user select data when charts are created manually.

Throughout this chapter, we use the controls presented in this section and show how different settings can be used. We do that through four examples. Table 16.2 offers a quick overview of the controls used in each example.

16.2 OVERVIEW OF THE CONTROLS USED IN THE EXAMPLES OF SECTION 16.4.

	TextBox	ComboBox	ListBob	CheckBox	OptionButton	ToggleButton	Frame	CommandButton	MultiPage	SpinButton	Image	RrfEdit
People Information	X			X	X		X	X				
Select Background Picture			X					X	X		X	
Selecting Flights		X	X					X				
Running Experiment	X				X	X	X	X		X		X

16.2 Event Programming

One thing is to be able to add a number of controls to a user form, but if you need the user form to perform some task, you will have to write some code to make it do so. In order to do that correctly you need to understand the topic of *Event* Programming.

Up to this point, all your code has been located in modules – and only in modules. With one exception: In Chapter 11, you were told to place two short procedures directly under *ThisWorkbook* for the purpose of automatically creating and removing a toolbar when an Add-In was opened and closed, respectively.

Event Programming is all about writing subs that are triggered by some event. Maybe you want the content of sheet 1 to be updated automatically from a database when you open a specific workbook. Maybe you want new sheets to be automatically renamed using current date and time when you add them to your workbook, or maybe you want a go-home check list to be displayed when Excel is closed. You can do that using event programming.

Using *Event Programming* you can also control the controls in your user form. Furthermore, you can place controls, for example a *SpinButton,* directly in your worksheet and use *Event Programming* to let the user use that to change the value in a cell.

To understand *Event Programming*, consider the screenshot in Figure 16.3. In the Project Explorer, we have double-clicked on *ThisWorkbook*. Above the code window you see two drop-down lists. Select *Workbook* in the leftmost list. Now the rightmost list contains all the event triggers that are available for the current workbook. Selecting an event trigger will automatically insert the title line of a sub. The name of the event triggers are self-explanatory. The code will automatically be executed when the event trigger is met, for instance when the workbook is opened. Note that these events are related to the current workbook only.

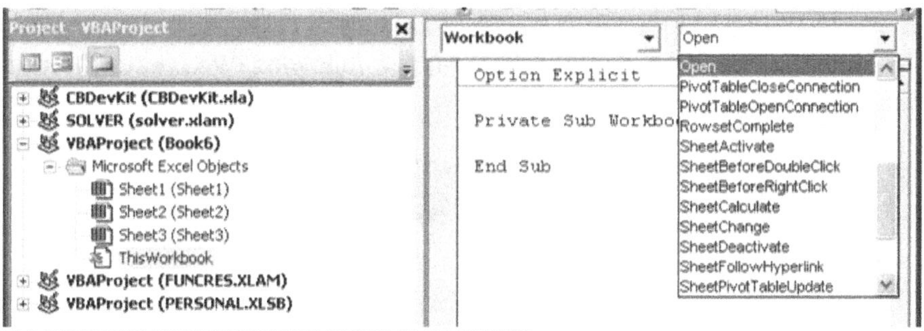

16.3 SELECT THE EVENT TRIGGER IN THE DROP-DOWN LIST.

To create code that is related to a specific sheet, double-click that sheet in the project explorer and select worksheet in the leftmost list to obtain a list of the event triggers related to a specific sheet.

Placing controls directly in a sheet adds those controls to the leftmost list as shown in Figure 16.4. Selecting the single control will provide you with a list of possible event triggers for that specific control.

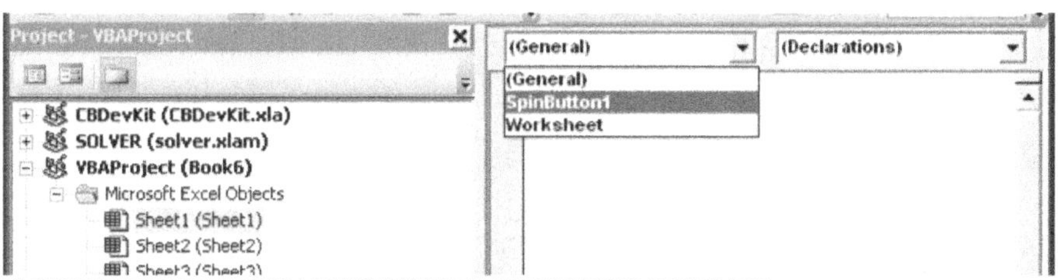

16.4 THE SINGLE CONTROLS APPEAR IN THE LEFT MOST DROP-DOWN LIST.

Some triggers are very obvious like *Click* or *Change* where the latter refers to the user changing the value of that particular control. But there are also more exotic event triggers like *PivotTableUpdate* for a worksheet. The best advice is to carefully inspect the list of event triggers to find one that suits your needs.

To program a user form you do exactly as above: activate the code window of the user form, select your control in the leftmost list and select a trigger in the rightmost list. Alternatively, you can double-click on the control to select it. In the next sections you will learn how that is done.

It is possible to use event triggers at application level, i.e. in Excel itself, to automatically execute some code when a new workbook is created, for example. But that topic is beyond the scope of this book.

16.3 Designing the First User Form

In this section, we show how to create a user form and how to make it perform the task we want it to. For this purpose, we use an example of obtaining information about people. In the following, we create the user form shown in Figure 16.5.

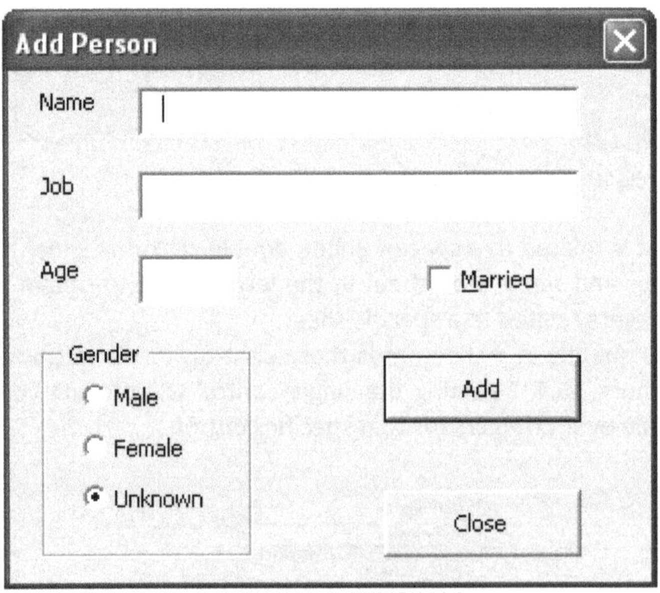

16.5 THE USER FORM TO BE CREATED IN SECTION 16.3.

To keep the code in this first example relatively simple when the Add button is pressed, we transfer the information in the user form to the worksheet as shown in Figure 16.6. Next, the user form is cleared such that new information can be entered. When the close button is pressed, the user form should be closed without information in the form being transferred to the worksheet.

E	F	G	H	I
Name	Job	Age	Gender	Married
Peter Hansen	professor	58	Male	TRUE
Jens Sørensen	mechanics	24	Male	FALSE
Lisa Høj	teacher	37	Female	TRUE
Carl Nielsen	Sales assistant	28	Unknown	TRUE
Lise Gade	student	21	Female	FALSE
Claus Petersen	Coordinator	48	Male	TRUE

16.6 INFORMATION OF THE USER FORM WILL BE TRANSFERRED TO THE WORKSHEET.

Note that we revisit this example in Section 16.4.3 where we will show how to check that all necessary information is provided in the correct format by the user.

16.3.1 Insert the User Form

You insert a user form in your workbook in the same way as you insert a module. As you know by now, there are many ways to do this. One option is to right click on the workbook in the Project Explorer in the VBA editor, choose *Insert* and select *UserForm*, as shown in Figure 16.7. Alternatively, you can select *UserForm* from the *Insert* menu in the toolbar.

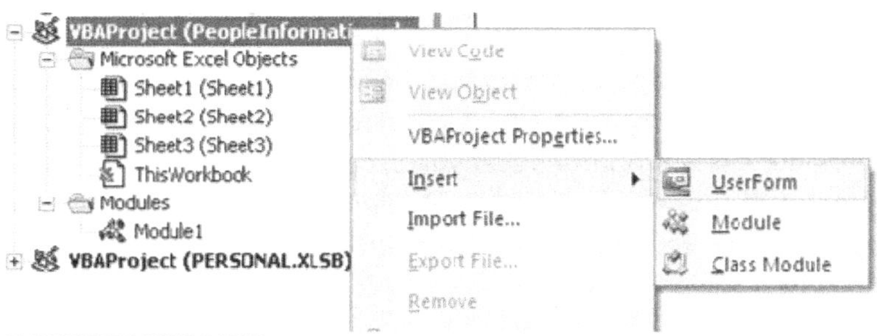

16.7 INSERT A USER FORM.

After inserting a user form, you will see an empty form in the code window as shown in Figure 16.8. Grid points are shown to ease designing the user form. They are only shown when working with the user form in the VBA editor. They will not be shown when the user form is displayed during execution of your program. In the project explorer you will see the new user form appear under *Forms* in your workbook.

The user form object you just inserted contains both the form itself and the code belonging to it. You can think of this code as being behind the user form or at the backside of it. There is no code behind the user form when it is first created. By right clicking on the name of the user form in the project explorer, you can swap between viewing the form and the code. Alternatively, you can view the code by double-clicking on the form itself.

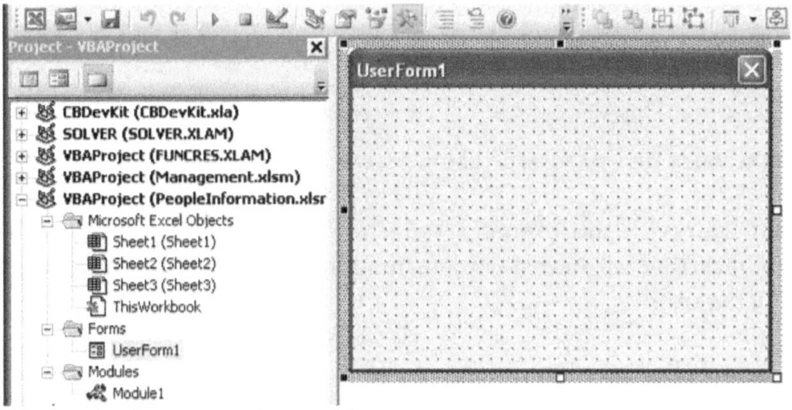

16.8 THE USER FORM APPEARS IN THE CODE WINDOW.

16.3.2 Changing the Appearance of the User Form

When a user form is created, it has a default size. The size can be changed in two ways, by dragging the border of the form or by changing the properties directly. It is easier to adjust the size of the form after adding controls to it.

Clearly you can also change the color, the text font, the border style, and many other things, most of which you are probably never going to use, but there are a few properties that you probably will need.

At this point, if you do not see the *Properties Window* in your VBA editor, open the *View* menu and select *Properties Window* or press *F4* to open it. Activate your user form by selecting it in the project explorer to see its properties in the properties window, which is shown in Figure 16.9.

In the top of the properties window, the drop-down list contains all controls on the current user form and the form itself. Here, you see the name of the control and information regarding the type of control and can select the control whose properties you want to view or change.

The *name* of a user form is the name that you will have to use in your code to refer to the user form. You probably agree that the default name, which is something like *UserForm1*, is not very descriptive. The *Name* property is always in the top of the list in the left-hand side of the properties window. Change the name in the right-hand side from *UserForm1* to for example *PeopleInformation*. Note that the name may only include letters and numbers and no spaces.

The *Caption* of a user form is the test being displayed in the blue top bar of the form. The default text is something like *UserForm1* – just like the name. Change the *Caption* property to something more descriptive, for example *Add Person*.

16.9 USE THE PROPERTIES WINDOW TO CHANGE PROPERTIES OF USER FORMS AND OF CONTROLS.

16.3.3 Show the User Form

While creating the user form, the easiest way to display it is to activate it in the VBA editor and press *F5*. When a user form is displayed, it can always be closed by pressing the red *X* in the upper right corner.

Eventually the user form should be displayed from your VBA code. For this purpose, insert a module in your workbook and create a procedure like the one shown in Figure 16.10. You should replace *PeopleInformation* with the name of your user form.

```
Sub run()
    PeopleInformation.Show
End Sub
```

16.10 USE THE SHOW METHOD TO DISPLAY A USER FORM FROM YOUR CODE.

When the user form is displayed, control is passed to the form. When the user form is closed, control returns to your procedure. If you want control to stay in your procedure while you display a user form, you can use the keyword *vbModeless* to do so.

You can include as much other code in the procedure as you want and you can show as many user forms from the same procedure as you want to. You can also show one user form from the code of another.

16.3.4 Adding Controls to the User Form

It is now time to add *controls* to the user form. Do that by dragging the control you want from the *Toolbox* to the user form. If the *Toolbox* is not shown when the user form is active, you can display it by choosing *Toolbox* in the *View* menu. Start by adding three *Labels* and three *TextBox* controls to make the user form look something like the one shown in the left-hand side of Figure 16.11.

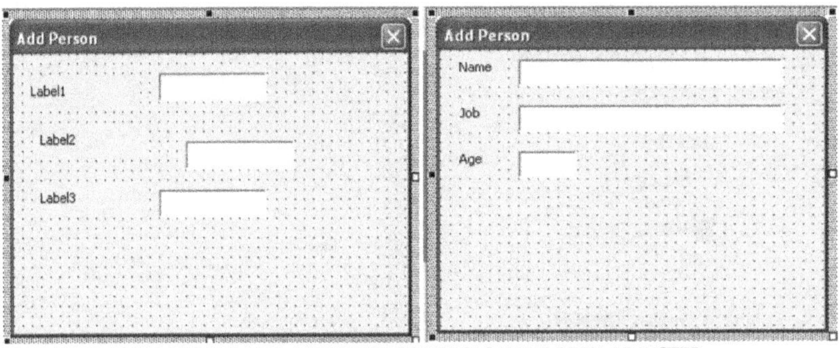

16.11 USER FORM BEFORE AND AFTER THE CONTROLS HAVE BEEN ADJUSTED.

Change the *Name* property of the three *TextBox* controls to something more descriptive. We have used the names *FullName*, *Job*, and *Age*, respectively. If you use other names, remember to change the code that we show in Section 16.3.8 accordingly. To activate the control whose property you want to view or change, either select it in the drop-down list of the properties windows or select it on the user form.

As a general rule, if a *Label* is just text and you do not need to refer to it in your code, you do not need to change the name of it, but if you need to refer to it at some point, you should give it a more descriptive name than the default. Change the *Caption* property of the three labels to be *Name*, *Job*, and *Age*, respectively.

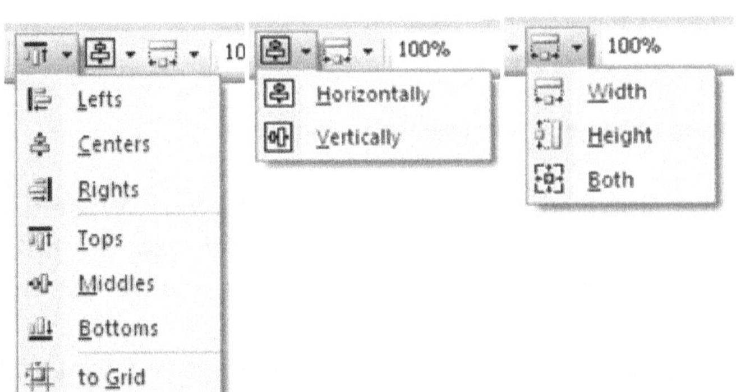

16.12 TOOLS TO ADJUST SIZE AND LOCATION OF CONTROLS.

To adjust the size and the location of each control, you can use the three menus shown in Figure 16.12. If you do not see them in your editor, make sure that the *UserForm* toolbar is displayed. After carefully adjusting the size and location of your first six controls, the user form should look approximately like the one in the right-hand side of Figure 16.11.

Place a *CheckBox* control on your user form and change the *Caption* property of it to *Married*. Change the *Name* property of the *CheckBox* to something descriptive: *Married*, for example.

The Gender area of the user form is created using a *Frame* control and three *OptionButtons*. If you place the *Frame* first and then drop the *OptionButtons* onto it, it is automatically ensured that only one of the *OptionButton* can be selected at a time. Change the *Caption* property of the Frame to be *Gender*. Change the *Name* property of the three *OptionButtons* to something descriptive: For example *GenderM*, *GenderF*, and *GenderU*, respectively and change the *Caption* property to *Male*, *Female*, and *Unknown*, respectively.

Finally, place two *CommandButton* controls on the user form. Change the *Caption* properties to *Add* and *Close*, respectively and the *Name* properties to something descriptive: *BAdd* and *BClose*, for example. Then adjust the size and location of the controls to make the user form look like the one in Figure 16.5.

16.3.5 Properties

The properties of each control on a user form can be set while designing the user form such that the user form will look and act correctly when displayed. They can also be changed through code using *Event Programming* while the user is filling in information. For example, our user form could have had a *TextBox* for the name of the person's spouse. This could be disabled when the user form was first displayed but if the user selects married, the *TextBox* for the spouse name would become enabled. Throughout this chapter we have several examples of working with control properties through the code.

You have already changed the *name* and *caption* properties of your controls to change the look of your user form and to ease referring to controls in the code. While moving and adjusting the controls, you changed the *left*, *top*, *width*, and *height* properties, even though you did not do so directly.

When including *OptionButton* controls on a user form, it is recommended to let one of them be selected automatically when the form is displayed. That way it is ensured that one of them will always be selected as one option can only be unselected by the selection of another one. Here, we select *Unknown* to be pre-selected. To do that, activate the *GenderU OptionButton* and change the *Value* property to *True*.

For most built-in dialog boxes, the *Enter* key can be pressed instead of clicking an *OK* button and the *Esc* key can be pressed instead of clicking the *Cancel* button. Here is how that is done: We want the *Add* button to correspond to pressing *Enter*, so select *BAdd* and change the *Default* property to *True*. We want the *Close* button to correspond to pressing the *Esc* key, so select *BClose* and change the *Cancel* property to *True*.

16.3.6 Tab Order

Try to open any built-in dialog box, for example the one used for printing. Now, press the *tab* key a number of times while observing how focus shifts from control to control. The order in which the controls are visited is the *Tab order*.

Each control has a *TabIndex* property and a *TabStop* property. The latter is of Boolean value. If the *TabStop* property of a control if False, that particular control will be skipped when the user tabs his way through your user form. If it is True, that control will be visited.

The controls whose *TabStop* value is True are visited in increasing order by the value of their *TabIndex* property. Therefore, the tab order can be changed by changing the *TabIndex* property of every single control.

Frame controls group controls together. The tab order of the controls within a Frame must be handled separately. In our example, when considering the whole user form, the *Frame* control is in the tab order, but the *OptionButton* controls in it are not. They are in the tab order of the *Frame* control. That way, tab orders also work in a hierarchical manner.

To set the tab order in our example, we start with the *Frame*. Select the three *OptionButton* controls in turn and change their *TabIndex* to 0,1, and 2, respectively.

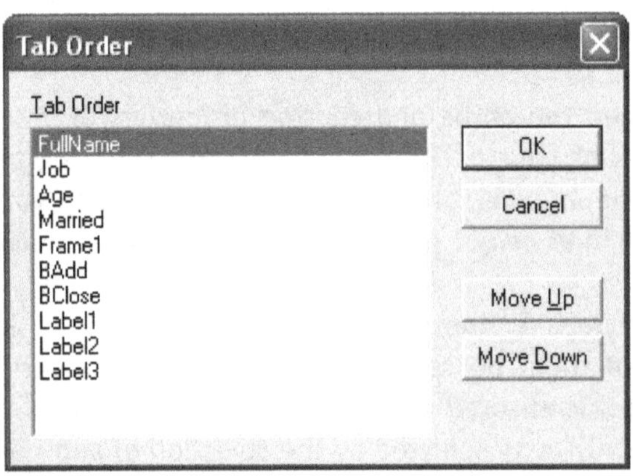

16.13 CHANGE THE TAB ORDER.

Labels should not have focus, so in our example we change the value of the *TabStop* control to *False* for the three labels. Notice that they will still have a *TabIndex* and be in the tab order even though they are not visited.

The easiest way to set the tab order is the following which is used to set the tab order of the remaining controls. Select *Tab Order* from the *View* menu. Use the *Move Up* and *Move Down* buttons to obtain the order shown in Figure 16.13. We have placed the labels last, but as they are not visited they could have been placed anywhere in the order.

16.3.7 Short Cut Keys

Try to open the *Print* dialog box in Excel again. If you look closely, you will see that one letter is underlined in the text supporting each control. If you press *Alt* + such a letter, focus will jump to the corresponding control.

We illustrate this by setting a short cut key for the *Married CheckBox*. Do this by selecting it and changing the *Accelerator* property to *M* or any other letter in the *Caption*.

CommandButton controls often have short cut keys, but in this example it is not necessary as they are already reachable by *Enter* and *Esc*, respectively.

16.3.8 Automating the User Form

By now the user form looks quite professional and focus changes as it should when tabbing or using short cut keys, but so far it is not useful for any practical purpose. In order to get the information out of the user form, we must add code to it. Note that even though in this example the code is relatively simple, the issue of adding the correct code to a user form is, by far, the hardest part when creating user forms. That will be evident when we show more advanced examples in Section 16.4.

Swap to the code part of the user form by right clicking the user form in the project explorer and selecting *View Code* or by double-clicking on the user form itself.

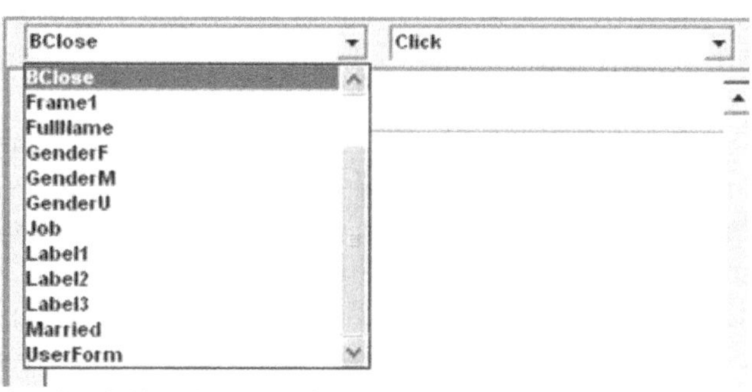

16.14 THE DROP-DOWN LIST OF THE PROPERTY WINDOW SHOWS ALL CONTROLS OF THE USER FORM.

Right above the code window you see a drop-down list containing all controls on the user form and the form itself as shown in Figure 16.14. By selecting a control in the list you can see a list of available events to the right.
Note that the editor is very eager to insert event procedures in the code window. Feel free to delete any procedure that you do not need.

In this first example, we need to control the two *CommandButtons*. To start with the easy one, locate *BClose* in the list and select the *Click* event. The only action to perform when the *Close* button is pressed, is to close the user form. A user form is closed using the keyword *Unload*, followed by the name of the form to close. Alternatively, if it is the form containing the code itself that needs closing, it can be done by the command *Unload Me*. The procedure is shown in Figure 16.15.

```
Private Sub BClose_Click()
    Unload PeopleInformation
End Sub
```

16.15 USE UNLOAD TO CLOSE A USER FORM.

See Figure 16.16 for the code that is executed when the *Add* button is clicked. As previously stated, the information of the user form should be transferred to the worksheet where the index of the first free row is determined.

The text entered by the user in a *TextBox* control is obtained by the *Value* property. Note that we use the name of each control to refer to it. Because the code is in the user form itself, we do not need to specify that we are referring to user form controls because it is assumed. The full path to the first value would be *PeopleInformation.FullName.Value*.

The *Value* property of a *CheckBox* control is True if it is selected, False otherwise. Hence, we can also use the *Value* property to transfer the status of marriage to the worksheet.

Because the three *OptionButton* controls are in a *Frame* and because we initialized one of them to True, exactly one of them will always be True. In the next part of the code we check which one is True and write the appropriate information to the worksheet.

After transferring all the information to the worksheet, the only remaining task is to reset the user form for the next person to be added. Note that if we had closed the user form at this point, it would automatically be reset before it was shown next time.

We clear the value of the *TextBox* controls, un-checks the *CheckBox*, and set the gender to *Unknown*. Finally, we set the focus to the first *TextBox*.

```
Private Sub BAdd_Click()
    Dim r As Integer
    Worksheets("Sheet1").Activate
    'Find first empty row:
    r = Range("E1").CurrentRegion.Rows.Count + 1

    'Write information to the sheet:
    Range("E" & r).Value = FullName.Value
    Range("F" & r).Value = Job.Value
    Range("G" & r).Value = Age.Value
    Range("I" & r).Value = Married.Value

    'Write gender:
    If GenderM = True Then
        Range("H" & r).Value = "Male"
    ElseIf GenderF = True Then
        Range("H" & r).Value = "Female"
    Else
        Range("H" & r).Value = "Unknown"
    End If

    ' Clear Form:
    FullName.Value = ""
    Job.Value = ""
    Married.Value = False
    GenderU = True
    Age.Value = ""
    'Set the focus to the first textbox:
    FullName.SetFocus
End Sub
```

16.16 CODE TO BE EXECUTED WHEN THE ADD BUTTON IS PRESSED.

16.4 User Forms in Action

In this section we explore the creation of user forms further. We will focus on the issues of automating the forms through code. This is done through four examples.

16.4.1 Example: Selecting Flights

In this section, we consider an example of obtaining prices for flight combinations. For this purpose, we construct the user form shown in Figure 16.17.

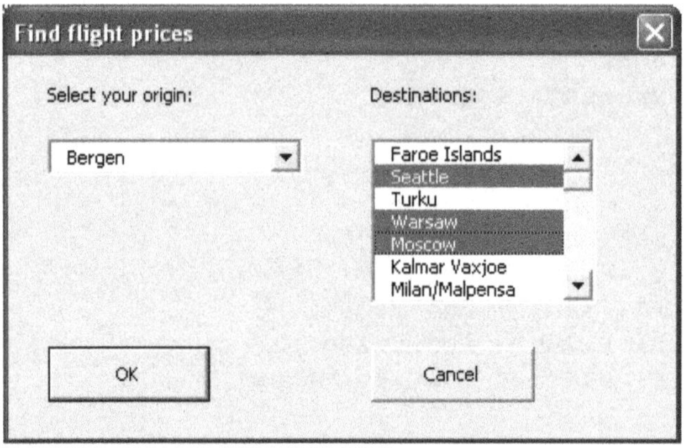

16.17 USER FORM FOR FLIGHT SELECTION.

In the left-hand side, the origin is selected from a *ComboBox*. After the selection, a list of all possible destinations from the chosen origin is shown in the *ListBox* in the right-hand side. One or several destinations can be chosen. Pressing the *OK* button will display the chosen destinations along with the price of each in a message box like the one shown in Figure 16.18.

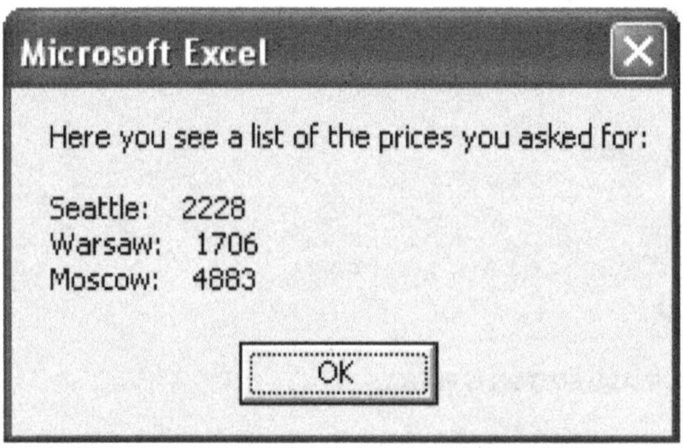

16.18 MESSAGE BOX DISPLAYING THE SELECTED FLIGHTS.

In the program, we use three global variables shown in Figure 16.19. They are defined in a module of the file, and the procedure showing the user form contains code for obtaining all available flight routes and their prices. The information is stored in the arrays such that for any index *k*, a flight from *Origin(k)* to *Destination(k)* costs *Price(k)*. Note that these arrays are public, and hence can be reached from anywhere in the file, also from the code of the user form.

```
Public Origin() As String
Public Destination() As String
Public Price() As Integer
```

16.19 GLOBAL VARIABLES.

We construct the user form as pictured in Figure 16.20. Table 16.3 gives an overview of all controls on the form except the labels. The controls are listed in top-down order, first the left-hand side then the right-hand side.

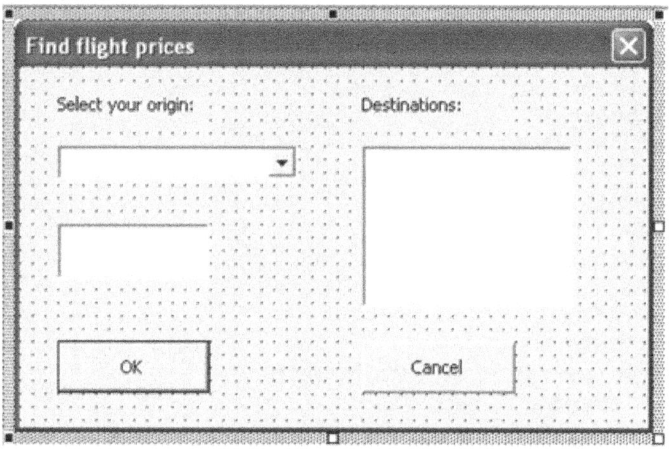

16.20 THE APPEARANCE OF THE USER FORM WHEN BEING DESIGNED.

Note that the *ListBox LBP* is made invisible which explains why it does not appear in Figure 16.17. This list is used to hold the prices corresponding to the destinations shown in *LB_Destination*. That way we save the time it would have taken to find the prices in the very long array *Price*.

Note also that the chosen *MultiSelect* setting of *LB_Destination* ensures that more than one destination can be selected simultaneously.

16.3 CONTROLS OF THE FLIGHT USER FORM.

Control	Name	Property
ComboBox	CB_Origin	
ListBox	LBP	.Visible = False
CommandButton	But_Ok	.Caption = OK
		.Default = True
ListBox	LB_Destination	.MultiSelect = 2
CommandButton	But_cancel	.Caption = Cancel
		.Cancel = True

The initialization procedure shown in Figure 16.21 is automatically executed immediately before the user form is shown. First *UBound* is used to determine the length of the *Origin* array which corresponds to the number of possible flights.

The purpose of the remaining part of the code is to ensure that each city appearing in the *Origin* array is added to the *ComboBox CB_Origin* exactly once. Hence, for each index in the array, we consider every preceding index to check if we have already seen that city. If it is the first time we see the city, it is added to the *ComboBox* using the *AddItem* method.

```
Private Sub UserForm_Initialize()
 Dim n As Integer
    Dim k As Integer
    Dim j As Integer
    Dim found As Boolean

    n = UBound(Origin)
    'Consider each origin
    'Add the origin if it is not already there
    For k = 0 To n - 1
        found = False
        For j = 0 To k - 1
            If Origin(j) = Origin(k) Then
                found = True
                Exit For
            End If
        Next
        If found = False Then
            CB_Origin.AddItem (Origin(k))
        End If
    Next
End Sub
```

16.21 INITIALIZATION OF THE FLIGHT USER FORM

When the user selects an origin in the *ComboBox*, a list of all possible destinations to be reached from that origin should appear in the *ListBox LB_Destination*. This is handled by the procedure in Figure 16.22 which is automatically executed when the *Value* property of *CB_Origin* changes.

```
Private Sub CB_Origin_Change()
    Dim ori As String
    Dim k As Integer

    ori = CB_Origin.Value
    LB_Destination.Clear
    LBP.Clear

    For k = 0 To UBound(Origin) - 1
        If Origin(k) = ori Then
            LB_Destination.AddItem (Destination(k))
            LBP.AddItem (Price(k))
        End If
    Next
End Sub
```

16.22 CHANGING THE ORIGIN SHOULD AUTOMATICALLY CHANGE THE DESTINATION LIST.

We start by remembering the origin and removing previous data from the destination *ListBox* and from the invisible price *ListBox LBP*. Next, we consider each element of the global *Origin* array. If the element in the array equals the chosen origin, we add the corresponding destination and price to their respective *ListBox*.

Now, the only thing missing is the creation of code for the two buttons. This is shown in Figure 16.23. The *Cancel* button should merely close the user form which is taken care of in the first procedure in the figure.

```
Private Sub But_cancel_Click()
    Unload Me
End Sub

Private Sub But_Ok_Click()
    Dim s As String
    Dim k As Integer

    s = "Here you see a list of the prices you asked for:"
    s = s & vbCr & vbCr

    For k = 0 To LB_Destination.ListCount - 1
        If LB_Destination.Selected(k) = True Then
            s = s & LB_Destination.List(k)
            s = s & ":     " & LBP.List(k) & vbCr
        End If
    Next

    Unload Me
    MsgBox s
End Sub
```

16.23 CODE OF THE ACTION BUTTONS.

When the *OK* button is pressed, a message box like the one shown in Figure 16.18 should appear showing the selected destinations. For this purpose we iterate through the elements of the destination *ListBox*. Note that *ListBoxes* in user forms are always indexed from zero and the *ListCount* method gives the number of elements in the list.

For each element, indexed by *k*, we check if it has been selected, in which case the *Selected* property of that element is *True*. If so, we use *List(k)* to obtain the *k*'th element, i.e. the name of the destination. Prices are obtained similarly. Finally, the user form is unloaded and the message box is displayed.

16.4.2 Example: Select Background Picture

In this example, we create a user form for selecting and previewing an image before it is chosen as background picture for a worksheet. For this purpose we use a *MultiPage* control with two pages. The first page is shown in Figure 16.24. Here, the user can select an image from the list or select *No picture*.

16.24 THE FIRST PAGE OF THE SELECT BACKGROUND USER FORM.

Depending on the selection on the first page, the user will see one of the two versions of page 2 shown in Figure 16.25. Independently of which page is displayed, pressing the *OK* button will set the selected picture as background of sheet1 in the active workbook. If *No picture* is selected, any existing background picture is removed from that sheet.

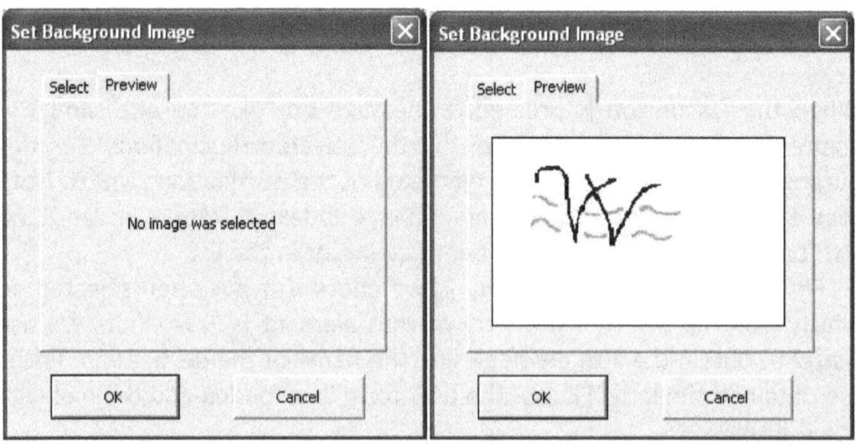

16.25 THE TWO VERSIONS OF THE SECOND PAGE OF THE SELECT BACKGROUND IMAGE USER FORM.

The user form is created by first adding the *Multipage*. Each page of it can be reached by selecting the tab. New pages can be added using the right click menu of the tabs. Pages are indexed starting at zero. The *Value* property of a *MultiPage* determines which page is shown. We add controls as shown in Figures 16.24 and 16.25 and set the properties as shown in Table 16.4.

16.4 CONTROLS OF THE SELECT BACKGROUND USER FORM.

Control	Name	Property
MultiPage	MP	
ListBox	List	.MultiSelect = 0
Image	Im	
CommandButton	B_ok	.Default = True
		.Caption = OK
CommandButton	B_cancel	.Cancel = True
		.Caption = Cancel
Label	NoImage	.Caption = "No image was selected"

The user form is initialized to ensure that the available pictures are listed in the *ListBox* on the first page. As illustrated in Figure 16.26, we assume that a list of available pictures can be obtained from sheet2 in the workbook. Setting the *Value* property of the *MultiPage* to zero ensures that the first page is shown when the user form is displayed.

```
Private Sub UserForm_Initialize()
    Dim R As Range
    Dim c As Range

    Set R = Sheet2.Range("A1:A6")
    For Each c In R
        List.AddItem (c.Value)
    Next
    List.Selected(0) = True
    MP.Value = 0
End Sub
```

16.26 INITIALIZE THE SELECT BACKGROUND IMAGE USER FORM.

When the user swaps to the preview page, we must ensure that the correct image is shown, if any. This is handled by the code in Figure 16.27. The variable *s* contains the value of the *ListBox*. If *No picture* is chosen, the *Image* area on the preview page is made invisible and the *NoImage Label* is made visible. On the other hand, if a picture is chosen, the *Image* area is made visible and the *NoImage Label* invisible. Furthermore, the image area is set to contain the picture given by the full path of the picture. It is assumed that the image files are contained in the same folder as the file of the code.

```
Private Sub MP_Change()
    Dim s As String
    s = " "
    s = BG.List.Value
    If s = "No picture" And BG.MP.Value = 1 Then
        BG.Im.Visible = False
        NoImage.Visible = True
    ElseIf s <> "No picture" And s <> " " Then
        BG.Im.Visible = True
        NoImage.Visible = False
        s = ThisWorkbook.Path & "\" & s & ".jpg"
        BG.Im.Picture = LoadPicture(s)
    End If
End Sub
```

16.27 WHEN THE PAGE NUMBER IS CHANGED THE CONTENT OF THE SECOND PAGE SHOULD BE ADJUSTED.

Finally, the code to control the buttons is given in Figure 16.28. The *Cancel* button simply unloads the user form. The *OK* button ensures that any existing background image is removed if no picture is chosen. If a picture is chosen, it is set as background picture. Furthermore, the gridlines are adjusted accordingly.

```
Private Sub B_cancel_Click()
    Unload Me
End Sub

Private Sub B_ok_Click()
    Dim W As Worksheet

    Set W = Worksheets("Sheet1")
    ActiveWindow.DisplayGridlines = False

    If List.Value = "No picture" Then
        W.SetBackgroundPicture ("")
        ActiveWindow.DisplayGridlines = True
    Else
        W.SetBackgroundPicture ( _
        ThisWorkbook.Path & "\" & List.Value & ".jpg")
    End If

    Unload Me
End Sub
```

16.28 CODE OF THE ACTION BUTTONS OF THE SELECT BACKGROUND IMAGE USER FORM.

16.4.3 Example: People Information - Revisited

When creating user forms, the programmer should put quite a lot of effort into making the user form stable with respect to the actions taken by the user. It should be checked that all necessary information is entered in the correct format and ensured that the user is prompted if this is not the case.

After creating a user form, it should be carefully tested. Try to make it crash and include code to fix the soft spots of it. At some point though, you will probably have to accept that no matter how much you take into account, it will probably never be perfect.

In the people information example of Section 16.3, we used a number of *TextBox* controls where the user was supposed to enter *name, job* and *age*. In that example, we accepted any information that the user wrote and we accepted if no text was entered. The result was a user form that worked correctly if the correct type of information was entered, but which gave no warning if misused.

In this section, we return to that example and add code to make the user form more stable. The code shown in Figure 16.29 is added to the *BAdd_Click* procedure before the information is written to the worksheet.

```
'Check Name:
If FullName.Value = "" Then
    MsgBox "Please enter a name."
    FullName.SetFocus
    Exit Sub
End If

'Check Job:
If Job.Value = "" Then
    MsgBox "Please enter a job."
    Job.SetFocus
    Exit Sub
End If

'Check Age:
If Age.Value = "" Then
    MsgBox "Please enter the age."
    Age.SetFocus
    Exit Sub
End If
If Not IsNumeric(Age.Value) Then
    MsgBox "The age must be a number."
    Age.SetFocus
    Exit Sub
End If
If Age.Value < 15 Or Age.Value > 70 Then
    MsgBox "Only persons between " & _
        "15 and 70 can join."
    Age.SetFocus
    Exit Sub
End If
```

16.29 CODE TO CHECK THAT THE USER INPUT IS OF CORRECT FORMAT.

When using *TextBox* controls, the main issue is to ensure that information is provided by the user. For the name and the job, we check that the value is not an empty string, meaning that nothing was entered. If this is the case, we set focus in the corresponding *TextBox* and exit the sub. That way control returns to the user form and the user can fix the problem. We also display a nice little message box explaining to the user what the problem is.

If a string is entered, we do not test it further. Hence, we accept letters, numbers, spaces, and special characters. At this point code can be added to ensure that every character is a letter, but then you would forbid *H. C. Andersen*. If you forbid numbers, you also forbid *King Christian the 4*th, but if you allow them you also allow *D23406MD3*, which is definitely not a name. So as you see, there is a tradeoff between what you forbid and what you allow.

Regarding the age, the task is easier: We first ensure that information is entered by testing that it is not an empty string. Secondly, we test that the entered information is numeric, and finally we test that the numeric value is within a pre-specified range. We do allow for the user to enter a fractional value.

Note regarding the gender that if one of the *OptionButtons* are pre-selected, the *Frame* ensures that exactly one of them will always be selected. Hence no further checking is necessary.

16.4.4 Example: Running Experiment

One of the hardest things regarding user forms is using several forms for obtaining information which is needed jointly afterwards. One way to get around this task is to sequentially call the user forms from a sub and temporarily store the information in a hidden worksheet, but that is not really good programming style.

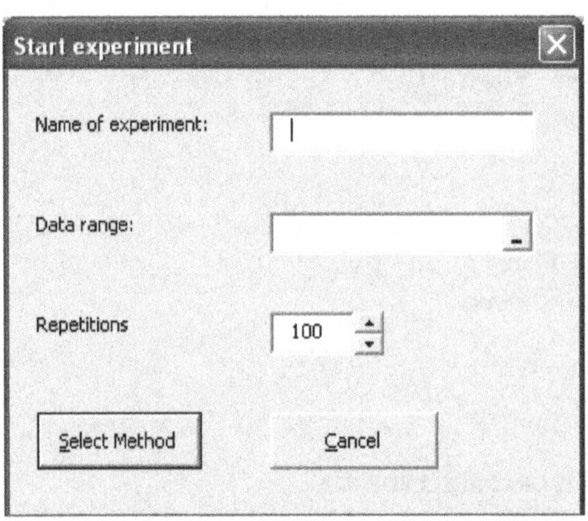

16.30 FIRST USER FORM OF THE EXPERIMENT EXAMPLE.

In this example, we show how to work with two user forms and have all the information available. The trick is the following knowledge: You can open and close one user form from another. You can obtain information from any open user form from any other user form. And finally, you can hide a user form without closing it. That way the user cannot see it, but you can obtain information from it because it is open.

For the purpose of illustration, we assume that an experiment has to be performed where we obtain the name of the experiment, a data range, and the number of repetitions from the first user form which is shown in Figure 16.30. Pressing the *Select Method* button should take the user to the second user form which is shown in Figure 16.31.

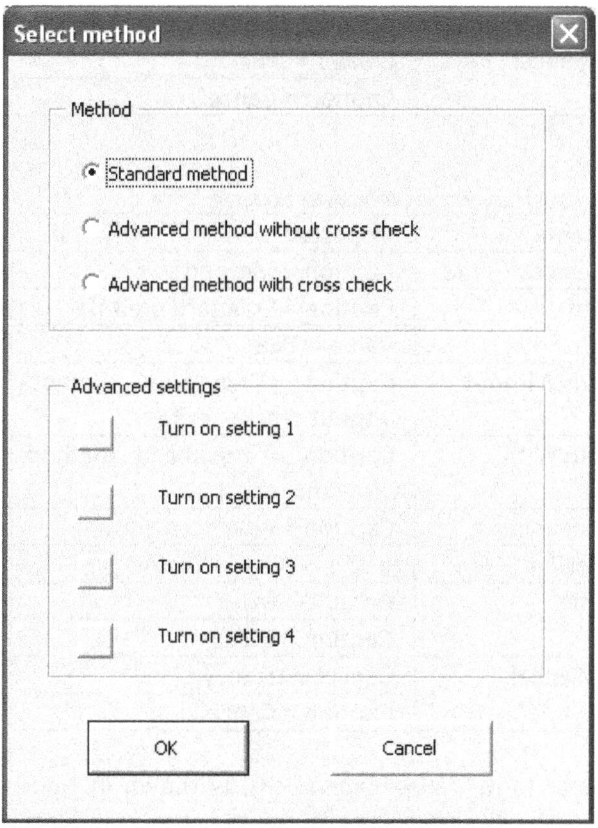

16.31 SECOND USER FORM OF THE EXPERIMENT EXAMPLE.

In the second user form, the user chooses between three different methods for performing the experiment and has the option of independently turning four settings on or off. Pressing the *OK* button should start the execution of the experiment. Pressing the *Cancel* button on either form should close the forms.

The property settings of the controls on each of the two forms can be obtained from Tables 16.5 and 16.6.

16.5 CONTROLS OF THE FIRST USER FORM IN THE EXPERIMENT EXAMPLE.

Control	Name	Property
TextBox	TBName	
RefEdit	Data	
TextBox	TBRep	.Value = 100
SpinButton	SBRep	.Value = 100
		.Min = 0
		.Max = 1000
CommandButton	BSelect	.Default = True
		.Caption = Select Method
CommandButton	BCancel	.Cancel = True
		.Caption = Cancel

16.6 CONTROLS OF THE SECOND USER FORM IN THE EXPERIMENT EXAMPLE.

Control	Name	Property
Frame	SelectMethod	.Caption = Method
OptionButton	Std	.Caption = Standard method
		.Value = True
OptionButton	AdvWithout	.Caption = Advanced method without cross check
OptionButton	AdvWith	.Caption = Advanced method with cross check
Frame	Advanced	.Caption = Advanced settings
4 ToggleButtons	Setting1 -4	(and 4 labels)
CommandButton	BOK	.Default = True
		.Caption = OK
CommandButton	BCancel	.Cancel = True
		.Caption = Cancel

The code of the first user form, called *Experiment*, is shown in Figures 16.32 and 16.33. First, if the *Cancel* button is pressed, the user form is unloaded. The next two procedures ensure that the *SpinButton* and the *TextBox* next to it works correctly. This is done be ensuring that when the value of one of them is changed by the user, the value of the other is automatically changed accordingly. Note how stability is built into the latter of the procedures.

```
Private Sub BCancel_Click()
    Unload Experiment
End Sub
```

```
Private Sub SBRep_Change()
    TBRep.Value = SBRep.Value
End Sub
```

```
Private Sub TBRep_Change()
    If TBRep.Value <> "" Then
        If IsNumeric(TBRep.Value) Then
            SBRep.Value = TBRep.Value
        End If
    End If
End Sub
```

16.32 CONTROLLING THE SPINBUTTON AND THE CORRESPONDING TEXTBOX.

When the *Select Method* button is pressed, the code in Figure 16.33 is executed. Here, it is first checked that a name has been provided and a range selected.

Next, the user form is hidden but not unloaded. Hence, the user cannot see it, but we can access the values of all the controls, including the information entered by the user.

```
Private Sub BSelect_Click()
    'Check input
    If TBName.Value = "" Then
        MsgBox "Please enter a name."
        TBName.SetFocus
        Exit Sub
    End If
    If Data.Value = "" Then
        MsgBox "Please enter a data range"
        Data.SetFocus
        Exit Sub
    End If

    Experiment.Hide

    Method.Std.Value = True
    Method.Setting1 = False
    Method.Setting2 = False
    Method.Setting3 = False
    Method.Setting4 = False

    Method.Show

    Unload Experiment
End Sub
```

16.33 CODE TO BE EXECUTED WHEN THE SELECT BUTTON OF THE FIRST FORM IS PRESSED.

The next part of the code prepares the second user form, called *Method*, by initializing a number of controls. Note how we can access the controls of the second user form from the code of the first one by placing the name of the second user form before the name of the control.

Next, we show the *Method* user form. Note that at this point control goes to the *Method* user form. First when the code in the procedure corresponding to the button pressed by the user in the *Method* user form is executed, will control return to the code in Figure 16.33. At this point the final line is executed and the *Experiment* user form closed.

```
Private Sub BCancel_Click()
    Unload Method
End Sub

Private Sub BOK_Click()
    Method.Hide
    If Method.Std.Value = True Then
        Call RunStdMethod( _
            Experiment.TBName.Value, _
            Range(Experiment.Data.Value), _
            Experiment.TBRep.Value, _
            Method.Setting1.Value, _
            Method.Setting2.Value, _
            Method.Setting3.Value, _
            Method.Setting4.Value)
    ElseIf Method.AdvWithout.Value = True Then
        Call RunAdvWithoutMethod( _
            Experiment.TBName.Value, _
            Range(Experiment.Data.Value), _
            Experiment.TBRep.Value, _
            Method.Setting1.Value, _
            Method.Setting2.Value, _
            Method.Setting3.Value, _
            Method.Setting4.Value)
    ElseIf Method.AdvWith.Value = True Then
        Call RunAdvWithMethod( _
            Experiment.TBName.Value, _
            Range(Experiment.Data.Value), _
            Experiment.TBRep.Value, _
            Method.Setting1.Value, _
            Method.Setting2.Value, _
            Method.Setting3.Value, _
            Method.Setting4.Value)
    End If
    Unload Method
End Sub
```

16.34 CODE OF THE SECOND USER FORM.

The code of the *Method* user form is shown in Figure 16.34. Here, the *Cancel* button closes the user form. If the *OK* button is pressed, the user form is hidden but not closed. The main part of the code checks which of the three *OptionButtons* has been selected by the user. Depending on the choice, one of three subs located in a standard module is executed. The value of each of the choices made on both the first and the second user form is sent to the sub as arguments. Note that these values can be reached because the user forms are still open. Finally, the *Method* user form is closed.

16.5 Exercises

16.1. Create the following Form:

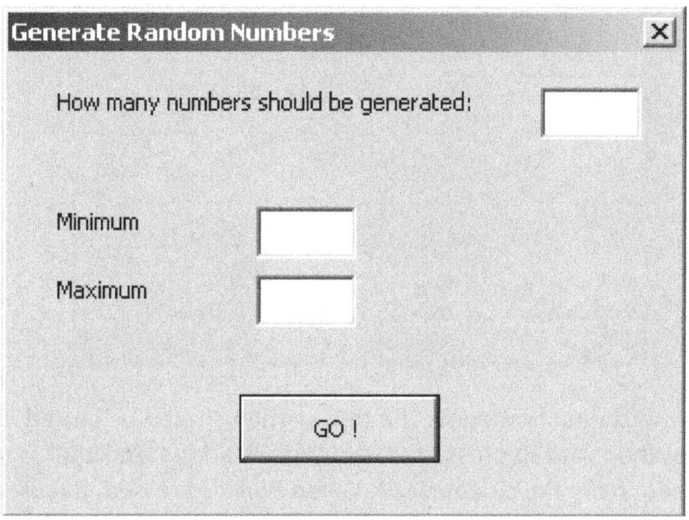

When *GO !* is pressed, random numbers between min and max should be generated and written in column A. You can use the worksheet function *RandBetween* to generate the numbers. Write a sub to display the user form and include a button for executing your sub.

16.2. Open the data file for this exercise. In that file you see a user form, which asks for the user's name, age, favorite food and the selection of a range. The information is transferred to the worksheet. Increase the stability of this user form by adding code to ensure that the input is correct.

16.3. This exercise assumes that you have read Chapter 12. Open the file for the exercise. Create a user form with a *ComboBox* and an *OK* button. When the user form is displayed the *ComboBox* should contain the names of the sheets in the workbook. When the *OK* button is pressed, the selected sheet should be activated and the user form should be closed.

16.4. Open the data file for this exercise. In the file you see a number of product codes and their corresponding prices. You can ignore the prices in this exercise but do not delete them as you need them in the next exercise. Make a user form to be used for typing in an order. Your user form should look like this.

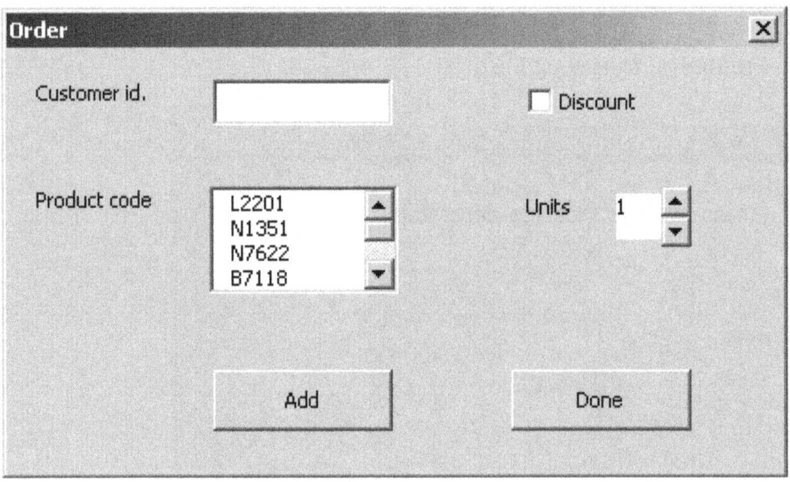

The following worksheet shows how the information should be stored in the worksheet: When *Add* is pressed, a new line is added and the user form is reset except from the customer ID. When *Done* is pressed, the user form is unloaded.

D	E	F	G	H	I
	Customer	Product	Units	Discount	
	DS34	N7622	4	discount	
		B7118	2		
	SM76	N7622	4		
		F3434	20	discount	

16.5. Open the file with your solution of Exercise 16.4. Expand your code to write the price of the selected product in column I. Assume for that purpose that the discount is 15% of the unit price. When *Done* is pressed, the total price of that customer's order should be calculated and written in column J.

16.6. This exercise assumes that you have read Chapter 12. Make sure that you have a number of Excel files in your current folder. Create a user form with the following:

- A List Box that displays the names of the Excel files in the current folder (only Excel files).
- An *OK* button.
- A *Cancel* Button.

When the *OK* button is pressed, the selected files should be opened

16.7. Open the file with your solution of Exercise 12.9. Change the code to obtain the information regarding the employee through a user form.

16.8. Open the file with your solution of Exercise 6.11. Include a manual strategy, where a user form is repeatedly displayed for the user with information regarding the amount of Euros left and the option of using a *ScrollBar* to specify the amount to exchange. When all Euros are exchanged the strategy of Exercise 6.11 should be used with the same exchange rates (possibly more if 500 have not been reached). Finally, a new user form should be displayed to tell the user how good or bad he performed. Supplement the information with a descriptive picture, for example a happy/sad smiley.

Chapter 17
Solver

Many problems within the areas of Management Science and Logistics can be solved by using linear programming (LP) or Integer Linear Programming (ILP). Examples of such problems are various types of distribution problems and production planning problems. The *Solver* Add-In for Excel is one of the engines for solving LPs and ILPs. There are several other Add-Ins for performing the same tasks, but since Solver is provided with Excel, we will use that.

In this chapter you will learn how to use the *Solver* Add-In from Excel. This will serve as a basis for the remainder of the chapter, where we go into detail about the use of Solver from within your VBA code. If you are not familiar with LP and ILP, you can consult the book's webpage, where you will find an introduction to the subject.

17.1 Introduction to Solver

We will use the example of a linear programming problem shown in Figure 17.1 to illustrate the Solver.

$$
\begin{aligned}
&Max \quad 3x_1 + 6x_2 + 7x_3 + 5x_4 \\
&s.t. \quad x_1 + x_2 \geq 20 \\
&\qquad x_1 + 3x_2 + 4x_3 + 3x_4 \leq 80 \\
&\qquad 2x_1 + 2x_2 + 2x_3 + 3x_4 \leq 100 \\
&\qquad x_3 + x_4 = 5 \\
&\qquad x_i \geq 0, i = 1,\ldots 4
\end{aligned}
$$

17.1 LINEAR PROGRAMMING PROBLEM USED FOR ILLUSTRATION.

17.1.1 Preparing the Worksheet

The first step is to enter the problem into the worksheet. In our example, we can type in the problem in a standard format as below. Note that for some problems, other formats are more appropriate. It should be mentioned that neither Excel nor Solver cares about the format in which the problem is typed. All they care about is that the cells are connected correctly through formulas. In Section 17.4.2 you will see an example of a non-standard format.

	A	B	C	D	E	F	G	H
1								
2								
3	3	6	7	5				
4								
5	1	1				>=	20	
6	1	3	4	3		<=	80	
7	2	2	2	3		<=	100	
8			1	1		=	5	
9								
10								

17.2 WORKSHEET WITH DATA FOR THE EXAMPLE IN FIGURE 17.1.

In Figure 17.2 all parameters of the example in Figure 17.1 are typed into the worksheet in standard format. The objective coefficients are placed in row 3, and row 2 is prepared to contain the value of the variables. Cell E3 will contain the value of the objective function. In this example, the overall goal of the problem will be to maximize the value of cell E3. Below the objective coefficients, though leaving row 4 empty, you will find the coefficients of the A-matrix in the range A5:D8. Just to the right of the A-matrix, we have left space for evaluating the left-hand-side of the constraints. Column E is for this purpose. Column F is for the human eye only and gives the nature of the constraints. Finally, column G gives the values of the right-hand-side coefficients. That completes entering the problem in standard form.

The only remaining task is to enter the formulas in order to calculate the objective value and to evaluate the left-hand-side of the constraints. When the LP or ILP is set up in standard format, the worksheet function *SumProduct* is very useful. The function takes as arguments two ranges of the same length, e.g. for the objective value in cell E3, we have *SumProduct(A2:D2;A3:D3)*, which is going to be calculated as A2*A3 + ... +D2*D3, which is precisely the objective function of the model in Figure 17.1. Fixing the row with the variables for the purpose of copying, we can write *SumProduct(A$2:D$2;A3:D3)* in cell E3. Copying the formula to each of the cells in range E5:E8 will provide us with the evaluation of the left-hand-side of the constraints. Note that the non-negativity constraints do not appear anywhere in the worksheet. They will be entered directly into the Solver user forms.

17.1.2 Using the Solver

Now that the worksheet has been set up, it is time to enter the problem into the Solver user form. In order to display the form, choose the menu *Data* and press *Solver* as illustrated in Figure 17.3. Note that if the Solver button is not displayed, it is most likely because the Solver Add-In is not activated. Please consult Chapter 11 to learn how to install an Add-In in Excel.

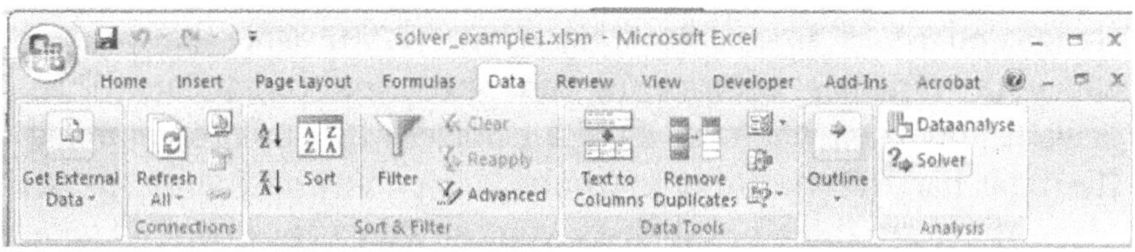

17.3 OPEN THE SOLVER FROM THE DATA MENU.

The Solver user form, which is also called the Solver dialog box, is displayed as in Figure 17.4. In the right part of the form, there are five buttons: The *Solve* button is used to perform the actual optimization when all information is entered. Hence, this is the final button to press. The *Close* button exits the Solver dialog box without performing any tasks. The *Options* button is where you control various settings. We will go further into detail about these settings later. The *Reset All* button clears all information from the dialog box and resets all settings to their default values. The *Help* button provides you with direct access to the Excel online help system.

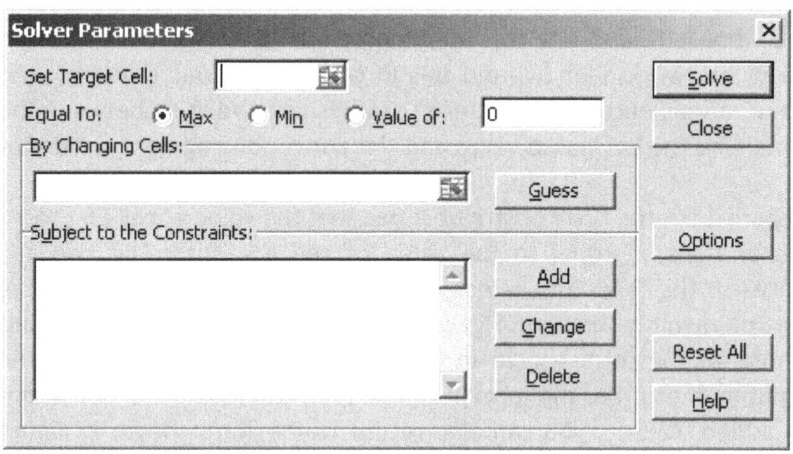

17.4 THE SOLVER DIALOG BOX.

In the left part of the form you will find everything needed for entering the LP or ILP into the Solver. Firstly, you have the *Set Target Cell*, which is where you place a reference to the cell containing the formula of the objective function. This is cell E3 in Figure 17.2. Right below the target cell you must indicate whether the goal is to *Maximize*, *Minimize*, or reach a specific value of the objective function. In the latter case, the value to be aimed for must be specified. In the next part of the form, indicated with the phrase *By Changing Cells*, you must specify the set of cells containing your variables. In our example, the variables are located in cells A2:D2. If the cells of your variables are not in adjacent cells, you simply write them as a range and use ";" as separator, e.g. A2:D2 ; G2:H2. Note that you must specify your variables before you can enter the constraints. This is particularly important when you integrate Solver with VBA programming.

The final part of the form is where you enter constraints for your problem. There are three possibilities: you can *Add* a constraint, *Change* a constraint that is already entered, or *Delete* a constraint which is not needed. The way a constraint is changed is similar to adding constraints. In order to add a new constraint to the problem, press *Add,* and the form shown in Figure 17.5 will be displayed.

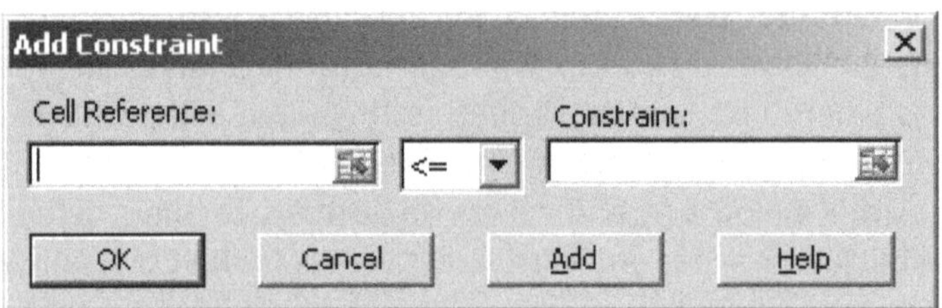

17.5 THE ADD CONSTRAINT DIALOG BOX.

Because the left-hand-side of the constraints are already evaluated directly in the worksheet (we did this in column E in our example), the constraint merely becomes a matter of establishing a relation between the cell containing the evaluated value and the corresponding right-hand-side value.

In Figure 17.2, the first constraint states that the value of cell E5 should be greater than or equal to the value of cell G5. Enter the two cell references in the form and select >= from the drop-down menu in the middle. The result is shown in Figure 17.6. Press *OK* to add the constraint and return to the form shown in Figure 17.4 or press *Add* to add the constraint and return to the form in Figure 17.5, where another constraint can be added. Clearly, you can also return to the form shown in Figure 17.4 without adding a new constraint by pressing *Cancel.* If several adjacent constraints have the same relation between left and right-hand-side, they can be entered jointly. An example of this is the cells E6:E7 and G6:G7 in Figure 17.8. If one or several variables must take on integer values, this constraint is also imposed using the form shown in Figure 17.5. This is done by selecting *int* in the drop-down menu. The right-hand-side field will automatically display *integer* as shown in Figure 17.7. In case of binary variables, *bin* is selected.

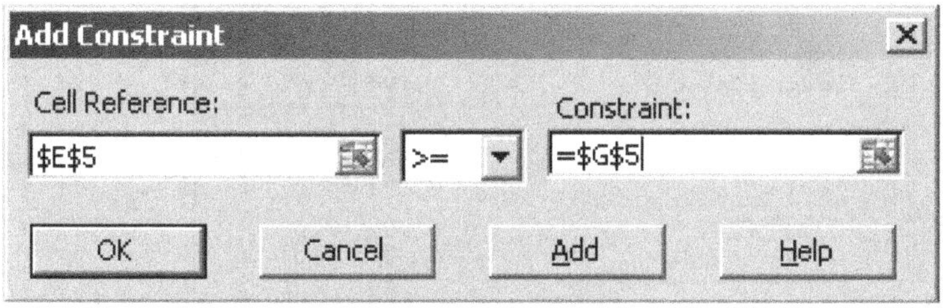

17.6 FILLING OUT THE ADD CONSTRAINT DIALOG BOX.

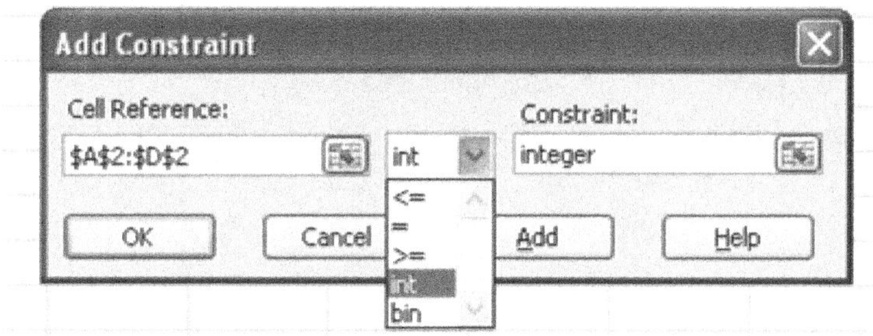

17.7 INSERTING AN INTEGRALITY CONSTRAINT.

Press the *add* button to enter the next constraint. Keep entering constraints until you have entered all four constraints and press *OK*. You now return to the previous picture and can see the constraints that you entered (note that I entered E6:E7 together to save work):

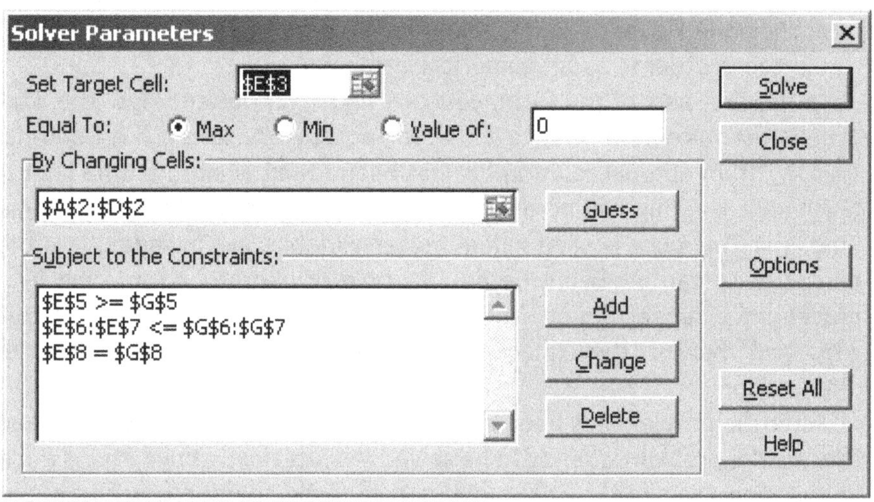

17.8 INFORMATION ADDED TO THE SOLVER DIALOG BOX.

By pressing *Options* in the solver dialog box, the user can control a range of settings for the optimization process. The form shown in Figure 17.9 is displayed.

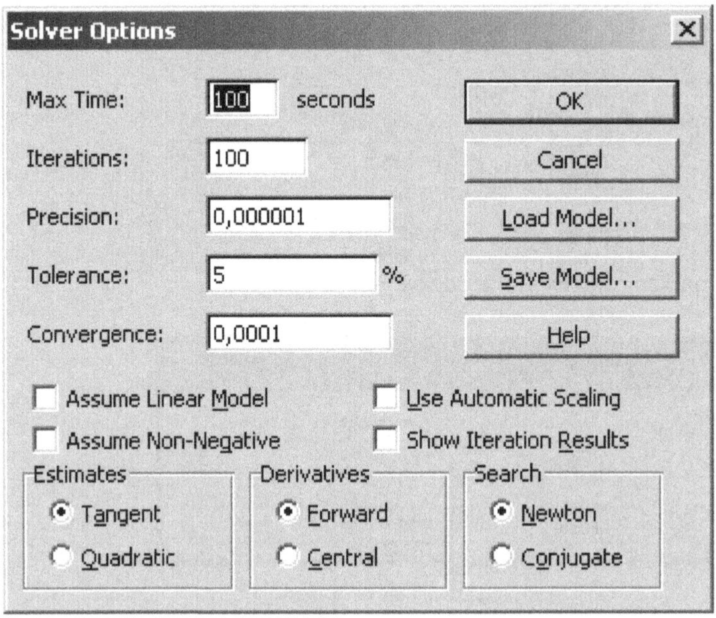

17.9 THE SOLVER OPTIONS DIALOG BOX.

In the second half of the form, the user can indicate that the problem is linear, i.e. it is an LP or ILP. This is also where you inform Solver that all variables must obey a *non-negativity* constraint. If some variables are allowed to take negative values, non-negativity constraints for the remaining variables must be entered as any other constraints using the form shown in Figure 17.5. It is recommended that *Use Automatic Scaling* is selected in order to avoid numerical instability.

In the first part of the form, you can adjust various settings. The *Max Time* is the maximum time that the Solver may use to reach an optimal solution. If an optimal solution has not been found when the time limit is reached, a warning will be displayed with the option of using additional time. The *Tolerance* is used when integer variables are included. It is the percent-wise gab between the best feasible solution found and the best proven lower/upper bound. The true optimal solution will be within this gap, and hence, the smaller the tolerance, the more exact the optimization.

After the problem has been entered and the correct options have been chosen, the problem is ready to be solved. As explained above, this is done be pressing *Solve* in the Solver dialog box. If the solution procedure was successful and an optimal solution was found, the dialog box shown in Figure 17.10 is displayed. Here the user can select which reports to view and stop the solver. If problems occur, or the problem is infeasible or unbounded, corresponding message boxes will be displayed.

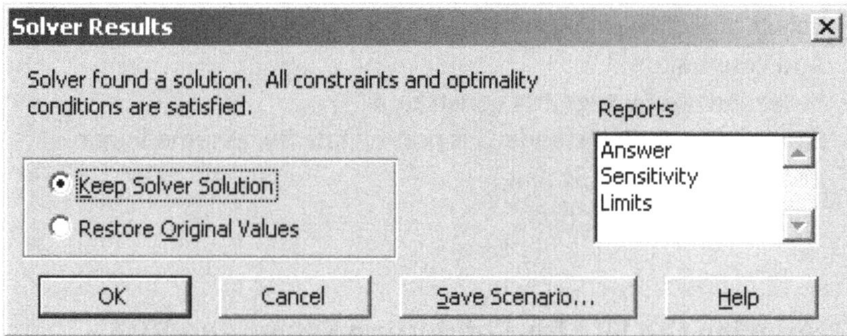

17.10 THE SOLVER RESULT DIALOG BOX.

After exiting the solver, the optimal solution will be displayed in your worksheet. This is shown for the example in Figure 17.2 in Figure 17.11.

	A	B	C	D	E	F	G	H
1								
2	37,5	7,5	5	0				
3	3	6	7	5	192,5			
4								
5	1	1			45	>=	20	
6	1	3	4	3	80	<=	80	
7	2	2	2	3	100	<=	100	
8			1	1	5	=	5	
9								
10								

17.11 OPTIMAL SOLUTION OF THE PROBLEM IN FIGURE 17.2.

In case the maximum time limit or other limits set by the user are reached before an optimal solution is found, the *Show Trial Solution* box as shown in Figure 17.12 is displayed. Here the user has the opportunity to terminate the solution process or to continue.

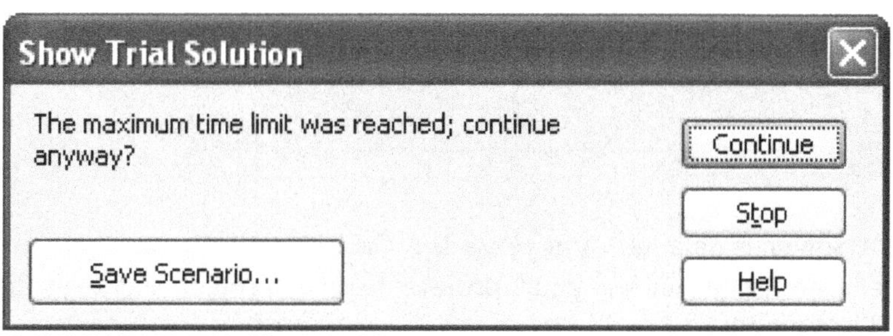

17.12 THE SOLVER TRIAL SOLUTION BOX.

Below follows a step by step guide on how to use the Solver.

1. Prepare the worksheet by typing in formulas
2. Open Solver dialog box
3. Set target cell.
4. Select objective (max/min)
5. Add constraints
6. If needed: add integrality constraints
7. Set solver options (standard is non-negativity, assume linear and use Automatic Scaling)
8. Solve and select reports

17.2 Preparing the File for Combining Solver and VBA

To be allowed to use the Solver functions from your VBA code, you must include a reference to the SOLVER.XLA or the SOLVER.XLAM, which is where they are stored. To do this, open the VBA editor and choose the menu *Tools* and choose *References*. The *Reference* dialog box shown in Figure 17.13 will be displayed.

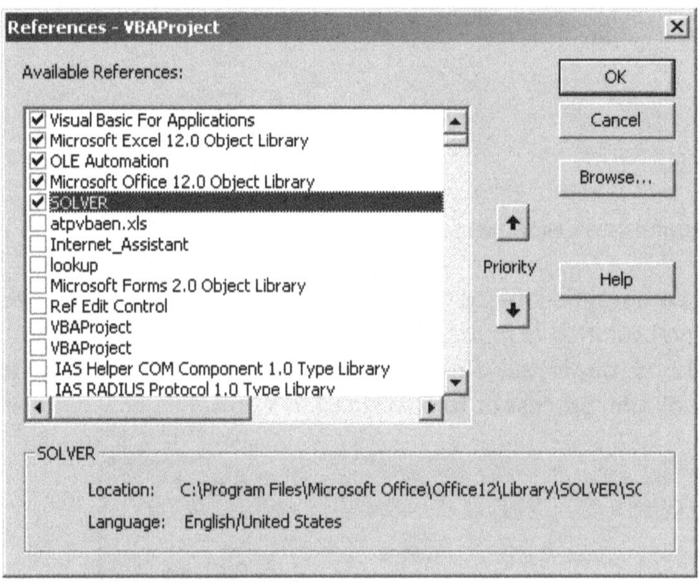

17.13 THE REFERENCE DIALOG BOX.

Make sure Solver is selected and press the *OK* button. You can now see the Solver reference under your project in the Project Explorer as illustrated in Figure 17.14.

If the reference to Solver is not displayed in the list in the reference dialog box, you can use the *Browse* button to locate the SOLVER.XLA file. Alternatively, you can return to Excel and open the Solver dialog box. Then close it and return to the VBA editor. Now Solver should appear in the list.

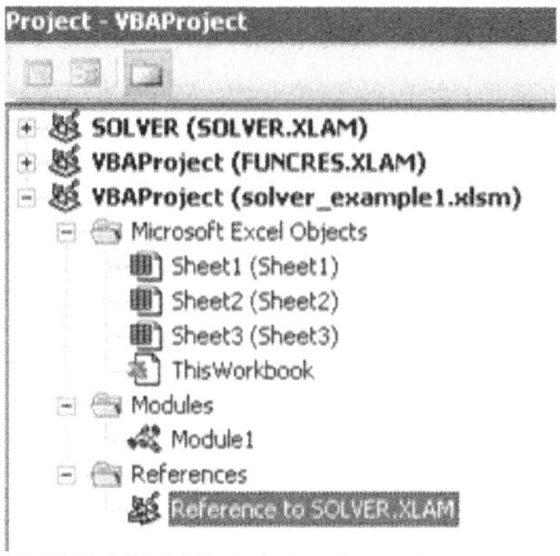

17.14 THE SOLVER REFERENCE MUST APPEAR IN THE PROJECT EXPLORER.

The location of the SOLVER.XLA file depends on the version of Excel as well as the installation. Therefore, if you open a file where the reference to Solver has already been set, it may not be correct on your computer. If you try to run a sub that uses Solver, an error message will be displayed.

The easiest way to solve the problem is to open the reference dialog box. Here you will see that the reference is not correct as illustrated in Figure 17.15. Remove the selection of Solver and press *OK* to close the dialog box. Return to Excel where you can open and close the Solver dialog box as explained above. Now you can return to the VBA editor and insert the correct reference through the reference dialog box.

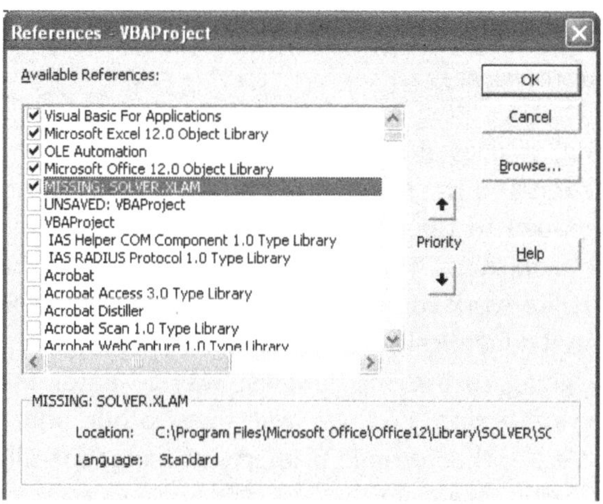

17.15 THE REFERENCE TO SOLVER MUST BE UPDATED.

17.3 Using Solver from the VBA Code

After having introduced the use of Solver directly from the worksheet, we will now return to the main purpose of this chapter, namely controlling Solver from within the VBA code.

17.3.1 A Small Example

In order to setup and solve an LP or ILP from the VBA code, we basically have to go through the same steps as we did when using the Solver dialog box. In the following, we will construct code for solving the problem in Figure 17.2 step by step. In Figure 17.16, the complete code is displayed.

```
Sub SolverExample1()
    'Preparing the spreadsheet:
    Range("E3").Formula = "=SUMPRODUCT(A2:D2,A3:D3)"
    Range("E5").Formula = "=SUMPRODUCT(A2:D2,A5:D5)"
    Range("E6").Formula = "=SUMPRODUCT(A2:D2,A6:D6)"
    Range("E7").Formula = "=SUMPRODUCT(A2:D2,A7:D7)"
    Range("E8").Formula = "=SUMPRODUCT(A2:D2,A8:D8)"

    'Reset:
    SolverReset

    'Objective and variables:
    SolverOk SetCell:="E3", MaxMinVal:=1, ByChange:="A2:D2"

    ' Adding constraints:
    SolverAdd CellRef:="E5", Relation:=3, FormulaText:="G5"
    SolverAdd CellRef:="E6:E7", Relation:=1, FormulaText:="G6:G7"
    SolverAdd CellRef:="E8", Relation:=2, FormulaText:="G8"

    'Set linear and non-negative:
    SolverOptions AssumeLinear:=True, AssumeNonNeg:=True, Scaling:=True

    ' No dialog:
    SolverSolve userFinish:=True
    SolverFinish KeepFinal:=1
End Sub
```

17.16 CODE FOR SOLVING THE PROBLEM IN FIGURE 17.2.

When the Solver is working, it uses the worksheet to recalculate the values of the objective function and the left-hand-side of the constraints. This means that it is not enough to calculate the value of the cells and then write the result to the worksheet. The formula itself must be in the worksheet in order for Solver to work correctly. Only in that way will the content of the cells be updated dynamically during the Solver process.

In this example we are going to use the simplest way to enter the formulas. In the examples in Section 17.4 we will show other, more dynamic ways of doing it. We use the *Formula* property of Range for this purpose. For the objective function we have.

Range("E3").Formula = "=SumProduct(A2:D2,A3:D3)"

Note that we are inserting the formula as a string of text containing the *SumProduct* function. The left-hand-side of the constraints are calculated in the same way.

When starting the solution process of a new problem, it is advisable to always reset the Solver into its default setting. This is particularly important, if another problem has been solved prior to the current one. Resetting the Solver is done by the function *SolverReset*.

When controlling the Solver from the VBA code, the set of variables, the cell containing the value of the objective function, and the nature of the goal are specified in a single command:

SolverOk SetCell:="E3", MaxMinVal:=1, ByChange:="A2:D2"

Here, the *SetCell* takes a reference to the cell with the value of the objective function. *MaxMinVal* takes a number indicating the nature of the goal. The 1 in this example states that the goal is to maximize the objective value. Finally, *ByChanging* takes a reference to the range of cells containing the variables.

Constraints are added to the problem using the function *SolverAdd*. The *CellRef* takes a reference to a cell or a range of cells corresponding to the left-hand-side of the constraints. *Relation* takes an integer indicating the nature of the relation. The 3 in this example states that the left-hand-side must be greater than, or equal to, the right-hand-side. Finally, the *FormulaText* takes a reference to a cell or a range of cells corresponding to the right-hand-side of the constraint. Note that the *FormulaText* can also take a number, which is very useful when only some variables need to be nonnegative, and hence, this relation must be imposed by adding constraints.

SolverAdd CellRef:="E5", Relation:=3, FormulaText:="G5"

Finally, the options must be specified. All options are set using the function *SolverOptions*. As in Section 17.1.2, we specify that the problem is linear by setting *AssumeLinear* to true. We require that all variables take nonnegative values by setting *AssumeNonNeg* to true, and finally we turn on the possibility of automatic scaling by setting *Scaling* to true.

SolverOptions AssumeLinear:=True, AssumeNonNeg:=True, Scaling:=True

Now, the problem is ready to be solved. This is done using two functions:

SolverSolve userFinish:=True
SolverFinish KeepFinal:=1

The function *SolverSolve* starts the actual solution process. The parameter *userFinish*:=True ensures that the dialog box is not shown after the solution process. The return value of the *SolverSolve* is quite important as it gives information about the success of the solution process. We are returning to that in Section 17.3.2.5. The function *SolverFinish* closes the Solver. The parameter *KeepFinal*:=1 ensures that the final values from the solution process are kept. Note that if the problem has been solved to optimality, this will ensure that an optimal solution is displayed.

17.3.2 A Walk Through the Functions

In order to control Solver from the VBA code, 13 functions are at your service. In the following, we will go through the most common functions in the order in which they are often used. Note that, for most cases, the () are not necessary.

17.3.2.1 SolverReset

SolverReset corresponds to choosing the *Reset All* button in the Solver dialog box. It clears all information about variables, objective function, and constraints. It also restores all Solver options to their default values.

Syntax:

SolverReset()

We recommend that this function always be called before any other Solver function in order to clear any old information that might remain. *SolverReset* can also be used to clean up, if several independent problems are solved iteratively. Note that if a set of problems is solved iteratively by adding additional constraints, *SolverReset* should not be used in between.

17.3.2.2 SolverOk and SolverOkDialog

SolverOk corresponds to specifying *Set Target Cells*, *Equal To*, and *By Changing Cells* in the Solver dialog box. Hence, the function is used to give Solver information about the variables and the objective function.

The function *SolverOkDialog* is similar to *SolverOk* except that the Solver dialog box will be displayed. It will be initialized with the values given as parameters to the function, but it will be possible for the user to change them through the dialog box.

Syntax:

SolverOk(SetCell:= , MaxMinVal:= , Valueof:= , ByChange:=)
SolverOkDialog(SetCell:= , MaxMinVal:= , Valueof:= , ByChange:=)

SetCell is a reference to a cell in the worksheet. This is the cell that evaluates the objective function. If *SetCell* is specified, then *MaxMinVal* must also be specified.

MaxMinVal is an integer stating the goal of the optimization problem. Table 17.1 shows the possible values along with their corresponding goal.

17.1 POSSIBLE VALUES OF THE PARAMETER MINMAXVAL.

Value	Goal
1	Maximize
2	Minimize
3	Goal value

ValueOf is a number. It is only used if *MaxMinVal*:=3, in which case the number specified will be the value that Solver tries to reach during the solution process. If *MaxMinVal* is different from 3, then *ValueOf* will be ignored even if specified.

ByChange is a reference to a range of cells in the Worksheet. These cells are the variables of the problem. This corresponds to the cells stated in the *By Changing Cells* part of the Solver dialog box.

17.3.2.3 SolverAdd

SolverAdd corresponds to pressing *Add* in the Solver dialog box. It is used to add constraints to the problem.

Syntax:

SolverAdd(CellRef:=,Relation:=,FormulaText:=)

CellRef is a reference to a range of cells in the worksheet. These are cells containing the evaluated left-hand-side of the constraints.

Relation is an integer number specifying the relation of *CellRef* to *FormulaText*. The possible values and their corresponding relationship to the right-hand-side are given in Table 17.2.

17.2 POSSIBLE VALUES OF THE PARAMETER RELATION.

Value	Relationship
1	≤
2	=
3	≥
4	Integer
5	Binary

FormulaText is either a number or a reference to a range of cells in the worksheet. This corresponds to the right-hand-side of the constraints. If *Relation* is either 4 or 5, the *FormulaText* should be left empty.

Note that if ranges are entered in *CellRef* and in *FormulaText*, the size of these ranges should match.

Because several constraints can be entered to the problem jointly as long as the relations of the constraints are the same, we recommend that you structure the problem with similar constraints adjacent in the worksheet.

17.3.2.4 SolverOptions

SolverOptions corresponds to choosing the options button in the Solver dialog box and specifying the settings.

Only options that should not be at the default setting should be specified. Options that are not specified will remain at their default setting.

Syntax:

SolverOptions(MaxTime:=, Iterations:=, Precision:=, AssumeLinear:=, StepThru:=, Estimates:=, Derivatives:=, SearchOption:=, IntTolerance:=, Scaling:=, AssumeNonNeg:=)

Tables 17.3 through 17.5 give the possible settings for each option along with an explanation.

17.3 SOLVER OPTIONS.

Option	Value	Setting
AssumeLinear	0 or 1	If 1, then Solver will use the simplex algorithm for solving LP. If 0, then Solver will use the GRG nonlinear solver.
StepThru	0 or 1	If 1, then the *Show Trial Solution* box will be displayed after every iteration. If 0, then the box will only be displayed when time limit or other limits are reached.
AssumeNonNeg	0 or 1	If 1, then an additional constraint is enforced on every variable to prevent it from taking on negative values. If 0, then no such constraint is imposed.
Scaling	0 or 1	If 1, then Solver rescales the constraints to the same order of magnitude. If 0, then Solver performs no such scaling.

17.4 SOLVER OPTIONS.

Option	Value	Setting
MaxTime	Integer greater than zero	Maximum time allowed before the solution process is terminated.
Iterations	Integer greater than zero	Corresponds to the Iterations box.
Precision	Number between 0 and 1	Corresponds to the Precision box.
IntTolerance	Number between 0 and 1	Maximal accepted gap between the solution claimed to optimal and the proven lower bound.

17.5 SOLVER OPTIONS.

Option	Value	Setting
Estimates	1 or 2	1: Tangent estimates are used. 2: Quadratic estimates are used.
Derivatives	1 or 2	1: Forward derivatives are used. 2: Central derivatives are used.
SearchOption	1 or 2	1: Newton search is used. 2: Conjugate search is used.

17.3.2.5 SolverSolve

SolverSolve corresponds to pressing the *Solve* button in the Solver dialog box. It starts the whole solution process.

Syntax:

SolverSolve(UserFinish:=, ShowRef:=)

UserFinish is a logical value and specifies whether the standard Solver result box should be displayed. If *UserFinish* is True, the standard Solver result box is not displayed. In this case, the return value of the function should be inspected and proper actions should be taken in any case. Note that *SolverFinish* must be called subsequently in order to close the Solver properly. If it is False, the standard Solver result box will be displayed and the user can manually choose the action to be taken.

ShowRef is a custom VBA function. If it is specified, Solver will call that instead of displaying the *Show Trial Solution* box at any point where this box would normally be displayed. If *ShowRef* is not specified, the *Show Trial Solution* box will be displayed as the standard option. Note that the latter requires user interaction.

Illustration

```
function MyShowTrialAction(StopReason As Integer)
    ' Here you add code to inspect the solution and take action
    MyShowTrialAction = True
end function
```

To use this function as *ShowRef* and avoid the need for user interaction, the *SolverSolve* function is called as

SolverSolve(True," MyShowTrialAction")

The argument *StopReason* is required. The possible values of this argument and the corresponding explanations are given in Table 17.6.

17.6 POSSIBLE VALUES OF THE ARGUMENT STOPREASON.

Value	Explanation
1	The function was called because the *Iterations* parameter in the function *SolverOptions* is 1 or because the solution process has been interrupted by the user (by pressing Esc). Note that if *Iterations* is 1, then the *MyShowTrialAction* function will be executed at every iteration.
2	The function was called because the maximum time limit was reached.
3	The function was called because the maximum number of iterations was reached.

The function *MyShowTrialAction* must return either True or False. If it returns True, Solver will proceed with the solution process. On the other hand, if it returns False, the solution process will be terminated.

The return value of *SolverSolve* gives you information about the solution status. The possible return values and their corresponding explanations are shown in Table 17.7.

17.3.2.6SolverFinish and SolverFinishDialog

SolverFinish corresponds to pressing the *OK* button in the Solver result box. It gives the possibility of displaying various reports and finally terminates the solution process.

The function *SolverFinishDialog* is similar to *SolverFinish*, except that the Solver result box will be displayed. It will be initialized with the values given as parameters to the function, but it will be possible for the user to change these through the Solver result box.

17.7 POSSIBLE RETURN VALUES FOR SOLVERSOLVE.

Value	Stopping condition
0	Solver found a feasible solution with all optimality conditions satisfied.
1	Solver has converged to the current solution with all constraints satisfied.
2	Solver cannot improve the current solution. All constraints are satisfied.
3	Stopped because maximum iteration limit was reached.
4	The objective value does not converge. This is the case if the problem is unbounded.
5	Solver could not find a feasible solution. This is the case if the problem is infeasible.
6	Stopped by user request.
7	Terminated. Assume linear was selected, but the conditions for a linear problem are not satisfied.
8	Terminated. The problem is too large for solver to handle.
9	Terminated. An error in the target cell or the constraint cells has been encountered.
10	Stopped because maximum time limit was reached.
11	Terminated. Not enough memory to solve the problem.
12	SOLVER.DLL is occupied. Try again later.
13	Terminated. An error has been detected in the model.

Syntax:

SolverFinish(KeepFinal:=, ReportArray:=)
SolverFinishDialog(KeepFinal:=, ReportArray:=)

KeepFinal must be either 1 or 2 and specifies whether to keep the final solution or to restore the previous values. If *KeepFinal* is 1, the final values of the variables are kept. If *KeepFinal* is 2, then the values are discarded and the previous values are displayed. The default value of *KeepFinal* is 1. Hence, if *KeepFinal* is omitted, the final values will be kept.

ReportArray is an array that specifies which reports to create after the solution process is finished. Table 17.8 gives information about the possibilities.

Any combination of two or three entries in the array will create the corresponding reports. If for example *ReportArray* = {1,3}, an answer report and a limit report will be created.

17.8 VALUES TO OBTAIN SOLVER REPORTS.

Array	Reports that will be created
{1}	An Answer Report
{2}	A Sensibility Report
{3}	A Limit Report

17.3.2.7SolverChange

SolverChange corresponds to pressing the *Change* button on the Solver dialog box. It is used to change the right-hand-side of an existing constraint.

Syntax:

SolverChange(CellRef:=, Relation:=, FormulaText:=)

Please refer to Section 17.3.2.3 concerning *SolverAdd* for an explanation of the arguments.

If the combination of *CellRef* and *Relation* does not correspond to any existing constraint, no action will be taken, and the function will return the value 4.

Note that *SolverChange* can only be used to change the right-hand-side of constraints. If the left-hand-side or the *Relation* needs to be changed, this is done by deleting the existing constraint and adding a new one.

17.3.2.8 SolverDelete

SolverDelete corresponds to pressing the *Delete* button on the Solver dialog box. It is used to delete existing constraints from the problem.

Syntax:

SolverDelete(CellRef:=, Relation:=, FormulaText:=)

Please consult Section 17.3.2.3 concerning *SolverAdd* for an explanation of the arguments.

In case the *CellRef* and *Relation* do not match any existing constraint, no action will be taken. In this case the return value of the function is 4. If the constraint is successfully deleted, the return value is 0.

17.3.2.9 SolverGet, SolverLoad, and SolverSave

SolverGet is used to obtain information about the current problem. *SolverSave* is used to save information about the current problem, and *SolverLoad* is used to load such information which has previously been saved.

These three functions are only used during rather advanced solution processes within the area of optimization. Therefore we will not explain these functions any further here.

17.4 Solver in Action

In this section, we shall illustrate some of the Solver features through three examples. The first example illustrates how additional constraints can be added and how several solutions can be saved. The second example is a transportation problem which is used to illustrate how problems can be solved when they are not entered in standard form. Finally, the third example is an example of a program that can solve problems of various sizes in a flexible way.

17.4.1 Example: Adding Additional Constraints

In this example we show how to add further constraints to a problem. The example is based on the problem presented in Figure 17.1 and uses the Sub for solving that problem as a subroutine. The code for solving the problem in Figure 17.1 is given in Figure 17.16.

```
Sub main()

    Call SolverExample1
    Range("A11").Value = "Initial solution is"
    Range("F11").Value = "Obj"
    Call CopyResult(12)

    Call SolveInteger
    Range("A14").Value = "Integer solution is"
    Call CopyResult(15)
End Sub

Sub SolveInteger()
    'Add Integer constraint:
    SolverAdd CellRef:="A2:D2", Relation:=4

    SolverSolve userFinish:=True
    SolverFinish KeepFinal:=1
End Sub

Sub CopyResult(i As Integer)
    Range("A2:D2").Copy
    Range("A" & i, "D" & i).PasteSpecial
    Range("E3").Copy
    Range("F" & i).PasteSpecial (xlPasteValues)
End Sub
```

17.17 CODE WHERE CONSTRAINTS ARE ADDED.

The purpose of the current example is to solve the problem, store the solution in the worksheet, add integrality constraints for all variables, and solve the problem again. Figure 17.17 gives a code for performing this task, and Figure 17.18 shows the resulting worksheet.

In Figure 17.17, we see that firstly the sub *SolverExample1* from Figure 17.16 is used to set up the LP problem and solve it. Next, row 11 is prepared for storing the solution. See Figure 17.18 for a preview. The sub *CopyResult* is used to copy the optimal values of the variables and the objective value to the row specified by the argument. In *SolveInteger*, the integrality constraint is added and the problem is solved again. Finally, *CopyResult* is used to copy the optimal values of the variables and the objective value.

	A	B	C	D	E	F	G	H
1								
2	38	7	5	0				
3	3	6	7	5	191			
4								
5	1	1			45	>=	20	
6	1	3	4	3	79	<=	80	
7	2	2	2	3	100	<=	100	
8			1	1	5	=	5	
9								
10								
11	Initial solution is					Obj		
12	37,5	7,5	5	0		192,5		
13								
14	Integer solution is							
15	38	7	5	0		191		
16								

17.18 RESULT OF EXECUTING THE CODE OF FIGURE 17.17

Note that when the problem is prepared to be solved the second time, only the parts that have changed need to be specified. Also note that Solver will initialize its search for an optimal solution using the current values of the variables. In particular for large integer problems, it is therefore advisable to initialize the problem with a good feasible solution in order to make the search for the optimum faster.

17.4.2 Example: Transportation Problem

BC A problem does not have to be set up in standard form for the Solver to be able to solve it. This example illustrates how a transportation problem can be solved. If you are not familiar with the transportation problem, you can consult the book's webpage for further information. A problem is given in

Figure 17.19 with 3 supplying factories and 4 warehouses to purchase the goods. The shipment cost is given in the range C7:F9.

	A	B	C	D	E	F	G	H
1	Transport problem							
2								
3	Shipping cost per truckload							
4								
5				Warehouse				
6			1	2	3	4	Supply	
7		1	464	513	654	867	75	
8	Factory	2	352	416	690	791	125	
9		3	995	682	388	685	100	
10	Demand		80	65	70	85		
11								

17.19 THE TRANSPORTATION PROBLEM.

	A	B	C	D	E	F	G	H
1	Transport problem							
2								
3	Shipping cost per truckload							
4								
5				Warehouse				
6			1	2	3	4	Supply	
7		1	464	513	654	867	75	
8	Factory	2	352	416	690	791	125	
9		3	995	682	388	685	100	
10	Demand		80	65	70	85		
11								
12								
13	shipments			Warehouse				
14			1	2	3	4	Total	
15		1	0	0	0	0	0	
16	Factory	2	0	0	0	0	0	
17		3	0	0	0	0	0	
18	Total		0	0	0	0		
19								
20								
21	Total cost			Warehouse				
22			1	2	3	4		
23		1	0	0	0	0	0	
24	Factory	2	0	0	0	0	0	
25		3	0	0	0	0	0	
26	Total cost		0	0	0	0	0	

17.20 WORKSHEET READY FOR SOLUTION OF THE TRANSPORTATION PROBLEM.

The worksheet is prepared for solution as in Figure 17.20. Range C15:F17 contains the variables to give the amounts to be shipped. Cell C18 is the sum of cells C15:C17, i.e. the total amount to be shipped to warehouse 1. Similarly for the other warehouses. Cell G15 is the total amount to be shipped from factory 1, i.e. the sum of cells C15:F15. Similarly for the other factories. Cell C23 gives the total cost of the goods that are shipped from factory 1 to warehouse 1 in the solution, i.e. it is the product of the amount to be shipped and the cost per truck load, i.e. cell C15 times cell C7. Similarly for the other cells in the range C23:F25. Cell G26 gives the total cost and it is the value to be minimized.

```
Sub SolveTransportation()

    'Reset:
    SolverReset

    'Objective and variables:
    SolverOk SetCell:="G26", MaxMinVal:=2, ByChange:="C15:F17"

    ' Adding constraints:
    SolverAdd CellRef:="C18:F18", Relation:=3, FormulaText:="C10:F10"
    SolverAdd CellRef:="G15:G17", Relation:=1, FormulaText:="G7:G9"

    'Set linear and non-negative:
    SolverOptions AssumeLinear:=True, AssumeNonNeg:=True, Scaling:=True

    ' No dialog:
    SolverSolve userFinish:=True
    SolverFinish KeepFinal:=1
End Sub
```

17.21 CODE FOR SOLVING THE TRANSPORTATION PROBLEM.

12							
13	shipments			Warehouse			
14			1	2	3	4	Total
15		1	0	20	0	55	75
16	Factory	2	80	45	0	0	125
17		3	0	0	70	30	100
18	Total		80	65	70	85	
19							
20							
21	Total cost			Warehouse			
22			1	2	3	4	
23		1	0	10.260	0	47.685	57.945
24	Factory	2	28.160	18.720	0	0	46.880
25		3	0	0	27.160	20.550	47.710
26	Total cost		28.160	28.980	27.160	68.235	[illegible]

17.22 SOLUTION OF THE TRANSPORTATION PROBLEM.

After having prepared the worksheet manually, a rather short code can solve the problem. The code is given in Figure 17.21. Clearly, the preparation of the worksheet can also be done through VBA just as we did in Section 17.3.1. Note, how the right-hand-side of the constraints refer back to the problem statement.

The optimal solution given when executing the code is shown in Figure 17.22.

17.4.3 Example: Solving Problems of Flexible Size.

In this example, we show how to make a Solver program flexible enough to solve problems of different sizes. Given a workbook with an LP or ILP of the form shown in Figure 17.23, our program should be able to solve the problem. The format is as follows: Cell A1 indicates the type of problem and cell A2 states the goal. Row 5 gives the variables, row 8 the corresponding objective coefficients, and row 6 states whether the variables are continuous, integer, or binary. The constraint matrix starts in row 12 and one empty column is given between the constraint matrix and the column giving the nature of the constraints. Neither the number of variables nor the number of constraints is fixed.

	A	B	C	D	E	F	G	H	I	J	K	L
1	ILP											
2	Max											
3												
4	Variable Name	x1	x2	x3	y1	y2	y3	y4				
5	Variable Value											
6	Variable type	cont	cont	cont	bin	bin	bin	bin				
7												
8	Obj	5	7	3	0	0	0	0				
9												
10												
11												
12	Constraints	1								<=	7	
13			1							<=	5	
14				1						<=	9	
15		1			-1000					<=	0	
16			1			-1000				<=	0	
17				1			-1000			<=	0	
18					1	1	1			<=	2	
19		3	4	2				-1000		<=	30	
20		4	6	2				1000		<=	1040	

17.23 EXAMPLE OF ILP.

The code for solving this Problem is given in Figures 17.24 through 17.26. The *FlexibleSolver* Sub in Figure 17.24 is the main program to be called with the workbook *w* containing the problem to be solved. Firstly *PrepareWorkbook* is called to initialize the workbook with the necessary formulas and to determine the number of rows and columns, respectively.

Note, in *PrepareWorkBook,* how the number of rows and columns are determined using the *CurrentRegion* property of Range. Also note how the *SumProduct* function must be given the address of the ranges, not the ranges themselves. This is also the case for the *SolverOk* function in *FlexibleSolver*.

The constraints are added in *SetupConstraints*, which is shown in Figure 17.26. Firstly the code iterates through the constraint matrix and checks the relation for each constraint. Next the variable types in row 6 are examined one by one in order to add integrality and binary constraints.

```
Sub FlexibleSolver(w As Workbook)
    Dim n As Integer ' variables
    Dim m As Integer ' constraints
    Dim V As Range
    Dim s As String, t As String
    Dim Reports() As Integer
    Dim status As Integer

    w.Activate
    w.Worksheets("sheet1").Activate
    Call PrepareWorkbook(n, m, V)
    'Reset:
    SolverReset
    'Set Options:
    SolverOptions AssumeLinear:=True, AssumeNonNeg:=True, Scaling:=True
    'Objective and variables:
    s = Range("B8").Offset(0, n).Address
    t = V.Address
    If UCase(Range("A2")) = "MAX" Then
        SolverOk SetCell:=s, MaxMinVal:=1, ByChange:=t
    ElseIf UCase(Range("A2")) = "MIN" Then
        SolverOk SetCell:=s, MaxMinVal:=2, ByChange:=t
    End If
    'Constraints:
    Call SetupConstraints(n, m)
    status = SolverSolve(userFinish:=True)
    'This is where solver status should be checked
    If UCase(Range("A1")) = "LP" Then
        ReDim Reports(2)
        Reports(1) = 2
    Else
        ReDim Reports(1)
    End If
    Reports(0) = 1
    SolverFinish KeepFinal:=1, ReportArray:=Reports
End Sub
```

17.24 MAIN SUB FOR SOLVING PROBLEMS OF FLEXIBLE SIZE.

```
Sub PrepareWorkbook(ByRef n As Integer, ByRef m As Integer, ByRef V As Range)
    Dim r As Range
    Dim i As Integer, j As Integer
    Dim s As String ', t As String

    n = Range("A4").CurrentRegion.Columns.count - 1
    m = Range("B12").CurrentRegion.Rows.count
    Set V = Range("B5", Range("A5").Offset(0, n))

    'Constraints:
    For i = 12 To 11 + m
        Set r = Range("B" & i, Range("A" & i).Offset(0, n))
        j = 2 + n
        s = "=SUMPRODUCT(" & V.Address & "," & r.Address & ")"
        Cells(i, j).Formula = s
    Next

    'OBJ:
    Set r = Range("B8", Range("A8").Offset(0, n))
    s = "=SUMPRODUCT(" & V.Address & "," & r.Address & ")"
    Cells(8, n + 2).Formula = s
End Sub
```

17.25 ENTERING VARIOUS FORMULAS.

The final if-construction in the code of Figure 17.24 is determining whether the problem is an LP, in which case two reports should be generated, or ILP, in which case only one report is generated.

```
Sub SetupConstraints(n As Integer, m As Integer)
    Dim i As Integer
    Dim s As String, t As String

    'Adding constraints:
    For i = 12 To 11 + m
        s = Range("B" & i).Offset(0, n).Address
        t = Range("B" & i).Offset(0, n + 2).Address

        If Range("B" & i).Offset(0, n + 1).Value = "<=" Then
            SolverAdd CellRef:=s, Relation:=1, FormulaText:=t
        ElseIf Range("B" & i).Offset(0, n + 1).Value = "=" Then
            SolverAdd CellRef:=s, Relation:=2, FormulaText:=t
        ElseIf Range("B" & i).Offset(0, n + 1).Value = ">=" Then
            SolverAdd CellRef:=s, Relation:=3, FormulaText:=t
        End If
    Next
    'Setting type of variables:
    For i = 1 To n
        If UCase(Range("A6").Offset(0, i).Value) = "INT" Then
                s = Range("A5").Offset(0, i).Address
                SolverAdd CellRef:=s, Relation:=4
        ElseIf UCase(Range("A6").Offset(0, i).Value) = "BIN" Then
                s = Range("A5").Offset(0, i).Address
                SolverAdd CellRef:=s, Relation:=5
       End If
    Next
End Sub
```

17.26 ADDING CONSTRAINTS TO THE PROBLEM.

17.5 Exercises

17.1. Use the Solver dialog box to solve the following LP problem:

$$\begin{aligned} \max \quad & 300x + 250y \\ s.t. \quad & 2x + y \leq 1600 \\ & x + y \leq 1200 \\ & x, y \geq 0 \end{aligned}$$

17.2. Enter the following LP problem into the worksheet and write a sub that solves the problem.

$$\begin{aligned} \max \quad & 300x + 250y \\ s.t. \quad & 2x + y \le 1600 \\ & x + y \le 1200 \\ & x, y \ge 0 \end{aligned}$$

17.3. Consider the LP from Exercise 17.2. Change your code to do the following:

1. Write the optimal solution (objective value and value of variables) to sheet 2.
2. Add the following constraint to the problem: $x + 1,7y = 1400$
3. Solve the problem again and write the new optimal solution to sheet 2.

D 17.4. Open the data file for this exercise. The file contains an Integer Linear programming problem, i.e. all variables must be integral. When a problem contains integer variables, you know from basic Management Science courses that no automatic Sensitivity Analysis can be performed. The only possibility is to vary the parameters manually. Here VBA can help automating the process.

1. The objective coefficient of X_2 (contained in cell C3) can vary from the value in J2 to the value in J3.

Write a sub that solves the maximization problem for each possible integer values of the coefficient of X_2 and writes the objective value and the solution (value of each variable) to the file.

D 17.5. Open the data file for this exercise. The file is set up as a standard inventory problem. It contains a sub for generating random demand for each week. Column B shows the number of items in the inventory at the beginning of each week. Columns C and D give weekly production and demand, respectively. Column E shows the inventory level by the end of the week. Columns G though J calculate the total cost which is a combination of holding cost and production cost. The total cost is shown in G2 and should be minimized. The ending inventory must be nonnegative. Write a procedure that uses Solver to calculate the optimal production plan given the demand in column D. The yellow cells are the variables, the red is the goal cell, and the only constraints needed are to ensure that ending inventory is nonnegative.

17.6. Consider the following problem:

$$\max \quad 3x + 2y$$

$$\begin{aligned} s.t. \quad & x + y && \leq b \\ & x + 2y && \geq 10 \\ & 2x + y && \geq 8 \\ & x, y && \geq 0 \end{aligned}$$

If *b* = 2, the problem is infeasible. If *b=12*, there is an optimal solution to the problem. Write a procedure that uses a For-Next loop to let *b* iterate through the values from 2 through 12. For each value of *b*, the problem should be solved. When the problem is feasible the first time, a message box should appear stating that this is the smallest feasible value of *b* and the looping should be terminated.

17.7. Open the data file of this exercise. The file contains a number of ILP problems that can be used for testing. Write a program that can read an ILP problem of flexible size based of a worksheet like the ones on the workbook. The program should display a message box stating the optimal value, the value of the LP-relaxation, and the ratio of the optimal value to the value of the LP-relaxation of the problem. D

17.8. Open the data file for this exercise. The exercise considers the transportation problem as discussed in section 17.4.2 and the file contains a number of such problems. Write a program that can solve transportation problems of flexible size. You can use a user form to let the user select which problem to solve. B D

Chapter 18
Simulation

In this chapter we discuss how to carry out a simulation study through VBA code. Just about any kind of economy based simulation study that you would like to carry out could be implemented in VBA. It should be noted though that there are programs specially designed for discrete event simulations, and we do recommend that you consider using such programs for that kind of studies.

Simulation in the form considered here is *what-if analysis* where simulation is used to analyze the consequences of one of several decisions in a situation where some elements are uncertain. An example of such a model is analyzing the net present value of an investment in a machine when the product to be produced faces uncertain demand.

The decisions to be analyzed could also be decisions regarding which strategy to use for planning production when production time is uncertain or which procurement strategy to use for a raw material when withdrawal from the inventory is uncertain.

In Section 18.1, we show how to work with random numbers in VBA. In Section 18.2, we consider the use of VBA when comparing decision strategies. In Section 18.3, we illustrate how the Excel Add-In *Crystal Ball* can be used for carrying out simulation studies, and in Section 18.4, we show how *Crystal Ball* can be controlled from the VBA code.

18.1 Generation of Random Numbers

Underlying any simulation study is the ability to generate random numbers. Most Excel users have tried to generate random numbers directly in Excel, and in this section we focus on the generation of random numbers in VBA. After introducing the subject and showing how to generate numbers from a couple of distributions, we leave it to the reader and books on statistics to extend the process to other distributions.

Random numbers are generated based on a sequence of numbers, therefore the *Randomize* statement should be used before generating any random numbers. This is illustrated in the code in Figure 18.1

```
Sub IllustrateRandomNumberGeneration()
    Randomize

    'Continuous uniform distributions:
    'between 0 and 1:
    Range("A1") = Rnd()
    'between 7 and 12:
    Range("A1") = 7 + (12 - 7) * Rnd()

    'Discrete uniform distributions:
    '7, 8,...,11:
    Range("A1") = Int(7 + (12 - 7) * Rnd())
    '7, 8,...,11:
    Range("A1") = WorksheetFunction.RandBetween(7, 11)
End Sub
```

18.1 USE THE RANDOMIZE STATEMENT BEFORE GENERATING RANDOM NUMBERS.

The simplest task regarding random number generation is to generate a random number between 0 and 1. For this purpose, the *Rnd* function can be used. By multiplying the function with a number, the size of the interval can be changed and by adding a number, the interval can be shifted. This is illustrated in Table 18.1, where we also show how to use *Rnd* to generate random numbers from a discrete uniform distribution by using the *Int* function. Finally, we show how the worksheet function *RandBetween* can be used for the same purpose. The use of these functions is illustrated in Figure 18.1.

18.1 GENERATION OF RANDOM NUMBERS FROM BOTH CONTINUOUS AND DISCRETE UNIFORM DISTRIBUTIONS.

Rnd()	Returns a random number in the interval [0;1).
4*Rnd()	Returns a random number in the interval [0;4).
5+4*Rnd()	Returns a random number in the interval [5;9).
Int(5+4*Rnd())	Randomly returns one of the values {5,6,7,8} with equal probability.
m+ (M-m)*Rnd()	Returns a random number in the interval [m;M).
Int(m + (M-m)*Rnd())	Randomly returns one of the values *m, m+1, m+2, ... M-1* with equal probability.
WorksheetFunction. RandBetween(5, 8)	Randomly returns one of the values {5,6,7,8} with equal probability.

Clearly, being able to create random numbers from uniform distributions is not enough in the world of business where many situations are modeled using a normal distribution. This can be handled by the worksheet function *NormInv* as illustrated in Figure 18.2. The first argument is a random number between 0 and 1 which we use the *Rnd* function to generate. The second and third arguments state the mean and the standard deviation of the normal distribution.

```
Sub IllustrateNormalDistribution()
    Dim demand As Double

    Randomize

    demand = WorksheetFunction.NormInv(Rnd(), 100, 15)
End Sub
```

18.2 GENERATING RANDOM NUMBERS FROM A NORMAL DISTRIBUTION.

Random numbers from other distributions can be generated in a similar way using their inverse function, for example *ChiInv*, *FInv*, or *BetaInv*. The first argument of these kinds of functions is always a number randomly generated by the *Rnd* function. The following arguments are the parameters of the specific distribution.

The exponential distribution is often used to model inter arrival times in, for example, queueing systems. Mathematically, we can generate random numbers from an exponential distribution with mean 1/λ using the formula -1/λ*Ln(randon number), which is shown in VBA code in Figure 18.3, where we generate random numbers from an exponential distribution with mean 10. In more common language, we generate inter arrival times where the average time between arrivals is 10 time units, i.e. on average there is 0.1 arrival per time unit.

```
Sub IllustrateExponentialDistribution()
    Dim customer As Integer

    Randomize

    For customer = 1 To 20
        Cells(customer, 1) = -10 * Log(Rnd)
    Next
End Sub
```

18.3 GENERATING RANDOM NUMBERS FROM AN EXPONENTIAL DISTRIBUTION.

18.2 Use Simulation to Compare Strategies

In this section, we consider two examples where simulation is used to compare the quality of different strategies. In Section 18.2.1, we consider a production planning problem where two planning strategies are compared and in Section 18.2.2, we consider an inventory problem where service quality and costs are compared for several order points.

In the first example we use the worksheet for handling data. This is clearly not recommendable due to the decrease in speed when large amounts of data are handled in a worksheet rather than being handled by internal data structures and it is only done to simplify the code in this first example. In the second example, the data is handled by internal data structures, mainly arrays.

18.2.1 Example: Production Planning

The first example is concerned with production planning and is based on Case 3, which is to be found on the book's webpage, but knowledge of the case is not assumed in the following.

In a production, a number of jobs are to be processed first on either machine 1 or 2 and then on machine 3 as illustrated in Figure 18.4.

The purpose of the simulation study is to compare the quality of two strategies for planning the production. The quality is compared based on several dimensions: The number of delayed jobs, the average delay of jobs as a whole and the average delay of those jobs that are delayed, the average time the jobs spend in the inventory for *Work in Progress*, and finally the *Make-Span*. Several other measures could be used in the comparison, for example measures focusing on the distribution of work between machine 1 and machine 2.

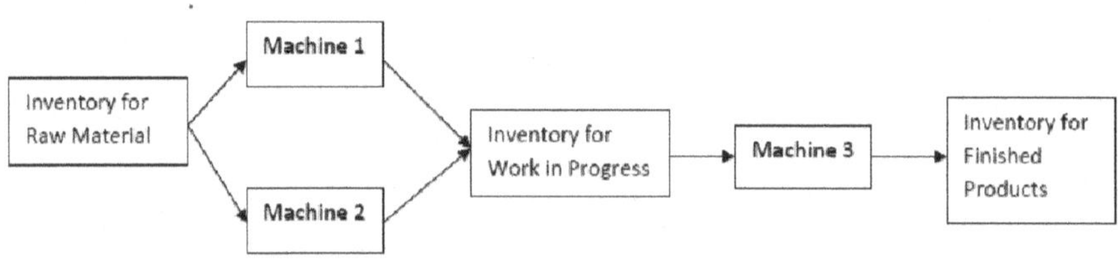

18.4 FLOW CHART OF THE PRODUCTION PROCESS.

The processing times for each job on each of the machines and the due times are given by a number of probability distributions. This information is created by a procedure called *GenerateData* and written to the worksheet as shown in Figure 18.5. We do not consider the generation of this data further as it should be clear from the material in the previous section how this can be handled. Note that the input data for the model consists of the number of jobs and the number of repetitions in the simulation, both stated in the worksheet.

Number of jobs		50		
Number of iteration		100		
	Due time	Processing Time		
	D_j	M^1	M^2	M^3
20	270	22	11	10
48	219	22	17	10
13	521	21	12	8
35	756	21	17	7

18.5 DATA TO BE GENERATED.

In order to compare the two strategies, a simulation study is carried out where we repeatedly generate a new set of jobs and create a production plan based on each of the two methods. Based on the production plans, quality measures are obtained and collected in a table like the one shown in Figure 18.6. Here *Plan1* and *Plan2* refer to each of the two strategies.

Based on the data in Figure 18.6, proper charts can be created and proper statistical information be calculated. We do not focus on that topic here.

Simulation Result

Number of Delayed Jobs		Average delay of jobs		Average delay of delayed jobs		Averate time in WIP		Make Span	
Plan 1	Plan 2	Plan 1	Plan 2	Plan 1	Plan 2	Plan 1	Plan 2	Plan 1	Plan 2
2	15	0,2	38,98	5	129,9333	36,72	42,2	425	444
5	18	1,6	65,7	16	182,5	103,14	68,42	496	518
1	14	0,16	22,52	8	80,42857	69,46	76,4	513	503
2	14	0,72	41,78	18	149,2143	73,94	56,7	477	485
0	13	0	28,9	0	111,1538	57,6	39,12	431	439
0	15	0	34,8	0	116	98,76	72,44	549	550
0	15	0	38,44	0	128,1333	42,86	27,42	389	413
1	11	0,06	30,24	3	137,4545	70,2	61,12	449	471
0	7	0	17,48	0	124,8571	97,3	95,94	527	527
0	13	0	23,84	0	91,69231	73,16	64,36	474	487

18.6 TABLE OF QUALITY MEASURES.

In order to determine the quality measures of the two strategies, a production plan based on each strategy should be created. Such a production plan is sketched in Figure 18.7 and includes an indication of the choice between machines 1 and 2, start and finish time for each job on the chosen machine and on machine 3 along with the time the job enters and leaves the inventory for work in progress. This is shown in columns H through Q in Figure 18.7.

Columns R through U give information for each job regarding time in inventory for Work in Progress, total time in process, an indication of whether the job is delayed, and the delay time of the jobs.

H	I	J	K	L	M	N	O	P	Q	R	S	T	U
						Inventory for WIP				Time		Job	Size
Job	Machine	Start M1	End M1	Start M2	End M2	Enter	Leave	start M3	End M3	Inv. WIP	Elapse T	Delayed	Delay
20	2			0	11	11	11	11	21	0	21	0	0
48	1	0	22			22	22	22	32	0	32	0	0
13	2			11	23	23	32	32	40	9	29	0	0
35	2			23	40	40	40	40	47	0	24	0	0
17	1	22	42			42	47	47	53	5	31	1	20
37	2			40	56	56	56	56	69	0	29	0	0
38	1	42	62			62	69	69	72	7	30	0	0
32	2			56	66	66	72	72	77	6	21	0	0
28	2			66	79	79	79	79	100	0	34	0	0
15	1	80	97			97	100	100	105	3	25	0	0

18.7 PRODUCTION PLAN.

We assume that the strategies only differ in the way they schedule the jobs on machines 1 and 2. Hence, the creation of the production plan for the first strategy is partitioned into a procedure, *ProdPlan1*, which handles the scheduling on machines 1 and 2 and thereby fills out the columns H through N in the table and a procedure *M3,* which handles the planning on machine 3 and fills out the columns O through Q in the table. We assume that the latter procedure also fills out columns R through U. We do not go into detail with the specific planning strategies as they are not important for the topic of this chapter.

```
Sub CalculateMeasures(w As Worksheet, r As Integer, _
                plan As Integer, jobs As Integer)
    Dim SumDelay As Double
    Dim AverageDelay As Double
    Dim AverageDelayDelayed As Double
    Dim SumWIP As Double
    Dim AverageWIP As Double
    Dim NumDelay As Double

    NumDelay = WorksheetFunction.Sum(Range("T7:T" & jobs + 6))
    SumDelay = WorksheetFunction.Sum(Range("U7:U" & jobs + 6))
    SumWIP = WorksheetFunction.Sum(Range("R7:R" & jobs + 6))

    If NumDelay > 0 Then
        AverageDelayDelayed = SumDelay / NumDelay
    Else
        AverageDelayDelayed = 0
    End If
    AverageDelay = SumDelay / jobs
    AverageWIP = SumWIP / jobs

    Call WriteMeasures(w, r, plan, jobs, NumDelay, _
        AverageDelayDelayed, AverageDelay, AverageWIP)
End Sub
```

18.8 CODE TO CALCULATE THE QUALITY MEASURES SHOWN IN FIGURE 18.6 BASED ON THE PRODUCTION PLAN IN FIGURE 18.7

After the creation of a production plan as displayed in Figure 18.7, the quality measures need to be calculated in order to produce the final table shown in Figure 18.6. This is done by the *CalculateMeaseres* procedure shown in Figure 18.8. The input arguments given to the procedure are the worksheet that should contain the table, iteration number, a number specifying the strategy which is used to write in the correct column, and finally the number of jobs.

The procedure first calculates the number of delayed jobs, the total delay time, and the total time of jobs in work in progress. Next, these are used to calculate the average delay of the delayed jobs, the average delay of all jobs, and the average time in inventory for work in progress. Finally, the measures are sent to a procedure called *WriteMeasures* with the only purpose of writing the information correctly to the table.

```
Sub Simulation()
    Dim w As Worksheet
    Dim iteration As Integer
    Dim jobs As Integer

    Set w = ThisWorkbook.Worksheets.Add
    Call PrepareSheet(w)

    ThisWorkbook.Worksheets("Main").Activate
    jobs = Range("C1").Value

    For iteration = 5 To Range("C3") + 4
        Call GenerateData

        Call ProdPlan1
        Call M3
        Call CalculateMeasures(w, iteration, 1, jobs)

        Call ProdPlan2
        Call M3
        Call CalculateMeasures(w, iteration, 2, jobs)
    Next
End Sub
```
18.9 THE SIMULATION MODEL.

The procedure that controls the simulation itself is shown in Figure 18.9 and is surprisingly short. First a worksheet for the table in Figure 18.6 is created and headings are entered by calling the *PrepareSheet* procedure.

The actual simulation consists of a for loop which iterates as many times as specified. In each iteration, we first generate new data, then for the first strategy we schedule on machines 1 and 2, then on machine 3, and finally write the measures to the final table. Next we plan with strategy 2: First machines 1 and 2, then machine 3, and finally calculate the measures.

Note that a procedure to create charts and perform various statistical calculations based on the final table can easily be inserted at the end of the procedure.

18.2.2 Example: Inventory Control

In this example we consider a classical inventory problem with stochastic demand. The goal of the example is to create a model that can be used in a simulation study with the purpose of providing decision support in determining the order point while taking the trade-off between cost and service level into account.

The model is based on the data given in the worksheet of Figure 18.10. We create the model to consider the inventory during 700 periods and start with an inventory level of 2000 units.

	A	B	C
1	Order cost, per order	12000	
2	holding cost per unit per time unit	0,3	
3	unit cost	25	
4			
5	Demand per time, normal dist		
6	mean	800	
7	std diviation	300	
8			
9	Reorderpoint	4000	
10	Lead time	3	
11			

18.10 DATA FOR THE INVENTORY MODEL.

The procedure in Figure 18.11 considers the inventory model over 700 periods once for a given order point. The first three input arguments are variables that are used to get return information from the procedure: The number of orders placed, the number of periods with inventory out of stock, and the total holding cost of the inventory over the 700 periods. The last two input arguments are the order cost and the holding cost per item per period.

First, information about the demand, the order point and the lead time is obtained and the order size is calculated as the economic order quantity.

For each period, *t, Order(t)* should be True if an order will arrive in that period and False otherwise. This is handled by setting the value of *Order(t+LT)* to True if we place an order in period *t*, where *LT* is the lead time. At any time the variable *OW* will give information regarding the number of orders that have been placed but have not arrived and *Inv* is the current inventory level.

In the main part of the code, we iterate through the periods. For each period, we update the inventory with arriving orders, determine the demand and withdraw it from the inventory, and if the inventory level plus orders placed is below the order point, we place an order. Furthermore, we update the first three input arguments throughout the process.

```
Sub Inventory(ByRef NOrder As Integer, _
        ByRef NOut As Integer, ByRef HC As Double, _
        OCost As Double, HCost As Double)
    Dim Q As Single ' Order size
    Dim OP As Integer 'Order point
    Dim LT As Integer ' Lead time
    Dim DMean As Double ' demand mean
    Dim Dstd As Double  'demand standard d.
    Dim t As Integer
    Dim P As Integer ' number of periods
    Dim Order() As Boolean
    Dim Inv As Double ' Current inventory level
    Dim Dem As Double  ' Current demand
    Dim OW As Integer ' Number of orders on wait

    DMean = Sheet1.Range("B6")
    Dstd = Sheet1.Range("B7")
    OP = Sheet1.Range("B9")
    LT = Sheet1.Range("B10")

    Q = Sqr((2 * DMean * OCost) / (HCost))
    P = 700
    ReDim Order(P + LT + 3)

    Inv = 2000
    OW = 0
    For t = 1 To P
        If Order(t) = True Then 'order arrive
            Inv = Inv + Q
            OW = OW - 1
        End If
        Dem = WorksheetFunction.NormInv(Rnd, DMean, Dstd)
        If Dem < 0 Then Dem = 0

        Inv = Inv - Dem
        If Inv < 0 Then NOut = NOut + 1
        HC = HC + HCost * Inv

        If Inv + OW * Q < OP Then
            'Order
            Order(t + LT) = True
            OW = OW + 1
            NOrder = NOrder + 1
        End If
    Next
End Sub
```

18.11 ONE ITERATION OF THE INVENTORY SIMULATION MODEL.

The code in Figure 18.12 is the main procedure. For each level of the order point, we repeat the experiment just explained 500 times. This is handled by the inner of the two for loops in Figure 18.12. In each of these iterations, we use the *Inventory* procedure to obtain the number of orders placed, the number of out-of-stock periods, and the total holding cost. These values are stored in three arrays.

```
Sub RunSimulation()
    Dim OCost As Double ' Order cost
    Dim HCost As Double ' Holding cost
    Dim UCost As Double ' Unit cost

    Dim N As Integer
    Dim j As Integer
    Dim k As Integer

    Dim NumOrder As Integer
    Dim NumOut As Integer
    Dim C As Double

    Dim Order() As Integer    ' Number of orders
    Dim Out() As Integer      ' Number of periods with stockout
    Dim HoldCost() As Double 'Calculated Holding cost

    N = 500
    Cells(9, 2) = 1500

    ReDim Order(N)
    ReDim Out(N)
    ReDim HoldCost(N)

    OCost = Sheet1.Range("B1")
    HCost = Sheet1.Range("B2")
    UCost = Sheet1.Range("B3")

    For k = 1 To 25
        For j = 1 To N
            NumOrder = 0
            NumOut = 0
            C = 0
            Call Inventory(NumOrder, NumOut, C, OCost, HCost)
            Order(j) = NumOrder
            Out(j) = NumOut
            HoldCost(j) = C
        Next

        Cells(k + 1, 5) = Cells(9, 2)
        Cells(k + 1, 6) = WorksheetFunction.Average(Order)
        Cells(k + 1, 7) = WorksheetFunction.Average(Out)
        Cells(k + 1, 8) = WorksheetFunction.Average(HoldCost)
        Cells(k + 1, 9) = WorksheetFunction.Average(Order) * OCost
        Cells(k + 1, 10) = Cells(k + 1, 8) + Cells(k + 1, 9)

        Cells(9, 2) = Cells(9, 2) + 100
    Next
End Sub
```

18.12 THE SIMULATION MODEL.

After running the experiment 500 times, we use the information to calculate the average number of orders placed, the average number of out-of-stock periods, the average holding cost, the average order cost and finally the sum of the last two. This information is written to the worksheet in Figure 18.13 along with the order point used in the experiment, where it corresponds to a single line.

Finally the outer loop ensures that the above process is repeated for every level of order points from 1500 through 3900 with intervals of 100. Based on the table created, an analysis can be made on the tradeoff between cost and service quality and a qualified decision regarding the best order point can be made.

E	F	G	H	I	J
Order point	av order	av out	Cost Hold	cost order	Total cost
1500	70,6	81,8	642241,27	847200	1489441
1600	70	68	681531,97	840000	1521532
1700	69,8	62,8	693133,46	837600	1530733
1800	70,6	57,8	708075,39	847200	1555275
1900	70,6	47,8	731812,25	847200	1579012
2000	70,6	40,6	755297,87	847200	1602498
2100	70,6	36	772796,99	847200	1619997
2200	70,4	33	798309,8	844800	1643110
2300	70,6	23,4	819925,85	847200	1667126
2400	71	21	837334,08	852000	1689334

18.13 OUTPUT DATA FROM THE SIMULATION MODEL.

18.3 Introduction to Crystal Ball

Crystal Ball is an Excel Add-In which provides a simple tool for simulation studies. It provides a wide range of distributions and is relatively easy to work with due to the graphical interface. Furthermore, when running the simulation, *Crystal Ball* automatically collects data and provides various statistical information. *Crystal Ball* is provided by *Oracle* and can be obtained from their webpage.

In the following we give a short introduction to the main tools in *Crystal Ball*, first when used through the graphical interface directly, then when used through VBA code. Note that we only give a brief introduction to *Crystal Ball*. An in-depth description of the Add-In is beyond the scope of this book.

After installing the *Crystal Ball* Add-In, a new menu appears in Excel. The two halves of the menu are shown in Figure 18.14. In the following, we introduce the tools of the menu that are used in this chapter.

The first control, *Define Assumption* is used to specify a probability distribution for a cell. The second control is used for decision making and is not used in this book. The third control, called *Define Forecast*, is used when indicating that statistics should be created for a cell.

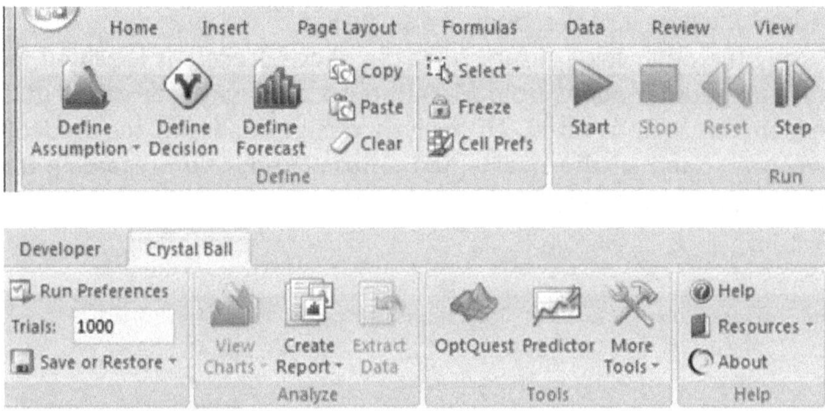

18.14 THE CRYSTAL BALL MENU.

When working with *Crystal Ball*, using the normal *copy* and *paste* tool or *Ctrl+c* and *Ctrl+v* will only copy the current number of a cell, not the underlying *Crystal Ball* information: The distribution or the statistics. To copy such information, the *Copy* and *Paste* controls on the *Crystal Ball* toolbar should be used. Similarly, the *Clear* control is used to remove the underlying *Crystal Ball* information of one or several cells.

The part of the menu that looks like a CD player is used to *Start* running a simulation and to *Stop* a simulation before it is done. The next control is used to *Reset* the simulation. Note that this should be done between every run and will be enforced by the program. The *Step* control will run a single trial of the simulation by drawing a new random value for every assumption cell. This is extremely useful for checking if everything seems to be working correctly.

From the part of the menu shown in the lower part of Figure 18.14, we only address the *Run Preferences* and the *Trials*, where the latter determines the number of times to repeat the experiment. Pressing the former of the two will open the *Run Preferences* dialog box of which the first two pages are shown in Figure 18.15.

Here a number of settings are specified. The main ones are the number of *trials* and a decision to stop if a certain confidence interval has been reached before the specified number of trials is reached. Furthermore, a seed number can be specified to enable replication of the sequence of random numbers generated.

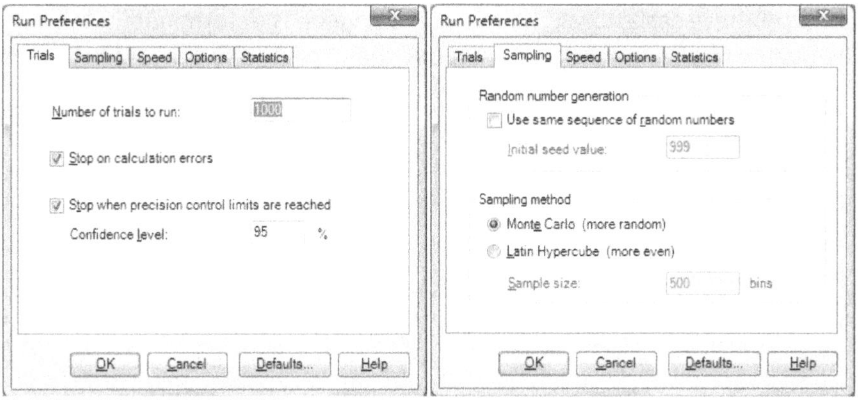

18.15 SET THE RUN PREFERENCES.

18.3.1 Example: Investment

The first example, which we use to introduce the use of *Crystal Ball* is concerned with analyzing the uncertainty in relation to the net present value of an investment in a production facility that is to produce a product with uncertain demand. Figure 18.16 gives the details of the investment which is to last for 10 years after which the scrap value is uncertain. It has been estimated that the scrap value can be obtained from a continuous uniform distribution. The discount rate is estimated to 10% and both sales price and variable costs are assumed to be fixed per unit.

	A	B	C	D	E	F
1						
2	**Total investment**	7910000		**Unit sales price**		375
3				**Variable cost**		97
4	**Time, years**	10		**Discount rate**		0,1
5						
6	**Scrap value**					
7	**Uniform distribution**	max	1420000			
8		min	250000			

18.16 DATA OF THE INVESTMENT MODEL.

The demand for the product is uncertain and is estimated to follow a normal distribution. For each of the ten years, a mean value of the expected demand is given in row 11 in Figure 18.17. The standard deviation is assumed to be 10% of the estimated mean value and is given in row 12 for each year.

Row 13 in Figure 18.17 is the demand drawn for each year in each trial from the distribution corresponding to that year. Based on the demand and the information in Figure 18.16, the remaining rows are used to determine the cash flow for each year with the totals shown in row 18.

Based on these cash flows, the net present value is determined in cell B20. The goal is to obtain information about the expected net present value of the investment when taking the above uncertainties into account.

9													
10	Year	now	1	2	3	4	5	6	7	8	9	10	scrap
11	Demand, mean		3000	11000	11000	7000	5000	3000	200	100	100	100	
12	Demand, std. Dev.		300	1100	1100	700	500	300	20	10	10	10	
13	Demand		3000	11000	11000	7000	5000	3000	200	100	100	100	
14	Revenue		1125000	4125000	4125000	2625000	1875000	1125000	75000	37500	37500	37500	
15	Fixed cost per year		50000	50000	50000	50000	50000	50000	50000	50000	50000	50000	
16	Variable cost		291000	1067000	1067000	679000	485000	291000	19400	9700	9700	9700	
17													
18	**Cash Flow**	-7910000	784000	3008000	3008000	1896000	1340000	784000	5600	-22200	-22200	-22200	250000
19													
20	**Net present value**	180374,92											
21													

18.17 CALCULATION OF THE NET PRESENT VALUE OF THE UNCERTAIN INVESTMENT.

We start by considering the scrap value which is to be contained in cell M18 and should be uniformly distributed between the values in cells C8 and C7. First activate cell M18, then select the *Define Assumption* control on the *Crystal Ball* toolbar. You will see the *Distribution Gallery* dialog box as shown in Figure 18.18. In the left side of the gallery you can choose to see all available distributions.

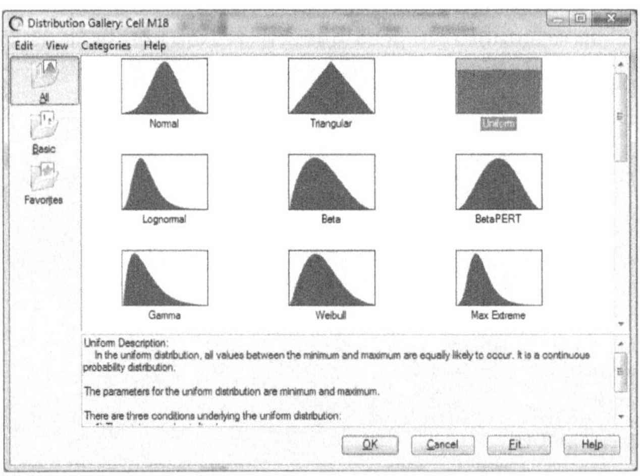

18.18 THE DISTRIBUTION GALLERY.

Note that continuous distributions are shown as green area charts, whereas discrete distributions are shown as green column charts. A description of the selected distribution can be found in the lower part of the dialog box. Select the continuous uniform distribution and press *OK*.

You now see the *Define Assumption* dialog box as shown in Figure 18.19. Here the parameters of the selected distribution should be entered. In this case the parameters are the minimum and maximum values. It is possible to enter the values directly, but to keep the model as flexible as possible, we recommend that you enter a reference to the cell containing the value instead. For this purpose the small tool next to the text boxes can be used. Use the *Enter* button to update the display and the *OK* button to accept and return to the worksheet. Note how the green color of the cell informs you that a *Crystal Ball* distribution is placed here.

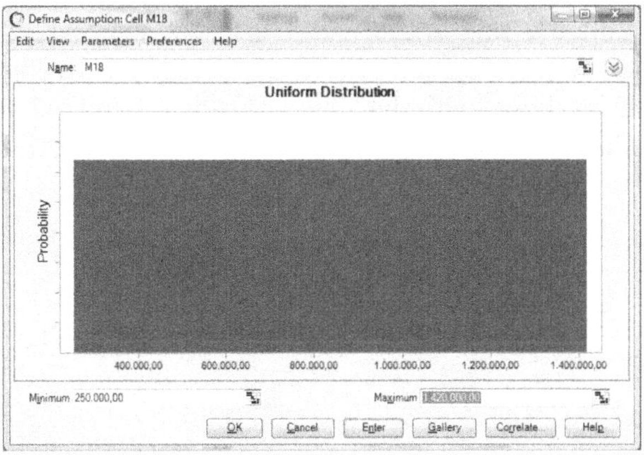

18.19 SET MINIMUM AND MAXIMUM VALUE FOR A UNIFORM DISTRIBUTION.

To enter a distribution for the demand of the first year, activate cell C13 and select the *Define Assumption* control to open the *Distribution Gallery*. Select the *Normal Distribution* and press *OK* to obtain the *Define Assumption* dialog box shown in Figure 18.20.

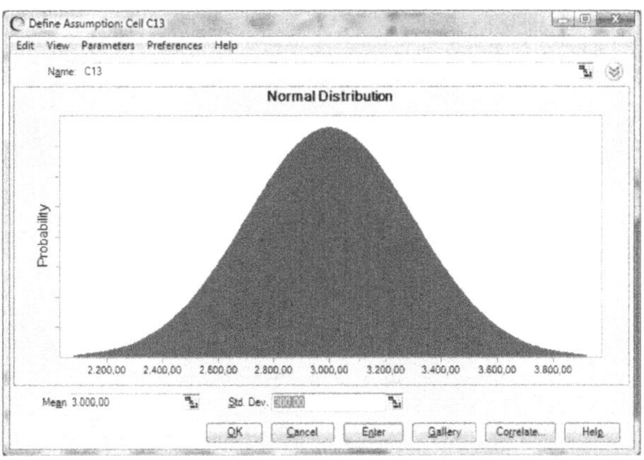

18.20 SET THE MEAN AND THE STANDARD DEVIATION OF THE NORMAL DISTRIBUTION.

To avoid having to go through the graphical interface for the demand in each of the ten years, we want to create the distribution for the first year in such a way that it can be copied to the remaining years afterwards. Therefore it is important to give references to cells C11 and C12 for the mean and standard deviation, respectively, instead of entering the values directly. Note that even though references are given, the value will appear. In the *Crystal Ball* framework, the $-sign can be used to give an absolute reference if needed. Press *OK* to close the dialog box.

To copy the distribution information to the remaining years, activate cell C13, i.e. the cell containing the distribution, and press the *Crystal Ball Copy* control. Then select cells D13 through L13 and press the *Crystal Ball Paste* tool. Then check that the references work correctly, activate for example cell J13 and select the *Define Assumption* control. Now the normal distribution should be shown with the values of cells J11 and J12. If that is not the case, use the *Clear* tool to remove *Crystal Ball* information and follow the above steps again.

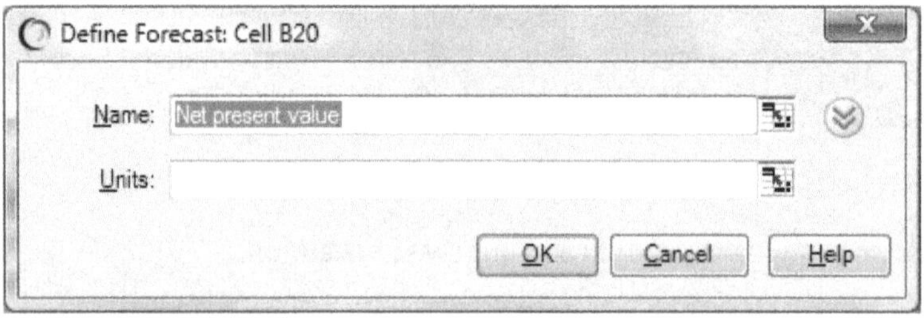

18.21 SET THE FORECAST CELLS.

To gather information about the net present value, activate cell B20 and select the Define Forecast control to obtain the small dialog box shown in Figure 18.21. Enter a name for your forecast and press *OK*.

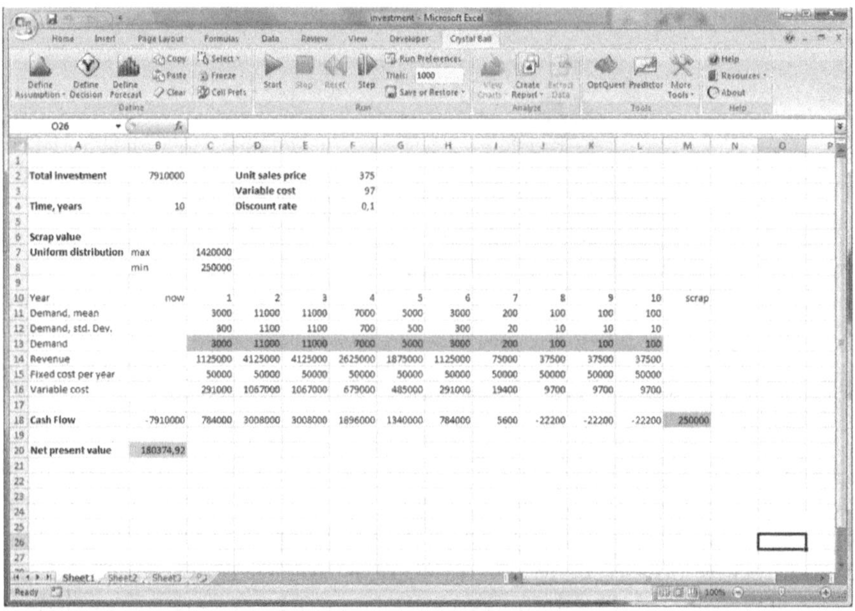

	A	B	C	D	E	F	G	H	I	J	K	L	M
1													
2	Total investment	7910000		Unit sales price		375							
3				Variable cost		97							
4	Time, years	10		Discount rate		0,1							
5													
6	Scrap value												
7	Uniform distribution	max	1420000										
8		min	250000										
9													
10	Year	now	1	2	3	4	5	6	7	8	9	10	scrap
11	Demand, mean		3000	11000	11000	7000	5000	3000	200	100	100	100	
12	Demand, std. Dev.		300	1100	1100	700	500	300	20	10	10	10	
13	Demand		3000	11000	11000	7000	5000	3000	200	100	100	100	
14	Revenue		1125000	4125000	4125000	2625000	1875000	1125000	75000	37500	37500	37500	
15	Fixed cost per year		50000	50000	50000	50000	50000	50000	50000	50000	50000	50000	
16	Variable cost		291000	1067000	1067000	679000	485000	291000	19400	9700	9700	9700	
17													
18	Cash Flow	-7910000	784000	3008000	3008000	1896000	1340000	784000	5600	-22200	-22200	-22200	250000
19													
20	Net present value	180374,92											

18.22 WORKSHEET AFTER INCLUDING CRYSTAL BALL INFORMATION.

The resulting worksheet is shown in Figure 18.22. Note how distribution cells are green and forecast cells are blue. The only remaining task is to set the number of trials and other preferences and press the *Start* control to start the simulation.

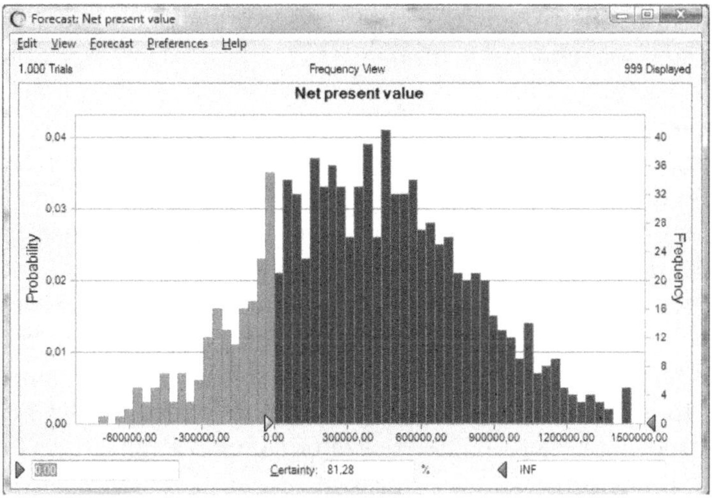

18.23 OBSERVATIONS OF THE FORECAST CELL.

Forecast: Net present value

Edit View Forecast Preferences Help

1.000 Trials

Statistic	Forecast values
Trials	1.000
Base Case	180374,92
Mean	373779,79
Median	369496,84
Mode	---
Standard Deviation	407426,55
Variance	165996394113,82
Skewness	0,0587
Kurtosis	2,73
Coeff. of Variability	1,09
Minimum	-923253,88
Maximum	1460909,19
Mean Std. Error	12883,96

Forecast: Net present value

Edit View Forecast Preferences

1.000 Trials

Percentile	Forecast values
0%	-923253,88
10%	-138161,20
20%	24128,83
30%	148367,71
40%	252284,95
50%	369301,92
60%	473266,41
70%	587305,90
80%	725120,74
90%	902013,82
100%	1460909,19

18.24 STATISTICAL INFORMATION OF THE FORECAST CELL.

At termination of the simulation, a *Forecast* like the one shown in Figure 18.23 will be shown for every forecast cell. In the main view, the distribution of the encountered values is shown. Below there are three textboxes. The middle one displays the portion of the values that falls into the range defined by the two other boxes. For example in Figure 18.23 it can be seen that 81.28 percent of the observations were positive. The blue columns in the display correspond to the given range.

By using the *View* menu, further information regarding the observed values can be obtained. Figure 18.24 shows the information given when selecting *Statistics* and *Percentiles*, respectively. By choosing *Split View*, all three displays can be shown simultaneously. This information can be used to support the subsequent decision making

18.3.2 Example: Sales

The next example illustrates how slightly more complicated matters can be dealt with in *Crystal Ball*. We consider opening of a food stand, and a decision must be made each morning regarding the number of meals to cook. During the day, the demand for meals is realized. It can be assumed that the demand for meals on any single day is normally distributed with a fixed standard deviation of one but where the mean depends on the weather. If it is raining, the mean is estimated to be 5 and if the sun shines it is estimated to be 10. This information is given in cells D7 through F9 in the worksheet shown in Figure 18.25. Price information is given in cells E2 through F4.

In this example, the goal is to build a model that can support the decision making regarding the number of meals to cook. For this purpose we analyze the consequences of each decision. When setting up the model we focus on the decision of cooking 12 (i.e. 1200) meals.

	A	B	C	D	E	F
1						
2					**Prices**	
3	**Number of meals cooked**	12			buy	10
4					sell	15
5	Mean of Norman distribution	5				
6	Demand for meals	4				
7					**Mean**	**Prob.**
8	Number of meals sold	4		Rain	5	0,5
9	**Profit**	-60		Sun	10	0,5
10						

18.25 THE SALES MODEL.

Because the mean of the normal distribution is itself uncertain, we start be letting the mean be defined by a probability distribution. Note that this distribution for the mean is given in cells D7 through F9. We activate cell B5 and select the *Define Assumption* control to place the distribution for the mean in this cell. In the *Distribution gallery*, select *Custom* as shown in Figure 18.26.

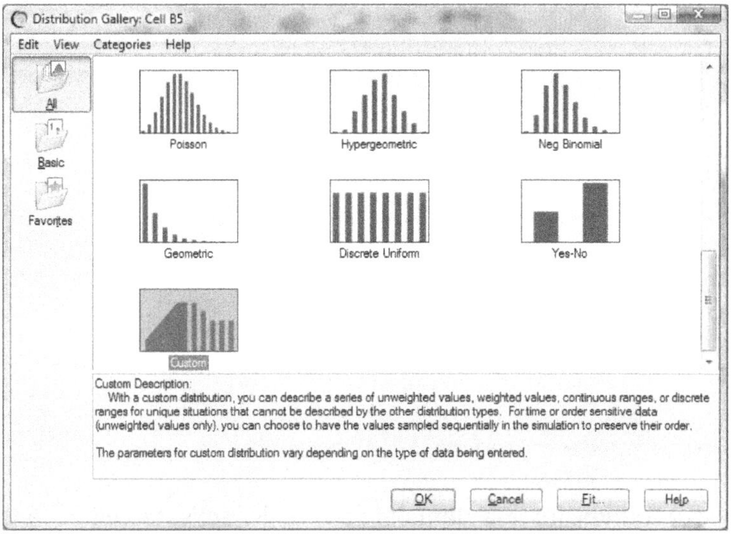

18.26 CHOOSE THE CUSTOM DISTRIBUTION IN THE DISTRIBUTION GALLERY.

In the dialog box for defining a *Custom* distribution, press the *Load Data* button in the right side of the form to display the *Load Data* dialog box as shown in Figure 18.27. If you do not see the Load Data button, press the double hat symbol in the upper right corner of the *Define Assumption* dialog box to make it appear. Enter the range =E8:F9 in the textbox or select the range in the worksheet. Press *OK* to confirm that the distribution looks like the one in Figure 18.28. Finally, press *OK* to return to the worksheet.

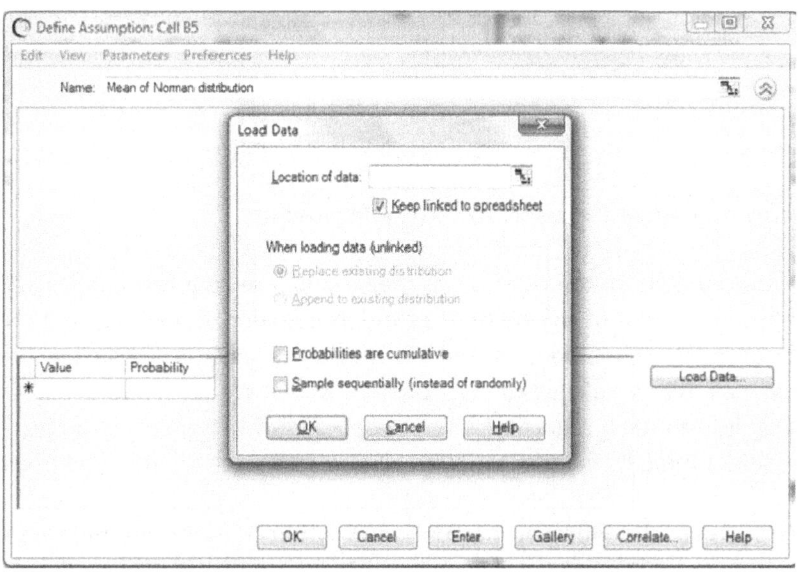

18.27 USE LOAD DATA TO SPECIFY A TABLE WITH A CUSTOM DISTRIBUTION.

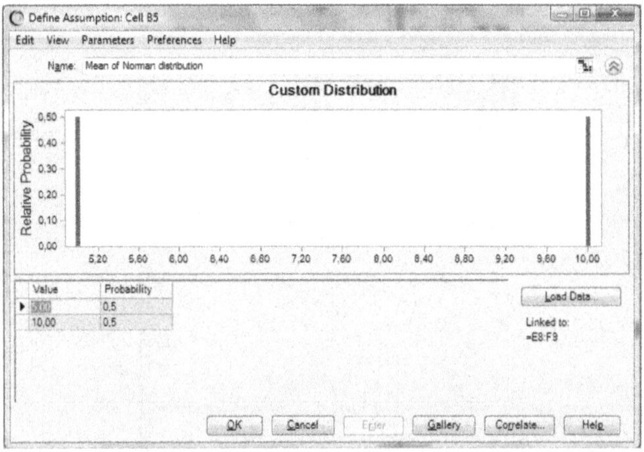

18.28 USE THE ENTER BUTTON TO GET A PREVIEW OF THE DISTRIBUTION.

To specify a distribution for the demand for meals, activate cell B6 and select the *Define Assumption* control and choose the *Normal* distribution. To specify the mean of the distribution, give a reference to cell B5 and let the standard deviation be one as shown in Figure 18.29.

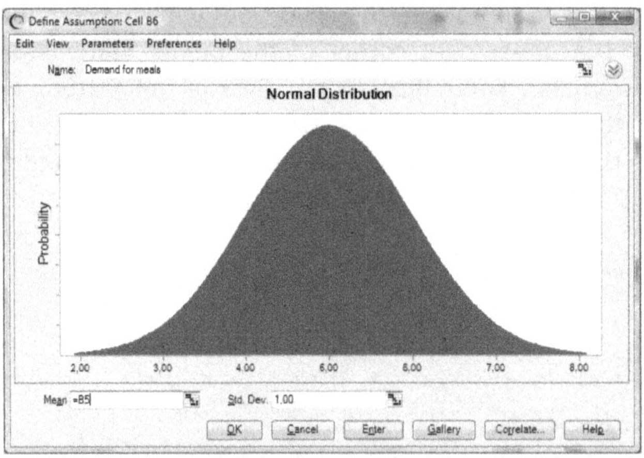

18.29 SPECIFY THE MEAN AS A REFERENCE TO A CELL IN THE WORKSHEET.

Cell B8 should contain the number of meals sold, hence a formula is used to give the minimum of the number of meals cooked, i.e. cell B3, and the number of meals demanded, i.e. cell B6, where the latter is stochastic. The profit in cell B9 is calculated as =B8*F4-B3*F3. We are interested in obtaining information regarding the expected profit. Hence we activate cell B9, select the *Define Forecast* control, enter a forecast name and press *OK*.

After setting the number of trials and other Run Preferences, the simulation can be started. The resulting distribution of the profit will look like the one shown in Figure 18.30. Note that the probability of obtaining a profit rather than a loss is only 49.43 percent and the mean value of the profit is negative.

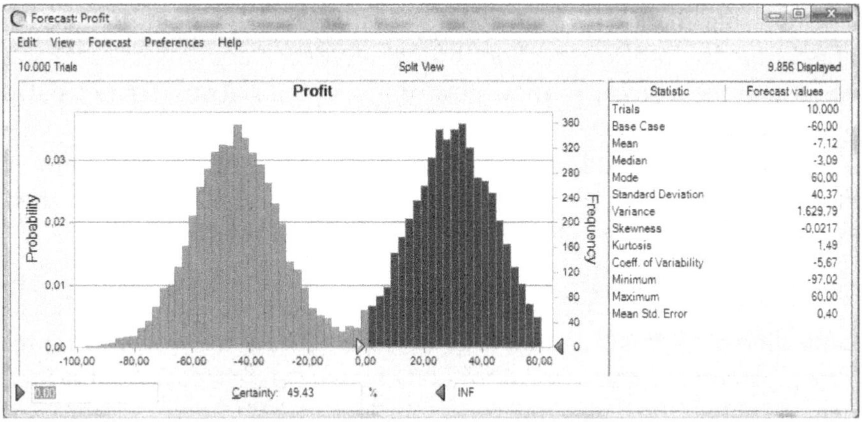

18.30 SPLIT VIEW OF THE PROFIT TO BE OBTAINED IF COOKING 12 MEALS.

For the purpose of comparison, Figure 18.31 shows the distribution of the profit obtained when only seven meals are cooked, and hence the value in cell B3 is changed to seven. Note here that the chance of obtaining a profit rather than a loss is 81.65 percent and the expected profit is 19.97.

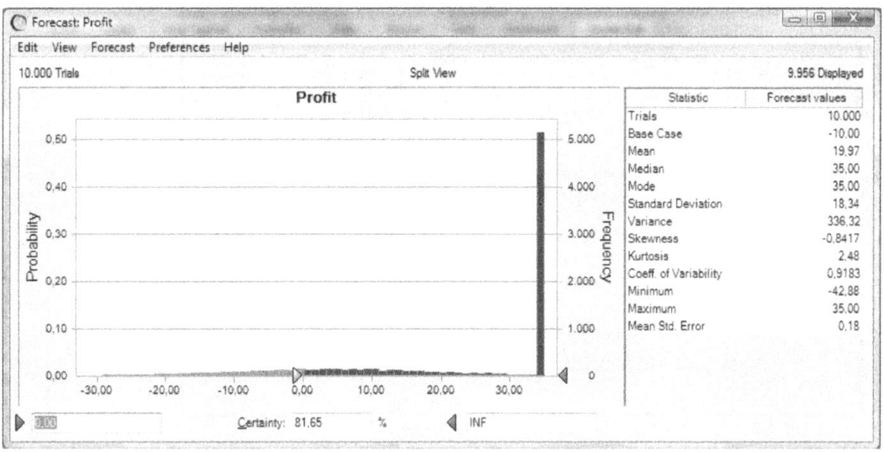

18.31 SPLIT VIEW OF THE PROFIT TO BE OBTAINED IF COOKING 7 MEALS.

To determine the best number of meals to cook, a simulation like the above should be performed for each interesting value in cell B3 and the resulting profit distributions should be compared. In Section 18.4, where we describe the use of *Crystal Ball* from the VBA code, we consider a systematic way of doing this.

18.4 Using Crystal Ball from the VBA Code

In this section, we focus on controlling *Crystal Ball* from the VBA code. We show how to create a simple simulation model and how to access the statistical information through code. In Section 18.4.1, we set up the sales model from the previous section through VBA code and in Section 18.4.2, we expand the analysis to show how to access the statistical data created by *Crystal Ball.*

The *Crystal Ball* Add-In offers an almost infinite number of methods and constants, and in the following we only use a small fraction of then. We point out that the *Object Browser* is very useful for obtaining the method or constant you need.

In order to use the material of the *Crystal Ball* Add-In in your code, a connection must the established. To do that, activate the workbook in the Project Explorer of the VBA Editor and choose *References* from the *Tools* menu to obtain the dialog box shown in Figure 18.32. Select *CBDevKit* and press *OK* and the file is ready for the use of *Crystal Ball* methods.

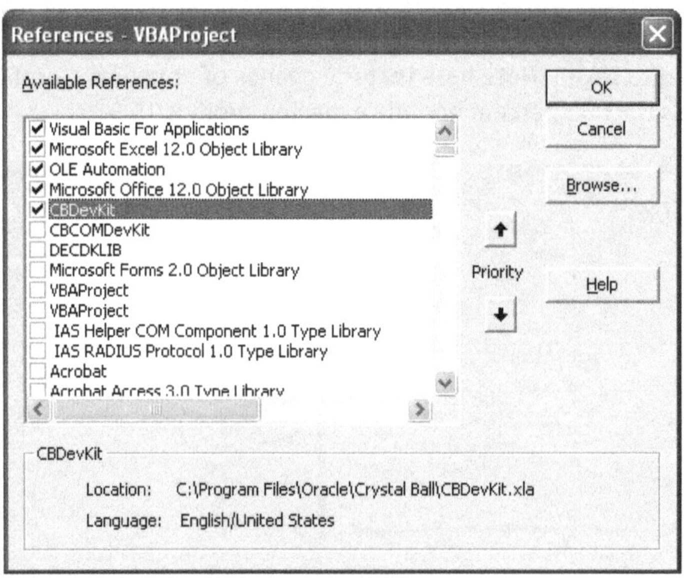

18.32 SET A REFERENCE TO THE CRYSTAL BALL ADD-IN.

18.4.1 Example: Sales – Revisited

In this example, we again consider the situation of Section 18.3.2, but here we set up and run the simulation through VBA code. We assume that the reader is familiar with the material in Section 18.3.

When using *Crystal Ball* from the VBA code the first step is to remove any information that might be stored in the system. This is done with the

Crystal Ball method *ClearDataNB*. To reset the simulation, the method *ResetND* is used. The NB part of the names is short for *No Dialog* and ensures that no dialog box will be shown. If you want the dialog to be shown, simply remove the *ND*. This is true for all the *Crystal Ball* methods ending with *ND*.

```
Sub Sales()
    CB.ClearDataND
    CB.ResetND

    Union(Range("B5"), Range("E8:F9")).Select
    CB.DefineAssumND CB.cbDfaCustom, False

    Range("B6").Select
    CB.DefineAssumND CB.cbDfaNormal, "=B5", 1

    Range("B9").Select
    CB.DefineForeND "Profit"

    CB.Simulation 10000
End Sub
```

18.33 CODE OF A SIMPLE CRYSTAL BALL MODEL.

From the VBA code, *Crystal Ball* works similarly to the way it works from the worksheet: First activate the cell then select the control. This is different from many other tools where the cell is given as input parameter.

To specify a distribution for a cell, we select the cell and then use the *DefineAssumND* method. The first argument of this method is a constant defining the distribution, and the following arguments are the parameters of the chosen distribution.

To start with the easiest, consider the part of the code where we select cell B6, which is the cell that should contain the Normal distribution. We use the constant *CB.cbDfaNormal* to specify a Normal distribution.

Since this is impossible to memorize, here is a trick: In the Object Browser, select CBDevKit and scroll through the long list of methods and constants. All distributions start with *cbDfa*. Other groups of information have other start letters, for example statistical information of a forecast cell starts with *cbFst*. Knowing that, it is not quite as hard to navigate.

The next two arguments are the parameters of the distribution, here the mean and the standard deviation. Note how we can enter the reference as a string containing whatever we would have typed in the textbox of the corresponding dialog box. Try to execute the code, then swap back to Excel and open the dialog box to see if it looks correct.

When defining a *Custom* distribution, the range to be selected should be the *union* of the cell where the distribution should be contained and the range containing the distribution table. We use *CB.cbDfaCustom* to specify that the distribution should be of custom type. The second argument, which is False, states that the data in the table is not cumulative.

To define a forecast cell, first select the cell then use the method *DefineForeND*. The first argument of this method is the name of the forecast which is stated as a string of text.

Start the simulation using the *Simulation* method with the number of trials as the only argument. The code explained here generates exactly the same chart as the method explained in Section 18.3.2.

18.4.2 Example: Sales – Extended Version

In the previous section, we introduced the use of *Crystal Ball* through the VBA code, but the reader probably agrees that the method in Section 18.4.1 was not a whole lot easier than the manual method used in Section 18.3.2. In this section we expand the example by performing analysis which is a lot easier to do using the newly introduced VBA method.

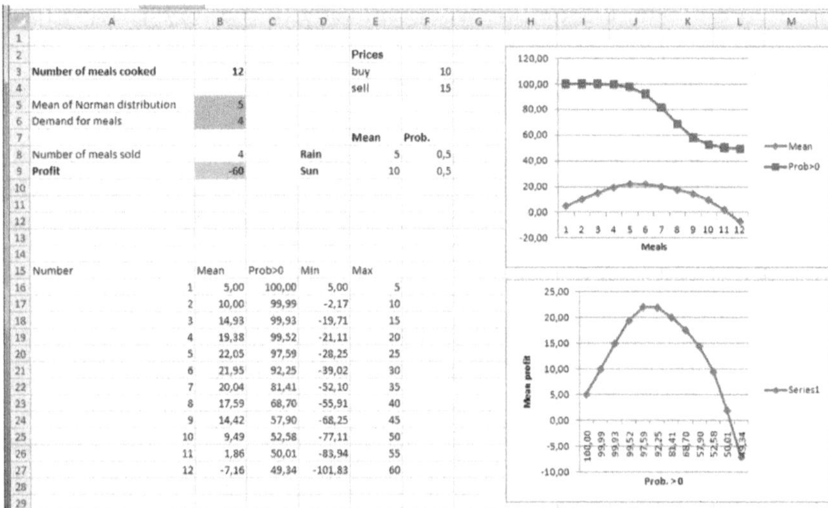

	A	B	C	D	E	F
1						
2					Prices	
3	Number of meals cooked	12			buy	10
4					sell	15
5	Mean of Norman distribution	5				
6	Demand for meals	4				
7					Mean	Prob.
8	Number of meals sold	4		Rain	5	0,5
9	Profit	-60		Sun	10	0,5
15	Number	Mean	Prob>0	Min	Max	
16	1	5,00	100,00	5,00	5	
17	2	10,00	99,99	-2,17	10	
18	3	14,93	99,93	-19,71	15	
19	4	19,38	99,52	-21,11	20	
20	5	22,05	97,59	-28,25	25	
21	6	21,95	92,25	-39,02	30	
22	7	20,04	81,41	-52,10	35	
23	8	17,59	68,70	-55,91	40	
24	9	14,42	57,90	-68,25	45	
25	10	9,49	52,58	-77,11	50	
26	11	1,86	50,01	-83,94	55	
27	12	-7,16	49,34	-101,83	60	

18.34 THE WORKSHEET TO BE CREATED BY THE CODE.

The goal of the Sales example is to analyze the consequences of the cooking decision in order to determine the best number of meals to cook. To do that, we need to run the above simulation with the number of meals to be cooked ranging from, say 1 to 12. Subsequently, the statistical data from these 12 experiments should be compared. The reader probably agrees that this would be rather tiresome to do using the manual method, but luckily it is not so hard to do through VBA code.

Figure 18.34 shows the worksheet we want to create with our code. Below the simulation model a table is created which for each number of meals cooked shows mean profit, probability of obtaining profit rather than loss, along with the smallest and largest profit value encountered during the simulation.

Two charts are created to ease the decision process. The upper chart displays the probability of obtaining a profit (upper curve) and the mean profit (lower curve) as a function of the number of meals to be cooked. Clearly, based on probability of profit alone, as few meals as possibly should be cooked. Whereas based on the mean alone, 5-7 meals should be cooked. The lower chart displays the mean profit as a function of the probability of profit. Based on this graph, we can conclude that only the 5 leftmost points, corresponding to cooking 1-5 meals, correspond to rational decisions. Which of those points to choose is a managerial decision based on risk willingness.

```
Sub Analysis()
    CB.ClearDataND

    Union(Range("B5"), Range("E8:F9")).Select
    CB.DefineAssumND CB.cbDfaCustom, False

    Range("B6").Select
    CB.DefineAssumND CB.cbDfaNormal, "=B5", 1

    Range("B9").Select
    CB.DefineForeND "Profit"

    Range("A15") = "Number"
    Range("B15") = "Mean"
    Range("C15") = "Prob>0"
    Range("D15") = "Min"
    Range("E15") = "Max"

    Call RunSimulation
    Call CreateCharts
End Sub
```

18.35 MAIN CODE TO CREATE THE MODEL AND SET UP THE TABLE.

Now it is clear exactly what should be created and the remainder of this section shows how it can be done. The code in Figure 18.35 exactly matches the code in Figure 18.33 except that the statement to run the simulation has been replaced with a couple of lines creating headings for the table and the call of two procedures which are explained below.

```
Sub RunSimulation()
    Dim meals As Integer

    For meals = 1 To 12
        Cells(3, 2) = meals
        CB.ResetND
        CB.Simulation 10000

        Cells(15 + meals, 1) = meals
        Cells(15 + meals, 2) = _
            CB.GetForeStat(Range("B9"), CB.cbFstMean)
        Cells(15 + meals, 3) = _
            100 - CB.GetCertainty(Range("B9"), 0)
        Cells(15 + meals, 4) = _
            CB.GetForeStat(Range("B9"), CB.cbFstRangeMin)
        Cells(15 + meals, 5) = _
            CB.GetForeStat(Range("B9"), CB.cbFstRangeMax)
    Next
     CB.ResetND
End Sub
```

18.36 CODE TO RUN THE SIMULATION NUMEROUS TIMES AND EXTRACT INFORMATION.

The code in Figure 18.36 iterates through the decisions of cooking 1 through 12 meals. For each decision, the number of meals to be cooked is changed in the worksheet, the simulation is reset using the *ResetND* method, and the simulation is activated using the *Simulation* method.

After running the simulation, we use the *GetForeStat* method to obtain information that is usually shown in the *Statistics* part of the *Crystal Ball* result chart. The first argument of this method is a range specifying the forecast cell to use, which in this case is the cell containing the profit. The second argument is a constant stating which type of statistical information we want. Here we use *cbFstMean* to get the mean value, and *cbFstRangeMin* and *cbFstRangeMax* to get the minimum and maximum value encountered, respectively.

To obtain the probability of the value being within a certain range, we use the *GetCertainty* method. The first argument of this method is again a specification of the forecast cell. The second argument is a number. The method returns the probability of the value being lower than the number specified in the second argument. Note that we subtract the number from 100 to obtain the probability of the value being above the number, which is zero is this example. Writing all this information to the worksheet creates the table.

```
Sub CreateCharts()
    Dim ch As ChartObject

    Set ch = ActiveSheet.ChartObjects.Add(400, 50, 300, 200)
    ch.Name = "analysis"
    With ch.Chart
        .ChartType = xlLineMarkers
        .SetSourceData Source:=Range("B15:C27")
        .Axes(xlCategory).HasTitle = True
        .Axes(xlCategory).AxisTitle.Caption = "Meals"
    End With

    Set ch = ActiveSheet.ChartObjects.Add(400, 300, 300, 200)
    ch.Name = "combined"
    With ch.Chart
        .ChartType = xlLineMarkers
        .SetSourceData Source:=Range("B16:B27")
        .SeriesCollection(1).XValues = Range("C16:C27")
        .Axes(xlCategory).HasTitle = True
        .Axes(xlCategory).AxisTitle.Caption = "Prob. > 0"
        .Axes(xlValue).HasTitle = True
        .Axes(xlValue).AxisTitle.Caption = "Mean profit"
    End With
End Sub
```

18.37 CODE TO CREATE THE TWO CHARTS.

The code in Figure 18.37 is executed after the creation of the table and creates the two charts. To the reader who is familiar with the material in Chapter 14 this should look very familiar. Note that in the second chart we specify the x- values to avoid having them interpreted as a separate data set.

18.5 Exercises

18.1. Open the data file for this exercise. Write a sub that uniformely generates *n* random numbers between *small* and *large* and writes them in column D.

18.2. Write a sub that draws 10000 numbers from a normal distribution and stores them in an array. Determine the minimum and maximum value and create 100 equally sized intervals between them. Determine the amount of numbers that fall into each of these intervals and use that information to create a chart. Your chart should look like a normal distribution.

18.3. Repeat Exercise 18.2 with other distributions to ensure that you master the generation of random numbers.

18.4. This exercise is about sequencing of jobs which was considered in Section 6.4.3. The exercise is based on the Greedy strategy presented in that section and the strategy for the same problem, considered in Exercise 6.12. Write a sub that generates random setup costs based on your favorite distribution (only positive numbers). The number of jobs is given in cell C1. Use your sub along with the subs for the two strategies to build a simulation model with the purpose of comparing the quality of the strategies.

The following three exercises are based on the inventory model presented in Section 18.2.2. When creating simulation models make sure to present your results in a useful way.

18.5. Open the data file for this exercise. The file is similar to the file used in Section 18.2.2 except that is includes a shortage cost per item per period the item is out of stock. Create a simulation model with the goal of determining the order point that minimizes the total cost.

18.6. Open the file with your solution of Exercise 18.5. Expand your model to include an analysis of the minimum total cost when the shortage cost per unit per period changes. Include code to present the results in proper charts.

18.7. Open the data file for this exercise. We consider an inventory model where the procurement price varies on a daily bases between the values V and M. The existing function generates the prices for you. Demand is fixed, the lead time is zero and orders have to be fulfilled immediately. Hence, if the inventory is empty, items must be bought even if the price is high. Let Q* denote the economic order quantity of the standard inventory model. Create a simulation model to analyze the total cost of the following two strategies:

1. Whenever the inventory is empty, order Q* items.
2. If the price is below $\sqrt{VM}$ and the inventory level is below 2Q*, order Q* items. Otherwise if the inventory is empty order Q* items.

The following two exercises are extensions for previous exercises. When creating simulation models make sure to present your results in a useful way.

18.8. This exercise considers the Traveling Salesman problem and extends Exercise 7.5. Open the file with your solution of that exercise. Create a simulation model with the goal of analyzing the quality of the following strategies for solving the problem:

3. The strategy of Exercise 7.5.
4. Visit cities in increasing order with respect to y-coordinate.
5. Visit cities in random order.
6. Visit cities in the order given by the Nearest Neighbor heuristics where the first city is chosen randomly.

18.9. This exercise considers planning of production and extends Exercise 7.8. Open the file with your solution of that exercise or the data file of that exercise. Create a simulation model that compares different strategies for planning the production. Based on your analysis, which strategy is best?

Index